Public Passions

Public Passions

The Trial of Shi Jianqiao and the Rise of Popular Sympathy in Republican China

Eugenia Lean

UNIVERSITY OF CALIFORNIA PRESS
Berkeley · Los Angeles · London

University of California Press, one of the most distinguished university presses in the United States, enriches lives around the world by advancing scholarship in the humanities, social sciences, and natural sciences. Its activities are supported by the UC Press Foundation and by philanthropic contributions from individuals and institutions. For more information, visit www.ucpress.edu.

University of California Press
Berkeley and Los Angeles, California

University of California Press, Ltd.
London, England

Library of Congress Cataloging-in-Publication Data

Lean, Eugenia, 1968–.
Public passions : the trial of Shi Jianqiao and the rise of popular sympathy in Republican China / Eugenia Lean.
p. cm.
Includes bibliographical references and index.
ISBN-13: 978–0-520–24718–5 (cloth : alk. paper),
1. Sun, Chuanfang, 1885–1935—Assassination. 2. Shi, Jianqiao, 1906–1979—Trials, litigation, etc. 3. Trials (Assassination)—China. I. Title. II. Title: Trial of Shi Jianqiao and the rise of popular sympathy in Republican China.

DX777.15.S92L43 2007
951.0'2—dc22 2006027327

Manufactured in the United States of America

15 14 13 12 11 10 09 08 07 06
10 9 8 7 6 5 4 3 2 1

This book is printed on New Leaf EcoBook 50, a 100% recycled fiber of which 50% is de-inked post-consumer waste, processed chlorine-free. EcoBook 50 is acid-free and meets the minimum requirements of ANSI/ASTM D5634–01 (*Permanence of Paper*).

To my parents,
Eric and Alice Lean

Contents

Illustrations

Acknowledgments

I have incurred innumerable debts in writing this book. To begin with, I was fortunate to work with several superb scholars during my graduate years at UCLA. The guidance of Benjamin Elman, my primary advisor, was, and continues to be, invaluable. In addition to being a model scholar and teacher, he is an excellent mentor who is able to provide his students with the intellectual space to develop their own strengths, even if this means encouraging them to pursue research projects far from his own interests. Richard von Glahn, Theodore Huters, and Miriam Silverberg were, in their very different ways, sources of inspiration and guidance. No longer just my teachers, they have also become good friends. More recently, my colleagues at Columbia have played a crucial role in making this book possible. In particular, I am grateful to Matti Zelin, Bob Hymes, Dorothy Ko, and David Wang, now at Harvard. Each provided assistance and wise counsel on a range of intellectual, professional, and institutional matters. I would also like to thank my colleagues at the University of North Carolina–Chapel Hill. Despite my short stay there before coming to Columbia, they were supportive and gracious, for which I will always be grateful.

Over the years, many friends and colleagues have supported me through the project. Some have read chapters, listened to my rambling thoughts, and helped brainstorm possible titles and research leads. Others simply offered friendship during trying moments of language training, writing, or research. I was lucky to find wonderful intellectual companionship at the University of California–Los Angeles. Ideas were born in exciting classroom exchange as well as in more casual, but no less invigorating, discussions held over coffee in the afternoon or beer at weekly happy hours. My dissertation-writing years were spent in Chicago, where the community involved in Chinese studies at the University of Chicago proved very welcoming. Faculty members, including Prasenjit Duara, Tang Xiaobing, and Judith Zeitlin, were generous with their comments on my work and their hospitality. The graduate students at the University of Chicago took me in as one of their own. While it is impossible to thank all the friends I met at UCLA and the University of Chicago, I want to extend my appreciation in particular to James St. André, Bao Weihong, Zvi Ben-dor Benite, Steven Day, Elyssa Faison, Lü Miaw-fen, Jason McGrath, Meng Yue, Hajime Nakatani, Bruce Rusk, Eugene Sheppard, Matt Sommer, and Zhang Zhen. Finally, during my years abroad, Yomi Braester, Karl Gerth, Annie Reinhardt, Erik Sahlin, Mark Swislocki, Edna Tow, and others provided much-needed companionship in morning language classes and dusty archives, as well as in more enjoyable settings.

Several people have taken the time to read chapters of the book manuscript and provide constructive criticism, including Michael Chang, Lee Haiyan, Rebecca Nedostup, Jonathan Ocko, Pablo Piccato, Teemu Ruskola, Kristen Stapleton, and Matti Zelin. I am truly grateful for their time and thoughtful comments. I presented my work at talks, conferences, and workshops at UCLA, Columbia University, Harvard University, Princeton University, the University of North Carolina–Chapel Hill, the University of Chicago, the University of California–Berkeley, the University of Pennsylvania, the University of Oklahoma, the Institute of Modern History (IMH) at the Academia Sinica, Taiwan National University, Beijing University, and Fudan University. My heartfelt appreciation is extended to the participants, organizers, and discussants of those meetings. Finally, my students at both UNC–Chapel Hill and Columbia University, with their astute questions and comments, have had a profound impact on the final form of this book.

Research for this project was made possible by several generous grants. A 1997 International Studies and Overseas Program Pre-Dissertation Fellowship and a 1998–99 Fulbright Institute of International Education (IIE) award funded dissertation research in Taiwan. A 1999–2000 grant from The Committee for Scholarly Communication with the People's Republic of China (PRC), administered by the American Council of Learned

Societies (ACLS), allowed me to conduct research in the PRC. While I was in Taiwan, Dr. Wu Jing-jyi and the Fulbright IIE staff ensured that my stay was most productive. Thanks are also due to the IMH at the Academia Sinica, which served as a host institution, and where I met several exciting scholars who were part of the Modern China Cultural and Intellectual History group. The librarians, archivists, and staff members at the Academia Sinica's IMH and Fu Ssu-nian libraries, the Kuomintang Party Archives, and the Academia Historica (Guoshiguan) all helped facilitate my research. During my stay in the PRC, the Shanghai Academy of Social Sciences (SASS) served as my primary affiliation, and Zhao Nianguo, my key liaison with SASS, proved resourceful and flexible in a variety of matters. Luo Suwen of the history institute at SASS pointed me in useful research directions. Librarians and archivists at the Beijing Municipal Archives, the Beijing Library, the Chongqing Municipal Archives, the Chongqing Library, the Nanjing Number Two Historical Archives, the Nanjing City Library, the Nanjing University Library, the Shanghai Municipal Library, and the SASS library offered invaluable assistance and service.

More recently, a Junior Faculty Research Grant and a Weatherhead East Asian Institute grant, both from Columbia University, have allowed me to engage in summer research trips necessary for the book revisions. In 2004–2005, the ACLS/Andrew W. Mellon Fellowship for Junior Faculty and the An Wang Postdoctoral Fellowship from the Fairbank Center at Harvard University made it possible for me to take a timely leave of absence from teaching and complete the manuscript. Reed Malcolm at the University of California Press deserves thanks for expressing enthusiasm about this project even in its earliest stages. He, Kate Warne, and Kalicia Pivirotto have been extremely efficient and professional in ushering me through the editing process. John Fitzgerald, Ruth Rogaski, and a third, anonymous reviewer read the manuscript in full for the University of California Press. I am grateful for their enthusiastic support and the insightful comments and criticisms they provided.

None of this would have been possible without my family. It is only fitting that I dedicate this book—a study of filial piety—to my parents, who have supported me unconditionally throughout the years and whose own achievements, big and small, have been a constant source of inspiration for me. I write in fond remembrance of my grandparents, Chung-Tao (C. T.) Kiang (1909–99) and Chien-yi Tai Kiang (1910–2004). My sister's encouragement, friendship, and humor have been crucial. Her suggestion that all I need to do to finish the dissertation is to write two words, “the end,” is only one of many comments that have reminded me of her uniquely sage advice. Finally, thanks go to Paize Keulemans. No one could ask for a better companion in things academic or in life. It is an understatement to say that this book would not be what it is without him.

Introduction

In the fall of 1935, a woman by the name of Shi Jianqiao discovered that her sworn enemy, ex-warlord Sun Chuanfang, had become a leading member of the Tianjin Qingxiu lay-Buddhist society (*jushilin*) on Nanma road.[1] Shi made several visits to the society's congregation site to learn of Sun's schedule, and on the morning of November 13, 1935, she planned to take action. Sun was scheduled to lead the sutra-recitation session that day, but things did not seem promising for Shi at first. The retired militarist was late because of the rain. And, when Sun finally appeared, Shi had to hire a car and rush home to the British Concession to retrieve her Browning pistol.[2] She later told authorities that she had been reluctant to carry a gun across the borders of the concessions unless she was sure Sun would be there. On her return to the lay society, Shi finally met with success. She positioned herself behind the kneeling ex-military leader and shot him three times. While the prayer hall descended into chaos and terror, Shi Jianqiao maintained her cool and triumphantly declared, "I have avenged the murder of my father. Do not fear. I will not hurt anyone else, nor will I run away." She then surrendered.[3] Newspaper accounts of the event described her attitude after the successful slaying as calm to the point of being uncanny.[4] One report stated that her disposition and behavior were solemn and dignified, as if nothing out of the ordinary had just taken place.[5]

Shi's extraordinary act of vengeance immediately became the focus of intense media interest. On the evening of November 13, only a few hours after the actual slaying, the *Xin Tianjinbao* (The new Tianjin), a local

Tianjin paper, printed a special edition to break the news. On November 14, 1935, the day after the assassination, Tianjin's *Dagongbao* (L'Impartial), described by contemporary social critic Lin Yutang as the only paper of reasonable quality during the Republican era, ran the headline "Blood Splatters Buddhist Shrine!!" The accompanying article had this to report: "At 3:15, as the devout were in mid-prayer, a woman devotee sitting behind Sun [Chuanfang] pulled a gun out of her sleeve and shot Sun in the back of the head. The first bullet went through the back of his skull to exit through his forehead. His brains were blown everywhere, yet Sun was still upright. Another shot was fired and the bullet entered his right temple, exiting his left forehead. The third bullet was shot at his waist and exited through his chest. Sun died immediately."[6]

The media reportage did not stop with the killing itself. In the following days, urban readers consumed details of the assassin's past and the case's connections to warlord politics. Media scrutiny focused on all levels of the protracted courtroom trial. Appealed twice to reach the Nanjing-based Supreme Court, the case generated a controversial final verdict of judicial leniency. Then, only two months later, the Nationalist (Guomindang) regime overturned this final verdict by issuing a state pardon. This rapidly unfolding series of events made the story of the avenging daughter front-page news for more than a year.

Other forms of media also contributed to the making of the case of Shi Jianqiao. The lively periodical press gave substantial editorial space to the debate among urban professionals and social critics advocating reform over the merits and demerits of filial revenge and the public support it drew. Fiction, radio plays, and theatrical productions inspired by the affair appeared in major urban centers. Shanghai residents could attend dramatic renditions, and readers in Tianjin and Beiping could read daily installments of serialized fiction based on the retribution killing.* Finally, the trial itself played as a spectacle. Observers flocked to the courthouses of both the district- and provincial-level trials to catch a glimpse of the female perpetrator. One commentator of the day dryly noted that whereas the public barely even registered news of the attempted assassination of Wang Jingwei, who was then head of the executive branch of government, Shi Jianqiao's seemingly insignificant case of vengeance had become the talk of the streets.[7]

*At the time of the Shi Jianqiao case, Beijing (Northern capital) was known as Beiping (Northern Peace). The name change occurred when the Nationalists took the reins of the central government in 1928 and moved the capital to Nanjing.

It is not at all clear why the media and the public became so fixated on a seemingly unimportant, familial affair. In 1927, the Nationalist regime had ostensibly brought an earlier chapter of internecine warfare to a close and initiated what is commonly known as the Nanjing decade by establishing China's new capital in the southern city of Nanjing. Yet, while the Nationalist regime was internationally recognized as China's legitimate ruling government, the Nationalists' goals to centralize, erect a functioning state apparatus, and firmly establish China's national sovereignty remained frustratingly elusive. Throughout the decade, Japan's increasing presence in Manchuria and North China threatened national sovereignty from outside. Communists who were organizing in both the urban centers and the hinterland, and regional militarists who were defiantly engaging in autonomous local rule in the Western, Southwestern, and most menacingly, Northern parts of China, posed threats from within. The daunting tasks of rebuilding society and establishing modern institutions of rule proved difficult; the regime was trapped between these goals and its desire to impose authoritative control over the very society and institutions it sought to reform.

Contemporary observers have continued to remark upon the media sensation caused by this Republican-era case, but have generally shed little light on why Shi's act of revenge engendered both overwhelming public sympathy and widespread controversy. A professional journalist reviewing his career, for instance, credited the sensational trial with providing him with his big breakthrough (Lin 1980). Another memoirist marvels in retrospect that Shi Jianqiao's story caused a stir both within and beyond China (Zheng 1992, 73–76). Regional historians of Anhui, Shi's native-place, claim her as an extraordinary daughter of their own (Wu 1990; Chen 1991), and compilers of remarkable and strange cases in Chinese history regularly include the quirky case of Shi Jianqiao.[8] Yet these accounts do not address exactly why the event was so controversial. Nor do they examine what larger sociopolitical implications the case may have had. Primarily interested in appropriating her fame to buttress Anhui's reputation, regional histories tend to present the avenger uncritically as a heroine. Popular historians and memoirists cite the affair of Shi Jianqiao as yet another example of the curious or, even worse, sordid times of the Republican period, merely using the case to dwell on the intrigue of the era's politics.

Differing from both celebratory treatments of Shi Jianqiao and accounts that treat the assassination as bizarre, my study uses this extraordinary event to argue that the female assassin's singular and violent expression of filial sentiment (*xiao*) helped give rise to a new communal form of ethical sentiment—"public sympathy" (*tongqing*). Concomitantly, it explores how the case of Shi Jianqiao prompted public dialogue over the relevance of sentiment (*qing*)—be it the assassin's ethical sentiment of filial devotion or the unprecedented collective emotionalism of an urban public—to Chinese modernity. Debate raged over whether filial heroism was suitable for a modern Chinese subject. Controversy swirled around whether the avenging daughter's motive of righteous passion should win either a judicial exemption or a pardon by the Nationalist state.

Furthermore, if Shi Jianqiao's motive of filial heroism garnered attention, the public sympathy that the daughter elicited became a source of particular social anxiety. For some, collective sentiment in the case constituted a powerful, new, communal form of sentiment based on a long-standing premise of the ethical authenticity of emotions. This communal sentiment could somehow serve as an antidote to an era of inauthenticity generated by slick mass media, the corrupt factionalism of the Nationalist regime, and the lack of justice in its courts. Others, however, regarded collective emotionalism as anachronistic and dangerous. For these critics, the widespread support represented a spontaneous expression of an unruly, feminized public that challenged "masculine" forms of modernity such as the rule of law or leftist narratives of historical materialism and social development.

I begin here by addressing some of the major historiographical and theoretical issues that this study of Shi Jianqiao engages. First, by examining public sympathy in this case, I readdress the public-sphere debate in the field of modern Chinese history. This book explores alternative ways of conceptualizing the development of urban publics in modern China within the context of a burgeoning consumer mass culture and growing political authoritarianism. Second, this study engages with studies of the complex notion of *qing* that have primarily been focused on late imperial culture, philosophy, and literature. While *qing* had been a crucial, if ambivalent, moral concept in Confucian cosmological discourses since antiquity, this case reveals that it continued to be central in debates over the articulation of modern China's post-Confucian social and political order. Finally, as an in-depth examination of a high-profile assassination case, this book extends our understanding of the culture of violence in the Republican era and explores how cases such as Shi Jianqiao's killing of Sun Chuanfang mediated debates over the role of ethical violence in modern justice.

PUBLIC SYMPATHY: BEYOND HABERMAS

A central concern of this book is to describe the rise of "public sympathy" (*tongqing*) by the 1930s. The compound *tongqing* has a long history, during much of which it did not mean "public sympathy." Han Feizi (c. 280–c. 233 B.C.E.), an important thinker who wrote during China's period of antiquity, was among the first to use the term. He writes in "Wielding Power," a chapter of his basic writings, that a good ruler needs to "compare names, differentiate events, comprehend unity, and identify [himself] with the Way's true nature (*tongqing*)."[9] As a leading figure of legalism, a school of philosophy that sought to promote the rule of law as superior to Confucian ideas of moral rule, Han Feizi believed that the ruler, surrounded by untrustworthy and self-interested ministers and sycophants, needed to cloak himself in secrecy and assume a "non-active" (*wuwei*) pose so as not to reveal his intentions. The ability to *tongqing*, or to know the nature or essence of a situation, was, along with a full set of laws, crucial among the methods of government in Han Feizi's world. Over the course of the imperial era, *tonqing* assumed several more meanings, including "having the same heart," "with the same intent," and "of like mind or reason."[10]

In modern Chinese *tongqing* is generally rendered as "sympathy" or, when used as a verb, "to sympathize with." However, I use "public sympathy" or "collective sentiment" here to indicate how by the early twentieth century *tongqing* had acquired an unmistakable collective connotation. Indeed, by the 1930s the term had come to denote explicitly the collective sympathies of an urban audience of the mass media. In discussions surrounding the Shi Jianqiao case, *tongqing* was frequently used interchangeably with other increasingly popular terms of the day, including national emotion (*guomin ganqing*), mass emotion (*qunzhong ganqing*), or public sentiment (*yüqing*).

"Public sympathy" was not the only "public" that was being conceptualized as a critical political and moral force in China's modern era. During the end of the Qing dynasty (1644–1911), reformers such as Liang Qichao avidly promoted the notion of "public opinion" (*yulun*), a concept that was adapted from Western political discourses and transferred to China as a neologism from Japan. Liang and others theorized that "public opinion" was to be the basis of imperial reform and modernization (Judge 1997). Like this late Qing conceptualization of a new collective, "public sympathy" in the 1930s was also perceived to function as a tribunal of sorts against which the caprices of officialdom were tried. Yet, while similarities exist, the two conceptualizations were fundamentally different in important ways. The earlier notion of "public opinion" embodied reason and progress, and arose in the pages of a new reformist press. Late Qing intellectuals promoted the concept and enthusiastically claimed that the opinion of the people could serve as an effective antidote to the late Qing state. In contrast, the later concept of "public sympathy" was explicitly grounded in the emotions of the people and was formed amid the sensationalism of the media. Furthermore, whereas late Qing intellectuals promoted "public opinion," left-leaning critics and urban professionals of the 1930s were highly suspicious of the rise of a mass public and condemned mass sentiment as feminine, emotional, and mired in superstition.[11]

If this study adds to our general knowledge of publics in modern Chinese history, it also allows us to rethink how the modern China field has approached the study of critical urban publics. The tendency of classical theory on the public sphere and civil society to disavow the realms of emotion and mass culture as legitimate conditions for the rise of "true" participatory publics has profoundly shaped the discussion of publics in modern Chinese history. The historiographic concern with the topic arose after the translation into English of Jürgen Habermas's *The Structural Transformation of the Public Sphere* (1989). In this important text, Habermas argues that the rise of capitalism enabled the creation of an ideal bourgeois public sphere in Western Europe in the eighteenth century. Located in the coffeehouses of England and the salons of France, this sphere was a realm of rational engagement in which people could uphold and defend their mercantilist interests against feudal hierarchy and state domination. Here they could also voice opinions critical of the social order. Laws and institutions that emerged from this public sphere embodied the principles of justice and humane values that its participants shared.

The translation of Habermas's text and the interest in civil society and the public sphere in the China field were related to historical events in the late 1980s and early 1990s. Whereas civil society played a crucial role in bringing down authoritarian regimes in Eastern Europe, in contrast, the Chinese Communist Party's violent repression of a student movement in 1989 elicited international shock and rebuke. The debates that then arose among modern China scholars were attempts to explain why civil society had "failed" in China. Much of the discussion tended to center narrowly on either promoting or refuting the presence of something similar to Habermas's formulation of the bourgeois public sphere in the Chinese historical experience.[12] While some historians began to problematize the tendency to make modern European history the basis of a standard yardstick of development, few have been able to move beyond the question of whether China had anything comparable to the public sphere in the West.

More recently, however, scholars have shifted from the highly charged question of whether an actual "public sphere" existed in modern China toward a more reasoned inquiry into the historically specific configurations of Chinese "publics" in late imperial and twentieth-century China. These scholars are concerned with understanding how new, or newly configured, urban institutions (e.g., mass media, civic organizations, labor groups, and an autonomy-seeking judicial profession), along with ongoing attempts to centralize state power, uniquely affected modern Chinese state and society relations (see, e.g., Goodman 1995; Tsin 1999; Xu 2001). These studies also investigate the idea that a public could be defined less in terms of place and more in terms of processes and practice. For example, while the discussion in the early 1990s hews closely to the Habermasian articulation of "public" in spatial terms, and focuses primarily on the social parameters of such a sphere,[13] more recent work explores the protean nature of urban "publics." This more recent scholarship considers how publics may have consisted of shifting realms in which participatory politics were indeed possible.[14] Some argue that publics in modern China were not necessarily permanent spatial realms but were in fact often "hailed" and interpellated into existence. In a recent discussion of how communist hunger strikers in the mid-1930s effectively used the mass media and scripts of moral resistance to bring about a moral public, Jan Kiely (2004) draws from Michael Warner's idea that publics "exist by virtue of being addressed."[15]

There is also an increased awareness that publics should be understood not merely in institutional and social terms but in their normative capacities as well. In his discussion of the pre-revolutionary French notion of *l'opinion publique*, Keith Baker (1987) effectively makes the case that publics should be understood not so much as sociological in nature, but as "imagined authorities."[16] China scholars have since also considered how publics were often more powerful as normative forces than as actual sociological entities. As mentioned above, in the late Qing period progressive publicists and constitutional reformists such as Liang Qichao envisioned the abstract "public opinion" (*yulun*) primarily as an ideal of reason and progress that could serve as a means to force the Qing dynastic government toward more open, contestatory politics. By the 1920s and 1930s, leftist writers producing Chinese reportage literature, a genre of literary nonfiction that described current events, persons, or social phenomena, effectively helped articulate the notion of China's "urban crowd." This crowd was imagined as participating in student and urban demonstrations and struggling against imperialist violence in the urban landscapes of the campus, the streets, and the factories. Neither late Qing "public opinion" nor the early twentieth-century "urban crowd" depicted in reportage literature had exact, discrete sociological referents.[17]

Yet, despite these inroads, Habermasian assumptions about "publics" persist among China scholars in unexpected ways. In particular, the belief that a critical, "authentic" public must be rational and "liberatory" continues to hold sway. This belief stems from Habermas's influence. Habermas privileges the bourgeois public sphere/civil society of eighteenth-century France, England, and Germany as a sphere that carves out a space for rational, bourgeois, male individuals to pursue their economic and political interests vis-à-vis the authoritarianism of absolute monarchy. Furthermore, in the second half of his work, which has received considerably less attention, Habermas asserts that mass culture and a public sphere are, in effect, incompatible. He describes how the bourgeois public sphere had degenerated by the nineteenth and twentieth centuries to the point of being a "mass" public, a passive audience, with little potential for enabling liberatory, critical participation in politics. By making such an argument, Habermas places himself squarely in the tradition of scholars of the Frankfurt school such as Max Horkheimer and Theodore Adorno, who, in their *Dialectic of Enlightenment* (1944), written in response to fascism in Europe, produced a withering critique of "the culture industry" and its effects on the masses. For all three, mass-produced and mass-consumed culture serves as an instrument of domination and social control.

It is this Frankfurt school legacy that has continued to inform historians of China who investigate the question of publics. Those interested in the question of a "public" in modern Chinese history have focused on finding evidence of an authentic rational, autonomous, and liberatory public, and they tend, therefore, to gravitate toward either the late Qing period or the 1920s. They find the late Qing to be a time when a critical, reformist press provided a promising space for nascent rational and engaged public debate. The 1920s is attractive too, as it was a period when national decentralization allowed for the development of more "autonomous" power for urban institutions.[18] In contrast, scholars view the

Nanjing decade as a highly unlikely point of departure for the study of Chinese "publics." The authoritarian tactics of media censorship and state terror adopted by the Nationalist government are seen as inimical to the development of autonomous civic power (see, e.g., Wakeman 1995, 1997). The highly sensational and commercialized media and entertainment circles of the 1930s have also struck many as dubious locations for a critical reading public.[19] Nor has Republican-era law appeared very promising. From the more conventional perspective of legal history, the Nanjing decade seems to provide only examples of limits in judicial reform (e.g., Phillip Huang 2001; Bernhardt 1994). It has also been characterized as a period of retracting judicial autonomy in the face of an encroaching party regime (Xu 2001).

While I do not want to suggest that the above assessments of the 1930s are wrong in identifying a retraction of judicial autonomy or increased Nationalist encroachment into society, I am arguing that the conditions of media sensationalism, state expansion, and a degree of civic retrenchment may not have rung the death knell for all forms of critical publics. In fact, as an era marked at once by commercial sensationalism and political authoritarianism, the 1930s provide us with an interesting position from which to consider how the sensationalism of the mass media might have helped to mobilize, or hail into being, a modern public that expressed a powerful critique of an actively centralizing regime. To this end, I build on some of the scholarship discussed above that recognizes the fluidity of "publics" and their ever-changing significance in state and society relations in the modern period. I move away from concern with the spatial or fixed social parameters of a "public" that predominated in earlier debates and focus instead on the processes that mobilize a "public" (sometimes working against the state, and sometimes initiated by the state).

In doing so, it is crucial to keep in mind the nature of Nationalist state power. Driven by a desire to end extra-territoriality and retrieve full Chinese sovereignty, the centralizing Nationalist regime aggressively sought to demonstrate its ability to monitor, control, and discipline Chinese society (Wakeman 1995). Yet the encroachment into civic society was always fractured. The competing political presence of imperialist powers in the cities and the warlords and communists in the hinterland speak to political division. Lack of resources and ineffectual strategies on the part of the Chinese regime only exacerbated the fragmentation of political power. Prasenjit Duara (1988) has aptly characterized Nationalist penetration into society as "involutionary," capturing the idea that increased investment in disciplining society only resulted in decreasing efficacy of Nationalist governance and control. In this context of fractured Nationalist authoritarianism, there was considerable room for a sentimental public to be hailed into being in urban China's robust consumer culture.

The public that I identify is sentiment-based and ambiguous in terms of its "liberatory" qualities. At the heart of this study, then, is the premise that reason and sentiment are not always mutually exclusive. The book problematizes the assumption that rational communicative action is *the* crucial component in the development of modern and critical "publics" and casts doubt on the assumed dichotomies between reason and sentiment and between reason and morality that underlie much of the existing literature and theory.[20] Could the attributes of a highly commercialized mass media and rising sentimentalism serve as the basis for articulating the "rational-communicative" elements traditionally associated with a Habermasian public sphere? How might media sensations prompt public explorations of the meaning of justice, the pillorying of public figures, and the adjudication of proper moral behavior for modern society and its subjects?

If we frame our analysis in these terms, it quickly becomes apparent that the sentiment-centered and sensation-creating case of Shi Jianqiao occasioned public activity that we could call "participatory" or even "critical" in nature. The trial, for example, made the public more aware of the workings of the courts, provided opportunities for the public to put forth alternative and what it deemed to be superior forms of moral justice outside of the court system, as well as to expose the limits of the existing justice system. Shi Jianqiao's actions prompted debates over the proper public role of women in society, and the gossip surrounding the warlord politics behind the scenes served as a forum where the public could judge the moral character of modern politicians and even the central regime. The political assassination of a warlord in a Buddhist lay-society exposed the collaboration between religious institutions and military leaders. The revenge also metaphorically imposed a sense of order in a period where legacies of the chaos of the earlier warlord era continued to generate deep social anxiety. The political implications of public sympathy were perhaps most evident in the Nationalist pardon of Shi Jianqiao. The central regime acknowledged explicitly petitions from civic associations demanding exemption for Shi Jianqiao and affirming the morality of her actions in justifying its decision to sanction the assassination. Finally, the charged passions and rampant sensationalism at the heart of the affair demonstrated the potency of the social issues under debate. Mass sensation prompted the urban audience not to remain passive, as Habermas would have it, but to participate, if passionately, by consuming information and commenting on the case. Indeed, public sentiment regarding the case became itself an object of obsessive commentary.

PUBLICS, CONSUMER CULTURE, AND GENDER

To avoid exaggerating the critical propensity of public sympathy, bear in mind that this new public was born out of consumer culture, and was thus permeated by a striking tension between expressing criticism while remaining susceptible to manipulation. To articulate this ambiguity more fully, it is helpful to review some recent scholarship that examines the relationship among urban publics, modernity, and mass consumer society in modern Europe. Interested in reconceptualizing the urban public and modernity, such scholarship has begun to put aside the freighted concepts of "public sphere" and "civil society," and to pay closer attention to alternative conceptual possibilities of "publics," or even "crowds," that are forged in the once-maligned realm of mass culture.[21] Vanessa Schwartz, a scholar of nineteenth-century Paris, for example, demonstrates the importance of new forms of mass media and cultural practices not only in transforming everyday life into spectacle, but in enabling individual spectators to come together as a new urban crowd to consume and delight in the visual representation of such spectacles (Schwartz 1998). Schwartz's crowd is made up of consumers of spectacles, or "spectacular realities," found in wax museums, the Paris morgue, and the daily paper. Viewing is thus seen as the basis of collective identity.

At the heart of Schwartz's analysis lies the prism of the spectator and the act of viewing. Such a focus on spectatorship stems in large part from the influence of Walter Benjamin, whose writings on urban mass culture are driven by a concern with the relationship between the rise of fascism and capitalism, with its attendant promises of democratic access to a technologically advanced modernity.[22] Inspired by Charles Baudelaire's poetic descriptions of the figure of the *flâneur*, Benjamin (1983) asserts that any possibility for critical distance from the allure of modern capitalist society lies metaphorically with the *flâneur*, a kind of antihero who, through his leisurely pace and powers of observation, can both be a part of and critically stand apart from the urban crowd. Like Benjamin's *flâneur*, Schwartz's crowd of spectators is somehow both part of the spectacle while at the same time commanding it through the act of viewing (Schwartz 1998, 10).

In this study of 1930s China, I want to retain the possibility suggested by the concept of the *flâneur* that crowds and publics might both be part of the urban phantasmagoria and yet resist the alluring power of the capitalist spectacle, but move away from the focus on spectatorship found in many of the studies inspired by Benjamin's work.[23] My use of the term *sensation*, rather than *spectacle*, in discussing the case of Shi Jianqiao speaks to the emphasis not on viewing, but on the moral authority of emotions in constituting modern publics and crowds. *Sensation* better emphasizes the affective quality of the affair and its ability to engage the sentiments of China's urban audience. When transmitted broadly via modern forms of mass media, news of the revenge, as I show, drew together a crowd of urban consumers who collectively engaged with the fate of the virtuous assassin on a deeply affective level. The media sensation surrounding assassin Shi hailed "public sympathy" into being, allowing urban denizens not simply to come together to *see* the event, or, alternatively, know it rationally, but to share their ability to *feel* it in very visceral terms. While the act of "seeing" was most certainly important in defining such a public, so too was the act of "feeling" or "sympathizing."

Yet, public sympathy in 1930s China converged with Schwartz's crowd of spectators in that both were products of consumer and mass culture. It is thus helpful for us to retain Schwartz's conceptual use of Benjamin's *flâneur* to explore how public sympathy was similarly characterized by an interesting ambiguity between being part of the spectacle (and thus, subject to manipulation by forces of capitalism and the state), and yet, under certain conditions, able to maintain a critical distance. As discussed above, public sympathy could be mobilized into a force that could sway legal proceedings, threaten the moral authority of cultural elites, mediate center-warlord relations, and influence the state's tactics in legitimating its power. At the same time, however, public sympathy in the Shi Jianqiao case always remained vulnerable to manipulation by higher authorities. As chapter 5 details, there were rumors that Feng Yuxiang and other major political players may have conspired all along in engineering the assassination, manipulating public sentiment for their own political purposes. Likewise, the Nationalist government used the pardoning of Shi Jianqiao as a means to appropriate public sympathy and redirect it to Nationalist rule. This susceptibility becomes more clear in the context of a stronger regime. If we move into the 1940s (see chapter 6), we can see how the exigencies of war allowed the Nationalists to be far more successful in rallying collective sentiment for purposes of patriotism.

Finally, gender played a critical role in constituting these new conceptualizations of publics and modernity. How publics were gendered is an issue that historians of modern China have barely begun to raise.[24] Once again, the lack of attention to gender is in part a legacy of the Frankfurt school, whose theorists tend to elide the issue of gender even while gendering as masculine their idealized public sphere and its attendant rational forms of communicative action.[25] Habermas discusses the crucial importance of the rise of the identities of *l'homme* and the (male) *bourgeoisie* in the making of the bourgeois public sphere. The bourgeois female is implicitly located in the domestic realm and involved only to the extent that she and the family help constitute the subjective identity of *l'homme*, an identity that is necessary for the public-sphere participant to feel compelled to defend the universal principles of humanism through rational engagement.[26]

In contrast, this work argues that Shi Jianqiao's gender was crucial in engendering public sympathy. With female bodies seen as dramatic sites upon which discussions of modernity could take place, the early twentieth century saw considerable social anxiety regarding the definition of the so-called "New Woman" (*xin nüxing*).[27] For many, Shi Jianqiao was a New Woman whose body and typically female *qing* served as effective forums for debate over Chinese modernity in the 1930s. Just as exemplary women in imperial China had long embodied the virtues and sentiment of the imperial collective, daughter Shi came for many to embody, and to gender as feminine, the virtues of a new martial nation. Shi's filial heroism effectively enacted the moral virtue of the new Chinese nation, and her ardent passions broadcast through the mass media mobilized, as well as symbolized, the collective sympathies of the authority of an emerging public (chapter 2). At the same time, critics of Shi Jianqiao were vociferous in their condemnation. As chapter 3 argues, left-leaning writers and judicial reformists became increasingly uncomfortable with the rise of a mass public and the threat this public posed to their own rational, "masculine" discourses of modernity. Both men and women may have avidly followed the affair, but these writers denigrated the collective emotionalism as foolhardy and feminine.

THE HISTORY OF *QING* AND ITS FATE IN THE 1930S

While I focus on emotions as the crux of a new public in 1930s China, by no means do I mean to imply that emotion-based publics are in any way more authentic than publics based on rationality. Nor do I mean to suggest that Western publics are "rational" and Chinese ones are "emotional." Rather, the primary goal of this study is to *historicize* exactly how an affective urban collective could gain the moral power it did in response to this 1930s Chinese media sensation. Why did moral sentiment, or *qing*, prove relevant in the making of a public in 1930s China? How did intimate domains—sentiment, familial virtue, and sexuality—figure in the making of nationhood, a new urban public, modern justice, and gendered subjectivity? To answer these questions and to better understand why the emphasis on gendered sentiment in the making of publics in 1930s China makes a great deal of sense, we need to consider the much longer history of attributing moral power to *qing*.

The concept of *qing* has a long and complex history. Referring to a constellation of meanings ranging from objective circumstance (*shiqing*) and disposition (*xingqing*) to, paradoxically, subjective feeling (*ganqing*) and even lust or desire (*qingyu*), *qing* in the imperial era, broadly speaking, could either be the basis of ideal social interactions or constitute selfish urges threatening to disrupt social harmony.[28] In imperial China's orthodox, Confucian moral system, reciprocal affective relations (*renqing*) between family members were thought to represent the relations of the larger political and cosmological order and thus served as the foundation of moral truth.[29] The virtues of filial piety and female chastity, when sincerely felt, could constitute forms of *renqing* and, thus, help create the ethical web that constituted the Confucian cosmological order.

While I refer here to sincerely felt virtues such as filial sentiment and wifely devotion as forms of Confucian ethical sentiment, fusing the notions of virtue and sentiment, the history of the relationship between virtue and sentiment in Confucian moral discourses is actually highly complicated and has long been characterized by considerable anxiety about the exact role of *qing* in forging these ethically valuable familial relations. I explore this anxiety and the relationship between virtue and sentiment in more detail in chapter 3. For now, suffice it to say that according to Confucian orthodoxy, ritual was the primary means for cultivating virtues such as filial piety, whereas sentiment was an ambiguous force. If contained and disciplined properly, sentiment could serve to signal the depth of the sincerity of the virtue. If not, *qing* could devolve into desire (*yu*) and thus foster chaos. These forms of ethical sentiment were thus systematically subject to state sanction. The imperial state's chastity cult, for example, memorialized and promoted female chastity through the granting of memorial arches, official biographies, and monetary awards to families and locales with chaste women (e.g., see Carlitz 1991; 1994). As the regular political endorsement of exemplary sons and loyal ministers effectively demonstrated, male filial grief and mourning were also esteemed forms of sentiment (Kutcher 1999). Finally, ethical sentiment could, in certain instances, take moral precedent over imperial law. In addition to the systematic legal endorsement of female chastity, in cases of filial revenge imperial law often recognized sincere filial piety as the basis for exoneration despite the crime of homicide.[30]

In the modern era, anxiety about *qing* did not wane. As scholars have long noted, the first quarter of the twentieth century saw the fall of Confucian orthodoxy and considerable shifts in the terms of imagining China's social order. Modern intellectuals found themselves urgently searching for ways to rearticulate the relationship between the individual and the social order. In the first decades of the twentieth century, antitraditionalist thinkers and writers who were part of the New Culture movement and the May Fourth Movement cast doubt upon the relevance of "traditional" bonds of moral sentiment (*renqing*) for a modern social order.[31] Filial piety and female chastity, in particular, were targeted and identified as the root cause of China's perceived failure to modernize. These New Culture and May Fourth writers then proceeded to consecrate new forms of *qing*—namely, modern emotions (*ganqing*), including romantic love (*aiqing*), and the related ideal of sexual liberation—as the basis of their new modernity and the core of a new, cosmopolitan subjectivity. New Women were identified as particularly effective bearers of these new forms of passion.

A great deal of scholarly attention has been paid to the New Culture and May Fourth attitudes toward *qing*. Yet, the May Fourth agenda did not represent the general population's attitude toward *qing* and modern subjectivity, nor was it immune to skepticism by the next generation of intellectuals. While anxiety about traditional *renqing* characterized more highbrow literary, moral, and political discussions, sentimentalism prevailed in much of China's urban consumer culture throughout the early twentieth century. Despite the trenchant iconoclasm of May Fourth writers that rejected forms of Confucian ethics, popular urban fiction of the early twentieth century unabashedly sentimentalized virtues such as filial piety to cater to the growing commercial market (Lee 2001). By the 1930s, as China's media became more "mass" in nature, the commercial success and popularity of ethical sentimentalism increased. Furthermore, critics and ideologues of the second quarter of the twentieth century grew increasingly ambivalent about the May Fourth iconoclastic agenda. In 1934, Jiang Jieshi (Chiang Kai-shek), leader of the Nationalist regime, initiated the New Life campaign, a regime-engineered movement that advocated a reconfigured form of Confucianism as the basis of national spirit and civilian discipline, prerequisites for the strengthening of society and the nation. Intellectuals started to move away from May Fourth ideals of explicit female passion and to emphasize more sublimated, virtuous forms of *qing* that more closely conformed to New Life standards.

In short, we must understand the controversy surrounding the Shi Jianqiao case within the context of the historically specific convergence in the 1930s of conflicting attitudes toward *qing*. Continued iconoclastic skepticism toward Confucian *renqing* coexisted with a revival of Confucian moralism and growing anxiety about May Fourth definitions of romantic love. Highbrow ambivalence toward the authority of *qing* grew, even while popular sentimentalism permeated urban consumer culture. Shi Jianqiao's case brought these tensions into sharp relief. As we will see, for regular consumers of popular sentimentalism in the urban media industry, the passionate female assassin deserved widespread sympathy (chapter 2). For writers who were moving away from the excessive emotionalism of May Fourth agendas toward a stronger emphasis on Confucian ethics, Shi Jianqiao and public sympathy for her actions merited furious critique (chapter 3). Finally, for the New Life regime, which was preoccupied with a renewed political interest in Confucian moralism as the basis of their nativist nationalism, the controversial assassin was worthy of a state sanction (chapter 5).

VIOLENCE, JUSTICE, AND THE ETHICAL AUTHORITY OF SENTIMENT

Shi Jianqiao's case allows us to investigate more than the making of a public and debates over *qing*'s significance in China's new social order. As a study of a homicide, the book also raises a host of issues concerning the relationship between *qing* and violence, the role of assassination in the broader culture, and the role of violence in constituting boundaries among ethics, justice, and political power. To address these issues, I examine the Shi Jianqiao affair in conjunction with a few other cases of Republican-era revenge and crimes of passion. These include a 1932–33 case of filial revenge in which a nephew, Zheng Jicheng, killed militarist Zhang Zongchang to avenge the death of his uncle (chapter 5); a 1935–37 crime of passion, where a woman, Liu Jinggui, killed her rival in love (chapters 3 and 4); and an explicitly nonviolent case of revenge where Xu Daolin in 1945 brought a lawsuit against Feng Yuxiang to avenge the death of his father (chapter 5).

In exploring the politics of *qing* behind these acts of revenge and homicide, this discussion differs from earlier studies of the early twentieth century in its treatment of violence. Previous scholarship has tended to treat violence as a straightforward use of might to achieve political ends such as consolidating control in cities, regional territories, and the national political arena. This focus on tactics of terror and violence as brute force characterizes, for example, histories of the Nanjing decade, and stems in part from the larger question that has long framed Republican-era studies, namely, whether the ubiquitous presence of violence and the state's sanctioning of violence can be taken as evidence of authoritarian, if not fascistic, Nationalist rule.[32] Unfortunately, much of this scholarship tends to assume that violence automatically had a destabilizing effect on society and does not consider how terror, or the sanctioning of terror, might function to constitute societal order or be seen as an integral, if unfortunate, part of political processes. There is no real in-depth inquiry into historically specific interpretations and meanings of violence nor, by extension, into the different motives for employing, sanctioning, or legitimating force. Nor have related questions been raised regarding how *qing* might be used as a strategy of legitimating terror or how certain forms of brutality became ideal expressions of *qing*.

To redress this neglect, I argue that we need to rethink our approach by shifting attention from a description of the straightforward institutional and political use of force and terror to an analysis of the *meanings* attributed to violence. Rather than automatically treating assassination as a sign of chaos or failed rule of law, then, this study asks how and why certain acts of assassination were deemed legitimate means of pursuing justice. It considers how acts of filial revenge have a long history of being considered as potent, if extreme, ritual expressions that, when endowed with *qing*, were pregnant with significance.[33] This approach helps us to understand how these acts became highly politicized as objects of struggle among different players. A single female avenger, an impassioned public, China's courts, the central regime, and regional politicians all sought to explain what these expressions of terror meant. For some, the degree of passion expressed in these acts authenticated the virtue of the motivations, rendering the act of brutal revenge legitimate and even above the law as a purer form of justice. For others, however, the emotional sincerity of the actors mattered little; they viewed the extreme violence as a mark of social destabilization and a sign of national chaos. The question of who had the right or power to define justice and to determine the exact relationship between *qing* and violence in modern society was central.

By taking violence as a thematic concern, this book also asks how impassioned acts of violence functioned to marshal collective subjectivity and political participation in twentieth-century China. While much of this study focuses on how ethically passionate revenge mobilized public sympathy in the 1930s and on the politics surrounding such a development, the book also investigates the significance of this issue for the 1940s and beyond. By following Shi Jianqiao's participation in relief efforts during the war against Japan, it examines how her individual reputation for violent passions remained symbolically charged and highly effective in drumming up Chinese patriotism in resistance efforts (chapter 6). While the regime succeeded in using promises of national retribution to mobilize collective sentiment against Japanese aggression, the use of impassioned violence for mobilization purposes was perhaps even more evident in the post-1949 era against internal enemies. By the 1960s, Shi Jianqiao found that her filial sentiment had become highly problematic in the new Communist order, and she had to launch a vigorous defense of herself and tailor her motive of moral sentiment into something that was not feudal and Confucian but in fact revolutionary (chapter 6). But, if filial revenge no longer had revolutionary cachet, class retribution and other forms of impassioned and ritualized violence functioned powerfully, and often tragically, in rallying the masses. In the conclusion, I suggest the possible implications of my findings by exploring how "public sympathy" for ethical violence laid the groundwork for the rise of "the sentiment of the revolutionary masses," a concept that proved crucial to post-1949 Chinese revolutionary politics.

EMOTIONS IN HISTORY AND IN THE STUDY OF HISTORY: A GLOBAL PERSPECTIVE

Scholars have rarely viewed the history of early twentieth-century China from the perspective of emotions and sentiment, with some notable exceptions in the field of literature (Link 1981; Lee 2001; Wang 1997). We can attribute much of this reluctance to a long-standing reticence about emotions in the general discipline of history. As a modern academic field, history is crucially informed by Hegelian assumptions regarding the importance of History in fostering the crucial force of a nation-state's march toward progress, namely, Reason, and historians have traditionally viewed their discipline as founded on the rational and objective ability to know the past. What may also have been a by-product of the Hegelian roots of the discipline is a strong sense of skepticism toward the historical study of emotions and the irrational. Only at the end of the twentieth century, with the post-structuralist critique of social science epistemology, and theoretical challenges from gender theorists, has this long-standing reluctance of historians to acknowledge the relevance of studying emotions begun to abate. Michel Foucault's writings, for example, have been among the most influential in endowing the inquiry of subjectivity, the body, and emotions with theoretical urgency. Concerned with historicizing or, in his terms, writing the "genealogy" of modern subjectivity, Foucault investigates the relationship between the structures of the modern self and the regimes of power and social practice, including the construction of the modern subject as both knowing subject and knowable object in modern social sciences.[34] Gender scholars, including Joan Scott (1988) and Judith Butler (1990), have drawn from post-structuralists such as Foucault to challenge the assumed metaphysical essence of gender and sexuality. In doing so, they shed light on the question of what historical processes lie behind the constitution of gendered and sexed identities, and in turn, how gender and sexuality might shape broader social and political structures.

Armed with these theoretical tools, historians have begun to study the history of subjectivity, gender, the body, and emotions. Modern Europeanists, for example, have been among those starting to take emotions seriously as a subject of historical inquiry. Challenging the long-standing assumption that sentiment was antithetical to the Enlightenment project, these scholars have demonstrated its crucial role in articulating the transition from an older aristocratic world order to a modern order. Leaving behind the earlier stratification of society by class and bloodlines, the modern era, they argue, sees the fundamental truth of emotional experience as the moral basis of bourgeois individuality. This innate human sociability, in turn, served as the foundation of the social solidarity that constituted a new civil society (Denby 1994). The rise of the sentimental novel and the cult of domesticity of the eighteenth century were also linked with the history of sexuality (i.e., gender difference), the rise of the middle-class bourgeois identity, and the carving out of public/private spheres (e.g., see Armstrong 1995; Goodman 1992). Only after playing a central role in the events of the French Revolution was sentiment increasingly relegated to the private sphere, as scholars promoted contractual and law-bound relations mediated by rationality as the basis of a new, masculine public sphere (see Habermas 1989; Landes 1988).

The historical significance of sentiment in the making of modernity was not specific to the modern West. If we consider some other works on sentiment and non-Western modernity, we can identify a global pattern among non-Western societies of the strategic employment of preexisting, "traditional" forms of virtue and sentiment in their creation of modern societies. This complicates previous interpretations of the "importation" of modernity from the West to other parts of the world. Understanding the similarities in the way different national consumer cultures and forms of mass media mobilized the masses and shaped modern societies gives us a better picture of the global impact of capitalism. Historians and anthropologists studying modern societies in non-Western countries other than China identify the crucial role of emotions and virtue in the construction of modernity and civic identity in, for example, Brazil (e.g., Caufield 2000). Others examine how poetic sentiment and a code of modesty shaped strategies of resistance among nomadic Bedouin women in modern Egypt (e.g., Abu-Lughod 2000). Still others look at how the domain of the intimate was intricately linked and implicated in the creation and maintenance of racial hierarchies crucial in modern colonialism (e.g., Stoler 2002). This study continues this dialogue as it explores the role of sentiment in creating an urban public, in imagining a post-Confucian social order, and in demarcating the boundaries among ethical, judicial, and political power in modern China.

ONE

The Assassin and Her Revenge

A Tale of Moral Heroism and Female Self-Fashioning in an Age of Mass Communication

1. I dare not forget the revenge of my father for a single
   moment;
It breaks my heart to watch my mother's temples turn gray.
I am loath to let her suffer any longer,
The opportunity should not be squandered.

2. I cannot bear to look back to ten years ago.
Things have remained the same, only the scenery has
   changed.
I arrive at the Society not to find the Buddha,
I seek death, not immortality.

Just after killing Sun Chuanfang, Shi Jianqiao distributed the poem above to witnesses at the crime scene. Composed by the assassin herself, the poem was in the form of seven-character, regulated verse (*qiyan lüshi*). As such, it was part of the tradition of lyrical poetry (*shi*), a literary genre long regarded as particularly effective both for expressing one's innermost thoughts and sincere feelings, and for arousing the emotions of others.[1] To an audience familiar with this poetic tradition, Shi Jianqiao's poem brimmed with passion and sincerity.[2] Shi's obsessive dedication to avenging her father is evident in the first line, and the mention of her mother's graying temples conveys her filial dedication to her mother as well. In noting how she was deeply troubled because the retribution had remained unfulfilled for ten years, the poem expresses the urgency of the matter and underscores the intensity of Shi's hunger for revenge. The mention of ten years, moreover, is meant to invoke the popular saying, "For a Gentleman seeking revenge, ten years is not too late," which alerts readers to the virtue of the act and suggests that one should bide one's time and wait for the right opportunity to seek revenge. In the next clause, "only the scenery has changed," is also significant, suggesting that the desire for revenge has remained unabated despite the passage of time. The last line dramatically turns the Buddhist temple, a site usually reserved for peaceful enlightenment, into a place of heroic karmic retribution. The poem presents filial devotion as the motive that drove Shi to such an extreme act of revenge.

This poem was part of a larger set of mimeographed materials that Shi Jianqiao had brought to the crime scene. In addition to the poem, Shi also distributed copies of a single-page statement of intent and a longer testament entitled *Gao guoren shu* (A letter to inform my countrymen [hereafter, *GGRS*]).[3] The succinct statement of intent was a list of four points:

Gentlemen take note:

1. Today, Shi Jianqiao (given name Shi Gulan) has killed Sun Chuanfang in order to avenge the death of her father Shi Congbin.
2. For concrete details of the situation, please refer to *Gao guoren shu*.
3. I have accomplished the great revenge, and am immediately turning myself in to the courts.
4. As for splattering blood onto the walls of the Buddhist hall and shocking everyone, my deepest apologies.

She signed the piece with "Female Avenger, Shi Jianqiao" and imprinted her fingerprint as a sign of authentication. The longer testament described in detail the tragic events that had led up to this final episode, including how ten years earlier Sun Chuanfang had ruthlessly decapitated Shi Congbin, a model military man and Shi's father, at the Bangbu, Anhui, train station. Ten years later, thirty-year-old Shi Jianqiao, a native of Tongcheng, Anhui, had finally come to avenge his death.

These richly suggestive materials showed how thoroughly the female assassin had strategically orchestrated this act of revenge. In an age of mass media, her revenge was available for public consumption from the start. The assassination was not an anonymous murder done on the sly, but rather a planned killing carried out in a lay-Buddhist recitation hall filled with people. With dozens of worshippers as her witnesses, Shi Jianqiao killed her sworn enemy and then distributed her materials, ensur-

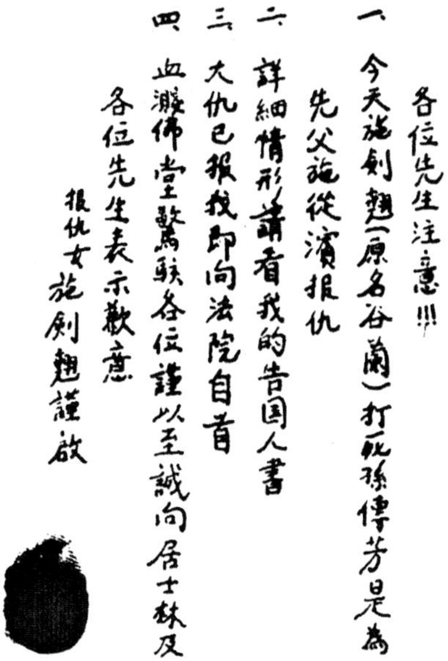

各位先生注意!!!
一 今天施劍翹(原名谷蘭)打死孫傳芳是為
先父施從濱報仇
二 詳細情形請看我的告国人書
三 大仇已報我即向法院自首
四 血濺佛堂驚駭各位謹以至誠向居士林及
各位先生表示歉意
報仇女施劍翹謹啟

Figure 1. Mimeographed pamphlet that Shi Jianqiao distributed at the crime scene, authenticated by her fingerprint. Reprinted in newspapers in the days following the assassination.

ing that not only the witnesses at the crime scene but a larger audience would learn the daughter's version of events. Almost immediately, the material was reproduced word for word for urban China's reading public to consume.

Shi Jianqiao's knowledge of public relations was evident throughout the course of the affair. The assassin continued to court the press after the killing. Upon turning herself in to the police, Shi gave a public statement and handed to authorities a preliminary will in which she had arranged for her mother and her children to be taken care of in the case of her demise.[4] Two days later, Shi held another press conference at the local police station and elaborated on the circumstances of the revenge. She began the meeting by saying, "There are discrepancies in each section of today's newspaper [coverage]," and went on to provide what she said was the true account of the event.[5] This meeting with the press was the first of several that she would hold during the lengthy trial.[6] Often right before the courts would announce a verdict, or at other crucial junctures in the legal case, Shi granted an emotional interview from her jail cell. She also on occasion released heartfelt poetry she wrote in prison.[7] Some of the poems described how she spent her time in jail studying classical poetry or engaging in admirable behavior, including teaching fellow inmates how to read. Others professed her concern and yearning for her mother and family.[8] The poems and jailhouse interviews punctuated the emotional peaks of her pursuit for justice, and were thus reminiscent of traditional opera, in which prose dialogue is often interspersed with poetry that was sung to represent the dramatic high points of the narrative. This tactic proved successful in gaining sympathy, with several observers lauding Shi's poems for powerfully conveying her genuine feelings. It also reveals the lengths to which the female assassin would go to influence media coverage.

In an era of modern communications, Shi Jianqiao managed to tap into the array of cultural and technological resources at her disposal to weave a highly compelling tale of ethical revenge. Every move appeared to be for public consumption. Shi vilified her enemy Sun Chuanfang, glorified her dead father Shi Congbin, and ensured that her self-presentation as a devoted daughter conformed to gendered assumptions about female heroism. Each public statement she made was imbued with great feeling and filled with gripping detail. The result was that much of urban China came to believe that the filial motive behind the revenge was sincerely felt, and public sympathy for her vengeful actions became remarkably widespread.

THE MASS MEDIA CONTEXT

Extraordinary cases had gripped the public imagination and elicited collective sympathy through theater and storytelling long before the case of Shi Jianqiao. However, with the appearance of modern forms of mass communication in the late nineteenth and early twentieth centuries, media sensations like the case of Shi Jianqiao became increasingly common and were unprecedented in their reach. Sensational cases were different from any before in their potential spread and the speed with which their impact was felt beyond the immediate communities involved. Local events were quickly transformed into universal tales that stirred the sympathies of urban or near-urban communities throughout China. By the 1930s, the media had expanded in scope and assumed the unprecedented characteristics of sensationalism and sentimentality befitting their mass audience.

The unprecedented impact of media sensations is a direct result of the tremendous growth witnessed by China's mass media in the early twentieth century. According to Perry Link, Shanghai's media industry expanded roughly sixfold from the beginning of the century to the early 1930s. During the same period, the urban literacy rate at least doubled (Link 1981, 10). Circulation by the third decade of the twentieth century was as high as a hundred and fifty thousand for some popular newspapers.[9] These highly circulated papers carried the news of the Shi affair. Major dailies that covered the event were not limited to those in the Shanghai-Nanjing and Beiping-Tianjin vicinities, but included those in Guangdong, Sichuan, Manchuria, and even Russia.[10] Nor was readership restricted to urban areas. Provincial communities surrounding urban centers also had access to newspapers covering the story.

Circulation figures alone, moreover, do not reflect the true extent of the media's influence. People commonly followed the news by sharing newspapers and reading those hung on public bulletin boards. Lin Monong (1980), a Republican-period journalist who writes about the impact of the Shi Jianqiao media event on his career, describes how as a student in Tianjin he had not been able to afford a regular newspaper subscription and instead read newspapers that were posted daily at important junctions throughout the city. Lin describes in detail how daily papers from both Tianjin and Beiping were made available in the afternoon when people would quickly crowd together, stand, and read. Of course, this group was still relatively limited. As Lin notes, those with the appropriate literacy level and leisure time were still in a substantial minority among Tianjin's overall population. Yet, although the habit of reading the daily newspaper may have been limited to a small group, information and news were available to much of the rest of the urban population. The introduction of the radio, for example, made news readily available beyond the literate audience. Leo Lee and Andrew Nathan report that Shanghai by 1937 had an estimated one hundred thousand radios (Lee and Nathan 1985, 374–75). But the true size of the listening audience, like that of the reading audience, was much larger. As Carleton Benson notes, owning a radio may have been a luxury, but many were able to listen to the radio in the factories where they worked or in neighborhood shops (Benson 1995, 123–27).

The sheer diversity of media had also increased dramatically. In the late nineteenth century, the eight-page *Shenbao* (The Shanghai daily) was one of the few sources of information for Shanghai industrialists and political elites. By the Republican era, all major urban areas had not one but several major dailies, some of which ran well over eight pages. These papers now contained argument and opinion, chronicled spectacular events, and served as a compendium of information for a targeted reading audience imagined to be far more inclusive than ever before. Urban readers could also choose from a variety of *xiaobao*, papers known in English as "mosquito presses" because of their unpredictable life spans and their reputation for reporting "biting" news. In the late Qing, when the genre first appeared, *xiaobao* provided information on the entertainment industry and courtesan circles to literati (*wenren*) readers. By the 1930s, while remaining short in page-length, *xiaobao* were catering to a much larger audience and reported on a myriad of topics, including ones that big papers omitted because of censorship or commercial reasons.[11] The periodical press had also grown substantially, and served as a forum for lively discussion on the case.[12] Journals ranged from those that were highly academic and specialized, read by a select few, to popular weeklies and magazines for the general urban audience. News and discussion of the Shi case appeared in all forms, from large dailies to mosquito presses, from popular weeklies to specialized journals.

In addition to the boom in journalism, different kinds of entertainment also proliferated, providing yet another forum in which information on the affair was disseminated. In the early twentieth century, China's urban audience increasingly consumed fiction, film, radio, and theater. After late Qing reformers like Liang Qichao had argued for the inspirational power of fiction, literary magazines of all stripes were founded in the first quarter of the twentieth century, and the popular fiction market greatly expanded. As the rise of commercial publishing houses continued to flood the market with affordable books in the following decades, readers could also simply open their newspapers to peruse literary supplements or read daily installments of serialized novels.[13] For fans of live drama, the theater world expanded in quantity and quality, especially in Shanghai. Audiences could choose from traditional opera, regional operas, reformed Shanghaiese theater, and modern spoken drama.[14] Finally, with the arrival of new technologies, leisure in urban China changed drastically. Radio modernized the "traditional" story-telling arts, while film completely revolutionized urban entertainment.[15] It was in this context of a burgeoning mass media that Shi Jianqiao held court.

THE ASSASSIN

Who exactly was this woman? Shi Jianqiao was born in 1906 in Tongcheng, Anhui.[16] In addition to her father, Shi Congbin, her immediate family included her mother, an elder brother, three younger brothers, and a younger sister. Her ancestral home was a small village near Tongcheng, called Shazigang. Her grandfather was a farmer and bean-curd seller. Her father, the eldest son in the family, and her uncle, the fourth son, Shi Congyun, became decorated soldiers in the early part of the twentieth century, raising the overall social status of the family. Shi Congbin, whose courtesy name, or *zi*, was Shi Hanting, was the deputy commander of Shandong's military affairs and served as a brigade commander to Zhang Zongchang by 1925, the year he was killed by Sun Chuanfang.[17] Shi Congyun, Shi Jianqiao's uncle, had served in a garrison of the Qing dynasty and died a martyr in the anti-Qing Luanzhou Uprising in 1911.[18] Shi Jianqiao had wed a fellow Anhui-native with the same surname, Shi Jinggong, who had been her cousin Zhongcheng's classmate at Baoding Military Academy and, by 1935, had bore him two sons, Jinren and Yuyao.[19]

Accounts of Shi Jianqiao's education differ, but it was very likely that she had a combination of both a classical and modern education, something quite common for privileged women at the time. According to a Shanghai *Shibao* (The eastern times) report printed in the days following the assassination, Shi had been educated at home, learning the proper womanly arts, including lyrical poetry.[20] The Beiping *Shibao* (Truth post) claimed that Shi Jianqiao had received an education in the classics and national literature at a private family school.[21] A retrospective account describes rather admiringly how she had been tutored at home along with her male cousin Zhongcheng in the Confucian classics, and how she had excelled as a pupil (Chen Jin 1991). Other reports note that she had graduated from Tianjin's Girl's Normal School (e.g., Wu 1990). The divergent accounts notwithstanding, it is clear that her upbringing and education were certainly marked by privilege and provided her with the cultural resources that she would later use in justifying her revenge. Her literary skill was needed to prepare the written materials she distributed at the crime scene and to write classical poetry while in jail. By displaying her knowledge of classical poetry and literature, Shi succeeded in implicitly likening herself to the classic figure of the *cainü*, or "talented woman" of the inner chambers of the late imperial period, a figure whose moral fortitude she no doubt would have wanted to claim.[22]

Given the complexity of the tasks at hand (both the assassination itself and the campaign to win public sympathy for her actions), one would think that Shi Jianqiao had backers in her quest. Yet the extent to which she received outside help to plot and engineer the revenge killing is still unclear. Contemporary observers of the case pondered over this precise issue. Some commentators wondered how she gained access to a mimeograph machine to prepare the printed material that she distributed.[23] The legal investigation inquired into how she acquired her Browning gun, the weapon with which she killed Sun.[24] Others speculated that Feng Yuxiang, a retired militarist turned Nationalist statesman, not only helped Shi secure an official pardon, but also had a hand in helping her engineer the whole affair.[25] Not until thirty years after the event did the avenging daughter openly address some of these questions. While she made no mention of Feng's role in planning the killing, she did acknowledge that she had conspired with her brothers and sisters (Shi 1987, 514). She also claimed that she had purposely left many of these issues ambiguous during the trial, since she had not wanted to implicate others in any wrongdoing.

THE RAPACIOUS WARLORD

Regardless of whether she worked alone or with backers, Shi Jianqiao won tremendous media attention and public support in part because Sun Chuanfang was the man she killed. In the atmosphere of growing distrust for warlords by the 1930s, her murder of Sun Chuanfang became significant beyond the death of Sun as an individual. As a retired militarist, Sun had the potential to serve as a symbol of China's national weakness. It was this potential that Shi Jianqiao sought to exploit.

After the 1911 Revolution, the promise of a new republic faded quickly. Sun Yat-sen, with no military power of his own, yielded political power to militarist Yuan Shikai. In his quest to establish his own dynasty, Yuan had failed to erect any lasting government system, and after his death in 1916 China effectively lacked a central government. A decade of warfare ensued, with regional militarists scrambling for power and seizing territory in the newly created power vacuum. Their internecine struggles ravaged much of China until the Nationalist Party launched its Northern Expedition in 1926, and nominally unified the country by 1928. Nationalist unification was, however, far from complete. Even as China's ongoing national weakness was being blamed on a prior decade of warlordism, militarists continued to hold sway over parts of China. The anti-Communist campaigns of 1934–35 sharply reduced the autonomy of many provincial militarists, but not until 1936 was the central state able to incorporate entire provinces of China that had been under regional militarist rule and consolidate political control over the greater portion of the nation. Even then, seven out of eighteen provinces in China proper continued to be essentially autonomous (Eastman 1991). Not surprisingly, social and political anxiety about both active and retired militarists persisted throughout the Nanjing decade.

Warlordism plagued the regime not only in reality, but also in symbolic terms. Edward McCord (1996) discusses the politics of anti-warlordism in early twentieth-century China and identifies the May Fourth movement, the 1919 patriotic mass movement, as seminal in coalescing public sentiment against warlords. During this period the term *warlord* (*junfa*) came to acquire unprecedented negative association with new forms of violence and imperialism (Waldron 1991). By the Nanjing decade, the Nationalist regime sought to capitalize on anti-warlord sentiment, but found this strategy to be fraught with political difficulty. On the one hand, smearing warlordism as a system that brought about China's internal disunity allowed the regime to justify centralization. By blaming remaining warlords for China's ongoing weakness, Nanjing could also absolve itself from failing to strengthen the country. On the other hand, a smear campaign could also result in a symbolic backlash. The demonized warlord became a trenchant sign of the central regime's inability to unify the nation. Furthermore, when attributing national disunity to remaining militarists, Jiang Jieshi had to distance himself from his own militarist past and establish that he had been fated from the beginning to assume Sun Yat-sen's mantle to rule.[26]

To resolve the dilemma of possibly implicating China's current leader as a "warlord," the public campaign against warlords shifted to target the specific group of militarists who lived in North China under de facto Japanese militarist rule (Waldron 1991, 1096). In the latter half of the 1930s, it was becoming increasingly evident that Japan was pursuing autonomous status for five northern provinces of China proper. To do so, the Japanese aggressively sought help from retired Chinese warlords and other local politicians. Rumors that "collaborationist" politicians and ex-Beiyang militarists were plotting their return and conspiring with the Japanese in North China quickly followed. It was in this Republican-era context that Sun Chuanfang's ascent and demise occurred.

A native of Licheng, Shandong, Sun Chuanfang (1885–1935), whose *zi* was Sun Xinyuan, was a major participant in the internecine warfare and alliance brokering among regional strongmen of the 1920s. His military education began under the Qing. He graduated from Beiyang military school around 1904 and was sent by the government to Japan for further training. Upon his return, he joined the Beiyang army and became part of the Zhili clique, one of the major groups vying for national control during the second decade of the twentieth century. Sun climbed the ranks quickly.

In 1924, Zhang Zuolin, the leader of the Fengtian forces, sent Zhang Zongchang southward to wrest control of the Yangzi provinces from the Zhili clique. In October 1925, Sun Chuanfang successfully launched a surprise counterattack against the advancing Fengtian troops, and on the fourth day of that month Sun captured Shi Jianqiao's father, Shi Congbin, and beheaded him (Boorman and Howard 1967–71, 3:160–62). Sun Chuanfang's successful campaign to rout the Fengtian forces resulted in the military leaders of Anhui, Hubei, and Jiangxi rallying to his support, and by December of that year, Sun proclaimed himself the commander-in-chief of the armies of the Five Allied Southeastern Provinces (Anhui, Jiangxi, Fujian, Jiangsu, Zhejiang). While still showing nominal deference to Wu Peifu, Sun had, in effect, become the strongest military leader of the Zhili group. By 1926 he had established the so-called Greater Shanghai Municipality and integrated the various Shanghai jurisdictions under his control. Sun continued to control the southeast until 1927, when Jiang Jieshi's forces swept northward from Guangdong to unify China. After being driven out of Shanghai, Sun returned to North China and allied with Zhang Zuolin and Zhang Zongchang in a last-ditch effort to oppose the Nationalists. When the military success of Jiang Jieshi proved inevitable, Sun retired from political life in 1928, took up Buddhism, and, together with ex-militarist Jin Yunpeng, established a lay-Buddhist society (*jushilin*) in Tianjin, where he was later killed by daughter Shi.[27]

At the point of his death, Sun's legacy was ambiguous. Some thought he clearly deserved to die because of his violent suppression of labor strikes in Shanghai, where he had been the military ruler from late 1925 to 1927. In a short piece entitled "Sun Chuanfang Should Die," writer Jun Zuo argued that, given his maltreatment of striking workers and citizens in Shanghai, Sun Chuanfang deserved his violent ending.[28] Yet his legacy in Shanghai was not entirely negative. The foreign community in Shanghai credited him for stabilizing the area. The English-language paper, the *North China Herald*, stated that "[Sun] stood out predominant in the administration of Shanghai . . . [and] his efforts at reorganizing the somewhat confused civic administration of Shanghai . . . are noteworthy."[29] Commenting on Sun's death in 1935, a Chinese commentator stated in a *Dagongbao* editorial that Sun's rule over Jiangsu and Zhejiang had been good and wondered why anyone would want to assassinate him.[30]

In North China, Sun's reputation and death were tainted specifically by rumors about his actions during the twilight years of his life. Despite his retirement into a life of Buddhism and his professed disavowal of all things political, accounts about his ambitions to reenter politics in Beiping circulated just months before his assassination. Specific rumors charged that Sun Chuanfang was scheming with Japanese collaborators, if not with the Japanese. Pamphlets circulated stories that Sun and Cao Rulin would share leadership of the North China movement for independence.[31] One editorial accused Sun of selling opium, a sure sign of his rapacity and evil nature.[32] Fictionalized accounts also helped generate the impression that Sun was participating in collaborationist politics. "Xiejian fotang" (A bloodbath in the Buddhist hall), a radio play based on the assassination, identifies Sun as a collaborator who had been betraying the country. Sun Chuanfang publicly denounced such reports as blatantly false and suggested that the Japanese were spreading gossip to generate social and political instability.[33]

Such rumors were fueled by Sun's association before his death with important North China players, many of whom were suspected collaborationists. Several attended Sun's funeral. He Yingqin was the Nationalists' minister of war who had negotiated the unpopular 1935 Ho-Umeza agreement. Cao Rulin was popularly perceived as a pro-Japanese official and, as a result of negotiating the disastrous "war loans" from Japan in 1917, had been the target of May Fourth protests in 1919; Wang Yitang had been among the first of the Beiyang politicians to cooperate with Japan and was a member in 1935 of the Hebei-Chahar political council that served as a buffer between the Nanjing government and the Japanese militarists in North China.

Given her own desire to portray Sun Chuanfang in as unflattering a light as possible, Shi Jianqiao built on the negative rumors about the retired militarist. To win popular support for her actions, Shi Jianqiao portrayed Sun Chuanfang as a potent symbol for the regional militarism of the 1920s and the lurking threat of warlord collaboration in the 1930s.[34] Shi Jianqiao did not hesitate to depict Sun Chuanfang as a depraved warlord. In her *GGRS*, Shi accused Sun of having "the heart of a demon" and being "lupine and rapacious in character." She smeared his reputation by contending that Sun's willingness to attack and decimate greatly outnumbered troops was evidence of his cruelty. She wrote that, "[Sun Chuanfang] deserves to die for his many crimes. . . . He calls himself 'commander-in-chief,' but he is really no different from a mere bandit (*dafei*)!" To emphasize Sun's cruelty, the dutiful daughter pointed to the ruthless decapitation of her father, which she argued was in violation of the fundamental principle of modern international warfare that the enemy's commander was never to be harmed. As a result, her father's beheading did not go unnoticed in the press. *Jingbao* editorialist Miao Wei followed Shi Jianqiao's cue and similarly found Sun Chuanfang's choice to decapitate Shi Congbin to be gruesome and his impaling of Shi's head on a stick at the Bangbu, Anhui, train station, unnecessarily humiliating.[35]

Blaming Sun for the social strife of the preceding decade was something of a risk. Shi Jianqiao's father had been part of the military imbroglios of the preceding decade as well, commanding highly unpopular mercenary troops. While this was gingerly acknowledged, Shi emphasized that her father's participation was under the orders of Zhang Zongchang and the northern government at the time. In contrast, Sun Chuanfang, she claimed in her *GGRS*, had been single-handedly keeping China weak and divided by unilaterally declaring himself the head of the Five Allied Southeastern Provinces in 1926 just when the northern powers had begun to erect a legitimate national government. Her father had dutifully served the internationally recognized Chinese government; her nemesis, however, was a member of a group of renegade militarists.[36]

LOYAL SOLDIER AND WRONGED FATHER

In contrast to the smear campaign she launched against Sun Chuanfang, Shi Jianqiao spent a considerable amount of energy depicting her father, Shi Congbin, in glowing terms. For many, Shi Congbin may have been less powerful than Sun, but he was still a Beiyang militarist. As the deputy commander of Shandong's military affairs and a brigade commander for Zhang Zongchang during the Second Fengtian-Zhili war, Shi Congbin was captured and killed by Sun in battle. Yet, in Shi Jianqiao's accounts, Shi Congbin was neither a mere casualty of war nor a minor warlord. Rather, he had been unequivocally wronged. By manipulating highly effective, if formulaic, characterizations of the moral uprightness of her father and fusing them with strategic personal detail, Shi Jianqiao told a powerful story of injustice against her father and thereby legitimated her choice to seek revenge.

For example, in her *GGRS*, Shi Jianqiao affirmed that Shi Congbin was an excellent father. She did so by reciting the exact words with which he had instructed her and her siblings: "You all have resolve in your heart . . . not to be idle or wanton, do not wallow in luxury. Curb your self and benefit the group. Do not abandon the people and you will benefit yourself. Be industrious and thrifty and you will lead a life of moral ex-

本市新聞

居士林內昨日駭人慘案

施從濱有女復讎
孫傳芳佛堂斃命

連發三槍皆中要害當場身死
行兇之後散發傳單坦然自首

[illegible]

孫傳芳

施從濱

Figure 2. Photos of Sun Chuanfang (top) and Shi Congbin (bottom) in the news coverage of the assassination, from the major Tianjin paper *Yishibao*, 14 November 1935.

cellence." These words invoked time-honored Confucian standards of how to be an exemplary human being. By attributing these words to her father, Shi implied that as a patriarch who was traditionally expected to serve as an exemplar for his children, Shi Congbin himself had embodied those virtues and fulfilled his duties. She also portrayed Shi as an exemplary leader. In the *GGRS*, she mentions his rule as a garrison commander in Caizhou: "The local people were strong and fierce, but many of the unemployed had become roaming bandits. My late father came up with a multi-level plan to establish a straw-hat factory. He absorbed the unemployed, taught them industrial arts, and let them become self-sufficient, saving innumerable lives. The trend of banditry was stopped and even until today, the business of the factory has not declined." Finally, she hailed him as loyal and brave, telling how in 1925 Shi Congbin had decided to stay in uniform upon the request of the Fengtian command. As she described at a press conference, "[By staying on, my late father] restored hope to the citizens and the state could rely on his council. It was not easy to let him go."[37] Since it was the courageous decision to stay on that proved fatal, the injustice against Shi Congbin was made even more evident.

Shi Jianqiao's account of her father's death was particularly compelling. On October 3, 1925, while leading the Superior Iron Brigade (*Tiejia jun*), a brigade of mercenary troops, in an attempt to capture Guzhen, Shandong, Shi Congbin was surrounded by Sun Chuanfang's troops with no support in sight. Shi's four thousand soldiers were slaughtered, while Shi himself was taken prisoner and beheaded the next day upon Sun's personal order. Shi Jianqiao related in heart-wrenching detail how her family would not have learned the truth except for the bravery and loyalty of one of Shi Congbin's personal servants. "Only a single servant was able to flee home. When we asked him about news from the front line, he threw himself to the ground in tears. We knew the news was not good."[38] The servant had been too grief-stricken to speak. Only after the Shi family had gone to Tianjin did they learn all the facts behind Shi Congbin's death.

The supporting cast in Shi's tale of revenge included the grieving widow and the suffering family her father had left behind. Even though there is little indication that the Shi family underwent any real financial strain, Shi Jianqiao nonetheless insisted that Shi Congbin's death meant that a poor widow and six children, four of whom were still young, were left to fend for themselves. Sun Chuanfang was directly to blame for her family's plight. The way in which Shi portrayed her mother was particularly important. Traditionally, dutiful daughters and chaste wives were expected to commit suicide if their fathers or husbands were killed unjustly. Such an extreme gesture was meant as an ultimate expression of loyalty and of protest against injustice. But in this twentieth-century tale, Shi Jianqiao did not commit suicide and, moreover, justified her decision to live in terms of her filial piety to her mother. She portrayed her mother as particularly grief-stricken by the affair and argued that she needed to right the wrong committed against her father on behalf of her mother. In her *GGRS*, Shi declared, "Although all I wanted to do was die, my elderly mother's illness gave me the will to live."[39] In her will, she stated, with similar effect, "To my dear mother . . . what I have been hiding from you for years, I can no longer hide. Our enemy has not yet been retaliated [against]. Father's death can no longer be obscured. . . . A sacrifice should be made for father's revenge. In the future, five children will still be able to wait on you. They are all dutiful."[40] Shi Jianqiao's act of revenge would be the ultimate gesture of filial piety, while her remaining siblings would be able to wait on her elderly mother in more mundane ways throughout the rest of her mother's life.

The decision to provide her will at the police station was a smart one.

As a document, the will was purportedly private, available to family members only, yet hers was widely circulated in the press. Thus, it revealed to the general public what ostensibly were her most sincere feelings, while at the same time addressing the mass audience in terms that made them feel as if they were privileged members of the Shi family. By showing how she had arranged to take care of her family in the event of her death, the document established her responsibility as an elder sister in the family. In the will, Shi directly addressed her siblings, along with her husband and mother, to explain her actions. She instructed her younger siblings to take care of their mother and to work hard at school. In specific comments to Zefan, one of her younger brothers, she explains why she decided to act alone, and couched her explanation not in terms of selfishness but in terms of selflessness. She argued that she acted alone for the sake of the whole family's well-being. "While father [belonged to all of us], and we intended to go on together, I did not want to sacrifice your future. Because you need to maintain a strong state and home, you have large burdens. . . . You should forgive your older sister in her reluctance to require others to undertake this task [of revenge]." She then lists a set of commands for him to follow in the case of her death, including taking care of their father's remains, writing a headstone for her, and telling him of the 3,000 *yuan* inheritance she has for her sons. She ends with "if we cannot meet again brother, follow father's teaching by diligently working towards the future. Make a big name for yourself in history. Do not lead an empty life."

THE REVENGE: RIGHTEOUS AND HEROIC

The portrayal of the revenge killing itself was crucial to the success of Shi Jianqiao's story. Specifically, it was important for her to cast Sun Chuanfang's murder not as a mere political assassination, but as a highly justified act of righteous revenge. By mobilizing a range of powerful cultural motifs that proved to have great emotional appeal, Shi did this with great effect. She deployed time-honored ideas about Confucian retribution, Buddhist karma, and popular ideas about female heroism and knight-errantry to establish the righteousness of the revenge. Furthermore, even while marshalling long-standing cultural beliefs, Shi demonstrated a tremendous capacity for updating them and making them relevant for the contemporary age.

Cosmological concepts of retribution had a long history in China. Cultural beliefs in reciprocity (*bao*) were rooted philosophically in Confucian classics, including the *Book of Rites* and the *Analects*, and had been central to the ordering of social relations in China since antiquity (Yang 1957). In China's literary tradition as well, retribution (*bao* or *baoying*) had long served as both a fundamental way of ordering social and moral relations in imperial literature and a central literary device that propelled literary narratives (Kao 1989).[41] From the start, Shi drew from these discourses. Her triumphant declaration at the crime scene, "I have sought revenge [to repay] my father" (*wei fu baochou*), immediately established the classical Confucian grounds of her actions. So too did her voluntary surrender at the crime scene.[42] By facing the legal consequences instead of running away, Shi demonstrated not only how sincere she was in seeking vengeance but also that she was willing to sacrifice her own freedom and potentially her life to do so. Confucian moralists had long viewed proper self-sacrifice (e.g., sacrifice for one's parent, husband, or virtuous ruler) favorably as an extreme expression of repaying one's moral obligations.

The Buddhist society as the site of the crime scene was also freighted with meaning. By killing her mortal enemy in the sacred shrine of a lay-Buddhist society, Shi unambiguously erected a religious framework in which she could become an instrument of karma and successfully establish that Sun's death was the inevitable result of his past sins (i.e., killing Shi Congbin in particular and killing innumerable others in general). She tapped into distinctly Buddhist notions of fated retribution (*baoying*) and the idea that one's past dictates one's fate (*houguo qianyin*). Not surprisingly, observers were quick to frame the event in Buddhist terms, and several explicitly used the idea *houguo qianyin* to explain Sun's death and justify Shi's actions. In an article entitled, "Bloodbath in a Buddhist Shrine," one writer noted that whereas Shi Jianqiao's actions were illegal according to the law, they were permissible according to Buddhist notions of karma. He concluded that no matter how much sutra-chanting Sun Chuanfang did, he could not avoid the fated reprisal for the evils he had once committed.[43] In Shi's narrative, the Buddhist site also worked nicely in tension with her classically Confucian act of filial revenge. In the increasingly tense atmosphere of the 1930s, Buddhist temples were often thought to harbor "retiring" warlords. In such a context, Shi Jianqiao's filial actions could easily be interpreted as blowing away the Buddhist cover of colluding warlords. Shi herself seemed to suggest as much in the poem she distributed at the crime scene, in which she stated that she "arrive[d] at the Society not to find the Buddha," but to seek Sun's death through filial revenge. Her Confucian act thus exposed the lie of Sun's Buddhist faith.

If cultural beliefs about Confucian ideas of virtuous retribution and Buddhist notions of karma helped Shi's case, what was perhaps most salient was the long-standing and vibrant tradition of knight-errantry (*xia*). Dissatisfied with the official legal system that had failed to punish Sun Chuanfang, the *xia* ethos celebrating a righteous heroism that could transcend even the rule of law was perfect for Shi. Found in political, literary, and historiographic discourses since as early as the Han dynasty (206 B.C.E.–220 C.E.), the classic, solitary assassin-retainer (*xiake*), characterized by skill in swordsmanship and heroic selflessness in righting wrongs, was an ambiguous hero.[44] His acts of righteous assassination and revenge were often at cross-purposes with the agenda of the imperial state. His tendency to wander (*youxia*), roam in bands, and fight for justice outside of the traditional family structure in the marshes (*jianghu*) threatened orthodox Confucian rule and signified the outlaw status of knights-errant.[45] His subversive, rogue identity was further underscored by a self-appointed sense of duty (*xiayi*) to protect the weak against the strong and claims to represent true justice where the official legal system failed to do so.[46]

The knight-errantry tradition thus not only legitimated Shi Jianqiao's decision to engage in extralegal actions to seek reprisal on her own, but also imbued them with a heroic flair. Not surprisingly, she consciously presented herself as a knight-errant. Her self-appellation directly conjures a sense of action and heroism associated with the *xia* personality. Whereas her given name was Shi Gulan, she chose "Jianqiao" as her sobriquet. The ideographs of *jian*, which has the primary meaning of sword or dagger, and *qiao*, which means either to raise or to be outstanding, made the *xia* connotation readily apparent.[47] Shi also included explicit allusions to the knight-errantry tradition in the material she distributed at the crime scene. She signed her single-page statement of intent with the flamboyant signature of "the avenging woman" (*chounü*). The first line of the poem that she had prepared was taken directly from the famous tale of the eponymous *xia* heroine, Yu Jiang, of the *Liaozhai tuyong*, a Republican-era pictorial version of Pu Songling's classic, seventeenth-century collection of the strange, the *Liaozhai zhiyi* (The strange tales from the Liaozhai studio). Observers were quick to make note of this.[48]

Shi Jianqiao was also no doubt attracted to the *xia* tradition because of the tremendous moral and political possibilities it offered women. Classical female heroines were at once subversive in their public lifestyles and orthodox in their embodiment of female virtue. While the male knight-errant might occasionally define his heroic virtue through filial duty, other principles of justice, including engaging in struggles against the oppression of the weak, personal revenge, or upholding loyalty among friends, often took precedent. In contrast, female knights-errant almost always took up arms and entered the marshes on behalf of male relatives.[49] Although technically not a knight-errant, Hua Mulan, the classical woman warrior (*jinguo yingxiong*), serves as an illuminating example of how female heroism turned on exemplary virtue. Upon learning that her aging father is being recruited by the state for battle, Mulan cross-dresses and takes his place, displaying remarkable filial piety.[50] During her years of war, she never reveals her true gender identity and becomes a war hero. Upon her return, Mulan rejects marriage to stay home and serve her parents faithfully to the end of their lives. This exemplary filial piety is crucial to the story. It validates her decision to cross-dress, cross boundaries, and engage in acts otherwise permissible only for men.

Within the Confucian cosmological order premised on the separation of gendered space, *xia* heroines who cross the boundary not only from normal society to the marshes, but also from inner chambers to outer society, have long generated deep social anxiety about the power of female sexuality and its potentially subversive threat to the larger cosmological order.[51] In her study of Pu Songling's classic, the *Liaozhai zhiyi*, Judith Zeitlin (1993) discusses *xia* women in particular, and argues that sword-wielding women have traditionally been moral paragons precisely because they needed to counteract any perceived threat posed by their sexuality.[52] Female gallantry in these stories, she argues, was predicated on the extreme lengths to which the female hero goes to live up to masculine standards of heroism and virtue. Pu's female protagonists, including Shang Sanguan, an avenger whom Shi Jianqiao explicitly cites as a source of inspiration, are heroic precisely in their gender dislocation and in their ability to be *like men* in their "high-minded spirit" and pursuit of justice. As a result, the female knight-errant has long been able to wander in the world at large and right a wrong without fundamentally disrupting the sexual economy underlying China's cosmological order.

Shi Jianqiao's self-portrayal as a *xianü* (female knight-errant) suggests that the standards of virtuous gender dislocation demanded of Shi's imperial predecessors remained remarkably relevant in the twentieth century. It was telling, for example, that Shi cited as her primary source of inspiration Shang Sanguan, a female knight-errant whose eponymous story was immortalized in Pu Songling's *Liaozhai zhiyi*.[53] In Pu's tale,

Shang Sanguan is both heroically dutiful and virtuously chaste. A young woman of sixteen, she rejects marriage and leaves home in order to avenge her father's murder. Her brothers have failed to achieve legal retribution, so she carefully plots for six months and then enters the home of the murderer during a party as a young male performer. At the close of the party, when all other guests take leave, she stays on, beheads the bully, and then dramatically hangs herself from the rafters as a clear sign of the selfless, sacrificial nature of her act. Shang upholds her chastity in a most miraculous manner. While hanging dead from the rafters after her revenge, her corpse dramatically repels a sexual assault, and Shang defends her chastity posthumously.

While she did not commit suicide, demonstrate any supernatural abilities, or even cross-dress like Shang Sanguan, Shi Jianqiao's moral character was still portrayed as unmistakably impressive. Like her classical counterparts, the modern-day avenging daughter took care to establish an impeccable reputation of sexual honor. Immediately after the slaying, details of her past reputation appeared in the press. The reading public learned, for example, how Shi had once been betrothed into a family whose patriarch was on trial for raping another daughter-in-law. Dubbed the Case of the Tongue because the daughter-in-law had used the part of the patriarch's tongue she had bitten off in self-defense as evidence in the trial, the case had caused a scandal. Rather than compromise her reputation and, by extension, tarnish that of her natal family, Shi Jianqiao immediately took the initiative and annulled the arranged betrothal. The press praised her for her deft handling of the affair and treated her extreme action to protect her honor as undeniable evidence of her *xia* heroism. One reporter wrote admiringly that while the Case of the Tongue had caused a stir in nine cities and would no doubt have brought shame to the Shi family if the betrothal had been upheld, Shi's swift and decisive action to annul the engagement had averted familial dishonor.[54]

The reputation of "chastity" established in the Case of the Tongue was evident again in Shi's description of her marriage, which showed the depths of Shi's devotion to her father and established the unquestionable sincerity of her motive. In traditional China, female chastity was very straightforward. Female paragons were either virgins or chaste widows who refused remarriage. Some protected their bodies from even the slightest hint of physical impropriety and were willing to kill themselves to do so. This sexual purity was a metaphor for their passionate devotion to their fathers or husbands and, by extension, to the patriarchy writ

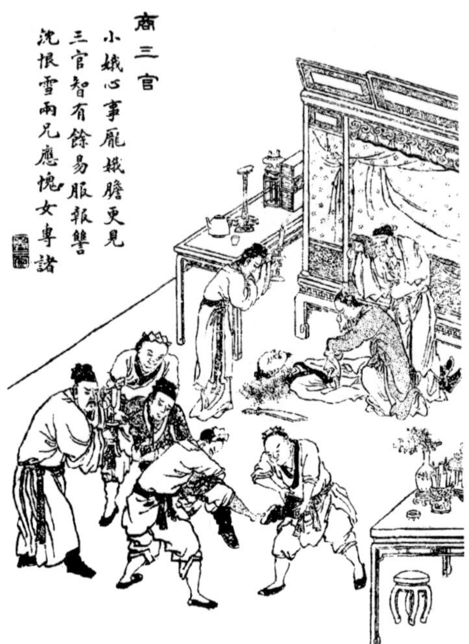

Figure 3. The story of filial daughter Shang Sanguan in the illustrated songbook of Pu Songling's *Liaozhai zhiyi*, 1914. (Lü Zhan'en 1914)

large, the emperor. Whereas, by the time of this twentieth-century case, the goal of demonstrating utmost loyalty remained the same, the proof of chastity had changed somewhat. Shi Jianqiao established a chaste reputation not by refusing marriage, but *as a result* of her marriage. The avenging daughter depicted her marriage to fellow Anhui-native Shi Jinggong as loveless and intended to aid her noble cause of revenge. She explained that she had agreed to marry not out of love but on the condition that her husband-to-be would help in her quest.[55]

Portraying her marriage as merely instrumental made her commitment to her father appear, in contrast, to be genuine and real, and her devotion to avenging her father's murder as all-consuming. Her portrayal was so successful that when news leaked that her husband was seeking a divorce while she was still in jail, commentators found his actions hypocritical. One *Ling Lung* writer stated that the husband clearly knew from the start she intended to seek revenge and not merely to serve as a "Good wife, Wise Mother" (*xianqi liangmu*). The commentator implored,

"How can Shi Jinggong not only claim that Shi Jianqiao's will to seek revenge does not adhere to the Womanly Way (*fudao*), but also use it as grounds for divorce? Clearly, Shi Jinggong is shallow and heartless."[56] In the end, her loyalty to her father was of the utmost importance, and not any loyalty to her husband. Shi Jinggong's failure to appreciate her filial piety only made him seem heartless in seeking a divorce.

It is interesting to note that Shi Jianqiao avoided citing more explicitly political female assassins as precedents. She was careful, for example, not to compare herself to any of the late Qing female assassins. A likely precedent was Qiu Jin, a highly flamboyant woman who was known for her cross-dressing and self-fashioning as a *xianü*, and who had gone to Japan in the twilight years of Manchu rule, where she fell in with anti-Qing anarchists and radical feminists. Also popular among late Qing radical circles were Western female assassins, including Sophia Perovskaia and Mme. Roland. Yet, Shi failed to mention any anarchist-feminist heroine, domestic or foreign. Whereas late Qing female heroism was explicitly political, Shi Jianqiao wanted to present her Republican-era heroism as something that was intensely personal and the result of a nonpolitical, private enmity. In doing so, she could more successfully capture the essence of classical martyrdom.

Although Shi Jianqiao sought to mobilize classical traditions, she hardly wanted to appear anachronistic. She thus added a strong dose of the modern to her actions. Leo Lee (1999) has described how the modernity of early twentieth-century urban culture in Shanhai was embedded in material objects like the telephone, Browning guns, Citroen cars, and even the Cheongsam (*qipao*) dresses seen on alluring calendar girls. Many of these same objects strategically appeared in Shi's tale of revenge and functioned, accordingly, to signal the "modernity" of the event. For example, Shi Jianqaio was a "modern" knight-errant in her choice of weapon and mode of transportation. As she made clear to the press, she had taken a cab from the temple to retrieve from her home her weapon of choice, which was not the traditional sword or dagger, but a Browning pistol.[57] Shi's appearance furthermore was imbued with an up-to-date cosmopolitan aura. It was that of a modest, but modern woman. In a photograph that was widely distributed after the assassination, her hair was styled in a bob cut, which in the first quarter of the century represented the radicalism of protesting female university students, although by the 1930s, it had become a proper style, conservative, yet contemporary. The gray-blue Cheongsam dress that Shi wore was also coded appropriately. Unlike the flower-patterned and shape-hugging cuts of the more sexual-

Figure 4. Undated portrait of Shi Jianqiao before the assassination of Sun Chuanfang.

ized calendar girls, Shi Jianqiao's outfit was modest both in color and in cut, establishing the virtuous ideal that conformed to both New Life ideology and female *xia* standard.[58] Her image was thus that of a modest, but clearly modern woman.

SENTIMENT, PREMEDITATION, AND THE TELLING OF A TALE

Beyond making sure that the content of her story conformed to familiar narratives, Shi Jianqiao also paid careful attention to the style of the telling. With the intent of maximizing an emotional response, the avenging daughter employed two seemingly paradoxical tactics in conveying her story. She delivered her sentimental narrative in a highly emotional manner while revealing in great detail exactly how she plotted her revenge. Such an approach differs radically from how female perpetrators of crimes of passion told their stories in modern French courts and society. In modern French courts, where the ideal standard of behavior was male rationality, such women often won judicial exemption precisely by stressing how their typically feminine characters, marred by irrationality and weak will, had led them to commit crimes of passion. In a study of the celebrated, turn-of-the-century, Parisian case of Mme. Caillaux, Edward Berenson (1992) illustrates how Mme. Caillaux formulated a successful defense that crucially turned on convincing the jury and the public that women's passions easily overwhelm their rational faculties. Mme. Caillaux and her lawyers carefully avoided revealing any evidence of calculation and planning in order to establish that it was her typically feminine passions of jealousy and rage that had caused her to lose her sanity temporarily and commit the crime. The end result was that she was absolved of wrongdoing and responsibility.

In Shi Jianqiao's case, however, emotion and premeditation were not at all mutually exclusive. This key difference from the French case stems from diverging ways of understanding sentiment. Whereas sentiment had implications for individual subjectivity and the larger cosmological order in both turn-of-the-century Paris and early twentieth-century urban China, the exact significance attributed to sentiment and the exact way in which the individual, society, and their inter-relationship were imagined differed considerably. In the Parisian trial, Mme. Caillaux's motive was clearly a motive of "passion" in the sense that it helped articulate rationality, the core of modern Western subjectivity, by serving as its counterpoint. Because Mme. Caillaux's feminine rage served as the deviant contrast that helped define the masculine norm of rational legal subjectivity, it was deemed the basis of judicial exemption. In contrast, in the Chinese case, while Shi Jianqiao's filial devotion was passionately expressed through an extreme act of violence, the crux of the controversy did not hinge upon the lack of rationality in her actions per se. Instead, attention was lavished on the question to what degree Shi Jianqiao's sentiment of filial piety continued to be *ethically* relevant in the shaping of gender, modern subjectivity, and early twentieth-century China's sociopolitical landscape. *Both* emotional urgency and rational premeditation underscored the sincerity of her virtuous sentiment.

In the telling of her tale, Shi Jianqiao first saturated her narrative with emotion. She also made sure that her public appearances were characterized by the expression of great feeling. For example, in the press conference held at the public security bureau just after the killing, Shi was overcome with emotion.[59] The *Yishibao* (The social welfare daily) headline the next day read, "Shi Jianqiao Tells Her Story with Tears."[60] At the opening sessions of both the first and second trials, the assassin wept uncontrollably in the courtroom. Each tearful display won full coverage in the press the next day.[61] During the first trial, Shi interrupted the prosecuting attorney who was conducting her cross-examination and demanded to know why the courts had failed to make public the personal statement she had distributed at the crime scene.[62] While the charged outburst drew media attention, so too did the heart-wrenching statement. When it was finally made available to the press a month later, the Shanghai *Shibao* referred to the testimonial as "Shi Jianqiao's 'Letter to My Countrymen;' Each Word, a Tear, Some One Thousand Words."

Though emphasizing emotion, Shi Jianqiao also explicitly raised the issue of premeditation and rational plotting. She emphasized exacting premeditation to demonstrate her sustained filial devotion and the sincerity of her actions. Not unlike her careful planning of the telling of the events, her preparations for revenge were presented as meticulous. Shi's accounts purposefully highlighted her preparation of materials for distribution at the crime scene. In her press conference just after the murder, she informed reporters, "Because I thought Sun's coming and going would involve bodyguards and that it was not in the cards for me to survive, my small pamphlets would make known my heart's intent, even if I were to die."[63] These pamphlets, along with ensuing press conferences and court appearances, detailed her preparations.

Entailing ten years of planning and a final year spent stalking Sun Chuanfang, the efforts that went into the plotting were impressive. Shi had first considered having her older brother, Zhongliang, undertake the assassination, but quickly realized that since he was not a soldier, he lacked the proper disposition to execute revenge. She then turned to a male cousin, Zhongcheng, whom Shi Congbin had raised like a son, but he too failed to take action. As mentioned earlier, in 1928, Shi Jianqiao married Shi Jinggong on the condition that he would fulfill the family's wishes for retaliation. But he was almost immediately dispatched to remote Shaanxi and shelved the task. By 1935, ten years had passed since her father's death, and all men of the household remained somehow indisposed.[64] Shi argued that the family had no one else to rely on but her, and stated, "I felt that [rather than] ask others I might as well ask myself."[65] These details about her male relatives failing in the task of revenge were particularly crucial. Only when all other alternatives were exhausted could the daughter justify entering the public arena to commit the revenge killing herself.

The twists and turns leading up to Sun's murder helped build narrative suspense. As Shi Jianqiao told it, she began in January 1935 by enrolling one of her sons in Tianjin's Peicai elementary school, which Sun Chuanfang's daughter, Sun Jiamei, was attending.[66] She accompanied her son to school each day until she eventually learned that Sun lived in Tianjin's French Concession. Buoyed by this information, Shi stiffened her resolve and sought to obtain a gun in her home province. She then returned to Tianjin in July only to find that Sun Jiamei had transferred to the Glorious China School in the British Concession. She used the enrollment of her brother's daughter in the Glorious China School as a pretext to investigate further and discovered Sun Chuanfang's license plate number. She sighted his car and then her target shortly thereafter, one evening outside of Tianjin's Guangming movie theater.

Not until September 17, 1935, did Shi Jianqiao obtain what turned out to be the fateful piece of information for her plans. Those following the affair learned that while attending the memorial services for her late father, Shi heard from the monk presiding over the services that Sun regularly assisted in leading sutra recitation at Tianjin's lay-Buddhist society. Armed with this piece of information, she then made visits to the lay-Buddhist society and discovered that Sun Chuanfang was indeed a leading member. She befriended a female member of the society, adopted the Buddhist name Dong Hui, and expressed interested in joining. Under the pretext that she wanted to observe the congregation in order to decide whether to become a member, she made several preliminary visits and, finally, went there on the fateful day of November 13, 1935. That afternoon she killed Sun. As she stated in her initial confession, "Today, just past 2 P.M., I saw only a few chanters present, and that Sun was not yet there. Just as I was talking with some other members, Sun's car arrived and he entered. I realized my opportunity to seek revenge had arrived. I had not brought my handgun, so I quickly took a taxi cab home, retrieved my gun and returned [to the hall]. . . . Immediately, I went to shoot Sun. I killed him with three bullets remaining in the gun. I could see in the distance that the police were about to arrive. I immediately turned myself over to the authorities and surrendered."[67]

CONCLUSION

There ended the avenging daughter's account. By exhaustively plotting all details of her performance, the heroine displayed an uncanny ability to manage the details of her visibility in the glare of the media's limelight. She moreover strategically inflected the story behind the revenge with seemingly genuine emotion, which proved essential to her ability to win public support. To be sure, Shi Jianqiao was not alone in using the media to court public opinion. Sun Chuanfang's family and supporters did as well.[68] Angered by Shi's claims of righteousness as well as her accusations of Sun Chuanfang, some of Sun's supporters made a public counterattack, defending Sun and discrediting Shi. In the days following the assassination, Jin Yunpeng, the fellow ex-militarist who had established the lay-Buddhist society with Sun in 1931, attested to the sincerity of Sun's Buddhist faith and his lack of interest in politics at the time of his death.[69] Beiyang militarist Zhang Xueliang also showed support for the Sun family with a telegram from Nanjing.[70] The well-attended memorial service for Sun organized by the Tianjin Shandong Native-place Association was yet another indication of support from powerful Shandong political figures.[71] Lu Xiangting, an old military colleague, was perhaps most vocal. Holding a press conference after the killing in the British Concession of Tianjin, Lu stated that he wanted to clear the air of rumors and correct the public record. He told reporters that while in battle during the Su-Lu war, he had learned from those who saw Shi Congbin die firsthand that Shi's death was merely another casualty in a period of intense chaos and nothing more. He further stated that for a military family to lose a father to war is hardly out of the ordinary, and thus there were no grounds for Shi's enmity (*chou*), much less for retribution (*bao*). He concluded by reminding the public that Shi Congbin was, in effect, just like Sun Chuanfang in having killed many innocent people during war.[72]

Yet, efforts by the Sun family and its allies did not have the same success that Shi enjoyed. Shi Jianqiao's success was all the more remarkable if we consider that women's appearance in the public arena in the Nanjing Decade generally remained a tricky proposition. Calls for moral restrictions and constraints on excessively public women had become stronger by the second quarter of the twentieth century, drowning out earlier calls for liberation.[73] Not surprisingly, several commentators noted Shi Jianqiao's ability to manage the press. A sympathetic writer compared a line of Shi Jianqiao's poetry with a dramatic performance by Tan Xinpei, one of Republican China's greatest Beijing opera performers. Alluding to Shi's superior skills of performance, the commentator wrote, "If one looks away for even a second, it would seem as if in front of you is the great work of a renowned actress" (Lingxiaohangezhu 1935a). Less sympathetic views were also expressed. One writer argued that Shi was a cynical operator exceptionally skilled in recognizing and appropriating customary ways to manipulate popular sympathy.[74]

In the end, however, the avenging daughter gave what proved to be a virtuoso performance. She proved capable of performing the delicate balancing act of taking full advantage of the media's power and reach, while at the same time never appearing to be doing so. Exhibiting impressive aplomb, she grasped the persuasive power of sentiment and brilliantly orchestrated her actions to weave a powerful and moving tale of sincere moral heroism that identified an unambiguous moral universe in which her crime of revenge was deemed genuine and virtuous. One writer thus noted, "All one has to do is look at the general media coverage, which includes a lot of laudatory phrases like 'unflinching composure' and 'ardent heroism,' to see just how widespread sympathy (*tongqing xin*) is" (Lingxiaohangezhu 1935a).

Shi Jianqiao's decision to assume the persona of the female knight-errant, in particular, paid off.[75] Sober and sensational journalism made reference to this persona by applauding the female assassin's virtue as sincere, heroic, and above all, like that of a man. One observer noted that even though she was in fact a fragile woman, her virtues of loyalty, wisdom, bravery, and righteousness were just like that of honorable men.[76] Another stated that since Shi Jianqiao showed steadiness in fulfilling her wish and, as a person, was ardent, straightforward, steadfast and brave; in short, she was manly in spirit.[77] Shi's masculine virtue also won her comparisons with previous *xia* women. One article cited as precedents both the heroine from Pu Songling's tale *Xianü* (1986b, 210–16) and the historical personage, Lu Siniang, or Fourth Sister Lu, of the Qing, a female knight-errant who was said to have assassinated Emperor Yongzheng.[78] Another noted that Shi's heroic virtue was simply uncanny (*qi*), a marvel that allowed her to qualify as a remarkable woman.[79] Like the classic female knight-errant, Shi Jianqiao's extreme filial piety, contained sexuality, and sublimated passion allowed her to transgress boundaries, engage in virtuous dislocation, and literally get away with murder.

Finally, while Shi Jianqiao undeniably displayed an astonishing knack for what we might today call public relations savvy, to conclude that she was *merely* a smooth operator underestimates the power and moral validity of her reasons for action. It is highly probable that even though Shi was a savvy player in a new era of mass communications, she also sincerely believed that she had the absolute moral right to kill Sun Chuanfang. It is easy to imagine how she was deeply frustrated. The chaos caused by years of warlordism had barred the way to any legal retribution. Adding insult to injury, Sun went on to enjoy a significant, albeit short, period in power as the leader of the Five Allied Southeastern Provinces and director-general of Shanghai after the battle in which Shi's father was killed. When he finally fell from political grace, Sun retired to a Buddhist temple where, from Shi's perspective, he continued to escape formal justice. The daughter most likely felt she had to rely on herself to achieve justice. With themes of filial piety, chivalric heroism, and fated retribution common to the social imagination of urban China at that time, she had a ready supply of resources with which to imagine an alternative way to seek reprisal. These themes most likely constituted the bedrock of Shi's own value system and provided her with the conviction needed to commit an act of murder.

TWO

Media Sensation

Public Justice and the Sympathy of an Urban Audience

> Filial daughter Shi Jianqiao avenged her father's death by killing single-handedly Sun Chuanfang, the Leader of Five Allied Provinces, in Tianjin's lay Buddhist society. . . . Her sincerity and purity are without limits; her filial revenge ranks in the top ten (in history) . . . learning of the news, the entire nation sympathizes with her.
>
> Jingbao *(The crystal), 8 December 1935*

> After assassin Shi Jianqiao killed Sun Chuanfang to avenge the death of her father, Shi Congbin, a national sensation ensued, and a sense of justice gladdened the hearts of the people; local theaters competed to perform the tale of the avenging daughter, and the force of the people's sentiment was truly great.
>
> Fu'ermosi *(Holmes), 6 November 1936*

In a decade when high-profile news events seemed to be the norm, the case of Shi Jianqiao managed to stand out. The 1930s saw several assassinations of political figures, and high-profile female murderers emerged with considerable frequency. The Nationalist regime relied upon an informal military corps to engage in political murder of its enemies, and revenge killings of militarists were not unprecedented. A strikingly similar case of filial revenge had taken place just three years earlier when Zheng Jicheng assassinated retired militarist Zhang Zongchang to avenge the death of his uncle (*wei shu baochou*).[1] Plenty of women were also engaging in public acts of violence. Just a few months before Shi Jianqiao killed Sun Chuanfang, urban China had witnessed a highly sensational crime of female passion in which a woman by the name of Liu Jinggui had assassinated her rival in love.[2] Yet, neither the killing of Zhang Zongchang nor the near-concurrent crime of passion by Liu Jinggui made as much of a splash as did Shi Jianqiao's case.[3] One contributor to *Ling Lung*, a Shanghai women's journal, wrote explicitly about the impact of the Shi case. "In recent years women who have surprised the entire country with a deafening blow have not been rare. But, recently, the matter of Shi Jianqiao shooting retired militarist Sun Chuanfang, now that is especially unique!"[4]

Though remarkably astute in her dealings with the media, even Shi Jianqiao could not have foreseen the extent to which the media would appropriate her tale, enlarge it, and turn it into a sensation. Journalists clamored to cover the unfolding case, and theaters fought over performing the story. The assassination and trial spawned serialized fiction in newspapers, reality-based novels, and sung performances on the radio. The photos of the case's protagonists were splashed across a variety of pictorial magazines and supplements.[5] Writers remarked about the reach of the case in retrospect. In his memoirs, Zheng Yimei describes in astonishment how the affair was covered in detail in the daily papers, adapted into drama, and even brought to the silver screen (Zheng 1992, 73–76). Although there is little evidence that a film was actually made, there were rumors of plans to make one. An article in 1936 stated that after Shi Jianqiao had been invited to the Huale theaters to view the film *Qingcheng shijiu xia* (Nineteen knights-errant of Qingcheng), talk immediately circulated that the Lianhua Studio of Shanghai was going to turn her story into a movie entitled *Xianü fuchou ji yingpian* (The account of the avenging female knight-errant). But, as the article noted, in the end there was no truth to such speculation.[6] It was simply that the sensation itself had made the news.

How do we understand the significance of such sensation? The quotations at the beginning of this chapter suggest that the widespread news coverage and adaptation of Shi Jianqiao's case into forms of entertainment were crucial in creating collective sympathy. The *Jingbao* contributor noted that once the nation learned of the news, it quickly came to sympathize with daughter Shi. The anonymous contributor to the *Fu'ermosi* forged a link between theaters adapting the story and the sentiment of the people becoming a "great force." This chapter explores the media events surrounding the case to understand how news coverage and fictional adaptations of the Shi affair created opportunities to explore topics that might otherwise not have found public airing in the increasingly repressive political environment of the period. It was in these arenas of fiction and theater that collective sympathy for the avenging daughter grew. This sympathy, in turn, validated the topics and norms being explored and promoted through the adaptations. As some of these norms carried implicit and, at times, not so implicit social and political criticism, public sympathy itself became politicized.

SERIALIZED FICTION, THE AVENGING WOMAN, AND MODERN ETHICAL SUBJECTIVITY

Fictional adaptations of the Shi Jianqiao affair appeared almost immediately. This section examines some of them, focusing in particular on one of the longer-running fictional series, the Beiping *Shibao's Xianü fuchou* (Avenging daughter). In these adaptations, Shi Jianqiao's persona as a female knight-errant proved to be a particularly powerful iconic vehicle through which the urban media audience could entertain new ideas of womanhood, modern subjectivity, and even national identity. Drawing from critical discussions on the role of "sentimental" literature in the modern world, I argue that these adaptations, in conjunction with the actual news story, helped turn the case of Shi Jianqiao into a compelling narrative of ethical sentiment. As such, the case helped articulate the ideal ethical and sentimental modern subject.

Scholars have for some time now examined the role of *qing*-based ("sentimental") fictional narratives in shaping early twentieth-century urban subjectivity in China. In one of the earliest English-language studies to pay attention to the issue, Perry Link (1981) classifies writing by a group of authors who printed their stories of love and romance from 1911 to 1918 in newspapers like *Libailiu* (Saturday) as "middlebrow fiction." Participants in the New Culture movement had disparagingly labeled this group the Mandarin Duck and Butterfly school because of their abundant use of the classical symbols of mandarin ducks and butterflies to connote lovers, and by the early 1920s, the label was further expanded to refer unsympathetically to all kinds of popular, old-style fiction, including not just love stories but also social novels, knight-errant novels, scandal novels, detective novels, and so on. Until Link's work, much of modern Chinese literary history had been shaped by this New Culture bias. Link's study is thus pioneering in its documentation of a whole category of long-neglected urban culture. However, his study stops short of examining the sentimentalism of these novels in any critical fashion. For Link, the sentimental nature of the literature had no real significance beyond enabling so-called Butterfly fiction to serve as a form of escape for China's urban *petit bourgeoisie* struggling with the uncertainties associated with the changes and vicissitudes wrought by modernization and reform.

More recently, scholars of literature have started to use *qing* less as a descriptive and more as a critical term to consider how *qing* might have played a more constitutive role in social history. Some have used the term *melodrama* to characterize such *qing*-based cultural productions of the late Qing and early Republican period. Properly speaking, *melodrama* is a term used to describe popular stories of sentiment that first appeared in post-revolutionary France. Peter Brooks (1976) identifies the melodramatic mode as being associated with French literature written between the dawn of the nineteenth century and the 1840s, when the authority of the church and state were on the wane, and a sense of the sacred was no longer possible. With traditional ethics and imperatives thrown into question, melodramatic tales, Brooks argues, helped legislate a "new regime of virtue" through the prism of personal morality and emotions.[7] Uniquely characterized by moral Manichaeism, hyperbolic gestures, high emotionalism, dramatized moral dilemma, and conflict between good and evil where one force must prevail, the literature rehearses this new moral regime in a post-sacred world.

The term *melodrama*, while not indigenous to China, is certainly useful when discussing vernacular fiction around the turn of the twentieth century, an arguably "post-sacred" period when the adequacy of the orthodox Confucian response to restoring societal and national strength was increasingly being questioned. Chinese translators of the late Qing were translating quintessential melodramatic texts from France and England, including Alexander Dumas's *La Dame aux Camelias*. Authors of that time, including Wu Jianren, drew from these translated novels when writing Chinese novels, such as *Henhai* [*The Sea of Regret*] (1905), to address the social and political perils of foreign imperialism. Such novels moreover initiated an exploration into the emotional and psychic landscape of individual characters as a way to articulate an alternative "regime of virtue" (Hanan 1995; Tang 2000).

The predominance of *qing*-centered narratives continued into the Republican era, though scholars differ on whether the term *melodrama* remains useful to describe these later narratives. The adaptation of novels like *La Dame aux Camelias* into film, along with other films that were characterized by extreme sentimentality, have prompted scholars like Paul Pickowicz (1991) to use *melodrama* to describe certain early twentieth-century Chinese films.[8] Other China scholars, however, have shied away from the term. In her discussion of Butterfly fiction, Haiyan Lee (2001) draws primarily from David Denby's (1994) work on eighteenth-century French sentimental literature to introduce the term *sentimentalism*. For Denby, melodrama requires a clear threat posed to virtue by a strongly personified villain or principle of villainy (e.g., peripety and deceit) and expresses a fear or reflection of desacralization in a new secular order.[9] Far more optimistic than melodrama, sentimentalism affirms the possibility of transcendence and locates that possibility in the moral authority of lived experience. Denby writes, "The individual (person, act, feeling) operates in the sentimental text as a sign, a cipher of abstract, universal categories. . . . [T]his weeping mother, this unfortunate child, and this dying father all refer beyond themselves to the whole of humanity" (89). Featuring individual stories of sentimental virtue in which new collective virtues are articulated, sentimentalism, argues Denby, lies at the heart of Enlightenment notions of community, middle-class bourgeois identity, public opinion, and even revolution.[10] For Haiyan Lee (2001), Chinese Butterfly fiction of the early twentieth century functioned in a similar manner. No longer faced with a sense of crisis that informed late Qing writers like Wu Jianren, Republican writers of Butterfly fiction were instead more concerned with the constitution of a new, urban, Republican identity. Whereas French sentimentalism promoted sentimentalized and sacralized virtues of the Enlightenment, Butterfly fiction promoted sentimentalized Confucian virtues such as passionate filial piety as the basis of both modern, urban Chinese subjectivity and the collective identity of a sentimental reading audience.

By introducing and promoting ideas of ethically sentimental individuals and national virtue, fictional adaptations based on the actual media story of Shi Jianqiao functioned as narratives of moral sentimentalism. These serializations read just like some of the sentimental Butterfly novels discussed by Haiyan Lee (2001). The cast of characters—a rapacious warlord, an honorable father, an avenging daughter—corresponds closely to Butterfly fiction archetypes. The themes of filial piety, heroic passion, and fated retribution are also ubiquitous in the Butterfly genre. Most notable is how these fictional adaptations, like the Butterfly novels, provided a model for subjectivity in the Republican era, which turned on a heroic and sentimentalized motive of virtue. Haiyan Lee discusses how Butterfly fiction sentimentalized the motives of virtue that drove its protagonists and shows how they moved readers to sympathize with the plight and actions of the characters. In fictional adaptations of the Shi case, the heroic daughter's virtuous motive was fused with emotion. Hardly a disciplined, ritualized expression of filial piety, Shi Jianqiao's devotion to her father was passionate and heroic; as such, it inspired readers to consider new ways of being.

To illustrate how this was so, let us turn in detail to some of the adaptations. Adaptations occurred in several different forms. One example was a pictorial series. The *Xiejian jushilin* (Bloodbath in the Lay-Buddhist Society), ran in the *Xin Tianjinbao* from 20 November 1935 to 11 January 1936 and recounted faithfully the key events behind the affair. Every day the series featured a lithographic image, accompanied by a brief written text, to tell the story over time. It recounted the dramatic assassination, moved through the history behind the revenge, and ended with Shi Jianqiao in jail. Scenes from the affair were depicted in dramatic, black-and-white strokes. Readers could both read about and see a visual depiction of Shi Jianqiao mimeographing materials for distribution at the crime scene. On the next day, they saw her taking a hired car. The day after, they learned of her retrieving the gun from her bedroom drawer. And two days later, they witnessed how Shi Jianqiao shot Sun Chuanfang in the head.

On the same day that this pictorial series began, the publisher of the *Xin Tianjinbao* printed the serialization ads for *Chantang liuxue* (The flow of blood in a Buddhist hall), a "reality-based" novel (*shishi xiaoshuo*) that was also based on the revenge case. From November 20 to December 19, 1935, newspaper advertisements promised that the book would reveal the true "causes and effects" (*houguo qianyin*) behind the event. These advertisements also granted a price break: while the book was normally priced at four *jiao*, customers who pre-ordered the book could get two for the price of one. It appears that the book was quite popular. On December 24, 1935, an advertisement informed the reading public that the first five thousand volumes, printed on December 10, 1935, were sold out and that five thousand more copies of the six-thousand word novel would be published because of further demand. Each copy of the second printing would sell for two *jiao*, and 5 *fen* would be added for postage. To urge consumers on, the ad read, "Not many copies left! Hurry and order now to get your copy soon."

Adaptations of the affair were not restricted to print. "Xiejian fotang" (A bloodbath in the Buddhist hall) was a *kaipian* performance that was broadcast on the radio a month after the killing.[11] *Kaipian* were originally the opening songs of *tanci*, longer prosimetric narratives that were part of a storytelling tradition known as *pingtan*. Probably appearing

Figure 5. Shi Jianqiao entering a taxi on her way to retrieve her gun, from the pictorial series *Xiejian jushilin* (Bloodbath in the lay-Buddhist society), printed in *Xin Tianjinbao* (Tianjin), 24 November 1935.

around the late Ming, *tanci* traditionally drew from recent events, were often associated with female authors and audiences, and were sung or chanted, often accompanied by a lute or banjo.[12] The genre proved easily adaptable to radio performances in the twentieth century, and by the 1930s, the genre of *kaipian* had become so popular that many radio stations dropped the main *tanci* program and performed *kaipian* alone (Benson 1995, 122–23). On air for almost a week in mid-December, "Xiejian fotang" was one such *kaipian*, and was performed on the radio station Huiling, number 1380 on the dial, from nine to ten in the evening, prime time for adults. In rhyme and verse, the piece addressed what it claimed were recent complaints about the lack of luminaries emerging from the women's quarters (*guige*). The song assured listeners that with Shi Jianqiao they redressed this lack and found a true woman warrior (*jinguo yingxiong*). The piece then went on to provide an explanation of Sun's violent death in the popular Buddhist terms of fated retribution, and described the tense moments before and during the killing and the dramatic details of the assassin's last-minute dash home to retrieve her gun.

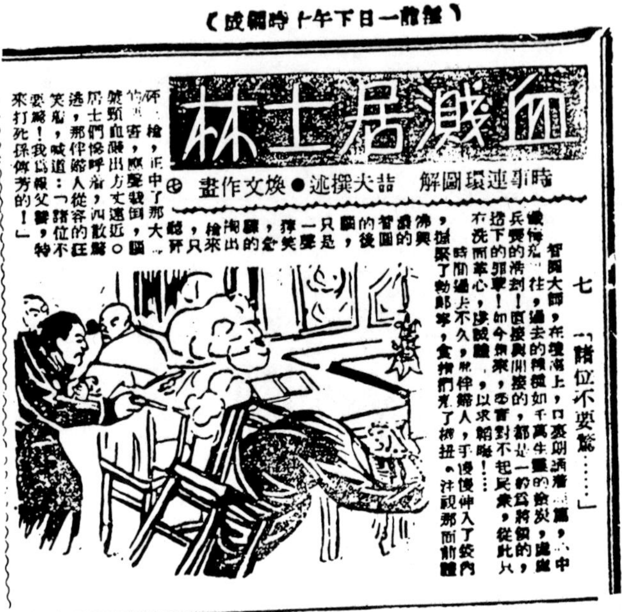

Figure 6. Shi Jianqiao shooting Sun Chuanfang, from the pictorial series *Xiejian jushilin* (Bloodbath in the lay-Buddhist society), printed in *Xin Tianjinbao* (Tianjin), 26 November 1935.

One of the most remarkable adaptations of the affair was a serialized novel in Beiping's *Shibao* (The truth post) called *Xianü fuchou* (The avenging daughter).[13] Given its length and richness as a text, it deserves closer attention and can illuminate well how fictional adaptations of the Shi case qualified as forms of sentimental narratives that helped shape modern subjectivity. Starting only a few days after the assassination and lasting until April of the following year, the novel chronicles on a daily basis Shi's life from the moment her father was still alive to the announcement of the verdict of her first trial. The generic structure of the series is a curious mix of popular love stories and martial-arts fiction. It also includes a chapter on Shi's dramatic trial that was reminiscent of the contemporaneous genre of detective fiction and its Chinese precedent, court-case fiction.[14]

In the story, Shi Jianqiao is portrayed as a *xia* hero who has the qualifications needed to transgress socially accepted norms to explore new ways of behaving as an exemplary New Woman. By acting under the auspices of filial piety, she avoids offending classical norms of female propriety. From the start, protagonist Shi displays a disposition of pure filial piety (*chunxiao xingcheng*). In the first few installments of the series, the heroine immediately proposes to sacrifice marriage to care for her parents. Then, upon finding out that her father is being called back to the battlefield despite his advanced age, she expresses a desire to follow her father into battle. In the second chapter, fittingly entitled "Learning of One's Parent's Death; Losing One's Will to Live," a servant who had loyally served her father in battle hesitates to break the news of Shi Congbin's tragic death to the Shi family because he fears that Shi Jianqiao, with her disposition of complete loyalty, will die of grief. When he does, Shi, despite being devastated, realizes that her own grief and paralysis would result in compounding the pain of her stepmother, Lady Li. Thus, instead of committing suicide, she decides to seek revenge.

Echoing Shi Jianqiao's real-life portrayal of events, the serialization has protagonist Shi assuming heroically active personae such as the woman warrior (*jinguo yingxiong*) and the female knight-errant (*xianü*). It is as both woman warrior and female knight-errant that Shi upholds the principle of exemplary parental devotion. But the two personae differ in terms of the objects of filial piety and the exact implication of this virtue. Shi Jianqiao as classic woman warrior acts for her *own* father and embodies in her filial piety the cornerstone of the family-based Confucian order. Shi Jianqiao as *xia* heroine exhibits more vigilante tendencies; she employs her impressive martial-arts skills in the pursuit of justice and for the purpose of upholding the universal principle of filial piety (*xiao*) indiscriminately. This shift in personae is marked in the series by a shift in narrative style. Shi is a dutiful daughter who models herself after the Mulan warrior when the series follows the events of the real case of Shi Jianqiao. When the protagonist assumes the *xia* persona, the series shifts to the narrative style typical of *wuxia* fiction at the time.

In this series, the term *jinguo yingxiong*, literally, "the hero in female military headgear," and often translated into English simply as "woman warrior," is applied to the character of Shi Jianqiao at two crucial junctures. At both points, she engages in extreme acts of filial piety that go beyond what a conventional daughter would do. The first time is when she feels uneasy about her father's purported military promotion.[15] She cites the virtuous Mulan as a model, offers to cut her hair, don military gear, and follow him into battle. While Mulan cross-dresses and enters battle, the modern series has the father bequeath to Shi the responsibility to stay home and care for her stepmother. The second time is when she hears the news of his untimely death and resolves to take on the noble task of revenge. As in the first instance, she expresses the desire to cut her hair, a symbolic gesture by which she reigns in her *yin*, or female, sexuality, a gesture necessary for her to transgress boundaries.

The series also showcases Shi Jianqiao as a *xia* heroine and scatters references to her *xia* nature throughout. Readers learn that Shi Jianqiao had acquired martial-arts skills in her youth, which she continues to pursue as an adult.[16] The story emphasizes that Shi is not merely schooled in the martial arts, but can also write poetry, an unmistakable attribute of the talented woman, or *cainü*, another celebrated female archetype. The fictional detail that Sun Chuanfang and her father were once sworn brothers (*mengxiong mengdi*) also functions to establish her *xia* nature, for by killing Shi Congbin, Sun does not simply murder Shi Jianqiao's father, he violates the venerable *xia* principle of brotherhood. Shi Jianqiao's alliance to Sun Chuanfang, a sworn-uncle (*mengshu*), is immediately displaced by intense hatred. He becomes the sworn enemy (*choudi*) and provides her with the opportunity to display her true *xia* colors.

One segment in particular detours from the style of a melodramatic social narrative into a style more reminiscent of *wuxia* fiction.[17] This shift is marked by a shift in time, in the setting of the story, and in tone. Whereas most of the story takes place in Tianjin and Anhui, the *xia* segment relocates the story back in time to Taiyuan, Shandong, where the real Shi had, in fact, lived for a few years. It leaves behind the emotion-laden description typical of love stories and adopts a more fantastic narrative tone common to the fanciful adventure of *wuxia* tales. It features action sequences that verify Shi's physical *wu* skills and focuses on the indiscriminate morality of the heroine's *xia* spirit. We are told at the beginning that Shi Jianqiao can do what even eight to ten strong men cannot do. To demonstrate this, the story tells how Shi Jianqiao once saved Lady Qian, an elderly neighborhood woman who is being abused by her wayward son and evil daughter-in-law.[18] As a young woman, Lady Qian marries into the wealthy Zhao family and serves them well by giving birth to a son. Unfortunately, this son, named Jinfu, is wild in his youth and not willing to be formally educated in Chinese boxing (*guoshu*) by his father. Instead, he befriends unsavory types, and brings home as his wife a Lady Sun who is from the circus and knows martial arts (*wuyi*) very well. Soon Jinfu's father dies, and the couple begins abusing the widowed mother, Lady Qian. In time, Lady Qian decides her only recourse is to make the abuse public. She sneaks out one day while the two are taking their mid-afternoon naps and happens upon the road where the famous *xianü*, Shi Jianqiao, lives. Upon learning of the old woman's plight, Shi

Jianqiao immediately becomes incensed and assumes the responsibility of helping this old woman. Lady Qian cautions Shi that both know martial arts and fears that she is asking too much from the female knight-errant. Shi responds by saying that she has no fear and has her own reasons for acting. In the next scene, Shi Jianqiao successfully makes the pair cower in submission with her courage and brilliant swordsmanship. Shi's reputation spreads even more widely as a result.

The shift to a more fantastical *xia* segment in the series assumes a crucial narrative function of illuminating the heroic qualifications necessary for protagonist Shi to be a modern woman in the "love-story" section. In other words, it is only through embodying the *xia* attributes of unmitigated bravery, an unstinting sense of moral justice, and absolute virtue that Shi proves capable not only of seeking filial revenge, but also of being a true modern woman. The fact that this series ultimately explores issues pertinent to modern womanhood is evident in several installments that focus on the heroine's involvement in two complicated marriage scenarios. The marriage theme was popular in urban fiction of the Republican period, including what Link (1981) calls the "love-story" genre. While the term suggests romance, Link defines this genre less by its romantic content (though many of the stories certainly included a strong dose of love) and more by its central preoccupation with the issue of free marriage versus arranged betrothals. This trend, of course, must be understood within the larger cultural context where marriage was a burning social issue. Redefining the institution as an antidote to the "traditional" arranged marriages that lay at the core of Confucian patriarchy, May Fourth intellectuals imbued the topic with particular urgency. They advocated an iconoclastic vision of the marriage union based on free love, romance, and individual choice. Marriage was to be a genuine emotional bond at the core of a modern nuclear family and, by extension, May Fourth cosmopolitanism. While by the 1930s the right to choose a marriage partner was still important, there was a discernable shift away from individual romantic love toward family reform that would benefit the Nationalist state.[19]

Xianü fuchou (The avenging daughter) is a love story in the sense that it explores the issue of marriage for modern women. In the first part of the series (the first three chapters), readers learn from daily cliff-hangers not about protagonist Shi's heartbreaks, but about how she resolves scandalous betrothals and arranges her own strategic marriage. Shi Jianqiao's handling of nuptial arrangements on her own becomes a mark of modern womanhood and is portrayed as a noble, even heroic (*xia*) task. In the fourth chapter, Shi Jianqiao boldly undertakes unconventional female behavior both to seek revenge and to arrange her own future. The scene unfolds the events leading up to Shi's decision to marry Shi Jinggong. At their initial meeting, she laments the lack of heroes in the world and states that she wants a husband who is a gentleman with the stomach and gall for *xia* justice. Shi Jinggong proceeds to win her heart by asserting that the ideals of a *xiake*, including helping the poor, repressing the strong, publicly encouraging good, and detesting evil, are the natural duties of humanity. What is most unconventional is that the protagonist then proposes to Shi Jinggong. The decision to propose is presented as heroic both in furthering the ultimate goal of revenge and as groundbreaking female behavior. The fictional Shi Jinggong expresses admiration for Shi Jianqiao's refreshingly bold behavior, and the plot makes clear that her action is yet another sign of her dedication to the pursuit of justice.[20] In short, by rejecting the traditional convention of going through a family matchmaker, Shi inverts gender roles and assumes the task of proposing—unusual behavior that would have been startling even in the most progressive circles of Republican China. Shi's moral passion for revenge serves both to offset any temporary moral impropriety and to introduce new, daring behavior for women to the reading public.

Heroine Shi's handling of difficult marriage scenarios moreover put forth a modern notion of individual responsibility in the High Republic. Defining moral character was a general didactic concern of Butterfly fiction at the time. In his discussion of modern *wuxia* fiction, Chen Pingyuan argues that a central artistic achievement of the twentieth-century martial novel is its focus on individual ethical sentimentality. Speaking specifically of chivalric and sentimental fiction (*xiaqing xiaoshuo*), Chen explains that the *qing* of these novels went beyond love and romance to include a more abstract sense of the moral sentiment at the core of being a person. As he puts it, *qing* was that which was necessary for the perfection of one's humanity or the realization of one's life's worth (Chen 1995, 116–19). The primary purpose of the *xia* hero then was not simply to engage in martial exploits and uphold justice, but also to acquire a *qing*-based personhood or humanity through his or her adventures.

Read in this light, the heroic undertakings of Shi Jianqiao in the *Shibao* series—be it filial revenge or arranging her own marriage betrothal—did more than introduce new norms of female behavior. They also showed that the basis of modern subjectivity revolved around, above all, ethical sentiment. This focus on individual subjectivity is evident as early as the first chapter, "The Annulment of Marriage to Uphold One's Moral Character," in which Shi decides to annul the betrothal despite her father's objections.[21] Presenting a fictional account of Shi's real-life success in disentangling herself from a scandalous betrothal, the chapter shows how, after discovering that her future father-in-law was involved in the Case of the Tongue scandal, Shi Jianqiao seeks to annul the prearranged marriage betrothal in order to defend her "individual moral character" (*geren renge*).[22] Her father objects to her handling the matter herself, but Shi Jianqiao insists that the situation is urgent enough for Shi herself to get involved. Shi prevails in the end and, moreover, convinces her father by arguing that society is more open, women are now liberated, and speaking about these issues as a woman is no longer shameful. In the end, she resolves the matter smoothly, wins the respect of outside observers, and saves face for her entire family.

As a tale of heroic and ethical transgression, Shi's story was thus centrally invested in locating a newly reconfigured notion of heroic filial piety at the heart of moral personhood in general.[23] Didactically powerful, it introduced norms that sought to *change* the social order in a new era when change was valorized. Previous scholars who have studied the "middlebrow" genre of serialized fiction tend to see an ambiguous conservatism with regard to the West as a distinguishing feature of the genre (e.g., Link 1981). In this series, while the tension between old (Shi's parents) and new (Shi Jianqiao as modern woman) is central to the story, filial piety and female *xia* heroism are hardly signs of conservatism or a return to the comforts of tradition.[24] Filial piety is the primary motivation for the protagonist's groundbreaking forms of female behavior and engagement in modern *xia* pursuits; it was the crucial ethical sentiment required for modern moral subjectivity.

The novel's emphasis on filial piety and the cultivation of a modern moral subject coincided with a more widely held belief that individual morality was linked with national strength. Whereas in May Fourth thought, individualism was as important as nationalism, by the Nanjing decade the more statist, corporatist discourse on the nation had taken hold, and individual morality was not celebrated as an end in itself, but was mobilized in the service of national collective morality. This tendency appears in a newspaper editorial entitled "The Morality Movement of the Republican Era" that appeared a little over a month after the killing of Sun Chuanfang (Wu 1935). Identifying the material and the spiritual as two central aspects of national defense, the editorial emphasizes the need to build moral fortitude before buttressing physical strength. Morality was crucial, it argues, because it serves as the lifeline of "individual moral character" (*geren renge*) and thus as the strength of the nation. This link between individual morality and national strength was at the heart of the state-engineered New Life movement. While the 1934 movement has been described as rather lackluster in retrospect, its goal of reviving the spiritual life and national strength of modern China by promoting individual Confucian virtues along with militaristic discipline and Christian spirituality was based on a genuine belief that national strength started with individual morality. In this larger political context, protagonist Shi Jianqiao was not simply a social exemplar in the High Republic. As a modern *xia* woman, her bold heroism, assertive confidence, and above all, filial and loyal motivation coincided with the virtues of an ideal nation.

THEATER AND PUBLIC JUSTICE

In addition to prompting fictional examinations of new womanhood and ethical subjectivity, Shi Jianqiao's case also inspired public exploration of forms of justice in the realm of theater. This section uses theatrical adaptations of the sensational affair to examine how, for theatergoers, Shi Jianqiao embodied a form of righteousness that could serve as an alternative to official definitions of order and justice. Differing from traditional Confucian norms of justice based on ethical reciprocity, as well as from reformist ideas of the rule of law, the form of justice served by Shi Jianqiao was rooted in chivalric righteousness (*xiayi*). It was, moreover, a form of public justice that was not provided by the courts (*ting*), but arose in the spectacular space of urban performance and theater, a realm of the *jianghu*, a term that is literally translated as "rivers and lakes," and metaphorically refers to the traditional imaginary setting where *xiake* roam and engage in righting wrongs. This examination, in turn, allows us to consider how dramatic and fictional adaptations of Shi's story cast doubt upon the justice meted out by the Nationalist state.

During the 1920s and 1930s, there was a proliferation of novels, newspaper serializations, radio plays, theatrical productions, and films that featured gallant outlaw heroes and assassins as self-appointed champions of justice. Scholars have noted how China's weak national image in the early twentieth century was a key reason for this *xia* renaissance. For example, Gu Mingtao, a writer of the Mandarin Duck and Butterfly school of the time, credited the popularity of the *xia* story with creating a picture of China's timeless martial vigor to compensate for the early twentieth-century international image of China as the "Sick Man of Asia"

(Link 1981, 14). The *xia* ethos was not merely a sign of an imagined martial vigor, but also a symbol for the idealism behind the Nationalist attempt to unify China and champion national justice. It may not have been a coincidence that the popularity of *xia* fiction peaked between 1927 to 1930, just around the time of the Northern Expedition (Link 1981, 22). By the mid-1930s, however, the euphoria of national reunification had worn off, and the looming presence of the Japanese in North China underscored the extent to which unification had failed. In this context, the *xia* ethos was no longer a quality ascribed to the ruling regime but had become increasingly associated with alternative expressions of national justice.

In the world of urban media and entertainment, adaptations of Shi Jianqiao's revenge qualified as one such expression. Public celebration of the Shi Jianqiao case as an expression of *xia* justice was particularly evident in theatrical renditions of the affair, which rendered the stage into a *jianghu*-like space. Specifically, theater provided the opportunity for a public exploration of real-life matters that was not possible in conventional journalistic venues subjected to state control at the time. This exploration is not surprising if you consider how theater in China had long been seen as a potential arena of illicit, heterodox activity, where the sentiment of the people could be easily stirred. Traveling troupes and street performers had long been characterized as being part of the *jianghu*. Discussing theater in the late Qing, Meng Yue (2000) argues that popular forms of urban theater beyond the control of officials and arbiters of taste often aggravated these elites. They described theater as a potential site for the moral corruption of women, as well as a place of danger with a potent ability to foster deviant emotions and morality. The tendency to draw on real life in its productions made late-Qing theater all the more problematic. As early as the 1880s, the Shanghai stage started to feature operas based on the "real," "the immediate," and current events (as opposed to traditional opera that featured highly stylized performances of the fantastically imagined past). Meng alludes to the increasing politicization of this new kind of "real-life" theater, writing that "the theater of the immediate later widened its means from *seeing* into *engaging*, [from] *showing* to *commenting*, and if only indirectly, criticizing" (301).

Early twentieth-century reformists came to appreciate the political implications of such "illicit" drama. New drama that first appeared in the late Qing, for example, appealed to reformist intellectuals because of its potentially powerful, if heterodox, ability to arouse the people (Mackerras 1975, 117). Late Qing reformist Liang Qichao, for one, promoted vernacular fiction and popular drama as a way to mobilize the "people." In his essay, "Popular Literature in Relation to the Masses," he wrote that "popular literature influences the way of the world . . . [and] arouses (*ci*, "to spur or pierce") people with the force of shock. . . . [N]othing delivers the astounding *ci* more powerfully than popular literature forms such as vernacular novel and drama."[25] In 1904, Chen Duxiu expanded upon Liang's argument, emphasizing in particular how theater was able to move audiences emotionally: "Theater . . . is an art form that can easily get into people's heads and touch their hearts. . . . Theater has the power to take possession of its audience, making it happy and joyful one moment and sad and mournful the next, making it dance in delirium one moment and cry in a flood of tears the next. It doesn't take much time to make incredibly great changes in people's minds."[26] By the May Fourth period, progressive dramatists found modern spoken drama to be particularly useful for commenting on society and contemporary affairs (Mackerras 1990, 104–12).

Drama in the 1930s continued to draw from current events, move the audience, and exhibit potentially heterodox, or *xia*, implications. Adopted into spoken drama almost immediately after the actual assassination, dramatic renditions of Shi Jianqiao's real-life story were examples of theater based on current events.[27] Given the unique size and nature of Shanghai's flourishing entertainment culture, it is hardly surprising that several plays based on the story appeared in Shanghai. *Shi Jianqiao Shoots Sun Chuanfang* was performed by the Period Drama Troupe at the famous Shanghai Public Stage playhouse run by gang boss Huang Jinrong. Originally planned for a limited, two-day performance on December 5 and 6, the show was extended for one extra day.[28] Another production with almost the same name, *Ms. Shi Shoots Sun Chuanfang*, was performed by the Daybreak Spoken Drama Troupe at the Southeast Grand Theater for a few days starting on November 25, 1935. It was then performed as a night show at the *Xinxin* garden theater, from November 29 to December 8, 1935. *The Chronicle of Sun Chuanfang's Assassination* played on November 29 and 30 at the Fujian-Anhui Traveling Theater and also had a short run at the Small World Theater from December 7 to December 10, 1935. One of the most extravagant and longest-running productions was *All About Sun Chuanfang*. Performed daily from December 20, 1935, until January 14, 1936, at the newly renovated Tianchan theater, the title of the production was suddenly changed midway in its run from *All about Sun Chuanfang* to *All about an Aveng-*

ing Daughter, perhaps because the theater realized that the story of a living female assassin would sell more tickets than the story of a dead warlord.[29] It was reported that troupes from other cities like Jinan and Qingdao also adapted Shi's story into dramatic performances.[30]

The exact reach of these theater adaptations is hard to assess, and reliable numbers for the audience are difficult to establish, but we can identify some characteristics of the audience. Audience members had enough leisure time and money to afford tickets. While they may not have drawn the vast crowds that traditional theater continued to draw, these plays were more inclusive than early spoken drama productions. Dominated by left-leaning dramatists, spoken drama in the 1920s generally tended to be fairly exclusive. By the mid-1930s, however, plays based on Shi's case enjoyed a broader appeal, catering to Shanghai's growing population of so-called petty urbanites (*xiaoshimin*), the same audience that read Butterfly fiction, lived in Shanghai's unique alleyway homes (*longtang*), and became the audience for early films.[31]

The broader appeal of many of these productions is apparent from their being performed at popular theaters. At the Public Stage playhouse's production of *Shi Jianqiao Shoots Sun Chuanfang*, tickets ranged from two *jiao* (twenty cents) for a seat upstairs to three, four, and even six *jiao* for more desirable seats downstairs. Ticket prices were thus reasonable, particularly compared to the cost of admission to films.[32] Furthermore, some of the advertisements suggest that, just as the real-life sensation appealed to a broad, mass audience, these productions were meant for "all circles of society" to enjoy.[33] Serious drama critics of the day had little to say about the artistic value of these adaptations, which suggests that these productions were decidedly not highbrow. At most, *Xishijiebao* (Theater world) would run a brief, formulaic write-up of the production. There were also roaming troupes that performed plays based on the Shi Jianqiao case, which meant that dramatic renditions of the case reached an even larger audience beyond Shanghai. Productions by roaming troupes were more likely to have been improvised without scripts, shared among troupes, and performed for only a few days at most in a given location.

Sources on popular culture in China have always been hard to come by, and unfortunately this case is no exception. Given the vernacular, and at times improvised, nature of productions based on the Shi Jianqiao case, scripts were not likely to be preserved. Playbills and advertisements printed in daily newspapers were, however, remarkably detailed and provide us with a sense of the shows. Many such ads appeared in the more commercial and major Shanghai dailies, including the *Shenbao* and the *Shibao*. Ads were also placed in theater-specific papers like the *Xishijiebao*. Overall, the ads promised productions that would enable the urban theater audience to enjoy a spectacle as well as to explore contemporary events.

An interesting tension between promises of spectacle and the guarantee of authenticity emerges from these advertisements. Theater production, in general, had moved toward portraying things more realistically. Whereas Peking opera was always highly stylized, so that a slight gesture of one's hand, the facial paint, or a wave of one's horsewhip was enough to hint at the action or meaning of a scene, Shanghai opera in the late Qing began drawing from real-life events and featuring "authentic" costumes and lifelike props. By the early twentieth century, new forms of theater were developed, including "civilization plays" (*wenmingxi*), which were forms of modern drama that had developed in the May Fourth period, and the more popular and spectacular forms of current-events drama (*shishi xinju*) and contemporary costume plays (*shizhuangxi*). The latter forms, in particular, were characterized by a tension between delivering both authenticity and spectacle, and were generic forms that were well-suited to the theatrical adaptations based on the Shi Jianqiao case.

Claims of authenticity in such advertising may have lent an air of heightened drama and emotional power to the promised performances. In an era when daily news and newspaper coverage was so highly sensational, a real-life drama could appear more intriguing and spectacular than an invented one. For instance, a preview advertisement for *Ms. Shi Shoots Sun Chuanfang* promoted the drama as a current-events play and claimed that this coming attraction based on actual events was well worth a look.[34] Other advertisements publicized the ability of such performances to provide accurate renditions of actual military battles and courtroom trials of the case of Shi Jianqiao. The theater bill for *All About an Avenging Daughter* boasted that the genuine story of the military struggle between Shi Congbin and Sun Chuanfang would be told once and for all. It guaranteed that the costumes were to be authentic, the sets lavish, and the props—from cannons to machine guns—like the real thing. The same theater bill advertised as its grand finale a dramatic courtroom scene and promised a realistic reenactment of the drama that was unfolding in the courts of Tianjin.[35] In short, while reality in the Shi case had become much like narrative convention, narrative convention readily drew from reality. Pledges of authenticity made in playbill advertising sold theater tickets. Drama based on a real case was readily marketable.

The ads also illustrate that the productions, while promising to deliver authentic accounts, were at the same time intended as crowd-pleasers. They were depicted as extravagant affairs that could affect audiences on a basic emotional level. By the 1930s, much of Shanghai entertainment culture was marked by spectacle. Meng Yue (2000, 436–98) has argued that as entertainment culture moved from Yangzhou to Shanghai after the Taiping rebellion, there was a shift in the history of "exhibition-type landscapes" from Yangzhou's extravaganza gardens (which had marked the city's power in the imperium in the pre-Taiping era) to the exposition centers for mass entertainment embodied by famous Shanghai playgrounds, such as the Great World Playground. These new entertainment centers were spatial reflections of a new era of Shanghai cosmopolitanism. They were spectacular in their ability to bring all types of theater and amusement from around the world into one space, in an exposition-like manner (439). Similarly, in a recent study of Shanghai film, Zhang Zhen (2005, 42–88) uses the linguistic term *yangjingbang*, originally applied to the pidgin Shanghaiese that incorporated foreign words and grew out of treaty-port culture where different language and cultures intermingled, to describe the cultural cosmopolitanism of Shanghai's migrant and working-class citizens. Slowly becoming the "petty urbanites" (*xiaoshimin*) of the city, this group displayed a voracious appetite for variegated attractions and experiences of play and entertainment. Such attractions included illustrated newspapers, amusement parks, rooftop gardens, teahouses, early films, and all types of theatrical performances.

Advertisements for theater productions based on the Shi Jianqiao affair reflected this vernacular cosmopolitanism of Shanghai. Some of these ads were themselves quite extravagant. Take, for example, the advertising for *All about Sun Chuanfang*, the play whose title was changed midway in its run to *All about an Avenging Daughter*. One of the regular commercials for this production was a lavish and variegated text that included visual material as well as textual information. At the heart of the ad were bold characters for *All about Sun Chuanfang*, and later for *All about an Avenging Daughter*. Above the name, in only slightly smaller characters, was "Tianchan Theater," one of Shanghai's major theaters for drama. Just under the title, ad copy strongly evoked the headlines about the case that were appearing in the same newspapers. These included "Injustice Done to Shi Congbin at a Train Station" and "Ms. Shi Sentenced to Ten

Figure 7. Advertisement for the theatrical production *All About Sun Chuanfang* (*Shenbao*, 26 December 1935).

Years." Finally, five large photographs competed to catch the eye of the viewer. At the middle, under the title of the show, was a photo of an elaborate scene from the production and its stage setting. The other four photographs were placed in the four corners of the ads and featured the actors playing the main characters of Shi Jianqiao, Shi Congbin, Sun Chuanfang, and Shi Zhongcheng, Shi Jianqiao's cousin. The title and theater name and the photographs were surrounded by text. Written both horizontally and vertically, the ad copy promised a wealth of attractions.

The content of this ad deserves some attention, as it gives us a sense of who in the theater world took part in such productions as well as the extent of the pageantry involved. The four oval photos show us the four main characters. We see the actors playing Shi Congbin and Shi Zhongcheng, dressed in military costume. The Sun Chuanfang character is dressed in a traditional robe, his hands folded as in prayer. The photo of Shi Jianqiao has Shi wearing an extravagant dress—far more extravagant than the simple dress worn by the real-life Shi Jianqiao in the pictures being circulated in the news—and is also highly dramatic: Shi's arms are extended, and she is pointing a gun. In addition to the four photos, the accompanying list of actors and their roles indicates that at least sixteen other actors had substantial roles, including some performing as prostitutes.

For those familiar with the theater world, several of these actors were well-known figures. The actor portraying Shi Jianqiao was a famous Shanghai *dan* actor, a male performer of female roles, by the name of Zhao Junyu (1894–1945).[36] Trained in Peking opera, by the 1930s Zhao had moved to more contemporary forms of drama, performing in famous *wenmingxi* (civilization plays), as well as in more spectacular *shizhuangxi* (contemporary costume plays). While *dan* actors commonly performed female roles in Shanghai's theater world, the gender politics behind a male actor playing a gender-bending female knight-errant was an interesting twist and added to the theatrical aspect of the whole affair. The actor who performed the role of Shi Congbin was Zhao Ruquan (1881–1961), another established Shanghai opera star, who specialized in the role of the *laosheng*, older, heroic, male figures, as opposed to younger romantic male leads.[37] By the 1930s, Zhao had become highly influential in the Shanghai theater world and was the head of the Shanghai United Actors Association. In addition to moving freely between opera and theater, he was also involved in directing, writing, and making the music and stage sets. His writing was often inspired by contemporary social news that he adapted into reality-based new drama (*shishi xinxi*), and it is possible that he was not merely performing in *All about Sun Chuanfang*, but had also written it.

The advertisement of figure 7 also vividly illuminates the elaborate nature of the actual production, shown in the center photo. To the right of the photo is the caption "the climactic scene of this production." The actors are dressed in seemingly authentic and up-to-date military garb, and cannons and live horses crowd the stage. The surrounding ad copy further emphasizes the pageantry that the image conveys. Marked by solid triangles are several sentences listed in a row on either side of the photo. These sentences promise "realistic and extraordinary settings," "absolutely new and complete military attire," "never before seen Russian-style troop movements," "live horses that ascend the stage," "heart-stopping cannons," "magnificent dance productions, both glamorous and sexy" and "better and more novel landscape sets." Just as the Great World Playground provided all sorts of entertainment within a single playground, this production, it was promised, would deliver all forms of drama and performance on one stage.

In addition to the various photos, the language of the ad copy employs a hodge-podge of discursive methods, echoing the mixed array of attractions being offered in Shanghai's entertainment culture more generally. Some of the text includes punchy, short promises such as "New production of Contemporary Sensation!" that echoed the headlines of newspapers. But some passages are written in the classical form of parallel couplets that liken the efficacy of this stage production to the power of nature in its ability to evoke a sensory response. They state that "the tense atmosphere of the drama is like the great Yangzi river; the more it flows, the more exciting it gets," and then claim that "the grandeur of the sets is like famous mountains and elegant rivers; the more you look at them, the more you love them." The ad also boasts that the event would be "exciting (*renao*) enough to render the atmosphere of the entire theater tense" and "comical (*huaji*) enough to bring laughter that would split your sides." In a review of another theatrical production based on the case, one *Xishijiebao* writer similarly guaranteed that the show would bring "laughter that rings through the heavens; you will laugh until your stomach hurts."[38] Without the actual scripts, we cannot determine what aspects of the beheading of Shi Congbin and the shooting of Sun Chuanfang would have been considered funny. Yet the convergence in these descriptions suggests that they were quite formulaic and indicates that these productions sought to present themselves as shows that would entertain all.

The ad copy hints at how the experience of going to theater was itself a thrilling experience, and how the producers of the play were somewhat anxious about this. The ad for *All about Sun Chuanfang*, posted on December 26, 1935, alludes to the teeming crowds at the theater. In an apology to theatergoers at the bottom, the text explains that because the crowd the night before had been larger than anticipated, some customers had to be regretfully turned away at the doors. Though it is impossible to determine whether this was true, the comment stirred up sensation by suggesting that there was great demand for the performance. Even while noting the unexpected crowds, the advertisement took care to define and discipline a new theatergoing audience. It urges theatergoers to get their tickets early, not to crowd, and to show up on time. The telephone number for reservations is provided. In one corner of the ad, the text says, "Take Note: *All About Sun Chuanfang* Starts Promptly at 8." Finally, lists of different ticket prices are included to educate readers. Evening shows are more expensive and different tiers of seats are priced accordingly, from 6 *jiao* for the most coveted seats, to 1 *jiao* for the seats on the third floor. If the audience did not heed such information, the theater-going experience could easily move from excitement to chaos.

Interestingly, these ads were selling the genre of current-events or contemporary costume drama as a form of cutting-edge entertainment. This was an era of new film technology, when film productions increasingly competed with drama for audiences and lured potential theater audiences away with the technology and thrills found in movie theaters. Live theater had to reinvent itself. It sought to remain competitive with the promise of being able to adapt current events into entertainment (far faster than a film could do), and the promise of live extravaganzas on stage. The ad for *All about Sun Chuanfang* explicitly refers to the theater world's need to renew forms of genre. For instance, it notes that this production "gets rid of the insignificant first act; (instead) the opening production will be a grand military spectacle (*da wuxi*), with more than 100 martial actors on stage at the same time." The other side of the ad claims that this production is like "vanguard troops that can smash apart a dull atmosphere" and constitutes "a vital new force (*shengli jun*) that revolutionizes hackneyed, stale theater!"

The military metaphors used in these phrases were particularly effective in promoting such theater. The 1930s saw an exaltation of military strength and general militarization. The New Life movement urged military rigor and discipline as means to strengthen the Chinese nation and society. Leftist discourse of the time was also increasingly militaristic, emphasizing struggle and revolution. The language in this ad clearly draws from this contemporary emphasis on militarization. The urgency and excitement of military action had penetrated commercial and cultural discourse and, in turn, such ads, like the theater they are promoting, domesticated militarism for purposes of consumption and entertainment.

Such military metaphors also help characterize this new popular Shanghai current-events theater as a *jianghu* space. The military metaphors in the ads highlight how Shi Jianqiao's story essentially revolved around martial issues, focusing on militarists and the battleground. These costume dramas of Shi Jianqiao's affair were directly linked to the contemporary situation of a post-warlord yet highly militarized regime under the Nationalists, and thus lent themselves to exploring real-life social concerns. For example, theater based on the Shi Jianqiao case might have shed rather unflattering light on the Nationalist regime's failure to control ongoing violence. By the mid-1930s, public anxiety regarding Jiang's rule was not limited to North China. In Shanghai and other southern cities, there was a growing sense that even though the arrival of the Nationalist state had put an end to the internecine regional fighting, it had not brought about any conclusive end to social turbulence. Urban centers were still rife with political insecurity. Underworld gang activity in Shanghai and elsewhere permeated society and hardly served as a harbinger of stable rule. Furthermore, the perception that the central regime was directly at fault increasingly gained currency. Jiang Jieshi's collusion with notorious gang bosses and paramilitary groups like the Blue Shirts was fairly well established, as was his tacit complicity with those engaged in political violence.[39]

In this context, dramatic treatment of the warlord period may have served as a metaphor for the Nanjing decade. By extension, in an era of skepticism toward the Nationalist regime, theater advertisements' emphasis on authenticity may have been intended to promote the dramas as a somewhat more "genuine" settling of accounts than the Nationalist regime was offering at the time. Ads for *All About Sun Chuanfang*, for example, guaranteed that audiences would see a lifelike rendition of the full story behind the killing. The drama would start with the warlord struggles of the 1920s and end with the district-level trial, which in real life had reached a verdict only a few days before the run of the show had begun.[40] Within the safe confines of the theater, the ads suggested, viewers could vicariously experience warlord disorder and then leave with a sense of restored control over the present situation, something that remained elusive in real life. Scenes of violence were to be staged and contrived to be *just like* reality so that they could be contained on stage just *as if* real disorder was being contained.

While the connotations of the plays cannot be firmly established without full access to their content, these dramatic performances were certainly often identified as more reliable sources of justice than the legal opinions of the regime's newly established courts. The public trial of Shi held in theaters and on street corners produced a sympathetic verdict far quicker than the legal resolution pending in real courtrooms. The court scene in *All about an Avenging Daughter*, for example, authoritatively sanctioned Shi's revenge during an evening performance a few days after her actual trial had only just initiated a complicated legal process that was to last for another nine months. Not surprisingly, one editorialist advocated the use of dramatic precedent to dictate the outcome of Shi's court trial, suggesting that extra-judicial forums like the theater were more effective than the real-life courthouse in providing proper justice (Lingxiaohangezu 1935b). Pointing out that the real-life trial had been stalled by petty judicial debates over Shi Jianqiao's surrender, this author argued that drama would provide more effective standards with which to try Shi. He cites as an example *Zhen'e ci hu* (Zhen'e kills a tiger), a drama set in the late Ming about Fei Zhen'e, an avenging heroine who, in the name of her emperor, assassinates Bandit Chuang, a traitor to China.[41] The writer reasoned that since Shi Jianqiao, like Zhen'e, had risked her life in the name of someone deserving, the judicial issue of surrender was moot, and widespread sympathy for the female assassin was reason enough for judicial exemption. Rather than listen to legal specialists pontificate endlessly, he concluded, one might do better by drawing moral lessons from the world of theater.

CONCLUSION

In a context where Nationalist courts were failing to persecute warlord traitors and ensure national security, the media celebration and public investment in Shi Jianqiao's killing of a militarist threatened to shed critical light on the ruling regime's failures. Celebrated in the media and entertainment worlds as a heroic *xia* undertaking, Shi's successful killing of a warlord was seen as an act of national redemption and as an expression of *xiayi*, or public justice. Traditionally, a classic *xia* hero appears in times of moral crisis and social chaos to bring about public order by both containing bandits (*fei*) and setting right inept officials (*guan*). Shi Jianqiao proved to be a modern *xia* hero who, like her traditional counterpart, appeared in a time of national crisis to bring about justice. She had successfully killed a reputed traitor and warlord, a modern day *fei*, and her success and popularity sharply contrasted with increasing public dissatisfaction with the Nationalist state, the modern inept *guan*. Whereas the regime's New Life campaign met with utter public apathy, Shi efficaciously embodied the virtues of a strong China as a modern *xianü*. While the central government appeared to be lacking in resolve and cowardly by accepting a policy of appeasement with regard to the Japanese, Shi's killing of a traitorous warlord suspected of collaboration was swift, determined, and heroic. If Jiang Jieshi's regime failed to deal with either the warlord past or admit to its complicity in urban violence in the present, Shi's revenge and ensuing trial successfully established a sense of national redemption. Public appreciation for the *xia* heroine, arising from the *jianghu* arena of media sensation, only made the failures of Nanjing all the more evident.

The media culture of the Republican period hardly seems a likely forum for the rise of a critical urban public. While not-so-subtle forms of control by powerful military patrons, influential families, and political parties had existed before the 1930s, it was in the Nanjing decade that a centralizing, modern state systematically began to contain and censor the press, periodicals, and the film industry.[42] The Nationalist regime used censorship to consolidate its rule from the start and imposed a restrictive publishing law in 1930 (Hockx 1998, 5). With state-building efforts proving only partially successful for the regime and rightists of the party increasing their sway over culture, the Nationalist authorities increased the suppression of "reactionary" cultural productions in the following few years. In 1934, comprehensive censorship regulations for books and periodicals were drafted (Hockx 1998, 5). In 1935, despite vociferous protests by journalists, harsh new press laws were enacted.[43] State censorship even became violent during this period. On November 14, 1934, Jiang Jieshi arranged for the assassination of Shi Liangcai, the editor of the *Shenbao*, who had consistently and openly criticized the official policy of appeasement with regard to the Japanese.

Scholars have not always agreed on their assessment of the impact of such censorship laws. Frederick Wakeman, for example, portrays the regulations as part of the Nationalists' attempt to squelch any semblance of an autonomous civil society (1995, 235–40). Michel Hockx (1998) directly challenges that assessment, suggesting that such views are colored by the successful campaign by the Chinese literary field in the 1930s to fight such Nationalist regulations, and that in reality such writers were quite successful in negotiating with censors a considerable degree of autonomy. Hockx concludes that literature in the 1930s was not significantly restricted by censorship and proved, in terms of literary output, quite lively. Hockx is, of course, speaking primarily about the censorship of literature, and there may indeed have been more restrictions on non-literary print media, especially in the case of political essays and commentary. Nonetheless, his caution against drawing a stark picture of extreme cultural repression under the Nationalist government is well taken. Despite an undeniable increase in attempts to censor cultural production, the focus here is less on illustrating repression as the inevitable result of such laws, and more on how censorship regulations reshaped the conditions under which political commentary could take place. While constrained, political commentary found alternative arenas for expression, including sensational media stories and forms of mass entertainment.

To be sure, the mass media of this period have conventionally been seen as regrettably sensational. Historians and literary scholars have long complained that Republican-era reporting and serialized fiction are too trivial or sensational to merit serious scholarly inquiry. These contemporary views are hardly unprecedented. Some of China's most influential critics of the Republican period disparaged the possibility of critical political debate during their day and despaired over the sensational nature of the mass media in particular. In 1936, Lin Yutang, for example, attributed China's lack of a critical public opinion to the overly commercial and sensational nature of the press. Citing Shanghai's *Shenbao* as an egregious example, Lin bemoaned that the market-oriented nature of newspapers resulted in an overwhelming presence of commercial advertisements, as well as a predominance of sensational news items like legal scandals and suicides (1968, chap. 11).

The result of such a view is that little thought has been given to how media sensation, didacticism, mass entertainment, and "trivial" news items might have played constitutive roles in shaping and politicizing a new urban public. What the study of the Shi Jianqiao affair suggests is that the very qualities of commercialism, sensation, and sentimentalism that Lin Yutang and others bemoan as evidence of political apathy were, in fact, prime conditions for the making of a critical public. It was precisely the sensationalism in Shi Jianqiao's case that enabled accounts of her affair to fly undetected under the radar of state censorship, and thus provide a forum for the public airing of pressing social and political issues. Not subjected to the kind of control exercised over conventional venues of "serious" journalism, serialized fiction based on the case allowed the reading public to explore radically new gender norms during a period when calls for constraints on female morality were increasingly strident among Nationalist ideologues. Dramas inspired by the killing were also not strictly policed. By celebrating Shi Jianqiao as the female knight-errant antihero and a superior bearer of national justice, theatrical productions could articulate alternative forms of public justice that lay outside the official court system.

It was thus precisely because the Republican era was characterized by aggressive state censorship and rampant media commercialism that its media and entertainment culture could serve as a *jianghu* space, where critical public explorations of otherwise taboo subjects could occur. Just as Shi Jianqiao manipulated the gendered *xia* identity to create space for herself to act in public as a woman, the *xia* idiom can also help us think about how media adaptations of the Shi Jianqiao case became an alternative space in which to explore issues in an era of state censorship. Or, put slightly differently, the *xia* concept of virtuous transgression embodied by Shi Jianqiao as an individual *xianü* became enlarged through the media to create a public whose sympathies for the avenging daughter were themselves expressions of *xia* justice able to deliver critical commentary in an age of media control. Attributing a subversive yet righteous quality to popular sentiment was certainly not unprecedented in Chinese history. As early as the fourth century B.C.E., Mengzi (Mencius) wrote about the apocalyptic "moral will of the people" as the basis of the right to rebel against tyrants. A more recent precedent can be found in the late Qing, when popular sentiment that served as the basis of political action in the Boxer uprising was mediated through rumors and transmitted via broadsheets and cultural practices such as martial boxing.[44] In 1920s rural Shanxi, as well, oral reports crucially mediated popular sentiment against the government at a point when newspapers were becoming a pulpit for regional ruler Yan Xishan (Harrison 2000). What this 1930s case illuminates is how sensational media coverage and entertainment surrounding a news event could function in a similar manner to broadsheets and rumors in the creation of sentiment in an earlier rural context. Not merely a mouthpiece for the government or modernizing elites, the commercial media and entertainment in the High Republic provided the consuming public with a forum from which their concerns could be addressed and their expression deemed "righteous."

In the end, however, public sympathy and its *xia* attributes were not welcomed by all. Precisely because of its rising influence, neither the state nor intellectuals were completely comfortable with the sensation-consuming, sympathetic public so evident in the Shi Jianqiao affair. While the state attempted to co-opt the new public with high-profile pardons, urban critics and left-leaning writers condemned both official attempts at co-optation and the role of mass media in generating irrational, feminized sentiments in the new mass audience.

THREE

Highbrow Ambivalence

Fear of the Masses and Feminized Sentiment

While admitting her actions are brave, we need to nonetheless consider the impact on society of such behavior. Even though I admit that from the perspective of China's knight-errantry (*yixia*) tradition, or from Europe and America's perspective of individual heroism, we can sympathize with (*tongqing*) [such behavior], we should not encourage it. This is because people exist for society and not for themselves. If we act out of our own emotions and harm someone else regardless for what reason, this is selfish (*zisi*).

Lin Gengbai commenting on a contemporaneous crime of passion, Chenbao, *20 March 1935*

Although it describes a contemporaneous crime of passion that featured a female assassin by the name of Liu Jinggui, a case to which I return in detail at the conclusion of the chapter, the epigraph for this chapter nicely illustrates how, despite public interest in them, crimes featuring passionate women caused considerable anxiety to elite observers. In contrast to the celebratory reception of the Shi Jianqiao affair in the urban media and the entertainment world, more "highbrow" social commentary published in newspaper editorials, legal journals, leftist periodicals, social and political weeklies, and the women's press took a rather negative view of the Shi Jianqiao affair and other crimes of female passion. While disdainful of female assassins, critical accounts acknowledged, even if somewhat begrudgingly, that such affairs were linked to larger social, political, and moral issues of the day. Commenting on the Shi Jianqiao case, Liu Shi summed it up nicely. While he had at first felt that the news of Shi was a private affair and not worth making a fuss over, he later changed his mind. Everyone was forced to pay attention, he argued, as the case had become the talk of the street (Liu 1935). Invested in shaping public response, editorialists and contributors to journals and magazines of all political persuasions took notice. The primary point of debate for this body of opinion-makers was the question of whether the female avenger's sentiment-based revenge should be praised as a public act of virtue morally beneficial to the nation or castigated as a private vendetta no modern society should ever condone.

As the dialogue unfolded, it quickly became clear that the focus of the debate was the moral and political question of how to establish a strong society and nation and what role sentiment should play in that process. Whereas in imperial China's cosmological order sincere expressions of morality made human relationships, social bonds, and even larger political ties meaningful and harmonious, by the 1930s sentiment and its moral and political relevance were under harsh scrutiny. Writers commenting on the Shi Jianqiao case showed little patience for either the assassin's sentiment of filial passion or the widespread public sympathy for the assassin. Both forms of *qing* were deemed selfish, particularistic, and traditional in nature, and were derisively associated with women. Left-leaning writers, promoters of national law, and other impatient critics, moreover, cast them in opposition to their own public-minded, universalistic agendas of modernity.

This chapter identifies several historical reasons for the antipathy toward sentiment among social commentators of the day. These include a sharp disillusionment with May Fourth discourses that had located modern liberation within progressive forms of female sentiment. Writers of the Nanjing decade advocated instead "rational" and implicitly masculine agendas, including the objective rule of law and the scientism of historical materialist analysis. Part of the antipathy toward sentiment also stemmed from the increasingly uncomfortable situation in which intellectuals and professionals found themselves in the 1930s. Critics and urban professionals found both their position as arbiters of social morality and their claim to professional expertise under siege as they were being wedged in between the increasingly powerful mass public, whose collective sentiment was created and spread by the thriving new mass media, and an aggressively authoritarian regime. To redefine their territory, these self-perceived molders of public opinion expressed considerable discomfort with or outright derision of what they perceived to be a feminized public and its fickle nature. They also decried any official attempt to mobilize public sentiment in bolstering central authority.

RITUAL, SENTIMENT, AND THE CHANGING SOCIAL ORDER

Sentiment was at the heart of discourses of reformist modernity in both the 1920s and 1930s, though in radically different ways. In the earlier May Fourth period, while a frontal attack on Confucian ethical sentiment was underway, refashioned notions of *qing*, including the concept of "love," or *aiqing*, remained central for many thinkers in their articulation of a May Fourth subjectivity. In contrast, in the Nanjing decade discussions surrounding Shi Jianqiao's revenge, romantic sentiment was increasingly deemed feminine and identified as antithetical to new, more masculine discourses of modernity that stressed rationality. In an era when the New Life movement dictated a renewed emphasis on Confucian moralism, and when judicial reform privileged the rule of law, all forms of *qing* came under doubt.

Ambivalence and shifting attitudes toward *qing* were nothing new to Chinese history. Anxiety over what exactly constituted *qing* and the degree to which *qing* should be regulated by more "rational" ritualism (*li*), or curbed by law or bureaucratic procedure, had been fairly constant since as early as the pre-Han era. Confucian thinker Xunzi (c. 335 B.C.E.–c. 238 B.C.E.) was among the first to frame the issue of the moral authority of *qing* in ambivalent terms. Known for having a more negative view of human nature than previous Confucian scholars, Xunzi, though acknowledging that *qing* was essential in defining moral character (*xing*), was most concerned with how best to mobilize *qing* without allowing it to become excessive desire (*yu*), and thus potentially disrupt social harmony. Ritual, or *li*, argued the thinker, was crucial in channeling *qing* into proper forms of expression and ensuring that *qing* remained virtuously contained. Xunzi writes, "I say that men are born with desires, which, if not satisfied, cannot but lead men to seek to satisfy them. If in seeking [to satisfy] their desires men observe no measure and apportion things without limits, then it would be impossible for them not to contend over the means to satisfy their desires. Such contention leads to disorder. . . . The ancient Kings abhorred such disorder; so they established the regulations contained within ritual and moral principles in order to apportion things, to nurture the desires of men, and to supply the means for their satisfaction."[1]

Initially codified in the Han dynasty (206 B.C.E.–220 C.E.) and then institutionalized through the civil service examination system in the Song dynasty (960–1279), imperial China's orthodox Confucian ethical system (*lijiao*) was shaped by this classical ambivalence toward *qing*. Imperial orthodoxy identified the Three Bonds—bonds between lord and subject, parent and child, and husband and wife—as crucial relations in maintaining social order. Even as prescriptive literature frequently identified sentimentality as a means to solidify these relations, ritual was always the crucial element in governing these bonds.[2] For example, while the sincere emotional experience of a filial bond rendered the parent-child relationship all the more successful in forging social order, the filial piety of a child was fundamentally an expression of ritual propriety rather than emotion.

By the late Ming, a philosophical and literary movement known as the "cult of sentiment," challenged this classical ambivalence toward *qing* by reversing the trend of placing emotion below ritual authority.[3] The cult included followers of the Wang Yangming school, commercial literati writers and dramatists, including, most famously, Feng Menglong and playwright Tang Xianzu, as well as female consumers and producers of *qing*-based literature and poetry. The cult's participants challenged *lixue* (ritual studies) orthodoxy. They decried the ritually prescribed, family-based *renqing* of *lixue* as obsolete and promoted spontaneous feeling, especially husband-wife love, as the foundational basis of subjectivity and moral harmony. For the first time, *qing* came to qualify as a form of Heavenly Principle, just as ritual and other important concepts such as human nature (*xing*) had long done.

With the fall of the Ming, the celebration of *qing* as a foundational moral force once again became problematic. Under the new Manchu regime, many Han literati-scholars underwent profound soul-searching and began to reexamine aspects of late Ming thought and society to understand what had led to the fall of Ming imperial rule. In such a reevaluation, a marked movement away from the cult of sentiment was discernible. As part of state and cultural consolidation under the Qing regime, *kaozheng*, or "evidentiary scholarship," set the parameters for the rise of classicism and ritualism, and spontaneous emotions were once again to be disciplined through ritual. This rise of ritualism was accompanied by the increasingly aggressive statecraft policies of mid-Qing emperors that increased the policing of passionate acts of filial piety and chaste suicide.[4] Eighteenth- and nineteenth-century evidentiary scholars, including Dai Zhen (1724–1777) and Ruan Yuan (1764–1849), who attacked the Wang Yangming school in order to promote their practical-studies approach, were representative of such trends.[5] The eighteenth-century novel, *Dream of the Red Chamber* (Honglou meng), while centrally featuring *qing*, explored far more deeply than any late Ming text the profound ambiguity of *qing* as a moral force.[6]

If the modern ambivalence toward *qing* echoes this long history of ambivalence toward emotion in premodern China, the epistemological terrain for the modern period was nonetheless considerably different. In her study of the genealogy of *qing* in modern literary discourses, Haiyan Lee (2002) identifies the introduction of an unprecedented model of personhood that inextricably linked emotion and interior identity by novelists, writers, and thinkers in the last decade of the nineteenth century and early twentieth century. Exploration of this new model of personhood first occurred in the late Qing, a period when Confucian orthodoxy was coming under assault. Just as the political factionalism of the late Ming had stimulated the rise of the cult of sentiment in literary and philosophical circles, in the late Qing the weakening of the Qing state in the face of internal and external pressures resulted in the revival of a cultural exploration with *qing*. Like their late Ming predecessors, late Qing writers found ritual studies and imperial statecraft increasingly ineffective, and started instead to translate Western novels of melodrama and to produce their own highly sentimental novels to mediate the vicissitudes of their day. What was unprecedented in the late Qing was the emerging idea that emotion constituted the interior space of one's individual psyche. In the late Qing novel *Henhai* (Sea of regret), writer Wu Jianren, for example, used interior monologues to explore in an unprecedented manner the affective and ethical interiority of his female protagonist, Dihua.

While the late Qing saw tentative explorations involving new notions of interiority and emotion, it was not until after the collapse of the imperial system and the dethroning of its attendant Confucian orthodoxy during the May Fourth movement that the notion of modern subjectivity predicated on an emotional core became the basis of an entirely new cosmological order. Haiyan Lee (2002) points to this genealogical shift by characterizing the late Qing discourse on *qing* as a "Confucian structure of feeling" that sought to assert the moral authority of *qing* in order to rejuvenate what was essentially a Confucian social order that rested on hierarchical ethical relations.[7] With May Fourth writers and thinkers increasingly drawing from Western Enlightenment thought and Romanticist discourses, Lee characterizes the latter era's discourse as an "Enlightenment structure of feelings." At the heart of this discourse lay the concept of an emotionally demarcated notion of interiority as the defining feature of the modern self. This modern *qing* was then the glue that united members in a new national republican order.

In their exploration of modern subjectivity, society, and the national state, May Fourth intellectuals most certainly grappled with the moral power and political significance of *qing*. To begin, thinkers vociferously discredited the modern relevance of past notions of orthodox sentiment (*renqing*). Chen Duxiu and Wu Yu, for example, wrote prolifically about the sins of family and filial devotion.[8] Others attacked female chastity.[9] Once unquestionable in the imagining of the imperial order, blind devotion to one's elders and absolute loyalty to one's husband were identified as the ethical core of the patriarchal family system that was the foundation of traditional Chinese despotism. Bearing the brunt of bitter, iconoclastic scorn, filial piety and female chastity became powerful metaphors for all that was wrong with "traditional" China; modern subjectivity, individual rights, and national liberation were to be achieved only with their full abnegation.

Although forms of human sentiment once held up as morally supreme had become fraught with moral ambiguity by the first quarter of the twentieth century, iconoclasts did not categorically reject the moral category of sentiment (*qing*). In fact, while desacralizing traditional forms of sentiment such as filial piety and female chastity, and, by extension, the classical Confucian cosmology in which familial sentiment was the cornerstone of an imperial social and political order, they were still promoting new forms of sentiment—shorn of traditional ethical constraints. In other words, May Fourth thinkers sought to put forth a radical reconfiguration of the relationship between sentiment and modern society. The May Fourth individual possessed psychological interiority and was part of a universal humanity in his or her ability to feel, to weep, and to fall in love.

Just as female paragons had embodied orthodox Confucian sentiment in the imperial era, the female body in the early twentieth century became the quintessential bearer of such modern sentiment. For many May Fourth writers, the New Woman (*xin nüxing*) was a model in her rejection of the strictures of Confucian arranged marriage and familial ritual obligation and her adoption of a life of free, romantic love and sexual liberation.[10] The famous debate over female chastity, which Zhou Zuoren initiated in *New Youth*, the leading reformist periodical of the day, was seminal in formulating such ideals of progressive female sentiment. Translating Yosano Akiko's "A Treatise on Chastity," Zhou raised the rhetorical question of whether a traditional morality that endorsed female chastity could ever exist free of hypocrisy in the modern era. He then urged "awakened" men to create a new morality appropriate for a new woman and a new day (Zhou 1918). In response to Zhou's rallying cry, Hu Shi contributed the essay, "The Question of Chastity," in which he vituperatively condemned traditional chastity and hailed sexual equality and romantic love instead as a truly progressive sentiment befitting a modern civilization.[11] In the piece, Hu repeatedly claimed that whereas traditional female virtue no longer followed the basic principle of human sentiment, romantic love and conjugal ties between two equal individuals did.[12] Implicit was the argument that the bonds of love that tied the New Woman to her progressive partner would, in turn, form the bonds of society. The new, progressive China was to be composed of national citizens who were bound not by ritual obligation but by individual emotions.

Even as notions of free love and liberated sexual relations were avidly promoted in this "Enlightenment structure of feelings," anxiety about these new forms of *qing* and the New Woman as bearer of that *qing* arose just as quickly. Ding Ling's famous 1927 story, "Miss Sophia's Diary" (Shafei nüshi de riji) is a telling example of how female intellectuals from the May Fourth generation expressed considerable doubt toward ideals of sexual liberation and romantic love. Ding Ling's protagonist, Miss Sophia, was stricken not only with tuberculosis, but also with modern *ennui* and the inability to connect emotionally in a meaningful way with any man (or woman, for that matter). The story ends with Miss Sophia lonely and estranged. Male writers also expressed ambivalence. In a famous essay, Lu Xun wondered what was to become of Nora after she leaves her home at the end of Henrick Ibsen's play, *A Doll's House*. His query into the fate of Nora encapsulated the anxiety about new prescriptions of womanhood in general. Leftist writers accused women's literature of being too moralistic and narrowly focused on the private realm of emotions and interiority, and called upon writers to be more engaged socially and politically (Larson 1998, 165). For others, the May Fourth exploration of the modern subject was fine as something endowed with both tremendous emotional and ethical capacity, as long as it remained in the realm of literature.[13] In contrast, the public arena was to be marked by "rational" discourses of science, democracy, and modern law. Intellectuals such as Hu Shi promoted the discourse of "Mr. Science and Mr. Democracy," and Chen Duxiu advocated the need for the objective rule of law against China's traditional system of the subjective rule of man. Debate and anxiety over the sentiment of modern love soon spread more widely through the mass media. Provocative opinion pieces, special journal issues devoted to the topic, and media coverage of crimes of passion or matrimonial affairs spawned larger public explorations of love and marriage (e.g., see Lean 2005; Goodman 2006).

By the second quarter of the twentieth century, ambivalence toward progressive forms of female *qing* had intensified. The promises of the 1911 political revolution and the 1919 intellectual revolution had not been fulfilled. Not surprisingly, skepticism about the basic tenets and ideas associated with the two movements became increasingly common. Just as Nationalist authoritarianism threatened the political ideals of 1911 republicanism, so too did New Life Confucian moralism threaten May Fourth ideals of romantic love. With Jiang Jieshi initiating the New Life campaign in 1934, Confucian virtues became necessary to strengthen the society and the nation. The cosmopolitan celebration of free love and liberated sexuality of the May Fourth period was being replaced with a stricter, more straight-laced emphasis on female virtue and propriety (e.g., see Lee 2002, 41; Edwards 2000). Similarly, anxiety grew around the public passions of women. Pundits and moralists of the era started to associate the New Woman with prostitution, the wanton sexual promiscuity of dance halls, and crass commercialism, and levied charges against her of libertine behavior, excessive individualism, and immoral norms of sexuality (Hershatter 1997; Fields 1999; Edwards 2000).

It was in this context of a fundamental rethinking of sentiment in the early twentieth century that critical commentary on the Shi Jianqiao affair took place. Skeptical writings on the case found the daughter's passionate motivation of filial piety to be seriously outdated, the vigilantism of her act of violence a sure sign of national chaos, and the emotional intensity of public support dangerously misguided. Spilling a substantial amount of ink on the affair, different groups of commentators bound by specific professional or political agendas (e.g., expertise in law, or a leftist or feminist agenda) published in specialized journals (e.g., journals dedicated to legal issues, publications of the leftist press, or women's magazines) and expressed a profound fear of national disintegration. As we will see, the majority used this case that so centrally featured sentiment as a counterpoint to what they believed was the ideal solution to China's national predicament. Thus, while the "backlash" to *qing* echoed some of the eighteenth-century retreat from the late Ming cult of sentiment, this early twentieth-century problematization of *qing* took place on a radically different epistemological terrain. Not geared toward bolstering a web of hierarchical ethical relations, the retreat from *qing* in the second quarter of the twentieth century was more centrally framed by growing concerns over the rise of unruly masses, how to demarcate China's new national order, and how to establish the legitimacy of "rational" discourses of modernity, including the rule of law and the scientism of historical materialism.

PRIVATE REVENGE AND NATIONAL STRENGTH

A palpable fear of national disintegration permeated nearly all the critical commentary on Shi Jianqiao. After two decades of failed parliamentary republicanism and warlord chaos, a sense of national crisis gripped the country, and intellectuals and politicians alike were consumed by the question of what a new, unified Chinese nation should look like. Many of these more highbrow observers of the case took exception to the media celebration of the daughter's filial revenge as legitimate grounds for national justice. Hardly offering closure, Shi's revenge, they argued, was instead concrete evidence that the chaos from the earlier period was threatening to engulf the Chinese nation in the present day. Commentary that specifically identified Shi Jianqiao's revenge as an act of "selfish retribution," or *sichou*, was particularly successful in invoking the moral urgency informing the discussion. The prefix of "selfish," or *si*, in the compound of "selfish retribution" (*sichou*), automatically conjured up the concept of "public," or *gong*. Both were part of a time-honored moral dyad that had long served as a rhetorical means to mark the moral parameters of China's social and political order. *Gong* identified actions perceived as ethically beneficial to the larger polity and *si* marked those deemed pernicious.[14] Thus, by identifying the revenge as an act of "selfish retribution," critics levied an unconditional denunciation of Shi Jianqiao's vengeful behavior.

Much of the moral venom was simply the sting of iconoclasm inherited from the May Fourth movement. The revenge was denounced as selfish because it was motivated by a dangerously outdated ethic of filial piety. Like their May Fourth predecessors, these modern men of letters refuted the validity of traditional forms of human sentiment, challenged the centrality of the reciprocal nature of personalized relations, and rejected the prominence of family ethics in envisioning China's polity. That said, the 1930s' writers also went beyond the earlier May Fourth critique, worrying about how the sentiment-driven revenge was a sign of continuing warlord intrigue that would harm a nation still struggling to unify. After a full decade of internal warfare, concerned observers during the Nanjing decade regarded Shi Jianqiao's vengeance as an ominous sign of the contemporary discord that continued to block national unity.

The study of the relationship between the 1920s and 1930s in modern China has largely focused on how the warlordism of the twenties gave rise to the nature of politics and militarism in the thirties. Little, however, has been done on how the politics of the Nanjing decade gave rise to competing memories of the preceding warlord era. Few, for example, have examined how the contest over the memory of the earlier decade was an important part of centralizing and imagining a nation in the later one. The Shi Jianqiao affair offers an intriguing entry into this issue. Competing interpretations abounded over whether Shi's revenge was a treacherous product of the earlier decade or an effective resolution of it, and the divergence in the two interpretations stemmed from differences in views about the national and moral implications of female sentiment in the 1930s.

Critical pundits denounced Shi's action as "selfish retribution" and made it clear that they felt her act to be part of the chaos. Several identified Shi Congbin as a minor warlord himself and argued that his death was simply another casualty of warfare between self-interested militarists.[15] Writing in *Funü shenghuo* (Women's life), one angry contributor called Shi Jianqiao's retribution one of many petty vendettas that dotted China's political landscape. They were pernicious, he claimed, because they prevented China from confronting imperialist beasts from abroad. Those beasts, he urged, were China's true national enemies and warranted national hatred as well as "public" forms of revenge.[16] This writer and others like him were troubled not only by Shi's actions, but also by the widespread endorsement of her revenge and the alternative moral discourses that made the revenge meaningful to so many people. One *Guowen zhoubao* (The national weekly) contributor explicitly blamed the widespread faith in filial piety. He wrote that the unquestioning reverence for the ethical sentiment obscured people's ability to see how this one act of revenge would only result in a wave of assassinations.[17]

The disdain for popular interpretations of the event was most evident in commentators' focus on religious narratives of retribution, which, like the act of revenge, came to be associated with twentieth-century warlordism. Shi's self-portrayal as an instrument of karma had struck a highly sympathetic chord with urban citizens who regularly read tales of fated retribution. Public intellectuals, in contrast, harbored extreme resentment toward Buddhist notions of reciprocity. Elite skepticism toward Buddhism was, of course, nothing new. As early as the Tang dynasty (618–907), when Han Yu wrote his classic condemnation of the use of the Buddha's bone in court ceremony, literati discourse had warned that Buddhism was heterodoxy, a façade for immoral behavior, and a sure sign of moral and social degeneracy.[18] Retreat into Buddhism had long been perceived as a selfish escape from the world. And, in fiction, monasteries were seen as spaces where suspicious things happened. Not merely a place of revelation and enlightenment, the Buddhist monastery was also often portrayed as a site where conspirators lurked and illicit sexual behavior took place.

Disdain for Buddhism persisted into the twentieth century and also acquired several layers of unprecedented connotations, several of which appeared in the commentary on Shi Jianqiao. For example, while it echoed some of the ominous warnings penned centuries earlier, the Marxist logic that Buddhism was a sign of feudal thinking that kept the masses benighted was new. In his colorful and multifaceted harangue in the leftist journal, *Dazhong shenghuo* (Mass lifestyle), critic Liu Shi, for example, discredited several arguments in favor of the female assassin, but reserved his sharpest criticism for the belief in karmic retribution or the Buddhist idea of "you reap what you sow." He reasoned that when these beliefs were brought to their logical conclusion, they made no sense. If Sun Chuanfang's death had been fated because of his past misdeeds, then Shi Congbin's fate of decapitation should likewise have been due to a dubious history. Barely hiding his contempt, Liu concluded that these interpretations were no more than pedestrian nonsense (Liu 1935).

In the Shi Jianqiao case, an elitist critique of Buddhism was also shaped by the fear of national chaos and warlord betrayal. In the general cultural imagination of the day, the Buddhist monastery was often imagined to be a site for harboring warlords and a place for the warrior-in-exile to wait for comeback. Not surprisingly, skeptics questioned whether Sun Chuanfang's proclaimed Buddhist desire to purge his sins was sincere, and rumors swirled of his comeback. In their writings on the case, commentators uncomfortable with Sun's newfound faith used long-standing literati stereotypes of Buddhism to express their antipathy for him. For example, critic Ping Xin maligned not only Sun but also all militarists like him. He accused warlords like Sun of chanting sutras and abiding by a vegetarian diet while at the same time forcing women into bed, treating them like playthings, and then casting them away once their own needs were sated. Ping ranted that while these militarists claimed to be monks wanting to enter nirvana, they actually served as hired ruffians for imperialists and engaged in rapacious criminal behavior. Ping concluded by cautioning that while they might "put down their knives for Buddhism" with the greatest of ease today, they could just as quickly "put down the sutra and pick up the knife" tomorrow (Ping 1935). Writer Li Ying similarly charged that Sun was a wastrel, hiding away uselessly in retirement.[19]

Moreover, at the heart of these charges lay a belief in Buddhist hypocrisy. Ideologically speaking, Buddhism had long taught that any attachment to worldly desires had to be completely extinguished in order to reach enlightenment. Yet, in the Shi Jianqiao case, commentators accused Buddhism of the opposite, namely, with encouraging desire for very real worldly attachments such as military power. Buddhism, they contended, provided militarists like Sun Chuanfang with the ability to erect the façade or illusion of retreating from the corrupt world of politics when, in reality, they were simply biding their time. Such accusations of Buddhist hypocrisy were not reserved for Sun Chuanfang alone. Ping declared that Shi Jianqiao had committed a moral crime that was just as serious as that of Buddhism. Like the faith, he wrote, her revenge merely created an illusion of national redemption while in reality it only generated further moral and national degradation (Ping 1935).

FEMINIZED SENTIMENT VERSUS MASCULINE RATIONALITY

Like the pundits who viewed any endorsement of Shi's filial motivation as hopelessly retrograde and the widely held belief in fated retribution as dangerously hypocritical, left-leaning writers and advocates of law also found the sentiment-based discourses in which the female assassin's filial actions were grounded fundamentally offensive to their sensibilities. A rationalistic tone characterized their respective agendas of modernizing society and the nation, and developing the rule of law. These post–May Fourth men of letters were deeply disturbed by the way these discourses of sentiment proved extremely persuasive and empowering to others. As self-perceived molders of public opinion, they also had little patience for both the growing autonomy of public sentiment and the central regime's willingness to endorse that public.

From Sentiment to Society: The Chinese Left

Left-leaning critics wrote prolifically on the Shi Jianqiao case, and their criticism was among the sharpest. Voicing profound disgust for the sentiment at the heart of this case, these critics sought to defend their own standing and worldviews in their commentary on Shi Jianqiao during an era when, on the one hand, the sympathies of a mass public were gaining unprecedented power and, on the other hand, an authoritarian government was steadily imposing its control in the arena of intellectual activity. To this end, leftists condemned the popular reception of the traditional Confucian cosmology of familial ethics that validated Shi Jianqiao's filial act. Instead, Chinese leftists placed tremendous faith in a modern concept of "society," whose development was grounded on structural shifts in economic relations of production rather than on foundational human relations dictated by ethical forms of sentiment. Accordingly, left-wing commentary on the Shi Jianqiao case identified *qing* not only as part of the epiphenomenal realm, but also as part of the superstructure of the feudal past.

Discussing the changes in meaning of *society* (*shehui*) from the late Qing, when the term was first translated into Chinese political thought as a neologism from Japan, Michael Tsin (1997) argues that from the start a close discursive link was forged between nation and society. Liang Qichao, for example, defined society in the late Qing as the coming together of individuals motivated by "public morals" and then identified such a society as the basis of a strong nation. During the May Fourth period, socialist writers like Chen Duxiu continued to emphasize society's central importance for the nation, while redefining the term as a sphere in which individuals could act as independent units outside of a family or clan system. But, as Tsin points out, it was not really until the 1930s that the term *society* gained a truly foundational status. Whereas Liang had identified "public morals" and Chen had identified a progressive New Culture as the glue that held people together as a society, critics and intellectuals of the 1930s were really the first to bestow a truly ontological status upon the concept of society, viewing it as a body that was both segmented into sections and yet was a unified organic entity that could propel national development. The social had become not merely one factor among many in creating national vitality, but its most fundamental condition.

This new notion of society and its definitional opposition to family ethical sentiments like filial piety were not exclusive to the left. Cultural conservative Feng Youlan also attributed a great deal of explanatory power and moral authority to the social by opposing it to what he described as an outmoded notion of filial piety. In a 1938 essay entitled "The Origins of Filial Piety," Feng explicitly called for people to disavow their beliefs in filial piety because it was the symbol of the regressive, Confucian, family-state cosmology. He urged that they should invest instead in the modern idea of "society," a space wherein individuals could fully realize their national potential. He wrote, "If the societal sphere constituted that of the nation, people of the country could then amass into a single national body."[20]

If the term *society* gained currency in the political discourse of the

1930s in general, Marxism played an especially prominent role in defining the parameters of the modern discourse surrounding the term. Having matured significantly since the initial forays into anarchism and socialism during the May Fourth period, Chinese Marxism of the later decade articulated a more sophisticated narrative of historical materialism, at the center of which was the concept of society.[21] Through the lenses of social analysis, historical materialism offered a comprehensive way of understanding the past that, in turn, would explain the problematic present. It moreover provided a linear progression of history that appealed to writers obsessed with China's national development and divided history into major stages of socioeconomic development. The study of society thus promised a scientific blueprint with which to build a national future. Finally, its claims to objectivity conferred an alluring sense of inevitability on the progressive unfolding of national history, and gave ontological status to the notion of society.

Not surprisingly, leftist writers readily applied their narratives of development to discredit Shi Jianqiao's act of filial revenge. Dividing Chinese history into stages of modes of production, critic Tian Xing, for example, drew from historical materialism to explain the significance of the case. Tian argued that the revenge made apparent China's failure to close the gap between progressive shifts in society on the one hand and the ongoing feudal condition of the epiphenomenal realm of consciousness on the other hand. Explaining his assertion, he first laid out an interpretation of historical development: during the earlier hunter-gatherer period, the elderly were useless, and during the following long stage of small-farm agriculture, the elderly came to be highly valued for their experience in farming, so that filial piety became preeminent. He reasoned that while filial piety was crucial in the historical stage of small-farm agriculture during the imperial era, that stage had ended, and Shi Jianqiao's action only meant that filial piety was exerting its presence in China's modern era anachronistically. Tian thus urged that China needed to alter its consciousness in accord with shifts at the base level of society. Just as Confucianism was implemented as the dominant ideology when the new landlords replaced the aristocratic landlords of the Warring States period, a new ideology was now needed to replace Confucianism as the new landlord class had collapsed. He warned against nonaction, saying, "If we fail to take on the task [of putting aside feudal beliefs] ourselves and catch up, we would be allowing the imperialists to force us into changing our consciousness; this would be tantamount to being fettered by yet another yoke of [imperialist] consciousness" (Tian 1935, 93). Invoking the specter of imperialism, Tian sought to prompt China to abide by the Tianjin courts' rulings, even though their decisions were ultimately informed by Western capitalism and imperialist thought. Feudal sympathy for Shi Jianqiao's filial piety, he reasoned, would prove to be the greater tragedy.

The sharp condemnation of the Shi Jianqiao affair by leftists also stemmed from their increasing exasperation with the growing power of the urban masses in an age of mass media. Uncomfortable with the public's irrational nature, leftist writers sought to discredit the new collective by pointedly gendering it as feminine and heaping scorn upon its affective quality. It has been well documented that, despite their political sympathies for the masses and the proletariat, leftist intellectuals in Europe and the United States have historically often expressed profound skepticism toward popular culture and have consistently been subjected to the charge of elitism. One scholar has argued that the critique of mass culture in the United States was, in effect, an attempt on the part of America's liberal intellectuals to define their status as an intellectual cadre in an emerging mass democratic society (Gorman 1996). Andreas Huyssen (1986) has also written about European intellectual anxiety about the masses in Europe's age of declining liberalism during the first half of the twentieth century. He argues that left-leaning intellectuals like Theodore Adorno were strongly ambivalent about mass culture and its role in fascism, and therefore derisively gendered that culture as feminine and inferior in order to articulate modernist aesthetics as a superior, masculine antidote.

In 1930s China, Chinese Marxists displayed similar tendencies. Believing that collective emotion posed a serious threat to the Chinese nation, these critics envisioned the new affective public as the inferior feminine "other" with regard to the superior discourses of masculine rationality. In the case of the Shi Jianqiao affair, left-leaning writers bitterly complained that the widespread public sympathy for the avenger was feudal, an obstruction to national modernization, and often associated with women. For example, columnist Meng Zhuo cited Shi Jianqiao's revenge along with several other recent sensational instances of filial piety as evidence of the insidious influence of traditional literature on the modern populace. Meng was not only disdainful of Shi's own admission that she was inspired by Shang Sanguan, but also expressed utter disbelief regarding another case in which a dutiful son had taken the saying "gegu liaoqin" (cut one's flesh to heal a loved one) literally and cut a piece of his flesh to cure his mother's pains. Meng proceeded to demand that educators and governmental authorities eradicate all old and unreasonable ways and establish a fully modern consciousness (Meng 1936).

Writing in the journal *Dazhong shenghuo* mentioned above, Liu Shi was among those who most explicitly associated public sympathy with women. Liu first noted scornfully that the filial avenger was a woman. He then grimly remarked how those flocking to line up outside the courthouse of both the district and provincial trials in the Shi affair were primarily schoolgirls and women.[22] This situation, he stated, proved how young girls were particularly susceptible to the old Confucian belief in "loving one's own flesh and blood," which threatened to entice them into the pit of ignorant filial piety. This viewpoint, he asserted, was an anomaly. "If this kind of filial vengeance is considered a virtue, it is the virtue of past times. Since it has no social significance for today, we can only deem [the case] an aberrant affair" (Liu 1935, 70) Liu Shi concluded the essay by tapping into a long-standing discourse of the relationship between female education and the moral plight of Chinese society, asserting that the case of Shi Jianqiao was a sure indication of the failure of modern female education. Liu's message was ominous indeed. It was the persistent hold of a feudal consciousness on the minds of Chinese women in the modern era that continued to keep the Chinese nation weak and impoverished.

Intellectuals in general were not only faced with an increasingly powerful public, but also an aggressively centralizing regime. Accordingly, in addition to discrediting popular sentiment, the Marxist opprobrium in this case also carried pointed antistate connotations. The harsh condemnation of Shi Jianqiao's filial piety clearly served as an implicit critique of the central regime's decision to sanction the avenging daughter. The vociferous denigration of filial piety, a classic Confucian ethic, contrasted sharply with the New Life campaign's promotion of Confucian values. In condemning the Shi Jianqiao affair for being no more than an act in the costume drama of the "return to antiquity" faction, Liu Shi's allusion to the conservative New Life agenda was, for example, barely veiled. The critical tenor of the leftist commentary on the case was made even more evident by the fact that it was primarily conducted in *Dazhong shenghuo*. This journal was known for its frequent criticism of the regime, and its editor, Zou Taofen, rarely hid his dissatisfaction with Nationalist rule.[23] In addition to being a full-fledged member of the Communist Party by the late 1930s, Zou was a key player in organizing the Shanghai National Salvation Association in December 1935, an organization whose manifesto demanding substantial action against the Japanese had enraged Jiang Jieshi.[24] For Chinese leftists, criticism of the sentiment-laden case of Shi Jianqiao was thus an effective way to express profound anxiety with both the rising urban public and the encroaching power of the central regime.

From the Rule of Sentiment to the Rule of Law

Leftists were not alone in voicing dismay. Judicial reformers as well admonished against the sentiment-centered affair. With imperialist powers demanding in exchange for relinquishing extraterritoriality the establishment of a modern Chinese judiciary, reformists were highly committed to promoting what they argued was an objective "rule of law" to improve China's national fate. Writing in trade journals and publications on law, advocates of legal reform commented on this case to express grave reservations about granting sentiment a fundamental role in justice and governance, and sought instead to promote a nonsubjective, rule-based notion of law for the modern nation. Furthermore, by questioning the authority of uneducated public sentiment, they promoted instead their own brand of professional, rational expertise.

The prioritization of the superior rule of a legal code involved a fundamental rethinking of the long-standing configuration that had posited human sentiment (*qing*) as the moral core of the general principles of the universe (*li*), which, in turn, formed the basis of the codified regulations of the body politic (*fa*). Throughout most of Chinese history, sentiment and law were, at least, in normative terms, rarely in contradiction, and when they were, sentiment was supposed to curb the excessively stringent application of legal code. Japanese historian Shiga Shuzo, for example, has written that, at least for imperial civil law, legal stipulations were, in principle, authoritative interpretations of part of the "larger ocean" of human sentiment (*renqing*) and universal reason (*tianli*).[25] Even as late as the end of the Qing dynasty, when debates on constitutional reform were taking place, this theoretical principle remained unquestioned. Late Qing debate centered primarily on the question of whether reform proposals violated the moral authority of human sentiment and did not critique the principle of sentiment itself.[26] Reformists like Shen Jiaben argued that Western ideas of human rights and equality qualified as forms of sentiment and should only thus be incorporated into Chinese law. The rival conservative faction advocating an ethical foundation for law protested, however, that such proposals were fundamentally antithetical to basic moral principles, failed to accord with basic human sentiment, and should not be implemented.

This theoretical formulation that saw sentiment giving rise to principle, which in turn defined law, persisted in nonreformist discourses into the 1930s. Take, for example, Hu Baochan, one commentator on the Shi Jianqiao affair, who reduced the controversy to the simple triad of sentiment (*qing*), moral principle (*li*), and legal code (*fa*). Hu asserted the highly unpopular view among modern legal experts that public sentiment—based on the belief that there was no closer bond than the one between parent and child—should reign supreme (Hu 1936, 6). When speaking of the legal code, he stated, one should refer to moral principle, and when referring to moral principle, one should begin with human sentiment.

Most legal observers of the case, however, were left aghast at the thought that sentiment should ever take precedence over the faithful application of the legal code. Even supporters of Shi Jianqiao recognized the potential conflict between public sentiment and China's national code. Wang Guifang, for example, acknowledged the possibility for conflict, but ultimately decided that national sentiment should dictate the fate of the filial assassin (Wang 1935, 3). He acknowledged that from the perspective of the law, Shi's behavior was no more than a personal vendetta that severely compromised the integrity of the legal system. But, reasoned Wang, from the perspective of the people, sympathy for Shi's vengeance was defensible and, in fact, a moral imperative. Shi's actions did not simply avenge her father's death, they also provided vindication for the nation, accomplishing what continued to remain elusive in official channels of justice.

Whereas supporters Hu and Wang were adamant about the need to privilege sentiment above what they saw as an ineffectual legal system, critics were just as absolute in their conviction that the two were irreconcilably in conflict and that the legal code had to supersede emotion at all times. In his comments on the decision to pardon Shi Jianqiao, published in the *Falü pinglun* (Law review), Da Quan reversed Wang's argument. He stated in bold and simple terms, "While there is human sympathy, [the] legal code is another matter" (Da 1936, 1). Whereas the pardon for Shi Jianqiao was defensible from the perspective of sentiment, he elaborated, it was highly inappropriate according to the principles of jurisprudence. He concluded that the failure to uphold the law would result in the ideology of revenge (*fuchou zhuyi*), a characteristic specific to the Middle Ages or half-civilized societies.

In the law-oriented commentary on the case, sentiment also assumed the unprecedented judicial meaning of "public sympathy" that was specifically contrasted to the specialized domain of professional, modern jurisprudence. The term *sentiment* in imperial discourses of jurisprudence had as one of its several meanings the notion of common human sentiment or even the common sense of the people. Yet the 1930s' notion of public sympathy diverged from this imperial connotation of *qing* in a few significant ways. To begin with, public sympathy arguably referred to a community that was far larger in scope, given the growing reach of the mass media that mediated its constitution. Second, "public sympathy" was frequently juxtaposed to the rational knowledge of specialists and professionals. This second characteristic was particularly important in prompting the attack on public sympathy in the Shi case by advocates of legal reform.

What was at stake for judicial reformers was no less than their autonomy and professional *raison d'être*. In imperial China, law fell under the purview of the central government and never functioned as a separate or autonomous institutional structure. By the early twentieth century, however, urban China had witnessed an increasing professionalization of the legal world. The positions of judges and lawyers had become modern occupations, defined institutionally through standardized training, professional associations, and trade journals.[27] An autonomous judicial sphere was slowly being carved out. Yet, while the Nanjing decade was purportedly characterized by judicial reform, legal reformers were wary of the Nationalist regime's expansion of its power over the legal system. Recent scholarship suggests that this state encroachment indeed took place. Xu Xiaoqun (1997) has argued that the Nationalist state quickly peeled back the layers of judicial independence that were only barely established in the preceding few decades. The government did so by appointing party members to key posts in the judicial system and requiring exams for lawyers to include party doctrine throughout the Nanjing decade. It even established the Emergency Law, through which it granted itself the right to "try" a person it felt was a threat to the nation directly without going through normal judicial procedures.[28] The regime's right to pardon served as yet another mechanism whereby the Nationalist regime could directly interfere with the authority of the courts.

Given their desire to retain some judicial autonomy, we can see how writers on judicial matters became interested in this case. In an earlier case of a revenge killing by Zheng Jicheng, the Nanjing-based government had already identified sympathetic appeals from public organizations as the moral and political basis of its decision to grant the assassin a state pardon. Writers commenting on the Shi trial were concerned that the state would once again use public sympathy to justify an official decision to overrule any court decision. Not surprisingly, legal professionals immediately turned the affair into a platform from which to issue a counterattack and argued that a pardon based on public sympathy for Shi Jianqiao undermined the integrity of the modern judicial system. In an article written for the *Duli pinglun* (Independent review), a liberal reformist weekly founded by Hu Shi, author Zhu Wenchang, for example, argued that modern nationalism hinged upon the establishment of a judicial system within which a more universal, transcendental notion of law was paramount.[29] The application of modern law, Zhu went on, should not make exceptions for either the age-old concept of moral human sentiment or the newer phenomenon of public sympathy. Commenting on both the Shi Jianqiao case and the Zheng Jicheng case, Zhu described China's legal system, with its tolerance for vigilante acts of revenge, as dangerously weak. Yes, he acknowledged, human sentiment had long played an important role in Chinese culture. Yes, China had long promoted ruling the country through filial relations. And yes, wrote the observer, the philosophy of seeking revenge continued to live on in the repeated telling in radio plays, fiction, and songs of the heroic revenge of fictional characters like Lin Chong and Wu Song.[30] Yet, in the end, Zhu exhorted, justice must not be based on public sympathy for the classic human sentiment of filial piety; such an idea was foolhardy and had already helped exacerbate the situation in North China.

Whereas some insisted that any extra-legal treatment based on sentiment would compromise a strong judicial system, others were less strident and made concerted efforts to portray law and sentiment as not necessarily mutually exclusive. Writing on the Zheng Jicheng case in *Falü pinglun*, commentator Hu Changqing recognized that the people's sympathy might conflict with the national code (Hu 1932, 3). This contradiction, he noted, was not only apparent in the Zheng affair, but also lay at the center of several other sensational cases. One case concerned a patriot named Yun Huifang, a member of the Shanghai-based boycott group known as With Blood and Spirit, Fight National Traitors, some of whose members, out of righteous anger (*yifen*), had hurled a bomb at a store that sold contraband Japanese goods and had gained the sympathy of the population at large.[31] Another example concerned Nanjing's Japanese Resistance Association, which had evoked a great deal of support when it imposed the death penalty on one of its own, a certain Chen Jiashu, who had accepted bribes from the Japanese. By citing as his examples acts of patriotism with which everyone could sympathize, Hu gave public sentiment a great deal of emotional validity. Yet, while striking this more conciliatory tone, Hu was still convinced that, in the end, the legal code should remain superior. By acknowledging that judicial procedure should occasionally recognize public emotion, Hu was seeking to expand the scope and capacity of the rule of *fa*.[32]

Like that of the leftists, the stinging assessment by advocates of law stemmed first from a modern disdain of *qing*. Whereas the scientism of Marxism condemned the populist faith in classic forms of human sentiment as feudal, proponents of legal reform found sentiment problematic because, in their eyes, it represented the "traditional" legal system that subordinated the rule of *fa* to orthodox sentiment. As a special-interest group faced with a serious threat to their professional autonomy, they viewed sentiment in the sense of public sympathy as problematic. To counter this threat, these writers asserted that China's national success required the establishment of a nonsubjective, transcendental notion of law, which only they, as judicial specialists, were qualified to accomplish. Finally, just as leftist commentary on the Shi case chastised the agenda of the central regime, so too did commentary by promoters of legal reform, for whom executive interference with the judicial system was a real threat. Thus, while these two groups differed in their specific agendas, their respective evaluations of Shi Jianqiao were very similar. Both sets of commentary contributed to the complete reversal of the long-standing Confucian view in which social and political truth stemmed from classically sanctioned moral sentiment. Now, more than any eternal Confucian virtue, modern notions of society and a rational legal code stood at the center of imagining the larger polity.

In reviewing the leftist and reformist responses to the Shi Jianqiao case, a picture of active debate and critical public dialogue emerges that contrasts sharply with the conventional image of the 1930s as a barren period lacking critical activity compared to the May Fourth period and the late Qing. Although hardly covering the critical intellectual terrain of the decade in any comprehensive manner, this review has demonstrated how commentators of divergent political affiliations and interests were drawn together by a common preoccupation with sentiment. While this sensational crime of female passion appears at first glance to be an unlikely object of critical concern, during a period of censorship intellectual commentators found it ideal in its capacity to provide them with a discreet opportunity to articulate critical views and alternative solutions to the nation's problems. Thus, discrete groups of critically minded professionals and political pundits were avidly contributing to the growing urban press of the day, making their concerns and opinions on Shi Jianqiao and other related matters heard. Even while they did not all agree on the exact significance of sentiment, nor on what the moral core of the new nation should be, this group successfully differentiated its views (particularly through barbed attacks on the validity of public sympathy) from those of the centralizing state as well as those of the increasingly powerful new public. The final irony of all this was that while these critics decried both the feminine emotionalism and the collective sympathies of the media-consuming public, their own opinions were delivered with the utmost moral conviction and ardent passion.

THE WOMEN'S PRESS AND SYMPATHY FOR HEROIC FEMALE VIRTUE

It is worthwhile to point out that not all of the editorial commentary on the affair was entirely negative. Commentary published in the women's press tended to be more sympathetic.[33] These writings also tended to pay comparatively more attention to the significance of Shi Jianqiao's gender, which was only derisively mentioned by the critics discussed earlier. While this "ghettoization" of concern for Shi Jianqiao's gender may in part have been due to the specialization of journal publishing in the 1930s, it also indicated how discourses of modernity were being gendered. For leftists and advocates of legal reform, Shi Jianqiao's crime of female passion was the counterpoint to their implicitly masculine discourses of modernity. In contrast, a small coterie of writers in the women's press proved vocal, if measured, in its praise and focused intently on her gender. Specifically, these minority pundits identified Shi as a symbol of their feminist agenda, which promoted women's rights as the basis of China's modernity and national strength. Yet even though these supporters diverged from other critics in their explicit focus on gender, they nonetheless shared in the general highbrow aversion to excessive sentiment by taking extra care to endorse the assassin not as a passionate New Woman, but as a starkly desexualized, virtuous, female hero of the nation.

This advocacy of explicitly straight-laced, female virtue was part of a larger backlash against discourses of modernity that focused on sentiment, passions, and overt sexuality. By the 1930s, feminist writers were seeking to distinguish themselves from earlier May Fourth thinkers and contemporaneous commercial discourses on new womanhood. The May

Fourth agenda of identifying the sexually liberated, romantically free New Woman as a harbinger of modernity had failed, and notions of unbridled female sexuality and desire associated with May Fourth cosmopolitanism increasingly smacked of bourgeois liberalism and selfish individualism. At the same time, witnessing the rise of a morally ambiguous, hypersexualized, and highly commodified image of the New Woman in consumer culture, reformist intellectuals of the Nanjing decade were increasingly dismayed by their loss of control over the interpretation of the powerful trope (Edwards 2000). In this context supporters of Shi Jianqiao in the women's press shied away from touching upon her sexuality and focused on her heroic motive of virtue instead.

China's women's press started in the late Qing and was borne of patriotism and reform. While individual publications often had short runs and faced tremendous challenges in finance, distribution, and censorship, the women's press overall proved highly influential in China's early twentieth-century print culture. The earlier publications of the late Qing addressed such issues as the education of girls, the abolition of foot-binding, and equality for men and women. In the Republican era, the women's press continued to link women's issues with concerns of national salvation as well as more concrete social and political topics of the day. Like the women's press in Japan and the West around the same time, these journals were not solely edited or consumed by women, but had a mixed-gender readership and editorship.[34] In terms of class and region, the journals were generally restricted to a more educated readership and urban environments. By the 1930s, with increasing censorship and publishing restrictions, several major titles of the women's press folded. Nonetheless, the remaining publications, including *Funü yuebao* (Woman's monthly), *Funü shenghuo* (Women's lifestyle), and *Funü gongming* (Women's voices), all of which published commentary on Shi Jianqiao and are cited here, continued to express an explicit concern with the relationship between women's issues and larger political questions, and were written and read by both women and men.

Some of the commentary in the women's press on the Shi Jianqiao case coincided with the general political attempt to marshal classic virtues for national purposes. Echoing the New Life movement's emphasis on Confucian moral propriety, conservative moralists concerned with defining womanhood promoted ideals of chaste femininity, upright womanly behavior, and pure and classic female virtue as the basis of the collective salvation of national China (Diamond 1975). Female commentator Xiao Yu did so in her writings on Shi Jianqiao. Paying attention to Shi's scrupulous moral record and her decidedly wholesome filial piety, Xiao argued that Shi deserved to be lionized as a woman of distinguished and virtuous valor: "During a period when morality is worsening daily, human lust runs amuck, and ethics are dying, Shi, a mere frail woman, is still able to give up her husband and children to fulfill her filial duty. Is she not a moral exemplar?" (Xiao 1936).[35] For Xiao, Shi was heroic not because of any embodiment of iconoclastic ideals of sexual liberation but because of her pure, classic virtues and her brave embodiment of sacrifice.

The moral conservatism evident in some of these female writers did not mean that they rejected the feminist agenda. On the contrary, Xiao Yu took care to note how Shi Jianqiao was a model of gender equality. To this end, Xiao drew an effective and sharp contrast between Shi's frailty as a woman and the heroics of ethical sacrifice. Commonly used in other sympathetic accounts to describe Shi Jianqiao, the term *frail woman* (*ruonüzi*) contrasts sharply with the image of the strong New Woman of the May Fourth period, which was itself defined vis-à-vis "traditional" female frailty. The New Woman had been the woman who could liberate herself and, by extension, all of China from the literal binding of the feet and the figurative enslavement by Confucian patriarchal norms that had for so long kept Chinese women and the nation weak. Yet, in laudatory accounts of Shi Jianqiao, her physical frailty was purposefully highlighted. Such an emphasis on her weak physical state functioned as an illuminating contrast with her strong, nonphysical virtue. Not surprisingly, Xiao contended that Shi's upright character was so exemplary that she was extraordinary not merely among women, but also among men. Triumphantly, Xiao concluded that Shi's virtue proved how nonsensical was the long-standing tradition of celebrating the birth of a boy with jade and the birth of a girl with mere tile (Xiao 1936).[36]

In contrast to moral conservatives like Xiao Yu, several supporters of the avenging daughter in the women's press took care not to celebrate her classic filial piety, yet still sought to appreciate Shi as a feminist hero. These writers were aligned with more conservative types in that they expressed their appreciation of Shi's womanhood in decidedly desexualized terms. *Funü yuebao* (Women's monthly) writer Li Ying, for example, used glowing terms to describe Shi's embodiment of both feminist and national heroism. Li hailed the assassin as "a personage whom our women's world should admire" and glorified her as a "brave and extraordinary woman, truly rare and remarkable." The essayist declared her "the pioneering leader of a woman's world" and contended that "Shi's survival would ensure glory to the nation!" (Li 1935, 3).[37] The only passion that was apparent at all was sublimated into national heroism. The distrust of sexual passions and emotions so prominent in the leftist and reformist writings on Shi Jianqiao thus also characterized much of the commentary published in the women's press. Sympathizers also made sure to avoid appreciating Shi Jianqiao's chaste sentiment in any way that was reminiscent of sexualized celebrations of the New Woman, focusing instead on discourses of chaste female virtue, pure heroism, and national collectivism.

CONCLUSION: HIGHBROW ANXIETY, NEW WOMEN, AND THE MEDIA AGE

The Shi Jianqiao case clearly generated a substantial amount of critical commentary, but it was not the only female crime of passion in the 1930s to do so. The contemporaneous affair of Liu Jinggui provides an illuminating point of comparison. Like Shi Jianqiao, Liu Jinggui became a high-profile woman by committing an act of extraordinary passion that generated media frenzy and whipped up tremendous public sympathy. In both cases, the presence of sentiment—both of the individual women and of the mass public—greatly alarmed social critics whose visions of modernity were based on sentiment's antithesis, namely, a rationally defined society and public order. By considering the two cases together, we can better see how writers and critics systematically used commentary on crimes featuring passionate women to serve their larger agenda of promoting rationality in the post–May Fourth period. Such highbrow dismay over public sympathy was symptomatic of the critics' larger unease over their decreasing influence on the moral direction of society in an era when the power of China's mass media was rapidly expanding.

On March 16, 1935, Liu Jinggui, a twenty-four *sui* female student at North China's Fine Arts Academy,[38] entered the faculty dormitory of Beiping's Zhicheng All-Girls Middle School where Teng Shuang, her rival in love (*qingdi*), resided. Fooling the dormitory guard into believing that she was a student's mother, Liu entered the dorm, found Teng, pulled out a Browning pistol, and pumped seven bullets into Teng's body. Teng died immediately, at the age of twenty-nine *sui*. Liu fled the school grounds and ran into the back alleys of the surrounding neighborhood. The school guard, who had heard the gunshots and saw her flee, ran after her and apprehended Liu in the Fengsheng alley. She was then brought into custody. Liu's trial began on April 23, 1935, and went

Figure 8. Photo of assassin Liu Jinggui after being captured (*Xin Tianjin huabao*, 24 March 1935).

through several appeals before the final verdict of life imprisonment was issued on May 5, 1937.

Liu Jinggui killed Teng Shuang out of jealous rage. Both women had been involved with the same man, Lu Ming, a medal-winning athlete of thirty-four *sui*. Liu Jinggui and Lu Ming were from the same town in Xuanhua county in Hebei province, and on April 11, 1933, they were engaged to be married. However, a few months later Lu Ming met Teng Shuang at an athletics conference and fell in love with her. Lu married Teng on November 1, 1933, and the two of them offered Liu six hundred *yuan* in compensation for dissolving her betrothal to Lu. On February 11, 1934, Liu Jinggui agreed to accept the money and dissolve her engagement to Lu. But in March Liu and Lu started an exchange of letters, which resulted in a five-day romantic tryst in a hotel on the outskirts of Beiping. As she later testified in court, Liu realized then that Teng Shuang was her rival in love (*qingdi*) and vowed to kill her.

There were many differences in the two cases. The Shi Jianqiao affair featured a classical female hero who acted out of filial passion. The Liu Jinggui case featured modern personalities (*xin renwu*), including Liu Jinggui, the female student; Lu Ming, the male athletic star; and Teng

Shuang, the female athlete. Yet there were many similarities. Both cases generated tremendous public interest and controversy. Moreover, much of controversy turned on the significance of *qing*. Filial passion gripped the public interest in the Shi case, and love was at the heart of the storm surrounding Liu's. The press regularly referred to the Liu Jinggui case as a crime of passion (*taose qingsha'an*), and its love triangle (*sanjiaolian*) generated special attention. As in Shi Jianqiao's case, *qing* generated anxiety in much of the highbrow commentary on the Liu case. Critics commented both on *aiqing*, or love, the central motive behind the crime of passion, and *tongqing*, collective sympathy for the murderess. Questions about whether love was an appropriate emotion for young Chinese men and women in what many were calling an "age of excess" (*guodu shidai*) were raised. These questions were linked to larger anxieties about new concepts of marriage, modern women's access to divorce, and the moral direction of urban society in general.[39] Rational behavior (*lixing* or *lizhi*) was regularly promoted as a force of moderation that could counter such excessive emotionality (*qing*).

Public sympathy (*tongqing*) also drew criticism. It was with respect to collective sentiment that one author explicitly compared Liu Jinggui's revenge with both the Shi Jianqiao affair and Zheng Jicheng's assassination of Zhang Zongchang. The writer commented disparagingly, "Our society has always sympathized with these avengers, thought their actions to be entertaining (*renao*), and applauded them for no reason, crying 'bravo!' Indeed, every time a criminal acts with determination, people in the street have strained their necks shouting 'good!'" The author then argued that from both legal and rational perspectives, neither the revenge killings nor the sympathy they elicited should be tolerated (Da 1935). In the *Yishibao*, a major Tianjin paper, another contributor lamented that "the hearts of the masses are blind." The writer expressed dismay at the fact that, whereas Liu Jinggui had unexpectedly elicited a great deal of sympathy for her act of revenge, Lu Ming's first wife, whom he had shamelessly divorced and cast away, was utterly forgotten by society (Yi Mu 1935).

The critical commentary on public sympathy in the Liu case perhaps demonstrates even more explicitly than the commentary in the Shi case how elite ambivalence toward public sympathy was intricately bound to anxiety about the growing power of mass media and authoritarian politics. In "Comments on the Homicide Case of Liu Jinggui," a piece published in the reformist journal *Duli pinglun*, Yu Dacai advised feminist groups in particular not to indiscriminately express public sympathy in the Liu affair and argued that the defense of a woman like Liu would result in antipathy for the entire women's movement and might even put the future of China's women's movement at risk (Yu 1935). Citing Hitler's Germany as an example of a fascist regime appropriating the woman's movement for dubious purposes, Yu conveyed the message that if China's feminist movement failed to make moral distinctions among women and arbitrarily supported any woman simply because of her gender, it too would be susceptible to the manipulation of militaristic regimes. While the Nationalist regime was not mentioned explicitly, Yu warned against authoritarianism implicitly, "If the women's community were to use *qing* to support this kind of murderer . . . and seek protection behind the slogans of feminism, could this [sort of behavior] ever hope to win society's approval? . . . If we do something foolish and [do] not focus on being a human, do we not give future reactionaries material? Do we not give future Hitlers some reason to limit women's rights?" The specter of fascism in China was raised.

Commentary on Liu's case emphasized that, as products of the new media, New Women were seen by critics to be especially prone to be deluded by mass emotions. One contributor to the Beiping *Chenbao* wrote an article entitled "The Analysis of Two Acts of Tragedy" in which the Shanghai-based Ruan Lingyu suicide case and the Beiping-based Liu Jinggui homicide case were discussed together. At the heart of the article was a warning against the dangers of excessive *qing* embodied by New Women. Jun Ji, the author, commented on the Liu Jinggui case, stating that Lu Ming's crime was capriciousness in love; Teng Shuang's, blind devotion to the wrong man; and Liu Jinggui's, imprudent anger and the squandering of courage that resulted in the wrongful death of Teng. Jun then warned that such erroneous use of emotions had implications for the fate of society and asserted that of the three, the most tragic was Liu Jinggui's mistaken anger. Liu could have directed her energy into building the nation, but instead had sadly channeled her sentiment into private *qing* and enmity. The author concluded, "This [case] is an example of emotions misguiding a person and causing . . . [her] to erroneously follow a deviant path" (Jun 1935, 11).

Jun Ji then proceeds to use the Ruan Lingyu case to connect excessive *qing* with the dangers of media-saturated, urban modernity. Ruan Lingyu was a glamorous Shanghai movie star who tragically committed suicide in 1935. Having starred in the 1934 film *The New Woman* (Xin nüxing), she was arguably one of the quintessential New Women of the Republican era.[40] As such, Ruan's life and death garnered tremendous media attention. Her rise to fame as an actress depended upon the new film industry, which was also seen as the cause of her tragic fall and suicide. As several scholars have noted, Ruan's death was widely attributed to the media-created pressures of stardom (e.g., Chang 1999). Observers of the day also felt that Ruan Lingyu had literally been hounded to death. The intrusion of the public into her personal affairs had been so great and the power of the press in her case so pernicious that it prompted the famous writer Lu Xun to write an essay on the affair entitled "Gossip Is Fearful" (Zhao Lingyi [Lu Xun] 1935). Writing about her death, Jun Ji contended that both her individual *qing* and the collective *qing* of her fans were direct products of the age of mass media and crucial reasons for her death. Jun argued that Ruan's susceptibility to the desire for fame, a direct product of her being a media star, caused her to be deeply affected by public speculation about her remarriage to Tang Jishan. Echoing Lu Xun, Jun declared that collective gossip and public disgrace had ultimately killed Ruan Lingyu.

Linking the Shi Jianqiao affair and the Ruan Lingyu case, commentary on the Liu Jinggui case crystallizes some of the profound ambivalences felt among highbrow critics toward sentiment, New Women, and the power of the new media. In a decade when new anxieties were arising about overly public women, the pernicious influence of new forms of mass communication, and the lack of moral sincerity in urban society, Ruan Lingyu, Liu Jinggui, and Shi Jianqiao all drew considerable attention. For many critics, these high-profile women embodied excessive *qing* in their individual actions (e.g., murderous *qing* on Liu's part, vainglory on Ruan's part, and feudal filiality on Shi's) and, moreover, elicited wild collective emotionalism, a highly problematic force in a new age of mass communications. Yet, regardless of the anger expressed on editorial pages, cultural critics fought an uphill battle. Public sympathy that was aroused so effectively in these cases of New Women became a considerable judicial and political force. As I show in the following two chapters, neither judicial actors nor the executive branch found that they could ignore public sentiment in the Shi Jianqiao case.

FOUR

The Trial

Courtroom Spectacle and Ethical Sentiment in the Rule of Law

When one's father has not undergone [a proper or just] execution, the son may take revenge on his behalf. But if the father has been [legitimately] executed, and the son then takes revenge [anyway], this is the way of [the] thrusting sword, which cannot remove the danger.

He Xiu (129–182), Gongyang Commentary *to the* Spring and Autumn Annals

The accused has been in great pain regarding the tragic circumstances of her father's death . . . [By seeking revenge], she was clearly fulfilling the wishes of her deceased father and sacrificing herself; she accomplished this exemplary behavior with a purely filial heart. Thus, if we examine the circumstances, they are indeed worthy of sympathy.

Supreme Court Verdict # 1207, August 25, 1936

The trial of Shi Jianqiao turned out to be a highly complex legal affair. The court case began on November 21, 1935, only eight days after the assassination, with the local prosecutor filing an official charge against female defendant Shi Jianqiao in the Tianjin District Court. The document presents the facts of the assassination in a fairly straightforward manner: ten years earlier, Sun Chuanfang captured and killed the defendant's father, Shi Congbin. The defendant had harbored a desire for revenge ever since. Not long before the killing, she bought a Browning handgun and six bullets from an unknown retired soldier, and secretly carried the gun and bullets to Tianjin, where she waited for a chance to act. Her time came when she discovered Sun Chuanfang's whereabouts at the Tianjin Lay-Buddhist Society. She promptly made arrangements to attend services at the monastery while Sun Chuanfang was there and killed him. After the murder, she proclaimed success in avenging the death of her father and asked the society's janitor Liu Shuxiu to call the police. When patrolmen Wang Hua'nan and, later, Qu Hongtao arrived after hearing shots, the defendant calmly handed over her Browning and the remaining three bullets, and surrendered herself to the authorities. The text then assures the reader that the investigation of the assassination was carried out according to the letter of the law and includes a forensic report for further verification of the thoroughness of the investigatory procedure.[1]

Citing Article 187 of the 1935 Revised Criminal Code, the complaint charges Shi with "possessing a gun with intent to use," a crime that mandated a punishment of imprisonment for not more than five years. It also charges Shi with the crime of homicide. The document cites Article 271 to state that most crimes of homicide are punished with "death or imprisonment for life or for not less than ten years." In conclusion, it recommends imprisonment for life or not less than ten years, citing Article 55, which reads, "Where one and the same act constitutes several offences, or where the means employed in committing one offence or the results of the commission of such offence constitute another offence, only the heaviest of the prescribed punishments shall be inflicted."[2]

The actual court proceedings began on November 25, 1935. Tu Zhang, the prosecuting officer of Tianjin's District Court presented orally what appeared to be an open-shut case. The accused had killed Sun Chuanfang with a gun in front of a crowd of worshippers and immediately confessed to the crime. Witnesses Fu Ming and Dong Hai, two monks of the lay-Buddhist society, and Wang Hua'nan, the first patrolman to appear at the crime scene, all corroborated that it was indeed Shi Jianqiao who had committed the murder. The written material distributed by the assassin after the killing, the Browning pistol used in the crime, and the remaining bullets were presented as irrefutable evidence of Shi Jianqiao's guilt.[3] Yet, despite the array of evidence, the trial proved far more complicated than most anticipated. Appealed all the way to the Supreme Court in Nanjing, the case included a dramatic reversal of the lower court decision, and eventually resulted in a decision of remarkable leniency.

The complex nature of the case became evident right after the Tianjin District Court announced its sentence of ten years for the defendant. On December 17, 1935, justices Kong Jiazhang and Ye Dejing, and court prosecutor Wen Renhao issued the verdict for Complaint #622 and ruled for limited leniency on the grounds of her voluntary surrender. While expressing personal sympathy for her filial ardor, they decided to bracket any moral compassion and deny the admissibility of the defense's argument that the circumstances of Shi Jianqiao's filial vengeance deserved judicial mercy. Both the prosecutor and Shi's legal team immediately appealed the lower court's decision. The defendant's representatives objected to the court's decision to deny that the filial motive constituted a mitigating circumstance. The prosecution objected to the decision to grant any leniency at all.[4] The case was retried in the Hebei Superior Court in Beiping. Convened on February 6, 1936, and presided over by Mao Yaode and an accompanying judge, Jing Xingzhen, this second trial lasted six days, and on February 12 the higher court annulled the lower court's decision, basically turning the District Court's ruling on its head.[5] The higher court ruled that the lower court was wrong both in acknowledging that the defendant had in fact established a clear intent to surrender and in failing to recognize that the female defendant's revenge was righteous and deserving of judicial compassion. Since the code stipulates a less severe sentence for crimes committed under mitigating circumstances than for those in which the criminal voluntarily surrenders, the end result was that Shi's sentence was reduced from ten to seven years. Both sides appealed again, and the case was delivered to the Supreme Court in Nanjing.[6] On August 25, 1936, the Supreme Court upheld as final the Superior Court's light sentence of seven years and the decision that her righteous vengeance constituted "mitigating circumstances deserving of judicial compassion" (*qing ke minshu*).

While the twists and turns of this complex courtroom drama are themselves complex and fascinating, this legal case came to represent much more than the pursuit of justice in an individual instance. The very notion of modern law itself was at stake. Showcasing both the individual ardor of the perpetrator as well as the collective sympathy of the urban audience, the case effectively forced the larger question of when executors of modern law should show judicial compassion and grant legal exemption. The principle actors in this case, including defendant Shi Jianqiao, her defense lawyers, prosecutors, and the judges presiding over the trial, were all forced to consider the authority of sentiment (*qing*) and ritual propriety (*li*) in their strategies for these proceedings in particular and for their determination of modern justice (*fa*) in general. In a period of legal reform, should judicial exemption ever be granted for a ritually prescribed motive of filial passion? Should the collective emotions of an ever-observant urban audience—in other words, public sympathy (*tongqing*)—be treated as a mitigating factor that might bear upon the outcome of the trial?

The trial fostered a spirited public discussion of the moral authority of *qing*, the relationship between public sympathy and the "rule of law," and the national significance of filial piety. With the intent to stir public passions, the defense team evoked the rule of ritual propriety, or *li*, to make the argument that judicial exception should be made for the moral authority of Shi's filial sentiment. In contrast, the prosecution and representatives of the Sun family opposed any recognition of the authority of either Shi's filial piety or public sympathy and pressed for an uncompromising rule by law instead. In the end, the courts struck a compromise of sorts. While granting leniency and implicitly acknowledging the power of public sympathy, the judges of the trial grounded Shi Jianqiao's righteous motive of passion in what they claimed was a moral right to due process and thereby turned the sensational event into an opportunity to reassert the foundational power of law.

TWENTIETH-CENTURY LAW: SENTIMENT, RITES, AND REFORM

The interrelationship among legal code (*fa*), the rule of ritual propriety, or rites (*li*), and the moral authority of human feeling (*qing*) has a long and complex history in China. In classical Confucian formulations of legal and, by extension, cosmological order, imperial law was grounded philosophically in two traditions of social control, namely, the Confucian rule of *li*, or moral suasion by rites, and the Legalist rule of *fa*, or coercion by law. Both rites and law were seen as articulations of universal or heavenly principles (*tianli*) and deemed necessary instruments of control. But imperial Confucian orthodoxy ultimately accorded to ritual—especially in its ability to accommodate and govern proper human sentiment, or *qing*—a more fundamental, if ambivalent, level of moral truth than either of the other two. Law was treated as a more limited set of incomplete and rigid rules that could never encompass the innumerable human and moral situations that could possibly arise. The rule of rites could thus function to curb overly stringent application of the law.[7]

While Confucian orthodoxy tended to identify sentiment and ritual propriety as more fundamental sources of truth that could help moderate the harsh application of law, the potential for tension rather than symbiosis among sentiment, rites, and legal code was often apparent in the practice of law. Such a potential was particularly evident in cases of righteous revenge and had been recognized as a problem since the period of antiquity (Dalby 1981; Lewis 1990; Cheng 2004). On the one hand, the rule of sentiment, rites, and morality recognized that concrete feelings of filial anger and loss could serve as a moral imperative for vengeance. On the other hand, the desire to sanction the moral authority of filial sentiment in acts of revenge contradicted and potentially undermined the law's obligation to punish all acts of homicide no matter how righteous. While the legal code did eventually recognize the legal right to revenge, beginning in the Yuan, the imperial state could never completely reconcile upholding the law with recognizing the tradition of revenge.[8] This discomfort increased over time, and, by the Qing, while the legal right to virtuous revenge was still recognized, the code took great care to define in strict terms the more narrowed and constrained conditions under which vengeance was morally and legally permissible.[9]

Although discomfort with the right to seek revenge grew steadily over the imperial period, the twentieth century saw the tension between the rule of law and the rule of rites and sentiment heighten to an unprecedented degree. Motivated by an acute sense of "traditional" China's failure in law, reformists of the late Qing and early Republican periods started to subject imperial law to harsh scrutiny and literal revision. The 1898 reform movement launched a devastating attack on ritual and scriptural Confucianism in general. Starting around the turn of the century, reform-minded jurists accorded considerable moral and political power to the rule of law while discrediting the previously authoritative role of ritual and moral teaching (*lijiao*) in jurisprudence.[10] An imperial commission led by Shen Jiaben took the lead in purging China's criminal code of any moral teachings (Meijer 1967, 79).[11] The rule of rites had come to be seen as an extra-judicial strand that needed to be expunged. By the 1911 Revolution, the rule of rites was, at least nominally, dethroned.[12]

If *li* and *fa* were rendered mutually exclusive in the late Qing, the New Culture period saw the rule of law dichotomously opposed to the rule of sentiment. Iconoclastic thinkers like leftist Chen Duxiu were among the first to move away from the issue of *li* and focus instead on emotion, or *qing*, as the definitional antidote to modern jurisprudence. In the formative *New Youth* article, "Differences of Basic Thought between Eastern and Western People," Chen argued that reactionary "rule of man" (*renzhi*) had been the core of the Chinese legal tradition and was exceedingly vulnerable to emotions. In contrast, the progressive "rule of law" (*fazhi*), associated with the modern West, was deemed objective, and thus above subjective interference (Chen 1915). Such iconoclastic attacks categorized all traditional Chinese law as being subject to the whim of human emotion and obliterated any memory of the complexity of the relationship between sentiment and law that had characterized much of the imperial period.

Despite growing reformist antipathy toward the role of emotions and rites in law, the exact relationship among sentiment, rites, and law nonetheless continued to riddle public discussions of modern judicial reform in the High Republic. Shi Jianqiao's trial was often at the center of such discussions, especially because the motive of filial piety, which fused emotionality with morality, was a lightening rod for debate. Specifically, the Shi trial forced jurists to address the question of whether the defendant's actions should be evaluated in terms of ritual propriety or law. In a New Life era when Confucian ethics were being promoted as the basis of national rejuvenation, this case raised the question of whether *li* should be incorporated into formalistic aspects of Republican law despite late Qing and early Republic jurists' attempts to expunge it. Could modern law tolerate ethical revenge as a ritual act, or did such an act constitute vigilantism and fall into the realm of extra-legal behavior?[13]

What was also at stake in the trial was the place of human sentiment in modern jurisprudence. In imperial jurisprudence, *qing* referred to several things.[14] In one sense, *qing* had the meaning of "truth," and the compound *qingli* meant the "circumstances or facts of the case at hand."[15] In another sense, *qing* pointed to the sentiment of various juridical actors and was potentially perceived to be in tension with the authority of the code. It could refer to the sentiment (*renqing*) behind the perpetrator's actions or motive and, as such, was evaluated in a manner that, if expressed in accordance with the rule of rites (*li*), could serve as the basis of judicial leniency. The judicial concept also denoted the collective feelings and expectations of ordinary people, which could be identified as morally authoritative and as something the application of law should not necessarily contradict. A third connotation was the judge's capacity for judicial compassion, and in this sense it encouraged magistrates to give sympathetic consideration to the particular circumstances of each case. In the Nanjing decade, when Shi's trial took place, at least three classic interpretations of *qing*, namely, the sentiment of the perpetrator, the feelings of ordinary people, and the judgment of the magistrate based on *renqing*, were under reconsideration. The judicial authority of a motive of filial piety was highly problematic in a post-iconoclastic era when "traditional" female virtues were far more controversial than ever before. The feelings and sympathies of the ordinary people had gained new significance in the era of mass media and growing urban publics. Finally, the imperial ideal of the moral authority of the judge's compassion as the basis of intervention came under much harsher scrutiny during a period of judicial reform when the rule of law was increasingly being promoted as absolute.

THE COURTS, THE PRESS, AND THE NEW PUBLIC

The tension between *qing* and the rule of law was not unique or specific to the Shi Jianqiao case. One commentator on the 1932–33 high-profile case of Zheng Jicheng, who, motivated by filial piety, had killed warlord Zhang Zongchang, spoke more generally of such tension and why it was heightening in the early twentieth century. In an editorial for the *Shandong Minguo ribao* (Shandong Republican daily), the writer said that the fundamental contradiction at the heart of the Zheng case was between the "theory of law" (*falü lun*), which asserted the need to abide by the letter of the law, and the "theory of emotion" (*ganqing lun*), which acknowledged the moral authority of the national sentiment expressed in the press in direct response to the affair.[16] Indeed, by the 1930s the tension between *qing* and rule of law had grown considerably given the new relationship between the public and the courts, as mediated by Republican China's thriving mass media.

Early twentieth-century urban China witnessed unprecedented developments in the relationship between the courtroom and the public as the burgeoning mass media of urban centers came to mediate a growing public interest in the drama of court proceedings.[17] A unique combination of factors converged to allow courtroom trials to become subjects of public fascination. The growing presence of an inquisitive mass media, attempts to reform the court system as a relatively autonomous institution, and a growing preference by the reading public for narratives of sentiment helped turn Republican China's courtrooms into forums for public debate on judicial matters related to the specific cases on trial and to larger social and moral issues . In turn, the relentless glare of the mass media's spotlight on the courtroom became itself a pressing issue as the question of how trials were to be tried in the media age arose.

As a self-proclaimed modernizing government, the Chinese Republican state self-consciously sought to present its legal system's institutional procedures as transparent and thus as a symbol of "modern" governance. Modeling its judicial system after that of Germany, Republican China did not establish a jury system, but had a panel of judges to decide cases.[18] Reforms also included making the courtroom seem more visible and "open" to the regular public. There is evidence that during the imperial period, interested observers could witness court proceedings. Court-case (*gong'an*) literature and storytelling, which often describe ordinary people in attendance at trials, functioned to create at least an expectation of openness in the imperial period.[19] However, what was unprecedented with the arrival of the mass media in the late nineteenth and early twentieth century was the scope of public access to the courtroom. As early as *Shenbao's* first trial coverage in the 1870s, detailed reports of the courtroom proceedings were included for consumption by a much wider audience. In the first half of the twentieth century, Supreme Court sessions remained closed, but press coverage of the legal proceedings at both the district and provincial levels was comprehensive and ensured that detailed information and verbatim transcripts could be distributed quickly to a reading public as trials unfolded. Live attendance at trials was also possible. Though some felt that the courts should restrict the number of live observers of high-profile cases, these proposals tended to stem from a concern with the potential for chaos in the courts and not from anxiety that public opinion might unduly influence court proceedings (e.g., Jian 1936).

Many groups benefited from a more transparent courtroom. Judges used the newly accessible courtroom to display their administrative abilities and moral standing in meting out justice and upholding social order. Lawyers, who were a new and increasingly powerful occupational group in urban China, could use the courts to showcase their professional *raison d'être* of pursuing justice on behalf of their clients. Yet, for the central government, absolute transparency was somewhat problematic. Indeed, while professing to be making its governing institutions less opaque, Nanjing nonetheless enacted censorship laws that restricted media coverage of particularly sensitive trials. For example, on July 12, 1935, a revised version of the press law was passed by the legislative branch of the central government stipulating that court cases could not be criticized in the press before judgment was rendered.[20]

Notably, in the Shi Jianqiao trial, press controls did not seem to hinder coverage. This lack of control may have been due in part to censors who felt that the trial was not particularly sensitive. Indeed, at the district and superior levels, Shi Jianqiao's case was very much in the public eye. On the day before the opening session of the Tianjin proceedings, more than one hundred bystanders gathered. On December 25,

1935, the actual opening day, more than two hundred showed up.[21] The courts proved well equipped to deal with the mobs of people, suggesting that the observers had been expected and the bureaucratic procedures to deal with them had already been established. The courtroom was filled in an efficient and orderly manner. The defendant was ushered in at 7:30 A.M. The observers were allowed to file in one by one starting at 8:10. Only after the public had entered did judge Wen Renhao, court recorder Liu Zaihua, and prosecutor Tu Zhang, enter. Legal representatives of both sides followed, and court was then officially called to order. The son of Sun Chuanfang did not arrive until the interrogation of witnesses had already begun.[22] Fewer onlookers were present during the opening session of the second trial on February 6, 1936. Reports on the opening session claimed that tickets for auditors had been limited to only thirty and that the crowd was smaller than the crowd at the Tianjin trial because of a big snowfall the night before. Nonetheless, security was still tight and, as the *Dagongbao* noted, the interest of observers at the court was no less intense.[23] Finally, like the articles by elite commentators, the media coverage tended to feminize the public. The Shanghai *Shibao*, for example, remarked explicitly on the amount of female observers outside the courts.[24]

Live observers, while symbolically significant, were obviously not able to generate public interest or disseminate news about trials widely. This role fell to the media. In the Shi Jianqiao case, for example, Shanghai's *Shibao*, Beiping's *Shibao*, as well as Tianjin's *Dagongbao* and *Yishibao* are only a few of the key urban papers that covered the proceedings of the legal event in detail.[25] Reporters attended the live courtroom sessions. Outside of the courtroom, they could use cameras. Inside, they wrote detailed accounts of what unfolded. Readers could learn the details of the proceedings the next day. Some papers included anecdotal accounts or columns of case-related trivia or human-interest tidbits, with titles like "Small Episodes at the Court."[26] Others included verbatim transcripts of the interrogation of various principles of the case. Such coverage not only familiarized readers with the technicalities of modern law involved, but also presented the moral issues at hand, further piquing public interest in the unfolding fate of the female assassin.

Finally, the legal trial clearly catered to a public preference for the theatrical. Just as Shi Jianqiao won public sympathy by conforming her account to the urban public's taste for the sentimental, her trial lawyers wove highly moralized arguments that carefully avoided legal technicality to present their case in terms that were compelling to the courts and to the public. Packed courtrooms on opening days and several unexpected antics, including tense emotional outbursts by various parties, heightened the overall suspense. Some of the most memorable moments came when Shi Jianqiao and Sun Jiazhen, Sun's eldest son, visibly expressed their grief. One of the Shanghai *Shibao's* headlines about the opening session of the Tianjin trial read, "Ms. Shi and Sun's son, each grieving their father's death, faced each other in the courtroom and wept bitterly."[27] An account two days later ran a similar headline: "Ms. Shi and the Son of Sun Wail in Court."[28] The article describes how, in reply to the judge's question about how her father was killed, Shi Jianqiao let out a large sob as she uttered the single word, "decapitation." These spontaneous shows of grief reportedly moved observers in the court to tears.[29] Readers of the near-verbatim press coverage of the proceedings were, no doubt, meant to weep as well.

Thus, what high-profile trials like Shi Jianqiao's suggest is that early twentieth-century courtrooms were becoming highly performative spaces. This is not to say that the performative elements in this trial precluded proper rational procedures. Nor do I mean to suggest that republican China's trials were more performative in comparison to the rational bureaucratic law of the West, which includes its own rules of performance and ritual regarding proper behavior in the courtroom, including what counts as "evidence," how documents are "authenticated," and so on. Rather, the point here is to show how the presence of the press in the courts inflected courtroom behavior in ways that encouraged participants in the proceedings to attend to an attentive public. Just as the dramatic adaptation of the courtroom trial in Shanghai theaters heightened public sympathy for Shi Jianqiao, the increasingly theatrical courtroom trial similarly helped fuel public interest.

THE DEFENSE: AN OFFICIAL STRATEGY OF SENTIMENT

The presence of a public audience shaped strategies and arguments at all levels of Shi Jianqiao's complex trial. An awareness of the media and sensitivity to the potential influence of an emotionally invested public was particularly evident in the defense team's approach to the case. Delivering gripping moral arguments and avoiding tedious interpretations of minute matters of law, Shi Jianqiao's lawyers hoped that the urban public, although unable to imagine actually committing such an extreme act as a revenge killing, would be able to experience it vicariously. They also counted on observers to sympathize with the ethical motive behind the revenge.

To be sure, the stakes were high for Shi Jianqiao. The prosecutor's case initially appeared ironclad, and her actions were potentially punishable by death. At the very least, Shi faced a long prison term unless her lawyers could establish grounds for leniency. To secure the best possible outcome, Shi Jianqiao hired Yu Qichang and Hu Xueqian, two of the most high-powered legal representatives available in North China at the time.[30] Yu Qichang, in particular, was well established and influential in judicial and academic circles. Born in 1882 in Shaoxing, Zhejiang, Yu graduated in 1911 from the law school of Japan's Imperial University. After graduation and the establishment of the Republic, Yu returned to China to serve in several high-ranking legal posts, including Chief Justice of the Supreme Court in Beijing (*Daliyuan*). In 1928, he became a professor at the law school at Beijing University and started taking on cases as a lawyer.[31]

It is not clear how Shi Jianqiao's family was able to procure trial lawyers of this caliber.[32] With a temporary residence in Tianjin's British Concession and a home in Tongcheng, Anhui, their native place, Shi's family was clearly not wanting economically, and could very well have had the necessary connections and ability to hire lawyers like Yu.[33] Or the affair may simply have been so notable that lawyers like Yu were eager to sign on. The trial was an opportunity that would not only help build their own reputation, but also help to legitimate the new occupational status of lawyers in general. As Shi revealed in an interview, she had received several letters from lawyers offering their services. Some of her late father's friends wrote letters stating that they were highly affronted by the injustice of Shi Congbin's murder and would represent her for free in order to "stand by an old friend and help in the pursuit of righteous justice."[34]

Whether they took on the case out of principle, for the money, or for the guaranteed publicity, Hu Xueqian and Yu Qichang were a formidable team. In fact, their professional stature and influence was apparently an issue. One retrospective account of the case noted how many of the judges and officials had been the students of Shi Jianqiao's head lawyer and thus susceptible to his influence. The author, who was a journalist at the time, described Yu's presence in court as follows: "When he was in court, his arrogance was great, and he put pressure on all officials. If he found out that court proceedings were not favorable, he would immediately stand up and appeal to the judge . . . in a tone of instruction; judges could not but heed him" (Lin 1980).[35] Shi's lawyers were not the only ones able to wield influence. Sun's family also had resources both in Tianjin and Shanghai, and hired highly reputable lawyers.[36] One of their attorneys was Zhang Shaozeng, a prominent Tianjin lawyer who was on the editorial board of the *Journal of the Tianjin Attorneys' Association*.[37] Zhang's reputation was powerful enough to elicit charges from the Shi camp that he was buying and influencing the trial at the start of the Hebei proceedings.[38]

Even if personal connections shaped the trial proceedings, they could not by themselves have determined the outcome in a case that involved such intense public scrutiny. The formidable influence of Shi's defense lawyers stemmed less from their existing power and status and more, I argue, from their ability to put forth an effective legal argument and command public sympathy. Specifically, the defense team devised a highly compelling legal strategy that was grounded in the Republican Code, the rule of rites, and in the moral authority of communal sympathy (*tongqing*) for the defendant. The defense consisted of two parts. The first part sought to establish that the assassin had voluntarily and immediately surrendered. This fact alone, Shi's lawyers argued, mandated a lighter sentence. The second part aimed to persuade the court that mitigating circumstances were involved. The defense contended that the ethical and political relevance of Shi Jianqiao's filial piety—that is, the motive for her revenge, which stemmed directly from the unethical and unlawful treatment of her father—constituted a mitigating circumstance and deserved judicial sympathy. To this end, the defense emphasized the moral authority of Shi's motive by appealing to the paramount role of rites, once deemed dead by legal reformists in the final decade of the nineteenth century and the first quarter of the twentieth century. Shi Jianqiao's devotion to her father was furthermore portrayed as an emotion with which everyone could sympathize.

The defense's argument that Shi Jianqiao's voluntary surrender deserved judicial leniency proved highly persuasive at the initial district court level, but it did not work with the higher courts. Nonetheless, it is worth considering here, as it illuminates the defense's overall strategy of using classical sanction to buttress its legal argument as well as to win public sympathy. In the 1935 Revised Criminal Code, voluntary surrender (*zishou*) is dealt with in Article 62, which stipulates, "If a person voluntarily surrenders and makes a confession and submits himself for trial for an offense not yet discovered, the punishment shall be reduced; provided that if special provision has been made therefore, then such provisions shall apply" (*ZHMGXF* 1935, 21). According to the defense, Shi Jianqiao had turned herself in to the janitors of the lay-Buddhist society before the authorities arrived, and thus met the legal stipulation of voluntary surrender.

Not content with simply citing the Republican code, however, the defending lawyers used several cultural and moral strategies to further their case. They first reminded the court that this recognition of voluntary surrender had a long history. They asserted that to encourage more criminals to turn themselves in, Chinese law had since the Tang granted leniency to criminals who had expressed a voluntary intent to surrender. Second, they claimed to cite ancient precedent with the following quotation: "All those who undertake revenge must report [their intentions] to the officials; therefore, for those who report their revenge to the authorities, it is just that they are exempt from their crimes."[39] While the lawyers attributed this quotation to the *Rites of Zhou* (*Zhou li*, c. 250 B.C.E.), only the first part of the quotation, "All those who undertake revenge must report [their intentions] to the officials" is actually from the classical text.[40] The second part of the statement is a modern elaboration of the subsequent clause in the original. The original reads as follows, "[then] the killing of the [original] offender will not be considered a crime." Despite the misquotation, the defense was nonetheless clearly appealing to the canonical text to ask the courts to consider the possibility that when an avenger confesses, he or she deserves more lenient judicial treatment.

In the end, the Hebei court overturned the original decision by the Tianjin district courts to accept the defense's argument for leniency based on Shi Jianqiao's voluntary surrender. The higher courts rejection of this line of defense may have been due to a general narrowing of offenses for which voluntary surrender was applicable. While Shi Jianqiao's lawyers made no distinction between the Republican code's treatment of voluntary surrender and that of the Qing code, Allyn Rickett (1971) suggests that the implications of the clause were qualitatively different. In imperial China, argues Rickett, voluntary surrender was in complete accord with the basic philosophy of law, which believed that punishment was merely an instrument whereby the harmonious balance of human and cosmic relations was to be restored after the disruption caused by a criminal act. Thus, if repentance canceled out the offense, there was no need for punishment. However, under the Republic, which had adopted Western legal premises that presumed that the nature of the act itself matters, any act that violated criminal law constituted an offense and had to be punished if the integrity of the code was to be preserved. This new understanding of the nature of the criminal act ushered in changes in legal practice with regard to offenses where restitution would be impossible (e.g., homicide cases), the granting of simple reduction instead of remission, and the use of considerable judicial discretion in doing so. It was thus increasingly common for the Republican era judge to refuse a reduction in punishment even when all conditions for voluntary surrender had been met.[41]

In the Shi Jianqiao case, however, the defendant's voluntary surrender was not merely an arcane issue of legal technicality. Debate over the issue also turned critically on whether the surrender was a sign of her sincerity. Press coverage of the charged courtroom exchanges over the issue of voluntary surrender was detailed, and debates over whether her surrender was such a sign were extensive. Newspaper readers learned that the Sun family lawyers had first suggested that Shi Jianqiao had been caught in the act and only then decided to confess since she had no other way out. They could also follow closely how the representatives for the Sun family suddenly took an entirely different approach to the legal issue, accusing the defendant of knowing all along that voluntary surrender would result in leniency to imply that her act of filial revenge was hardly committed out of absolute sincerity.[42] The spirited defense also appeared in detail in the press. Shi's team focused on establishing unequivocally that she had indeed surrendered voluntarily.[43] They counted Shi's verbal pronouncement upon killing Sun and her prepared written account of the revenge as direct admissions of culpability at the crime scene. They argued that her request to Fu Ming and Dong Hai to report her act to authorities on her behalf was further evidence of her desire to confess, even though the monks had failed to do so before a patrolman arrived at the scene of the crime.[44] Her full confession and testimony at police headquarters was offered as yet another instance of proof, and even her composure after the crime was claimed to show her willingness to surrender.[45] Shi, it was forcefully argued, had not expected leniency; she fully understood the severity of the penalty for revenge and still chose to act. This, they asserted, was the behavior of one inspired by "pure filial passion."[46]

The second part of the defense's strategy was intended to establish that Shi's passionate motive of filial piety and her act of righteous revenge constituted mitigating circumstances and thus deserved judicial compassion. The lawyers contended that since her father's execution had not been legitimate and her indignation was righteous (*yifen*), the particular circumstances behind the revenge should mitigate a strict application of the law. This line of argument technically turned on Article 59 of the 1935 Revised Criminal Code, which stipulates, "Punishments may be reduced by reason of extenuating circumstances" (*ZHMGXF* 1935, 21) and Article 273, which states, "Whoever out of righteous anger, then and there, commits homicide, shall be punished with imprisonment for not more than seven years" (*ZHMGXF* 1935, 98).[47] Yet, while the defense lawyers took care to ground their argument in the criminal code, they knew that the real strength of their case lay in their ability to evoke classical Confucian ritual propriety (*li*), in conjunction with modern New Life nationalism, to demonstrate that Shi Jianqiao's filial piety was a form of human sentiment worthy of legal sanction. To this end, they cited the Confucian classics, emphasized Shi's emotional sincerity, and promoted the political relevance of filial piety in a period of moral decay. The defense sought to appeal not merely to the compassion of the judges, but also to that of the public.

The defense team's strategy of appealing to the rule of ritual propriety and texts from antiquity in a period following the iconoclasm of the May Fourth era was hardly foolproof. It risked appearing anachronistic—a charge that the prosecution was more than willing to press. Nonetheless, the defense team took a chance. In their brief, Shi Jianqiao's lawyers explicitly cited what they claimed was a passage from the *Gongyang Commentary* to the *Spring and Autumn Annals*. "When one's father has undergone a [legitimate] execution, one cannot seek revenge. When one's father has not undergone a [just] execution, one can seek revenge."[48] Notably, the citation was not entirely accurate. The original passage from the *Gongyang Commentary* is given in the first of the two epigraphs for this chapter: "When one's father has not undergone [a proper or just] execution, the son may take revenge on his behalf. But if the father has been [legitimately] executed, and the son then takes revenge [anyway], this is the way of [the] thrusting sword, which cannot remove the danger."[49] The moderns had clearly paraphrased the ancients once again. Regardless, the clear implication of their apparent citation was that since the ancients had believed that the illegitimate killing of one's father served as legitimate grounds for revenge, so too should the modern courts.

Citing the *Gongyang Commentary* as an authority in matters of jurisprudence was hardly new. Imperial-era jurists had long turned to the ancient text of the *Gongyang Commentary* when the legal code did not directly apply or when the code would lead to socially undesirable consequences.[50] In his articulation of imperial ideology, Dong Zhongshu of the early Han dynasty developed the *Gongyang* tradition that recognized rites as better able to accommodate human feelings in matters of jurisprudence. In the Song, Wang Anshi returned to the text to comment further on conditions for legitimate vengeance. The *Gongyang* tradition retained its authority in Qing law and was often the basis of leniency.[51] This overall imperial history of relying on the *Gongyang Commentary* in matters of law indicates that ritual rule was not distinct from imperial law but inextricably intertwined with it. Thus, in the eyes of a public familiar with this tradition, the defense's recourse to the *Gongyang Commentary* evoked both legalistic and moralistic authority. Only in the eyes of reformists was such a strategy increasingly deemed nonlegalistic and a form of traditional moralism.

In referring to this *Gongyang Commentary* passage, Shi Jianqiao's defense team was clearly fully aware of the historical authority of the text. For the defense, Shi's filial revenge was justified precisely because it had occurred in a period of political and social chaos. The team was also aware of the elaboration of the tradition by Song-dynasty reformer Wang Anshi and cited him as follows: "As for he who kills to avenge a father or brother's death, it is within the Ruler's power to weigh the situation, forgive the assassin's passions, and permit (the revenge), if there are no authorities at the time to which one can report the revenge and if the perpetrator had never before been arrested for the crime."[52] In this quotation, Wang Anshi elaborates upon the *Gongyang Commentary's* acknowledgment that in times of state failure, official compassion can be demonstrated for virtuous revenge. For the defense, the decentralized chaos of the 1920s during which Shi Congbin's murder occurred qualified precisely as such an era of state failure. With legal recourse simply impossible during a time of chaos, righteous revenge was a viable alternative for Shi in order to right a wrong and uphold her filial duty.

To buttress their argument for the authority of rites, the defense linked the canonical sanction to the political context of the day. In one of the key legal exchanges during the initial trial, Yu Qichang, Shi's head lawyer, dramatically wondered aloud in court whether China could really afford to condemn the concept of filial piety. Was it not true, he demanded, that "of myriad things that are bad, lasciviousness is the worst; of things that are good, filial piety is the best?"[53] Should the circumstances of this crime thus deserve full compassion (*kemin*)? He concluded his argument by stating that he himself would never advocate an ideology that was against filial piety, especially since the country was in the midst of promoting reverence for Confucian values. Alluding to the ongoing New Life Movement of the time, he challenged the courts' sense of ethical and political responsibility.[54]

Having established that the very lawlessness of the 1920s had rendered Shi Congbin's death unjust and Shi Jianqiao's revenge worthy, the defense lawyers then blamed the conditions of the period on militarists like Sun Chuanfang. Echoing Shi Jianqiao's public depiction of Sun, Yu and Hu contended that Sun Chuanfang's savagery had perpetuated general chaos. They cited Sun's taking of prisoners as mere trophies and his failure to treat them with benevolence as evidence of how he had flaunted all standards of international warfare.[55] They also pointed to his barbaric decision to impale the decapitated head of Shi Congbin. They concluded that it was no surprise that when faced with the tragedy of her father's unjust death and a desperate family situation, the accused went from being a privileged young lady to being a focused killer seeking revenge. Sensing that the growing social resentment toward warlords in the Nanjing decade could work to their advantage, the lawyers sought to channel the widespread social frustration with China's national problems into public sympathy for Shi Jianqiao.

The defense's desire to embed a moral strand in the fabric of their argument was also evident in its decision to cite earlier legal cases that had become moral parables. For example, Shi's lawyers went back to the Tang dynasty, the classical period of imperial law, to cite the medieval case of Xu Yuanqing, a dutiful son who went to great lengths to kill Zhao Shitao, the official who had sentenced his father, Xu Shuang, to death.[56] Since Xu's revenge had been a sincere act of filial piety, Empress Wu Zetian had decided with great fanfare to commute Xu's sentence from the death penalty to the lesser punishment of banishment. The citation of a classical Tang tale of virtue suggests that the defense's strategy did not follow that of the narrowly legalistic arguments preferred by judicial reformers, but instead tapped into a classical tradition of jurisprudence that merged ritual and legal rule. Such a strategy was also more dramatic and better able to appeal to the sympathies of the urban public.

Finally, the defense displayed considerable agility in portraying Shi Jianqiao's filial piety to be not merely exemplary virtue, but also a form of passion. Shi Jianqiao's motive was explicitly identified as righteous anger and a sharp pain that she had harbored deep in her heart for more than ten years. This concept of "righteous anger" (*yifen*) and the idea that it deserved judicial compassion were not new to Republican-era law. In a larger discussion of the social vulnerability of widowed women with property in *The Death of Woman Wang*, Jonathan Spence describes a seventeenth-century case of two brothers who had committed a murder that they claimed was an act of filial revenge. The killing was, in actuality, an attempt to improve their chances to inherit a widow's property. In the end, the scheme was foiled because they had failed to realize that the vengeance clause in the Qing code granted leniency only when that vengeance was sought *immediately* in a fit of righteous rage (Spence 1978, 73–76). As Spence points out, the code was quite precise in defining the temporal circumstances of revenge murder, stipulating that if the revenge killing had been done right away in a fit of righteous rage, the perpetrator would receive no punishment; if done "after a slight delay," a punishment was to be imposed, but leniency would be shown.[57] Spence explains that the Qing state added time limitations to the code out of an official desire to limit the window of opportunity for socially disruptive acts of revenge.[58]

What Spence does not mention is that the immediacy of the act lent a degree of authenticity to the anger and thus to the virtue of the act. In other words, the legal stipulation regarding the immediacy of the act spoke to the moral authority of the *sincerity* of the anger. In the case of the two brothers, the temporal requirement functioned to check a fraudulent case of righteous revenge. According to the Qing code, because the brothers waited to seek revenge, their anger was no longer authentic and thus neither righteous nor deserving of judicial compassion. In Shi's twentieth-century case, authentic emotion was still important in marking the sincerity of a motive of virtue. If Shi's case had been tried under Qing law, Shi's motive would not have qualified as "righteous anger," given the ten-year time lag between the death of her father and the revenge itself. According to Republican law as well, "righteous anger" should only occur "then and there," at the scene of the crime. Yet by stressing that the passage of time during which her father's death went without revenge had caused her fury to become all the more righteous, Shi Jianqiao's defense sought to turn that legal handicap into a benefit. The frustration of not being able to seek recourse during such a period of political chaos rendered the anger harbored in her heart all the more sincere.

In short, the defense's appeal to the rule of *qing* was highly sophisticated, and the argument for mitigating circumstances was succinctly stated in the initial brief: "The defendant's father Shi Congbin should not have been killed, and yet Sun Chuanfang killed him. Thus, with such a sharp pain of losing her father, the defendant waited for an opportunity to kill Sun. The *Spring and Autumn Annals* sanctions the truth of righteous revenge. At this moment, morality is on the wane; it is a period that neglects filial piety. The defendant's sacrifice and exemplary behavior, however, are enough to set the moral trends of this era back on track. We should encourage this custom, and we should rule with leniency."[59] By mentioning the pain Shi Jianqiao suffered from her loss, this quotation provides us with a sense of how the defense sought to emotionalize Shi Jianqiao's filial piety. At the same time, we see how the team portrayed her motive of passion as both righteous and relevant. It evoked the rule of ritual propriety and used classical sanction to give the argument for filial piety the moral weight of tradition. The lawyers also proved contemporary relevance by enlisting New Life contemporary concerns for ethical renewal.

It was in their concluding remarks on December 12, 1935, that Shi Jianqiao's lawyers made the dilemma between appealing to the rule of ethical sentiment and the rule of law most explicit. Yu Qichang summed up the quandary with the following comment, "Although we cannot encourage murder, we cannot stifle exemplary filial piety."[60] Moral sympathy for a crime of righteous anger and the legal obligation to penalize homicide were in potential conflict with each other. Yet, the defense concluded by urging the court authorities to keep in mind not only that revenge had been permissible in [traditional] Chinese law, but that the Republican-era code could also accommodate the righteous act. With its clause of "mitigating circumstances," the modern code could assume a moral perspective, consider the exceptional situation, and grant judicial leniency.

The result of this approach was immediate. The press became obsessed with the defense lawyer's arguments, providing almost verbatim coverage of the each day's courtroom sessions. Editors were convinced that people wanted to read about the melodrama, and each aspect of the defense's moral argument would make the news. Headlines like "The Circumstances are Sympathetic and the Filial Piety Honorable" were printed to draw readers in.[61] Captions such as "The two attorneys, Yu and Hu, loudly orated and grandly debated in court, requesting a lenient sentence" featured the grandstanding tactics of Shi's lawyers to attract readers.[62] Finally, headings like "Each Circle of Society Sympathizes with Ms. [Shi]," punctuated the long articles, making public support explicit.[63]

THE DEFENDANT: COURTING PUBLIC SYMPATHY

While Hu and Yu launched an impressive courtroom performance, so too did Shi Jianqiao. Not content to leave matters in the hands of her defense team, the media-savvy assassin, while officially expected to assume a passive role as the defendant, proved remarkably active in trying to win public support for herself during the trial. Her lawyers were still obliged to make a legally grounded argument, even while they unmistakably shaped their legal arguments to appeal to the public audience. The defendant, in contrast, could flaunt expressions of emotionality at will.

With a keen sense for performance and a penchant for dramatic display, Shi Jianqiao made sure that each court appearance was replete with melodrama. She produced several moments of high drama marked by seemingly spontaneous emotional outbursts. For example, during the District Court trial, in response to the prosecution's allegations that her motive of filial piety was insincere, Shi cried in exasperation, "If it weren't to revenge my father, why would I even risk killing [Sun]?"[64] At another point that same day, Shi Jianqiao burst out in protest against Sun Chuanfang's eldest son's description of the bereaved family after they lost their father and husband. "He says his father's death is cruel! He doesn't even realize that my father dying in his father's hands is even worse."[65] At the close of the Superior Court trial a few months later, the Hebei court's decision to reverse the Tianjin court's ruling prompted the defendant to cry foul in a highly dramatic and public manner. In a courtroom filled with observers, Shi Jianqiao vocally objected to the decision: "If we can't establish in this case voluntary surrender, then we might as well have that article dropped from the Code. I made my intentions more than evident in the pamphlets I distributed at the crime scene. And, I told the monks to alert the police. If this is not surrender, I don't know what is!"[66] In all instances, her indignation was palpable, and her outbursts appeared genuine.

Like her legal representatives, Shi Jianqiao did not want the technicalities of law to overwhelm the moral component of the defense. At several points, Shi Jianqiao expressed frustration with arguments over legal particularities and sought to bring the debate back to the larger issue of her ethical right to seek revenge. For example, in the initial trial, after her lawyers had made their argument in favor of her having established a clear intent to surrender, Shi Jianqiao volunteered her opinion while on the stand: "As for my surrender, what is the meaning of the pamphlet I distributed? After I distributed it, could I have fled even if I wanted to? As for Sun Chuanfang capturing and killing my father, should this have been? My father at that time was acting under orders from the central government under the Fengtian clique. Who did Sun report to? Based on these points, it seems that a discussion of whether I should have taken vengeance can be put to rest!"[67] Fearful that the courts would get mired in the technical issue of determining whether she voluntarily surrendered, Shi Jianqiao quickly asserted that she did surrender and then immediately redirected attention to the injustice of Sun Chuanfang's actions. She wanted to remind the courts that because Sun's actions had been so brutal and outrageous, she had a fundamental moral right to seek recompense.

These dramatic expressions of emotionality produced concrete results in the courtroom. On December 28, 1935, Liu Shuxiu, the janitor of the monastery, and patrolmen Wang Hua'nan and Qu Hongtao, witnesses who had all testified that Shi Jianqiao had calmly turned herself over to the authorities at the monastery during the first trial, suspiciously failed to show up for the opening session of the appeals trial in the Hebei Provincial Court. The situation infuriated Shi, and she made her fury known to the press. Shanghai's *Shibao* reported on the following day that "Shi Jianqiao is disgruntled; all her powerful witnesses have left Tianjin, and no one knows of their whereabouts. The Sun family has money and power, the circumstances are suspicious."[68] In the end, Shi Jianqiao's public protestations clearly had some effect. When the Hebei Superior Court opened session again on February 6, 1936, patrolman Wang Hua'nan, one of the three missing witnesses, mysteriously reappeared.

Shi Jianqiao was just as relentless outside of the courtroom. She took advantage of a detail-hungry press by granting press conferences and interviews throughout the appeals process. During an interview after the initial verdict, Shi Jianqiao sought to clarify her virtuous motive, remind the public of her legal innocence, and make evident her disappointment with the court's decision not to recognize her righteous anger as mitigating evidence. Comparing her case to that of female assassin Liu Jinggui, a contemporaneous, high-profile case of a crime of passion (Liu killed the "other woman" in a love triangle), Shi Jianqiao pointed out that since the courts had recognized Liu's voluntary surrender and granted her a twelve-year sentence, her own sentence of ten years was too long. As an act of filial revenge, the circumstances of her crime, she reasoned, merited far more than the two-year reduction that Liu had received from her twelve-year sentence.[69] Ironically, Liu Jinggui's twelve-year sentence was later overturned upon appeal, and Liu was sentenced to life imprisonment.[70] Nonetheless, Shi Jianqiao was clever to link her case to the Liu case when she did. The final verdict of life imprisonment in the Liu affair had not yet been decided, and she was able to align herself with another female criminal who was winning public support. Moreover, this comparison helped keep Shi's trial newsworthy by winning headlines. In the December 19, 1935, issue of the Shanghai *Shibao*, the main headline screamed, "Ms. Shi, Not Happy!" and was followed by a smaller headline that further proclaimed, "Like Liu Jinggui, Voluntary Surrender Established. The Issue of Motive, Suspended. Result, Only Two-Year Leniency."

Shi Jianqiao even turned her jail cell into a site from which to press her case. For example, right before the verdict was reached in the initial trial, she strategically granted several interviews from prison during which she presented herself in a way that differed greatly from her feisty, almost defiant courtroom persona. The December 12, 1935, issue of the Shanghai *Shibao* began its coverage with the main headline, "Ms. Shi Chants in Jail; Thousands of Miles Away, She Thinks of Her Mother, in a Dream, So Distant."[71] The full article is an interview with the defendant. Printed in a question-and-answer format, it allowed readers to feel that they were engaged in an intimate dialogue with her. They meet a well-behaved and almost melancholy prisoner who calmly recounts how she is well fed in jail and spends much of her time either reading Chinese classical poetry or composing poems that express her sorrow at being separated from her family.

While Shi Jianqiao appeared to be resigned to her fate in jail during the interview, her answers were pointed with meaning. To begin with, the defendant was able to turn the interview into an opportunity to underscore her unique moral position, which helped reinforce her legal team's defense that her extraordinary actions merited sympathy and leniency. At one point, Shi deplores the lack of common sense among her fellow female inmates, most of whom had killed their husbands to escape miserable marriages because they had not known that they could turn to the courts of law to seek divorce. She states that this situation, symptomatic of the poor state of female education in China, has made her want to open a school for women after she is released from prison.[72] She goes on to emphasize that she is in a unique position to help those less fortunate women. "Although in my youth my education was the Three Followings and Four Virtues (*sancong side*), the typical education of a proper gentry woman, in the end I have turned out to [embody] the opposite, and today I can avenge the death of my father." By portraying

Figure 9. Undated photo of assassin Shi Jianqiao in jail, circa 1936.

her act of assassination as an indication of her liberation from the confines of traditional female education, Shi Jianqiao underscored her moral exceptionality. The success of Shi's theatrical self-promotion can be seen in the following day's Shanghai *Shibao*, which ran a section header that read, "A personality truly distinct from [that of] most other women."[73]

Having presented herself and her revenge as morally exceptional, Shi

Jianqiao proceeded to move the public discourse beyond the immediate concern of the upcoming court decision to introduce the idea of a possible state pardon. She did so in a seemingly modest, heartfelt poem that she had composed in jail. The title of the poem was "Under the Moon, Thoughts of My Mother," and the Shanghai *Shibao* printed the original, handwritten poem in its entirety. The poem reads as follows:

> The night is chilled like water; the moon is empty and cold,
> Yet my warm sentiment [to serve my mother] abounds.
> On what day will Heaven take pity on me and grant me an official pardon?
> Then, I can serve my dear mother and be by her side.
> Oh how my contentment will be complete.[74]

At first glance, the poem appears to be a straightforward sentimental expression of her sorrow. The disarming modesty of the poem, the emotional expression of filial piety, as well as the motif of homesickness under the moonlight helps lure the reader into sympathizing with the personal wishes of the author. Yet, despite its modest tone, the poem makes a fairly radical and strategic claim. With the line, "On what day will Heaven take pity on me and grant me an official pardon?" it introduced long before the trial was over the idea that the state should grant a pardon to help Shi pursue this personal, yet universal, desire of fulfilling her filial obligations.[75] And, indeed, in eleven months time, the idea that the state should become involved became a reality.

PROSECUTION: A STRATEGY OF LAW

The prosecution's approach could not have been more different from the approach used by Shi Jianqiao and her defense team. The newspaper *Yishibao* summed up the difference between the two approaches as follows: "The two sides build their case; the defense attorneys invoke the Classics; the prosecuting team analyzes the Code."[76] The in-house prosecutors and legal representatives for the Sun family decided to counter the defense team's moralistic argument for leniency with arguments for strict adherence to the rule of law as stipulated by the code. They vehemently opposed granting any judicial compassion and argued that the accused assassin deserved nothing less than lifelong imprisonment.

The prosecution's strategy drew from the general reformist trend of the early twentieth century to establish a powerful rule of law in China. By the 1930s, official encroachment into the legal arena was increasing. The Nationalist state, concerned with centralizing its own power, was highly distrustful of autonomous pockets of power in society and even within its own bureaucracy and sought to dismantle any semblance of legal autonomy erected in preceding decades (Xu 1997). Laws such as the "Emergency Law for the Suppression of Crimes Against the Safety of the Republic," which gave the Nationalist Party broad access to the judicial system on the grounds of punishing "counterrevolutionaries," were means by which the regime sought to "party-fy" (*danghua*) the judiciary. Yet, at the same time, official encroachment only seemed to stiffen the resolve of many reforming jurists, lawyers, and other advocates of law. As discussed in chapter 3, judicial authorities in the Republican period were concerned with carving out a degree of professional autonomy, modernizing the legal system, and redefining law as rational and the basis of national strength. During the 1920s reformists had made significant inroads by establishing bar associations and law schools, and by reforming the courts. A reformist commitment to the institutionalization of judicial autonomy continued into the Nanjing decade. Liberal reformers such as Hu Shi, for example, explicitly railed against the party government's movement into the judicial arena, though often not without cost. In a 1929 article entitled "Failure of Law in Nationalist China," published in the liberal journal *Xinyue* [The crescent moon] in the spring and reprinted almost simultaneously in Shanghai's *North China Herald*, Hu Shi condemned the increasing party control over the judiciary. In return, the Nationalist authorities issued a temporary ban on Hu Shi's writings.

It was in this tense context of official encroachment into the judiciary that the prosecutors of the Tianjin and Hebei courts as well as the lawyers for the Sun family formulated their strategy. Just after the assassination, the lawyers for the Sun family held a press conference in the British Concession and presented the major points of their strategy.[77] The first part of their strategy was to argue that Shi Congbin's death was merely a matter of war and not grounds for any kind of revenge. To recognize Shi's death as anything beyond a war casualty would, they warned, force society to acknowledge the right to revenge of the family members of all people killed during the warfare of the twenties, which would have tragic consequences. A second assertion was that modern law should not consider voluntary surrender a special condition for leniency regarding the crime of murder. To argue against voluntary surrender, Sun Guanche, one of the attorneys of the team, wrote an editorial for Shanghai *Shibao*, in which he explained that the voluntary surrender clause was obsolete in modern law.[78] The third part was to urge everyone to abide by the facts of the case and the law rather than public sympathy (*shehui tongqing*). To make this point, they enlisted the help of Lu Xiangting, a veteran of the warlord struggles of the 1920s and an old colleague of Sun. As mentioned in chapter 1, Lu held a press conference and acknowledged that although an act of filial vengeance wins the sympathy of society, the reality was that Shi Congbin's death had been a mere casualty of war, and his death did not merit revenge as a means to bring about true justice (*zhengyi*). Lu urged everyone to maintain an objective, critical outlook and a truthful understanding of the situation. He concluded ominously that support for the recent wave of assassinations, including Sun's, would only render National law useless and slowly erode societal peace.[79]

During the actual court proceedings, prosecutors and the attorneys for the plaintiff built their arguments on all three points, emphasizing the final warning that the failure to privilege the rule of law over the rule of sympathy would lead to social unrest. They showed little patience for the defense's strategy of appealing to the rule of *li* to justify judicial compassion. For example, in their formal complaint filed for the first trial, Zhang Shaozeng, Sun Guanche, and Wang Hao, the full legal team for the Sun family, reserved sharp criticism for the defense's use of the Confucian Classics.[80] While the lawyers acknowledged that revenge had a place during the period of antiquity when the concept of the nation-state was weak, they argued that the continued reliance upon revenge in China was highly problematic, as concepts of nationhood and societal peace had existed in China since the eighteenth-century. Classic texts promoting private revenge, like the *Gongyang Commentary*, were no longer applicable, they insisted. Rather than abiding by an anachronistic reverence for the moral sentiment of filial piety, the courts, the lawyers asserted, needed to respect national law (*guofa*).[81]

Xu Jiucheng, the Hebei Superior Court's in-house prosecuting official, made what was perhaps the most explicit statement regarding the problems that might arise if the courts did not follow the rule of law. Xu opined that there was an untenable tension between filial vengeance and modern law and social stability. While he was sympathetic with Shi Jianqiao's motive of filial piety and agreed that leniency based on mitigating circumstances was not completely unreasonable, he concluded emphatically that today's society could not afford to tolerate the highly disruptive action of violent revenge. The prosecutor stressed that it was the court's responsibility to penalize acts of revenge and overrule any sympathetic circumstances.[82] Zhang Shaozeng, one of the attorneys for the Sun family, suggested the same in his appeal to the Hebei Superior Court. "If we fail to punish [such an act] according to the letter of the law, in the future . . . it will be enough to harm the nation's order and agitate societal peace."[83]

Wanting only a strict application of law, court prosecutors and the lawyers for the Sun family implored the courts to treat the modern legal code as the ultimate source of judicial authority. Not surprisingly, whereas both emotion and melodrama pervaded the defense's approach, the prosecuting side struck a far more legalistic tone in their argument, emphasizing a literal and precise reading of the code. For example, in their complaint filed during the first trial, the legal representatives of the Sun family questioned the defense's interpretation of the code. Demanding faithful readings of the law, these attorneys pointed out that Article 62 of the Criminal Code states explicitly that voluntary surrender is possible only when it is done *before* the crime is discovered (*ZHMGXF* 1935, 21). In the Shi Jianqiao case, they contended, voluntary surrender was not established because the police, having heard the noise of the defendant's gunshot, had discovered the crime before Shi had surrendered. Their complaint stated, "Shi Jianqiao was like a bird in the cage, caught red-handed. How could this be voluntary surrender?"[84]

Like the Sun family attorneys, the court prosecutor's precise interpretation of the legal code sharply contrasted with the more theatrical and moralized interpretations of the law presented by the defense. In his complaint, he challenged in precise legal terms the idea that Shi's revenge had in fact been committed out of "righteous anger" (*yifen*) and thus merited judicial compassion. Citing article 273, "Whoever out of righteous anger, *then and there*, commits homicide, shall be punished with imprisonment for not more than seven years" (my italics), the prosecution argued for a literal reading of "righteous anger" as something provoked spontaneously at the crime scene. Since Shi Jianqiao had harbored the intent to seek revenge for ten years, he reasoned, her actions were neither spontaneous nor righteous. Instead, he advocated that she should be tried under the harsher penalty of not less than ten years for homicide as stipulated in Article 271 (*ZHMGXF* 1935, 98).

This strategy of strictly adhering to the legal code was also employed to rebut the defense's interpretation of texts of antiquity. In the Hebei Superior court trial, prosecuting attorney Zhang Shaozeng argued that even if the courts decided to acknowledge the authority of the *Gongyang Commentary* passage, the defense could not demonstrate that Shi Congbin's execution was illegitimate as required by the classic text. Zhang contended not only that Sun Chuanfang's decision to kill Shi Congbin, a prisoner of war, was an everyday occurrence during the 1920s, but also that Shi Congbin himself had committed crimes that deserved the death penalty. Zhang claimed that Shi Congbin had violated Article 34 of the Criminal Code of the Army, Navy, and Air Force by leading his White Russian mercenary troops in pillaging the local area and indiscriminately harming civilians. Zhang also cited Article16 of the Articles to Army Court Proceedings, which stipulates that even a criminal who is a prisoner of war must be tried in court, to argue that Sun, as the highest official at the front line, was legally responsible for the trying and punishing of Shi Congbin. He cited articles 7 and 8, which stipulate that in such cases on the front line, the military unit's judicial officials should organize the trial. Finally, Zhang pointed out that the newspapers of the day could verify Sun Chuanfang's fair treatment of Shi, since the original documents of the military trial were lost. As evidence, he pointed to a headline from a 1925 issue of the *Shuntian shibao* (The Shuntian times), which read, "Shi Congbin's Death Sentence; Sun Chuanfang Adjudicated."[85] Simultaneously vilifying Shi Congbin and justifying Sun's actions, this line of argument consciously alluded to the authority of legal codes and sought through example to promote law above sentiment.

THE COURTS: DUE PROCESS OF LAW

While the prosecution had launched an aggressive counterattack, the judicial outcome suggests that the defense's appeal to the authority of moral sentiment swayed the courts in the end. A few months after the Tianjin District Court refused to acknowledge that extenuating circumstances existed, the Hebei Province Superior Court reversed that decision. The Superior Court stipulated that there were in fact mitigating circumstances, and the Supreme Court upheld this decision in August 1936. At first glance, the results appear to indicate the success of the defense's argument that the defendant's righteous fury qualified as an extenuating circumstance. Closer examination, however, reveals a difference in emphasis between the defense's rationale for judicial leniency and that of the courts. Whereas the defense invoked the rule of *li* both to endow Shi Jianqiao's impassioned vengeance with moral authority and to win public sympathy, the higher courts proved to be skeptical of classical sanction as well as wary of granting public sympathy too much power. In fact, the judicial rulings stipulated that the extenuating circumstances of the case rested with neither the inherent moral value of Shi's filial passion nor the overwhelming amount of public support for the assassin, but rather with the unlawful death of Shi Congbin. By making such a distinction, the reforming courts turned the high-profile case into an opportunity to assert the primacy and objectivity of due process of law, and, in effect, to engage in a highly public act of institutional self-justification. In doing this, the courts sought to defend their authority vis-à-vis the encroaching presence of the Nationalist Party regime, and the rising power of a new public.

Despite the immense public appeal of the defense's approach, the judges were ambivalent, if not anxious, about granting too much authority to ritual propriety (*li*) and classical sanction. The verdicts of the higher courts took particular exception to the defense's attempt to cite the *Gongyang Commentary*. The Hebei ruling states, "Although it is written in the *Rites of Zhou* that 'for those who commit revenge and report their acts to the authorities, they are without crime,' modern law has long discarded this view, which the accused should be fully aware of."[86] The higher court judges thus agreed with the prosecution and the Sun family lawyers, and denied the admissibility of the ancient text.

Furthermore, for the Hebei and Nanjing courts, Shi Jianqiao deserved lenient treatment because her father had been denied a lawful execution. Rather than relying upon classical sanction for Shi's feelings of loss and anger as the moral justification for vengeance, the courts argued that the travesty in the case, and thus the basis of judicial leniency, was that Shi Congbin had died without a fair trial. The provincial-level verdict spent a great deal of time on the question of whether Sun Chuanfang had granted his prisoner of war, Shi Congbin, a fair hearing. The verdict began by recounting the full testimony of Sun's eldest son, Sun Jiazhen, who had testified that his father had in fact organized a full military trial and had therefore executed Shi Congbin in accordance with the letter of the law. But the verdict proceeded to note that incriminating reports had surfaced during the trial. These reports provided evidence that when Wu Peifu, the leader of the Zhili clique to whom Sun Chuanfang ostensibly reported, had telegrammed Sun to ask why he had killed Shi Congbin, Sun Chuanfang flatly denied any involvement in the matter. The verdict concluded that these reports of Sun Chuanfang's outright denial were evidence that Sun had, in fact, been fully aware that he had failed to grant Shi Congbin fair legal treatment and that the testimony of Sun's son was thus flawed.[87] Accordingly, the Hebei verdict states, "So, it is evident that Shi Congbin's death was not in accordance with the law. The accused has been in great pain regarding the tragic circumstances of her father's death and . . . [because her father] had been unable to clear these unjust charges. [By seeking revenge], she was clearly fulfilling the wishes of her deceased father and sacrificing herself; she accomplished this exemplary behavior with a purely filial heart. Thus, if we examine the circumstances, they are indeed worthy of sympathy."[88] The Hebei court concluded that Shi Congbin's unlawful death constituted circumstances worthy of sympathy. It was because her father had been denied fair legal treatment before his execution that Shi Jianqiao's pain was sincere, her filial piety virtuous, and her revenge deserving of judicial compassion.

Newspapers the following day quoted the judges as saying that since Shi Jianqiao had sincerely felt that her father did not die lawfully, her criminal behavior was excusable.[89] On August 25, 1936, the presiding judge of the Third Criminal Court of the Nanjing Supreme Court, Liu Jianying, decided to disregard the appeals from both Shi Jianqiao and the Sun family and upheld the decision of the Hebei judges as final.[90] Liu too zeroed in on Sun Chuanfang's denial to Wu Peifu as evidence that Sun had failed to follow proper legal procedure in the trial and execution of Shi Congbin. With final authority as the highest court of the land, the Supreme Court concluded, "Although according to law, this [situation] does not deserve sympathy, if we consider the circumstances, they are in the end forgivable." Shi Jianqiao's righteous fury stemmed not simply from the injustice of her father's death, but specifically from his being denied due legal process.

The court's desire in this case to promote an agenda of due process was important, given the context of increasing encroachment by the Nationalist Party in the early 1930s into the legal arena. As we will see in chapter 5, in this case, the regime was more than willing to sanction public support for Shi Jianqiao in order to strengthen its position vis-à-vis the courts by arguing that the regime was unique in its ability to bridge the gap between the rule of law and the reality of public sympathy. For justices committed to judicial reform and autonomy, it was important not to appear to be completely yielding to the regime's New Life agenda, which was promoting the rule of rites or ethics as supreme. Indeed, in the final court decisions the judges managed to find a compromise that promoted the need for due process. They demonstrated that the law did in fact have the mechanism to accommodate judicial compassion and grant exemption when due process was denied.

In addition to turning the verdicts into an opportunity to assert proper legal procedure, the courts also showed that they were reluctant to acknowledge explicitly the sway of public sympathy. No reference to collective sentiment was ever made in the verdicts. Yet, this silence becomes deafening when we recall the obvious ploys used by the defense to court public sympathy as a judicial force. A retrospective account of the trial also suggested that the Sun family was fully cognizant of the potential judicial power of public sympathy and actively courted the press and the public over the course of the trial. Chen Jin (1991), for example, accused the Sun side of both bribing the judges and shamelessly manipulating the media through press conferences. Furthermore, while the court documents were opaque about how public sympathy bore upon legal proceedings, outside commentators did not hesitate to remark upon the judicial role of a sentimental public. As noted in chapter 3, reformers and legal professionals writing in trade journals and specialized periodicals were gravely concerned with the potential influence of public sympathy in the judicial arena.

One skeptical commentator sounded a particularly dire warning in the *Guowen zhoubao* (The national weekly): "Because Shi Jianqiao made clear in her words and action that she was seeking revenge for her father, society applauded. This publication has received a lot of letters praising her poetry, including the seven-character regulated verse she had distributed just after she committed the crime. In general, however, we have refrained from publishing these materials since the recent praise supporting this assassination is not at all beneficial to public security or public interest."[91] This passage delivers a cautionary message. Praising the editorial decision not to publish any of the letters to the editor and poems in support of the assassin, the critic hinted at the deleterious effects of public sentiment on society. The author went on to argue that though public sympathy for Shi Jianqiao might be relevant according to popular custom, it was highly problematic for modern law. The article deplores the destructive cynicism of the assassin, who had known that achieving revenge through litigation might not have succeeded and had thus decided to act on her own rather than seek legal recourse. By extension, the piece reasoned, popular endorsement for Shi was yet another expression of an utter lack of faith in China's legal system. The critics were recognizing what the courts saw too—namely, that the potentially negative and powerful impact of public passions on the outcome of the legal case.

In short, while silent on the matter in their final written decisions, the judges had to grapple with the force of public sympathy when formulating their final decisions. They too were exposed to the articles and opinion pieces on the judicial influence of public sympathy and witnessed the defense's attempt to enlist collective emotions in the trial proceedings. The final judicial decisions can thus also be seen as an institutional gesture to contain the influence of the new sentimental public.

CONCLUSION: THE LEGAL CASE OF LIU JINGGUI

It is worthwhile to compare briefly the legal outcome of the Shi Jianqiao trial with the trial of the previously discussed and roughly contemporaneous Liu Jinggui case. As mentioned in chapter 3, having killed her rival in love, Liu's case came to be known as a crime of passion and attracted tremendous public interest. Like Shi Jianqiao's case, Liu's was complex. Liu's trial began prior to Shi's on April 23, 1935. On April 29, the District Court verdict granted her a sentence of a mere twelve years, half of the maximum amount, in an expression of judicial leniency based on sympathy. However, upon appeal, the Hebei Superior Court reversed the lower court's decision in May of the same year and sentenced Liu to life imprisonment. On May 5, 1937, the Nanjing Supreme Court upheld the Superior Court's decision as final.[92] From the beginning, Liu's case was intertwined with a case against Lu Ming, her lover. The prosecution had filed a case against Liu for premeditated murder and against Lu for offending public morality, given his improper relations with Liu Jinggui after the annulment of their engagement. Moreover, there was a fairly lengthy period between the Hebei trial and the final trial at the Supreme Court because Liu's defense lawyers decided to accuse Lu Ming of rape in an attempt to reverse the Hebei Superior Court's unfavorable decision to deny Liu judicial leniency. This meant that Lu had to be put on trial for charges of rape, and a trial within a trial took place. On October 28, 1936, Lu Ming was found not guilty. Love letters between Lu and Liu served as evidence to prove that the tryst was voluntary on Liu's part.

The Shi and Liu trials are worth comparing not only because they dealt with roughly contemporaneous crimes involving highly passionate women, but also because the legal strategies adopted by their respective defenses were nearly identical. Like Shi Jianqiao's defense described above, Liu Jinggui's was two-pronged. The first prong was the argument that the voluntary surrender of the defendant deserved leniency.[93] The trial was held in a period when the criminal code was undergoing revision, and Liu Jinggui's defense lawyer, Liu Huang, laid out a highly legalistic argument in support of voluntary surrender (*zishou*), citing several legal precedents and also pointing out that whereas the existing criminal code recognized *zishou*, the new code expanded the scope for reduction of the sentence on grounds of such behavior.[94] This legalistic argument proved successful at the district court level, and Liu Huang won his client a lenient sentence of twelve years. When responding to the Beiping district court's verdict in her own trial, Shi Jianqiao cited the Liu Jinggui case, whose initial verdict was announced eight months prior to hers, as a precedent on the *zishou* issue.

The other prong turned upon the logic that judicial compassion (*minshu*) for exceptional circumstances could mitigate the strict rule of law. As Shi's defense team did months later, Liu's lawyer urged leniency based on sympathy for his client's passionate motive. But whereas Shi Jianqiao's lawyers presented her motive as an expression of righteous anger (*yifen*), Liu Jinggui's lawyers portrayed her motive as tragic anger (*beifen*). To counter the prosecutor's earlier charge that Liu had tragically killed an innocent in the case, her defense lawyer wrote, "With her love and virginity stolen from her, Liu Jinggui had emotions that, at the time, resulted in [an act of] anger. . . . The occurrence [of her killing Teng] is tragic, and although it was the defendant who killed [Teng], the motivation was really caused by Lu Ming's deceitful rape; . . . thus, public opinion [*yulun*] for the defendant is sympathetic [*lianmin*], and, according to law, we should reduce the penalty."[95]

Several salient points arise when we compare these cases. First, the influence of public sympathy was not felt in the Shi Jianqiao case alone. As the quotation in the above paragraph reveals, Liu's defense lawyer did not hesitate to cite public opinion explicitly in his briefs. The outcome of life imprisonment for his client shows that invoking public sympathy in a legal battle did not guarantee victory. Yet, even while it was not the deciding factor, the opinion of the urban public was nonetheless clear to the court and a crucial component of legal strategy that could shape, if only implicitly, the legal decision. In the Shi Jianqiao trial as well, while the verdicts did not explicitly acknowledge public sympathy as a reason for leniency, the defense team clearly unfolded its case in a manner that would excite public sentiment. Taken together, these cases demonstrate that in a period of modern mass communications, Republican courts were fully aware of the public and its power.

Second, in an era of New Life morality, not all forms of female virtue and sentiment appeared to be equally appropriate in the eyes of the courts. Liu's defense lawyers failed to win exemption for their client based on judicial compassion for Liu's tragic anger, whereas Shi's lawyers, who showcased their defendant's filial ardor, met with success after their appeal to the Superior Court. What the two outcomes appeared to suggest was that the motive of love did not prove as compelling as the motive of filial ardor. To be sure, the courts in both cases ruled in explicit legal terms. In the Liu case, the crucial reason why the defense failed to win judicial exemption was the existence of a cache of love letters penned by Liu. These letters proved that Liu willingly met Lu Ming for a five-day romantic tryst at a hotel outside of Beiping even after he had broken off the engagement and was to wed Teng Shuang. Such a scenario did not support the argument that Lu Ming forced Liu into sex, and the exceptional circumstances that would have given rise to "tragic anger" were not established. In the Shi trial as well, while compassion was shown, the decision was anchored in legal, rather than ethical, terms and the courts carefully grounded their decision of exemption in terms of due process of law.

Yet, even with the legal logic evident in the respective court rulings, the decisions had connotations beyond what the legalistic interpretations might have intended. In other words, the final outcomes may have had the more general effect of sanctioning the "classical" female virtue of the filial daughter while failing to do so for the emotion of jealous betrayal exhibited by Liu.[96] Taken together, these legal outcomes distinguished between motives of female passion and at least appeared to endorse only those that were ritually prescribed and conformed to a New Life agenda.

While it might be easy to dismiss such high-profile trials as exceptional or mere sensations, I argue otherwise. It was precisely as exceptional spectacles of justice that these cases helped shape the parameters of twentieth-century Chinese law. First, in a period marked by the struggle for judicial autonomy and reform, both cases involved a very public contest among judicial players about whether law should accommodate the moral authority of *qing* or ritual propriety. Second, attempts to institutionalize the judicial system as a relatively autonomous branch of the government in the context of an increasingly inquisitive and sensation-hungry mass media turned the courtroom into a public arena for social and moral deliberation. Thus, just as the mass media had assumed an adjudicating function, the courts themselves had become a forum for spectacle, melodrama, and public debate. This, in turn, allowed a broader, mass audience to gain a voice in pressing social debates, including the public dialogue over womanhood and modernity. Whereas critics and intellectuals used more highbrow editorial, political, and fictional forums to make their opinions heard, the public found a pulpit in the trials, especially those featuring passionate women. Public emotions flared over the issue of whether female perpetrators' virtuous motivations or passionate heroism deserved judicial exemption, and had some influence on the process of adjudication itself. In the end, public sympathy not only influenced courts but also attracted the attention of the Nationalist regime. As we will see next, the executive branch of the government took an interest in the Shi Jianqiao case and responded to popular sentiment by using its pardon mechanism to discipline society and party-fy the judicial realm.

FIVE

A State Pardon

Sanctioned Violence under Nationalist Rule

[The killing of Sun Chuanfang] cannot be considered and discussed in the same manner as other regular homicides. Rather, it is reasonable to agree with telegrams that sincerely request the government to grant a pardon and, with evident righteousness, guard against traitors.

Chenbao, *23 November 1935*

Afterward, although there was a state pardon, the effect of the pardon was no more than the exemption of "executing the punishment" and not a fundamental revision of his guilt. . . . The final method of a pardon cannot satisfactorily answer the question . . . and is invalid in both name and reasoning. How can we ever explain away the doubts of the people's sense of justice? If this case is judged from the perspective of Party Doctrine (*dangyi*), we are more likely to find a method that is valid in name and reason.

Ju Zheng, *Dongfang zazhi, 1935*

On October 14, 1936, at two o'clock in the afternoon, the Nationalist government announced that it was granting Shi Jianqiao a pardon. This was not the first time that the central regime had decided to pardon such a criminal. The Nanjing government had issued a similar reprieve to Zheng Jicheng, who had appeared on the public stage in 1932 under circumstances that were remarkably similar. Like Shi, Zheng had killed a retired militarist to avenge the murder of a father figure. Whereas Shi had killed ex-Jiangnan military leader Sun Chuanfang, the son had killed northern militarist Zhang Zhongcang. While Shi sought revenge for her father, Zheng did so for his uncle. In both cases, public support for the assassin was overwhelming. For both assassins, the central regime issued high-profile pardons shortly after their cases had been adjudicated in the court system.

It is not obvious why the regime decided in two separate instances to grant pardons. Although public sympathy was widespread and the motives of the assassins honorable, these acts were after all still murder. By pardoning the two, the central government risked compromising its own legal code, which condemned all instances of homicide. For a government claiming to be "modern," the sanctioning of "traditional" revenge motivated by filial piety was hardly a natural choice. Yet Nanjing decided rather quickly to pardon these two killers, assuming that violent acts of traditional ethical revenge were indeed permissible in the modern state, and in both cases openly acknowledged public outcry for state sanction. The two pardons thus beg the following questions: Why did the state sanction these instances of violent retribution? Why did it do so in such a high-profile manner? Why did it give such a prominent position to public sympathy and the seemingly outmoded motive of filial piety?

Answers to these questions can be found in the official pardons, telegrams sent by public associations that demanded official grace, as well as a host of editorial and political commentary. As these documents show, the Nationalist regime issued pardons in order to expand and sustain central control, albeit with ambivalent results. By the 1930s, Jiang Jieshi, the leader of the Nationalist regime, had combined both the party apparatus and the state bureaucracy under his control to establish a corporatist, Nationalist Party-state regime, and was moreover aggressively expanding its reach into society.[1] Yet, despite these intentions to extend party-state power, the Nationalist regime was, in fact, merely one political actor among several vying for control over the meaning associated with righteous assassination. A complicated political landscape existed at the time of these assassinations, characterized by a range of social and political forces. There was widespread public sentiment for the two filial assassins as virtuous, if rogue, heroes. There were judicial reformers, who had steadily gained ground in the early quarter of the twentieth century and continued to defend that ground in the trials of the two perpetrators; civic associations flexing their institutional muscle in the aggressive lobbying for official grace; and finally, individual regional politicians involved in the intrigue surrounding the affairs who were seeking to sustain their autonomy vis-à-vis the center. On one level, these pardons were an attempt by the Nationalist regime to resolve tensions laid bare by the assassinations, both within the Nationalist regime and between the regime and elements in society. On another level, however, the pardons only made these tensions more apparent, occasioning a lively dialogue in print over the merits of official support of violence.

In examining the complex politics lurking behind acts of revenge and assassination, this project builds on but also diverges from the prevailing scholarly approach to violence in 1930s China. Those interested in the 1930s have long noted the Nationalist regime's tacit endorsement of a culture of violence in China's political world and characterized the state's relationship with violence as an extension of the personal politics and factional divisions under Jiang Jieshi's rule. Political murder was one of the more common uses of terror by which Jiang cowed political opponents and the general population into submission. Several famous assassinations occurred during this period, including the murder of Yang Xingfo of the Chinese League for the Protection of Human Rights and Shi Liangcai, the *Shenbao* newspaper editor, who was a regular critic of the regime and another member of the League for the Protection of Human Rights. There was also the spectacular, if unsuccessful, attempt on Wang Jingwei, Jiang's leading political rival in the Nationalist Party. In all these cases suspicion centered on Jiang himself. In his recent biography of Dai Li, the head of Jiang's secret service organization, Frederic Wakeman argues that such suspicion was hardly unfounded. He describes how Jiang had personally ordered Dai Li to arrange these killings, and how political terror became institutionalized as a standard policy of the Nationalist regime. Dai Li lead clandestine assassination units in the Special Services Department, staffed by men and women who, despite their self-portrayals as heroic rogues and individual heroes, were essentially "technicians of homicide" and used modern practices of secret service squads and group training units in the business of assassinating political opponents (Wakeman 2003, 173).

While the acts of violence at the heart of this study resemble in certain respects the politically motivated acts of state terror described by Wakeman, they differ in significant ways. Whereas political killings generated terror precisely because of their shadowy, clandestine, and illicit nature, the acts of violence under consideration here were explicitly public and portrayed as fully legitimate by the assassins, sometimes by the regime, and especially by the public. Public opinion in the 1930s condemned the political terror of Dai Li's squads for having a destabilizing effect on Chinese society. Wakeman (2003, 176–79), for example, discusses some of the public backlash and how the more high-profile "hits" resulted in galvanizing both national and international public outrage and condemnation of the violent excesses of the regime. In sharp contrast, the assassinations by Shi Jianqiao and Zheng Jicheng were widely perceived as restoring order. They were presented in the media as acts of retribution that would bring about public justice through the killing of notorious warlords. The two different forms of political violence also shaped state legitimacy in very different ways. Jiang's reliance upon political murder functioned to generate pervasive terror throughout the Nanjing political world, allowing the regime to cross the boundary from the realm of law into the realm of the illicit and from the realm of ethical rule into the realm of amoral expediency. In contrast, in sanctioning these two acts of assassination, the regime sought to bring two potentially illicit acts of private violence into the realm of the law, make a claim for its own merciful rule, and demonstrate how its power fell squarely within the bounds of judicial and ethical authority.

I begin this chapter by introducing the Zheng Jicheng case. I then review the two pardons to identify the different sources of authority the regime invoked to justify its decision to sanction the violence. The next section examines the symbolic meanings attributed to state-sanctioned revenge. Telegrams appealing for an official pardon sent by civic associations, women's groups, and other public educational facilities and military groups wove a compelling narrative about how virtuous revenge constituted a form of national authenticity and that state sanction would provide the Nationalist regime with an invaluable opportunity to promote its vision of New Life nationalism. In this context, we can understand the regime's final decision to pardon Shi and Zheng as an official attempt to channel the righteous sentiment at the heart of these revenge cases into loyalty to its rule. The pardoning process also affected political relations. Specifically, it influenced negotiations between the center and various political players, including civic associations, the judicial sphere, and restive militarists-turned-politicians.

THE 1932–33 CASE OF ZHENG JICHENG

On September 3, 1932, a young man by the name of Zheng Jicheng shot northern militarist Zhang Zongchang to avenge the death of his uncle, Zheng Jinsheng. Zhang, who had earned the nickname "the Dog Meat General" for his culinary preference, had been the military governor of Shandong from 1926 to 1928, during which time he had become the ruler of Zhili as well.[2] His rule had been notoriously corrupt, and his personal reputation was just as infamous. In addition to his well-known love of dog meat, Zhang was also known for his height (six and a half feet) and his harem of concubines from all over the world (they each had a wash basin with their country's flag on it). It was during his tenure as military governor that Zhang had killed Zheng's uncle.[3] Zheng escaped arrest only by taking refuge in Japan and England. He returned to China when the Nationalists successfully concluded the Northern Expedition to unify China in 1928.

In 1932, Zheng Jicheng had the chance to seek his revenge. It was the first time that General Zhang had been in Shandong since the Northern Expedition. After the Nationalist Revolution, the general had first taken refuge in Dairen and then in Japan, where an initial attempt on his life was made. In 1931, under general amnesty regulations passed by the Nationalist regime, Zhang had been able to return to Beiping. It was rumored that he led a life of excess while secretly plotting a comeback. In September 1932, the governor of Shandong, Han Fuju, invited Zhang to visit Shandong province. Zhang went to Jinan, the provincial capital, but his visit was cut short when he received sudden news that his elderly mother had fallen ill. On September 3, 1932, Zhang was thus at the train station waiting for train number 202 back to Beiping. He was accompanied by some twenty of his old friends and colleagues, a large handful of journalists, and several top officials of Shandong province, including Han Fuju's right-hand man, Shi Yousan. It was just short of six in the evening, only seconds after the general had completed his departure speech that Zheng emerged from the large crowd on the platform and opened fire, killing the retired militarist.[4]

The Zhang killing generated a tremendous media sensation. Like Shi Jianqiao, Zheng had a flair for the dramatic. Like daughter Shi, nephew Zheng had been clever enough to kill his victim at a site filled with people so that the assassination would lend itself to spectacle. Whereas Shi had chosen a crowded prayer hall, Zheng chose a commuter-filled train station in Jinan, the capital city of Shandong. He also knew enough to surrender immediately at the scene of the crime, for which he won public support. Media coverage of Zhang's assassination was instant. The press recounted how the two assassins (Zheng was accompanied by a loyal attendant) failed to kill Zhang immediately, describing in colorful detail how Zhang had fled through the train cars to jump off onto the tracks, with the assassins running in close pursuit, and Zhang's bodyguards chasing them. Accounts reported a second hail of bullets, during which Zhang was hit three times before he fell to the ground. He was then rushed to the Shandong provincial hospital, where he finally died.[5]

Like Shi's act, this killing generated sensational coverage. Some accounts were wildly inaccurate. Take, for example, the report of the event provided by Mrs. A. de C. Sowerby, a witness at the crime scene. Appearing as a special to the English-language *North China Herald*, the piece described the assassin's detainment at the crime scene as follows:

> Immediately, the crowd we had just passed scattered in all directions. My companion said: 'Must be a bomb, officials travelling, probably.' Then hell broke loose. . . . Just as I climbed up the steps I saw a nice-looking Chinese, well-dressed in a long gray gown, . . . but the soldiers and police pounced on him with a howl, took a pistol from him and then I saw the most sickening sight I ever beheld. The whole crowd fell on him, tore his clothes off and beat him with the butts of their rifles while maddened coolies tore at his face. It was horrible and I felt myself shrieking to them stop but, of course, we coud'nt [*sic*] do anything.[6]

While gripping and arguably indicative of Western perceptions of the barbarism of crowds and chaos in Chinese society, Mrs. Sowerby's report conveyed very little concrete information of who was involved and what actually occurred. In fact, parts of her report—including the lynching of the "nice-looking Chinese"—were simply not true. An article by the paper's own correspondent directly refuted her histrionic account: "Nor is it true, as a certain foreign newspaper asserts, that an enraged crowd attempted to lynch the murderers."[7] Regardless of its questionable accuracy, what this news story reveals is that there was great public interest in the murder. Given such public attention, it is hardly surprising that the Nationalist regime came to express avid interest in this case, as well as in the Shi affair a few years later.

THE PARDONS

It was not at an obvious choice for the new regime to pardon individual acts of revenge. The Nanjing-based regime was probably not too disappointed to find Sun Chuanfang and Zhang Zongchang dead. Sun and Zhang had both been anti-Nationalists. Both had joined northern warlord Zhang Zuolin in 1928 to establish the Coalition for a Peaceful Nation, a short-lived military alliance that opposed the Northern Expedition through which the Nationalists centralized their control over at least the Eastern seaboard of China.[8] When the two militarists were forced into "retirement" after 1928, neither fully pledged their support to Jiang

Jieshi, and both therefore remained the subjects of constant speculation throughout the early 1930s. Rumors abounded that one or the other was involved in plotting a comeback or colluding with the Japanese to establish an independent North China. Zhang Zongchang's return to China from Japan in 1931, for example, generated endless speculation about his reentry into the political world and, as mentioned in chapter 3, Sun Chuanfang, who had retired to devote himself to Buddhism after 1928, also constantly faced deep skepticism concerning the sincerity of his faith.

Ultimately, however, neither man posed a serious threat to Jiang, whose attention was drawn elsewhere. By the mid-1930s Jiang Jieshi was preoccupied with a host of more pressing political problems. Japan had invaded Manchuria in 1931 and was continuing to encroach ominously into North China. Obsessed with routing the Communists both in urban centers and in the rural hinterland, Jiang Jieshi refused to resist Japanese advancement with any determination. As a result, students took to the streets in protest. Mounting debt, factional infighting, and the challenges of unifying a society after a decade of internecine warfare were other issues that the regime could not afford to ignore. The decision to pardon these two assassins would hardly seem worth the attention and effort.

Finally, sanctioning acts of filial revenge would seem to present to the ruling regime with the classic dilemma between the impulse to mobilize righteous violence and the need to contain the potential disorder brought on by such violent behavior. Official sanction of virtuous revenge was nothing new in Chinese history. While specifics varied from dynasty to dynasty, the imperial state had a long tradition of viewing particular forms of violence not as transgressions of law but as extreme yet exemplary expressions of Confucian virtue. Since as early as the Han, for example, filial revenge and chaste suicides by women were not merely condoned but systematically celebrated as ideal forms of behavior (Lewis 1990; Elvin 1984). The motives of filial piety behind righteous revenge and chastity behind female suicide served as powerful metaphors for the political loyalty that crucially cemented the hierarchical relations of the Confucian sociopolitical order. The spectacularly violent quality of these acts further indicated the depth of such charged ethical ideals.

Yet, even while seeking to mobilize these violent displays of virtuous sentiment, imperial regimes also had to struggle with the less desirable implications of sanctioning brutality. Officials of the Han dynasty, for example, struggled to reconcile the Confucian demand for righteous requital with the Legalist understanding that under state law virtuous assassination was still an act of murder (Lewis 1990; Cheng 2004, 34–36). Such official ambivalence persisted into the Qing dynasty. As mentioned in chapter 4, when the Qing imperial state sought to tap into the symbolic potency of filial revenge, it feared that official endorsement of retribution might encourage violence and disorder. To reconcile these two impulses, the Qing legal code explicitly stipulated that only acts of filial revenge committed *immediately* after learning of the injustice done to one's parent deserved judicial lenience.[9] In chaste suicide cases as well, the Qing state during the Yongzheng reign raised the standards for chastity in cases of virtuous suicide in an effort to dissuade random acts of self-inflicted violence (Theiss 2001).

Like the Han officials who centuries earlier had been confounded by this classic dilemma, authorities of the Nanjing-based regime needed to proceed with caution when confronted with the cases of Zheng Jicheng and Shi Jianqiao. On the one hand, the assassins' heroic filial piety was no doubt attractive to a state that was engaged in promoting Confucian values for its New Life campaign, a movement initiated in 1934 by Jiang Jieshi to bolster national strength with an emphasis on a spiritual-ethical revival and the militaristic disciplining of society. On the other hand, the Nationalist state could hardly afford to encourage vigilante behavior. Faced with the momentous task of rebuilding authoritative government and societal institutions, including an effective judicial system, an endorsement of extralegal actions, no matter how virtuous, would certainly appear to compromise its fledgling courts and newly reformed law codes.

Given this context, the granting of these two pardons suggests that Nationalist authorities recognized the contradiction between the moral benefits of filial revenge and the need to uphold state law and sought to use the pardons to resolve the tensions. Evidence appears in the texts of the pardons themselves. Zheng Jicheng was pardoned in 1933 and Shi Jianqiao in 1936. Zheng's pardon reads as follows:

> According to the Judicial Yuan:[10] because Zhang Zongchang had murdered his [uncle] Zheng Jinsheng, Zheng Jicheng grabbed the opportunity to assassinate Zhang at a train station; after the incident, he turned himself into the authorities without resisting and allowed himself to be arrested; it was because he was avenging the murder of his [uncle] that he violated criminal law. Such extraordinary circumstances can be pardoned. At present, on the basis of appeals issued one after another by Party organizations of each county, city and province, and myriad citizens' groups, we should not execute the original sentences for said perpetrator and pardon him according to law. We should grant the approval [for an exemption]. By relying, in

> particular, on regulation number 6 of the Revised Rules of Organization for the Government of the Republic of China, we announce that Zheng Jicheng is granted a pardon and exempted from serving his original sentence of imprisonment for seven years. We thereby demonstrate sympathy. This is the order.[11]

Issued three years later, the pardon of Shi Jianqiao was nearly identical:

> According to the Judicial Yuan: because her father Shi Congbin had in the past been cruelly murdered by Sun Chuanfang, Shi Jianqiao, long pained with the desire to avenge her father, grabbed the opportunity to assassinate [Sun], and then, calmly declared [her revenge] and waited for the full force of the penalty of law. As for her murderous behavior, it constitutes a violation of criminal law. But if we consider that she was a lone woman acting upon filial thinking and with little regard for her own personal safety, then her intent merits commiseration and the extraordinary circumstances [of the crime] are forgivable. At present, on the basis of the various appeals for a pardon that schools and citizens' groups have issued one after another, we should not execute the original sentence for said Shi Jianqiao and pardon her according to law. Now, according to regulation number 68 of the Provisional Constitution of the Republic of China's Tutelage Period, we announce that we grant a special exemption for Shi Jianqiao's original sentence of imprisonment for seven years, and thereby, demonstrate sympathy. This is the order.[12]

Establishing the exact motivation behind the Nationalist pardons in these two cases is difficult. We do not have access to documents revealing behind-the-scenes decisions in drafting the pardons, and the official pronouncements themselves are frustratingly brief. Furthermore, both are strikingly similar in their language, format, and the type of information they convey. Yet, though brief, the two statements, if read carefully, actually speak volumes. In fact, it is precisely in the seemingly formulaic nature of the texts that we can see the regime invoking both the legal code and the authority of virtuous sentiment to justify the recourse to executive power, thereby papering over any apparent conflict between the letter of the law and ethical sentiment. In other words, executive pardoning—issued only after the due process of law had run its course—became the means to reconcile the classic dilemma discussed above.

To mobilize the authority of codified law, the pardon texts underscored the legal foundations of the regime's right to issue clemency. Both pardon announcements cited the specific legal or constitutional code upon which the pardon was based. The earlier text cited regulation 6 of the Revised Rules of Organization for the Government of the Republic of China, whereas the 1936 pardon used regulation 68 of the Provisional

Constitution of Republic of China's Tutelage Period. Given that the latter code was based on the earlier one, the regulations shared the same wording: "The Nationalist Government has the power to grant amnesties, pardons and commute sentences."[13] With Lin Sen, the Chairman of the National Government, and Ju Zheng, the head of the Judicial Yuan, signing both pardons, the executive arm and the judicial arm presented a unified front.[14]

Appeals were also made to forms of authority outside of written code. First, the pardons explicitly stated that the motive of filial piety, long celebrated as ethically and political valuable, constituted an extraordinary circumstance meriting exemption. The texts also took pains to note that both assassins had surrendered to the authorities. This helped to portray the filial devotion of the assassins as being genuine, leading them to carry out their revenge even in the face of stiff legal penalties. Second, in noting explicitly that various types of public organizations had "one after another" appealed for official mercy, the two texts appealed to the authority of public sentiment. While the use of filial piety as a justification for sanctioning violence found precedent in the imperial period, this appeal to public sympathy was new. State sanction could thus pay respect to the legal code and judicial process even while attending to the widely popular ethical appeal of righteous revenge.

ORTHODOX HEROES, FILIAL VENGEANCE, AND NEW LIFE NATIONAL ESSENCE

The Nationalist regime was not alone in making an argument for state-sanctioned violence. Civic groups, schools, and other organizations also outlined how official endorsement of filial revenge would prove politically expedient for the New Life regime. With the express purpose of lobbying for official action, these groups issued telegrams to the center requesting clemency for the assassins. To mobilize public support for their actions, they also had the telegrams printed in a range of urban dailies. While the state used the pardons to assert both the legal and ethical foundations of its right to sanction violence, these telegrams focused less on the legal basis of an executive pardon and more on the ethical and political argument for state endorsement. With China facing both the external threat of imminent war with Japan and the internal problem of domestic unrest, these requests built a convincing case that heroic ethical subjectivity could serve as the basis of national subjectivity. They portrayed the two assassins not as heterodox bearers of antistate justice but as proper heroes whose ethical motives had the sympathy of the public and represented a form of national authenticity befitting the New Life nation.

Nationalist discourses frequently feature a unique tension between the need to represent the nation as constantly developing and marching forward through time to its ultimate historical telos of self-realization and the need to anchor this constantly evolving entity in an unchanging permanence and essence. Partha Chatterjee (1993) discusses the tendency among colonized nations to portray the nation-state as both "modern" in its territorial sovereignty and political self-definition and "traditional" in its essential character. Focusing on India, Chatterjee describes how male nationalists rendered the authentic, pure Indian woman as a quintessential symbol of national essence. Embodying the inner, spiritual domain of the Indian nation that was separate from, and thus unadulterated by, the presence of colonialists, the "pure" Indian woman served this purpose well. Inspired by such theorists, scholars of China have started to investigate the relationship between Chinese nationalism and gender, arguing that Chinese ideologues similarly located the tension between modern national progress and unchanging permanence in the female body (e.g., Duara 1998). While they did not sanctify the home and domesticity as nationalists did in India, they did endorse Chinese women who redirected the female virtue of self-sacrifice into public service for the nation.

Although historians of China have focused on the symbolic value of the female body in articulating the national body, few have considered how certain forms of violence might have served the same purpose. To be sure, the general symbolism of violence in nationalist discourse has become a subject of scholastic inquiry. Henrietta Harrison (1998), for example, examines the complex cultural politics behind the valorization of violence committed for the *founding* of the nation. The ongoing commemoration of the Revolution of 1911 and its revolutionary martyrs and heroic generals in both the People's Republic of China and Taiwan provide plenty of examples of how violence is commemorated as a marker of the founding of the Chinese nation. The question of violence as a form of national essence, however, has not been seriously broached. Here, I redress this lack by demonstrating how these telegrams identified filial vengeance as a sign of eternal Chinese authenticity that diverged from the commemoration of revolutionary violence. Symptomatic of a wider concern for national consolidation rather than revolutionary overthrow, state-sanctioned revenge in the Shi and Zheng cases came to symbolize *both* timelessness and modernity. The ethically charged bodies of the two assassins further delivered a message that could metaphorically conform to an image of China as a strong, martial, and modern nation-state. The filial motivation of the two perpetrators came to be seen as representing uniquely Chinese qualities endowed with national significance.

Arguments for recognizing filial revenge as a form of Chinese authenticity could easily have drawn on a broader discourse on "national essence," or *guocui* in modern Chinese. This term came into currency during the late Qing, when the *Guexue baocun hui* (Society for the protection of national learning) and its journal, *Guocui xuebao* (Journal of national essence), were founded in 1905 by scholars and activists such as Zhang Zhidong. Editors of the journal declared that "a civilization has a vulnerable physical aspect (the *kuo*, nation) and a potentially enduring spiritual aspect (*ts'ui*, essence) which is capable of resuscitating the civilization after it has become moribund or physically destroyed" (Schneider 1971, 35). In the 1920s, members of the *Xueheng pai*, or Critical Review Group, a literary and cultural movement that revolved around the journal by the same name, *Xueheng* (Critical review), published between 1922 and 1933, continued to evoke the notion of national essence, though the term's meaning underwent drastic transformation.[15] For actors in the 1930s who were trying to establish a sense of cultural continuity in a China that was perceived as being in danger of losing its roots, *national essence* was a rich term: it could refer to spiritual elements with an enduring, if not universal, quality that could help to constitute the modern nation and guarantee national strength.

In this context, Jiang Jieshi's promotion of Confucian values, such as filial piety, was arguably an attempt at delineating China's national essence. In a secret speech given in the spring of 1932 to the paramilitary organization known as the Blue Shirts, Jiang stated, "Our organization [Blue Shirts] should take the responsibility for this fundamental cure—revival of our national spirit. . . . *Zhong* [loyalty], *xiaoshun* [filial piety,] *dexing* [virtue], *ai* [love], *he* [harmony] and *ping* [peace] should be our central guiding principles for the achievement of *li* [propriety], *yi* [righteousness], *lian* [purity] and *chi* [sense of shame]—which comprise the national spirit of China."[16] Jiang's 1934 New Life campaign more fully articulated this form of nativist nationalism. The movement was not meant to be a return to the past or a *restoration*, a term that has long implied a literal going back to the institutions of the once-revered Chinese antiquity. Instead, it was a revival, renaissance, or national rebirth that was to be achieved through the reconstruction or rejuvenation not of the old society but of its underlying, eternal virtues (Dirlik 1975). Filial piety was to play a central role in this national rebirth. An article published in the Nationalist propaganda organ *Zhongshan jiaoyu guan jikan* (Journal of the Sun Yat-sen Educational Institution) argued that since Sun Yat-sen had located national strength in China's essential, ethical familial system, the eternal virtue of filial piety was the most basic element of the moral foundation of a strong, forward-moving Chinese nation (Yang 1936).

The filial motivation of the two perpetrators thus came to be seen as representing essential Chinese qualities, as was evident in many of the telegrams sent to Nanjing appealing for the release of Shi Jianqiao and Zheng Jicheng. These telegrams linked the passionate actions of the assassins to the greater good of China, praised them for killing Chinese traitors, portrayed their personal vendettas as national ones, and appreciated their filial piety and heroism as an expression of national virtue. Support for Shi was particularly broad, coming from all types of organizations in several provinces. Telegram after telegram clamored for her release, praised her bravery, and showed wondrous amazement at the ability of a young woman to kill single-handedly a national menace like Sun. Organizations from Anhui, Shi's home province, and women's groups were among the most aggressive in their lobbying. The Anhui Alumni association was duly impressed with its native daughter, stating in its wire that even "as a fragile girl, Jianqiao was able to expel a traitor from the country as well as seek revenge for her father."[17] The Women's Association of Nanjing accused Sun Chuanfang of betraying the party and the nation, putting the lives of ordinary citizens in danger as a "true criminal of the Revolution." It then admired how "Shi Jianqiao, a mere wisp of a woman, had not settled for existing in the same world as her great enemy and thus sought revenge." The appeal linked her individual action to its implications for the national collective, concluding that she was not merely avenging an individual grievance but seeking "revenge for millions of comrades."[18] The Donghai Woman's Organization echoed the Nanjing group, issuing a detailed appeal that framed Shi Jianqiao's revenge for her father as a revenge for the nation (*wei guo chuhai*).[19]

Public support for Zheng three years earlier had been similarly vocal and had also consistently expressed appreciation for the larger implications of Zheng's personal vendetta.[20] One contributor to the "Unfettered Talk" column of the *Shenbao* remarked that because warlord Zhang

Zongchang had been so rapacious and had so fundamentally betrayed the country, the Chinese people were thrilled with the news of his death.[21] Another Shandong editorialist, recalling in detail Zhang Zongchang's cruelty, noted how all circles praised Zheng for his bravery and for seeking revenge on behalf of the entire province.[22] Zheng himself wrote, "I took the risk to assassinate [Zhang] first to bring glory to the Party-state, second to bring honor to the revolution, third to expel evil from Shandong, and fourth, to avenge my adopted father's wrongful death."[23] By underscoring the significance of his revenge for the party-state, Zheng was clearly appealing to the central regime.

Several telegrams demanded that Nanjing pay tribute to the filial devotion of the perpetrators as something uniquely Chinese. Insisting that the antiquity of filial piety attested to its national authenticity, the Anhui Fengyang Normal School's telegram, for example, reasoned that since Confucius's *Spring and Autumn Annals* specifically praised those seeking virtuous revenge, the central government should do the same.[24] The Anhui alumni association was even more explicit: "Our country has taken the spirit of loyalty and filial piety as the foundation of the country for several thousands of years; [thus, today's government should] preserve the righteousness of the national people and show leniency [for Shi Jianqiao] in the judicial arena. With a lenient sentence, one can both follow the public-minded Way and satisfy public sentiment."[25] According to this telegram, filial piety was hardly antiquated but was an enduring and thus relevant national virtue. Filial piety was part of the national essence because it proved itself constant through time, an unchanged and eternal part of the foundational spirit of the Chinese people throughout the ages.

Some of these telegrams directly established a connection between a pardon for filial vengeance and the New Life movement. The telegram from the Military Academy of Hubei condoned filial revenge in cases when one's father had been killed illegitimately. It first quoted a passage from the *Gongyang Commentary*, the *locus classicus* of the moral authority of righteous revenge.[26] It then proceeded to declare, "At this time of establishing a New Life Nation, it is particularly fitting [for the government] to laud and praise [Shi Jianqiao] along with promoting old virtues, in order to provide for constitutional rule." The point was clear. With Jiang Jieshi currently engaged in promoting New Life national virtue and modern constitutional rule, the Nanjing government should abide by propriety (*li*) and show compassion for the assassin, just as the ancients would have done centuries ago. Virtue was being promoted as the proper basis for constitutional rule.

The assassins' motive of filial piety was not the only significant aspect of virtuous revenge. The violent form that the ethical ideal assumed was also important, and the act of assassination itself could easily have been considered part of the Chinese "national essence," endowed with both eternal tradition and modern value. The "eternal" characteristic of assassination was based on the long-standing appreciation of virtuous violence throughout Chinese history. Since as early as Sima Qian's *Shi ji* (Record of the grand historian), the lone assassin, or *cike*, was celebrated for his martial vigor, bravery, and unrivaled sense of justice. Often acting with no regard for personal interest or safety, such an assassin was a martyr *par excellence*, and his revenge killing an ultimate expression of virtue and self-sacrifice. Far from being a transgression, his violence demonstrated how far he was willing to go for the sake of virtue and principle.

It was easy to see Zheng and Shi as the most recent examples of this long line of self-sacrificing assassins, Zheng and Shi updated the martial courage and upright sense of propriety of the lone-assassin archetype, linking its classic virtues to national heroism and modern-day patriotism. For example, the pardon of Shi and several supportive telegrams explicitly presented Shi Jianqiao as "a frail young woman" who could through sheer will transform herself into a powerful avenger and slay a ruthless warlord. Such a characterization echoed the heroic virtue of female knights-errant of the imperial past, memorialized in innumerable stories and tales. Yet, at the same time, Shi's embodiment of this heroic if not redemptive virtue made her a perfect symbol for the modern Confucian nation, which, despite its current problems, similarly hoped to transform itself into a powerful entity. One opinion piece summed up the updated patriotic implication of Shi's act, stating that with "great bravery and tremendous filial piety, [Shi] expelled a traitor on behalf of the country. . . . When our brothers and sisters heard the news, they arose, and in a unified voice, appealed for a pardon" (Zhang 1935).

If the classical tradition of ethical revenge imbued these twentieth-century acts of violence with meaning, so too did an entirely modern discourse on assassination. Assassination was not merely an antiquated relic of the past but had become a powerful, if ambiguous, symbol of the new. The modernity of this mode of violence was first firmly established in the anarchist discourse of the late Qing, which presented it as a progressive and vigorous way to engage in modern politics. Late Qing essayists and revolutionaries from Liang Qichao to Wang Jingwei harbored a deep distrust of mass action and drew instead from the ideals of nihilism and anarchism of the Russian populist movements.[27] Accordingly, they promoted assassination as a quintessentially modern technique of anti-Qing revolution. They organized assassination corps and engaged in both successful and aborted individual attempts. The modernity of assassination was given material form in the fetishization of the technology of explosives and bomb making (Krebs 1981). During the late Qing, assassins were no longer wielding swords or daggers like the classic *xiake*, but throwing bombs instead.

By the Nanjing decade, assassination was still perceived to be a contemporary form of violence, though key differences existed from the late Qing. The technology associated with assassination was no longer the bomb but the Browning pistol, the weapon of choice for both Shi Jianqiao and Zheng Jicheng. Whereas modern assassination was explicitly directed against the Manchu state in the late Qing, by the Republican period the act was, in fact, often symbolic of just the reverse. No longer antistate in meaning, political assassination came to be associated with the regime itself. As scholars have long noted, Jiang Jieshi consciously modeled the Nationalist regime after strong, fascist regimes in Europe, many of which celebrated militarism explicitly and state terror implicitly (e.g., Van de Ven 1997). Like its European counterparts, the Chinese regime sought to generate an atmosphere of terror and put state control and violence on display as a spectacular sign of its power. It did not hesitate to allow its own Special Forces to assassinate political enemies it believed were obstructing strong national rule.

Needless to say, the central government's use of political killings drew fire from critics.[28] Political assassination was strongly associated with both the political chaos and warlord strife of the 1920s and the state-sanctioned right-wing terror in the 1930s. Several critics were bold enough to criticize the regime's support of such brutality. In the *Duli pinglun*, a liberal, reformist weekly founded by Hu Shi, Jiang Yanfu charged that the regime's reliance upon assassination was a sign of its weakness (Jiang 1933). In a Shandong newspaper, Zhao Nan similarly identified the successful assassination of former vice minister of Foreign Affairs Tang Youren and the attempted assassin of Wang Jingwei as signs of chaos and disarray among Nationalist factions. According to Zhao, it was clear that Tang and Wang were targeted because of their pro-Japanese sympathies, even if confusion swirled around who engineered the assassinations. Reporting rumors that Dai Li, the head of the state's Special Forces, had carried out the assassination attempts on behalf of Jiang himself, the writer concluded that the suspicious lack of information on the two cases was symptomatic of the obfuscation that enveloped party politics in general.[29]

Some writers made an effort to distinguish virtuous assassination from political assassination. Shandong writer Zhao Nan contrasted the two cases of Tang Youren and Wang Jingwei with the assassinations of Zhang Zongchang and Sun Chuanfang. Whereas Tang and Wang were the victims of politically motivated murders, he claimed, the killings of Zhang and Sun were straightforward honorable cases of impassioned revenge. Zhao's sharp distinction between suspicious political execution and sincere vengeance belied, however, a growing sense of ambiguity regarding even so-called "virtuous assassination." Wang Shubi, for one, argued that revenge was an ancient tradition of heroism and martial vigor that continued to thrive in modern China with ambiguous results (Wang Shubi 1935). The author of "Assassination," published in the critical journal, *Dushu shenghuo*, traces the history of Chinese assassination from Jing Ke, the famous assassin who was thwarted in his attempt to kill the king of Qin, to the late Qing Revolutionary assassinations, including Wang Jingwei's attempted killing of She Zhengwang, which were inspired by the Nihilist Party assassinations aimed at the Czar of Russia. Yet, despite this legacy, this author ultimately voiced reservations about assassination in the modern era, mentioning Shi Jianqiao's case in particular. He argued that while Shi's purported motive of filial piety was elevated and noble, the assassination was hardly straightforward, and the politics behind it were far more complicated than they appeared.[30]

Ambivalence toward assassination notwithstanding, the interpretation of these two revenge killings as expressions of national essence was most likely highly compelling to the Nationalist regime. In part, avenging assassins as national heroes provided a powerful counternarrative to popular interpretations of the two as antistate, *xiake* rogue heroes. Zheng and Shi were not merely heroes avenging the wrongs of the nation, but had also won public support as *xiake*, gallant outlaw assassins, an interpretation that evoked the age-old tradition of renegade outlaw-heroes and heroic highwaymen who uphold justice when the state fails. As discussed in chapter 2, Shi Jianqiao was celebrated as a *xianü* who could accomplish in a few gunshots the kind of national justice that continued to elude the central state. Observers of the Zheng case also implicitly acknowledged the antistate implications of celebrating assassin Zheng as a *xia* hero. One article, for example, compares Zheng Jicheng to Zheng Huchen, a Southern Song assassin and a reputed *xiake* who was remembered for his success in banishing a notorious traitor to foreign lands, an accomplishment that gained significance in a period when the Song state was failing to drive out northern barbarians.[31]

Pardons identifying the assassins as national heroes would thus provide the Nationalist government with the perfect opportunity to attempt to control the spin of affairs, and contain less flattering interpretations. The two acts of revenge had the potential to serve as appealing metaphors for Nanjng's political role. As one commentator noted, Sun Chuanfang's cruel decision to impale Shi Jianqiao's father's head on a spike after an unjust death was a sign of the moral and political chaos of the 1920s.[32] By extension, Shi Jianqiao's revenge had dramatically returned things to order, just as Nationalist Revolution and rule were to lead China back to national order. Similarly, whereas Zhang Zongchang's rapacious rule represented the barbarity of warlordism in the earlier decade, Zheng Jicheng's retribution signaled a return to normalcy in the Nanjing Decade. In short, in a period when the Nationalist regime was desperately seeking to redefine the Chinese nation, all components of these two cases of righteous revenge—the filial piety, the reciprocity of relations (*bao*), and the extremity of virtue expressed through violent revenge (*chou*)—proved attractive. Both acts of revenge became sites of authenticity that confirmed the regime's self-image as a strong, martial, and modern nation-state. Both also became means for the state to harness the assassins' filial passion as well as the public sympathy they elicited for purposes of New Life nationalism. Bold avengers righting wrongs were representative of what the Nationalist regime could do for China.

ASSOCIATIONAL POWER, JUDICIAL AUTONOMY, AND PARTY DOCTRINE

Although the decision to sanction these acts of violence turned crucially on the symbolic weight of filial revenge, we should note that the pardons were at the same time concrete expressions of the *realpolitik* that characterized the political culture of the era. The pardoning of Shi Jianqiao and Zheng Jicheng allows us to see how actual state and society relationships were being negotiated in the 1930s. Specifically, the regime used the pardoning process to mobilize the authority of public sympathy in order to legitimate its attempts to exert its control over society and the judiciary, and to negotiate its relations with savvy regional players and retired militarists. The attempt to use the pardons in such a manner was ultimately fraught with ambiguity. Even as the pardoning process proved to be an opportunity for Nationalist authorities to consolidate their control over alternative pockets of social and political power, it simultaneously revealed the limits of the regime's ability to consolidate the full control it sought.

Party Doctrine versus the Letter of the Law

The pardons proved to be an opportunity for the central regime to negotiate its relations with its own judicial branch. By the 1930s, fierce debates were raging over how to define principles of justice suitable for a modern society. Legal reformers advocated the letter of law as the foundation of a modern society. Yet, as these two revenge cases show, popular sentiment passionately endorsed the ethical justice of filial revenge, posing a challenge to the code's interpretation that acts of homicide deserve punishment. The regime manipulated this tension between codified law and popular sentiment in its attempt to justify its expansion of power into the judicial arena. Upon rising to national power in 1928, the new Nationalist regime exhibited considerable anxiety about growing judicial autonomy and moved quickly to contain, or "party-fy" (*danghua*) the judicial sphere.[33] This "party-fication" included the ongoing efforts by the executive branch to secure its authority over the judicial branch of the government and its reformist elements. It also included attempts to increase state control over the new arena of professional groups of lawyers and justices, which had established a fragile semblance of judicial autonomy during the earlier decades. By providing the regime with the opportunity to claim that it could resolve the contradiction between law and popular sentiment, the pardons became yet another way for the regime to pursue its larger agenda of "party-fying" the judiciary.

The power to pardon was first established as part of Republican governance in 1912. The Provisional Constitution of that year gave China's president the power to grant pardons, amnesties, and other forms of exemption. Article 68 of the Provisional Constitution of June 1, 1931, gave the Nationalist regime with similar powers. While the article itself was very succinct and merely stated the regime's right to grant amnesties and pardons, a more elaborate explanation of how to interpret the article was provided in the *Zhonghua Minguo xunzheng shiqi yuefa xiangjie* (Detailed explanation of the provisional constitution of the Republic of China's tutelage period), a text that was published in Shanghai by the Law and Political Studies Press (Zhu Fang 1936). According to this text, the pardon (*teshe*) differed from amnesty (*dashe*) in that it was granted to an individual perpetrator rather than a group.[34] It was intended not to absolve the crime but merely to grant the perpetrator a reprieve from judicial penalty. The text further explains that the pardon was required by law to be granted only after the completion of the full adjudication process and was thus a means to supplement legal code. Procedurally, the Judicial Yuan worked with the executive branch in granting pardons. The head of the Judicial Yuan would first propose a pardon, and the executive branch would have the final authority to administer it.

The view that the pardon was a legitimate tool that the Executive Yuan could use to redress the limitations of the judiciary system was promulgated more widely in the 1935 Shanghai Commercial Press publication *Zhongguo dashe kao* (A reflection on the Chinese amnesty [Xu 1935]). In promoting the pardon, this text sought to identify its Chinese origins. To demonstrate that China had a long tradition of endowing leaders with the powers of exemption, much of the slim volume was dedicated to listing classical sanction and historical precedents for granting amnesties, pardons, and exemptions. In the section titled "Origins," the booklet explained that, throughout Chinese history, law had generally been perceived as limited in its ability to address all human situations; thus, pardons, amnesties, and exemptions were mechanisms that allowed the executive branch to compensate for or amend the judicial process when necessary. In the words of the text, "Since the Warring States Period, China has had leaders avail themselves of the powers of exemption if and when criminal administration loses its 'suitability'" (Xu 1935, 2).[35] Despite this publication's attempt to locate the origins of the modern pardon in Chinese history, a modern government's right to pardon was, of course, hardly specific to Republican China. The entry on pardons in the work mentioned above, *Zhonghua Minguo xunzheng shiqi yuefa xiangjie* (Zhu 1936), notes explicitly that in all modern countries including those in Europe, America, and Japan, the pardon fell under the purview of the chief of state or president (*yuanshou*).

To be sure, the right to pardon was something shared by many modern governments at the time. What was unique to these Republican-era pardons, however, was that they were inextricably bound up with the Nationalist agenda of extending the authority of the party above the law. Executive intervention after the courts had issued their final verdicts sent an unambiguous message that the judicial system could not account fully for the extraordinary nature of the circumstances behind the crimes. Yet, for some Nationalist authorities, the pardon mechanism, recognized explicitly in the Provisional Constitution as an executive privilege that did not overturn guilt but merely granted a reprieve, was not enough to ensure true justice. The two pardons became an excuse for some to weigh in on the larger reassessments taking place regarding the relationship between law and sentiment and between the Nationalist Party and the judiciary, as well as regarding the place of party doctrine, or *dangyi*, in achieving justice.

Take, for example, an erudite and spirited defense for the imposition of party doctrine on the judiciary (*sifa danghua*), that appeared in *Dongfang zazhi* (Eastern miscellany) and *Zhonghua faxue* (Chinese legal studies) in May 1935. The article was written by Ju Zheng, the Nationalist-appointed head of the Judicial Yuan, and uses the Zheng Jicheng case to argue that party doctrine was uniquely able to accommodate both the letter of the law and popular sentiment.[36] The Zheng case, wrote Ju, was particularly illuminating because it exposed a glaring tension between people's justice (*renmin zhengyi*) and the law of the land, namely, the Criminal Code of the Three People's Principles. On the one hand, the public had believed that the assassination was an ultimate expression of public justice and not a crime at all, since Zheng's filial motive was virtuous and Zhang Zhongcang a rapacious traitor. Yet, on the other hand, according to the Republican-era legal code, revenge was an act of premeditated murder. Moreover, Ju suggested that the executive pardon, which was merely the exemption of punishment and not a fundamental reversal of the guilty verdict, failed to adequately address the people's sense of justice. Party doctrine, contended Ju, was the only way to bridge this fundamental conflict between the authority of collective sentiment and legal stipulation and therefore had to be the final authority in this case. Party doctrine, he further explained, was committed to upholding national liberty (*guojia ziyou*), the founding principle of the Nationalist Revolution. This principle rested less on the need to defend individual liberties, the concern of the modern legal code and, instead, more on the need to promote the collective freedom of the Republic. In this light, he reasoned, since Zhang Zongchang's past history violated the rights of the group, his individual rights of protection under the law were no longer worth upholding. Zheng Jicheng's killing of a traitorous warlord, which had helped promote National liberty at large, deserved to be recognized as the higher principle of liberty and should not be prosecuted according to codified law.

This view that party doctrine was best able to bring about justice was echoed in a response to the Shi Jianqiao case. In the November 1935 edition of the Nanjing publication *Minsheng*, published just after the Sun assassination, author Wan Sheng revisited the earlier commentary by Ju

Zheng and cited verbatim Ju's rationalization of *dangyi* (Wan 1935). While I have not been able to identify who Wan Sheng was, his decision to publish in the journal *Minsheng*, which was known for disseminating the policies and views of the Nationalists, makes it clear that he was promoting views that accorded with the Nationalist regime.[37] In addressing the controversy surrounding the Shi Jianqiao case, Wan Sheng reminded readers that the Nationalist head of the Judicial Yuan had already argued for *dangyi* in the earlier Zheng Jicheng case. The implication was clear. In the Shi Jianqiao case as well, party doctrine would be the final arbiter and allow the Nationalist regime to rise above both codified law and constitutional definitions of the executive pardon to reverse the verdict of guilt. While there is no evidence that there was any actual movement to do this in either of these cases, the affairs nonetheless served as a forum for Nationalist authorities and other writers to promote party doctrine as the primary means of bridging the gap between public sentiment and the code of law, guaranteeing the collective interests of the nation, and ensuring that justice was truly served.

The Normative Power of Civic Associations

In addition to shedding light on party-judiciary relations, these pardons are also significant in that they reveal a growing recognition of the normative authority of civic associations and how that authority was wielded in negotiations of power. It is notable, for example, that in these pardons the Nationalist government located public support in approved societal groups. The pardon of Shi Jianqiao explicitly mentions that "schools and citizens groups" lobbied for the release of the assassin. Zheng's pardon as well noted how "myriad citizens' groups have issued [appeals] one after another." These phrases suggest the Nationalists' larger vision of society, which saw society's constituency not as the masses (*dazhong*) but as groups and associations (*tuanti*). Yet, even while the language used in these pardons served to legitimate a vision of society that the Nationalists were comfortable with, there were risks and unintended consequences involved in such a rhetorical maneuver. The civic associations themselves could gain from it a sense of institutional legitimacy. Other players, including regional militarists, who were not entirely aligned with the regime's agenda, could also mobilize the "authority" of associational power to pursue their own, possibly separate, interests.

The Nationalists had long been concerned about the rise of autonomous associational power. With the central government lacking clarity and coherence starting in the late Qing, civic groups and associations were acquiring considerable power and autonomy, and developing complicated relationships with central or centralizing powers (e.g., see Strand 1989; Xu 2001). Native-place associations, labor organizations, and other civic groups often found that, even as their autonomy increased, their interests and attempts to build the nation-state often coincided with or reinforced the agenda of centralizing powers (Goodman 1995; Tsin 1999). Yet, despite frequently overlapping agendas, the Nationalist Party was nonetheless displeased with the growing autonomy and power of these associations, starting as early as the 1920s (Tsin 1999). During Nationalist rule of Canton, Sun Yat-sen initiated methods that enabled the party to both mobilize and discipline the authority of these groups. By establishing a propaganda apparatus, forging links with school groups, women's organizations, and merchants' groups, and justifying such moves with his theories on corporatist politics and party rule, Sun sought to ensure Nationalist encroachment into society.[38]

By 1928, the new national regime intensified its desire to bring autonomous civic groups more securely into the Nanjing fold. Jiang Jieshi quickly moved to consolidate what had once been a fairly autonomous Nationalist Party into a state apparatus in order to create a much more corporatist party-state regime than had ever existed before. With the party under his control, he then sought aggressively to "party-fy" (*danghua*) urban society by expanding the regime's reach over merchant associations, civic groups, professional organizations, and societal circles.[39] Drawing from Sun Yat-sen's Three People's Principles and theory of three-stage revolution, Jiang argued that internal consolidation within the regime and the establishment of a corporatist party-state was the equivalent of moving from the military government stage, the first stage of the Nationalist Revolution, to the second stage of tutelage government, a period when the Nationalists would exercise state power on behalf of the people, and its party would rule the country (*yidang zhiguo*). To secure control over professional societies, the new regime required all groups to register and subjected them to a barrage of new regulations and mechanisms of control.

Scholars have recently demonstrated that in seeking to mobilize as well as regulate society, the Nanjing-based regime often generated what was perhaps the unintended consequence of conferring power and legitimacy on the very groups and "society" that it was seeking to rein in. In his discussion of Nanjing's attempt to police urban associations, Xu Xiaoqun has shown how the legal statutes and administrative regulation used to assert control at the same time reinforced the institutional boundaries of these groups. As he puts it, "Engaging in a corporatist social engineering, Nanjing sought to organize society into functional groups supervised by the party-state. Yet, the regulations and statutes enacted by the GMD to control urban associations also lent the associations legitimacy at the same time" (Xu 2001, 80). In an article on the use of petitions during the Nanjing decade, Rebecca Nedostup and Liang Hongming have similarly argued that petitions became opportunities for civic groups and even individual citizens to "turn [Nationalist propaganda] against its own authors" (2001, 207). Petition writers, they show, heeded the government's call to participate in the construction of the Republic by using petitions to seek redress when they believed it was not fulfilling its obligations. The act of petitioning was moreover meant to instill the idea of a tutelary government that rested on "a precarious balance of democracy and paternalism" (185). But it often became a means for petition authors to point out that tutelage carried both power and obligation beyond what was intended by the regime.

The pardons of Shi Jianqiao and Zheng Jicheng risked having a similar effect of conferring more power than was intended on the public groups being mobilized. By explicitly pointing out that many public organizations had demanded official grace, the pardons sought to weave a semblance of unity between the central government and the nation's far-flung civic groups. In doing so, the pardons intended to promote the Nationalist vision of society, namely, one that was divided into manageable and regulated groups. The pardons furthermore voiced the regime's claim that it was granting clemency *on behalf of* public sentiment. Such a rhetorical gesture allowed the government to present itself as representative of, and therefore in control of, the organizations from which it sought to draw its authority.

Yet, for civic associations that had issued telegrams, the pardoning process was an opportunity to assert their institutional *raison d'être* beyond that ascribed by the regime. Public organizations and civic groups flooded local, provincial, and national governmental and party organizations as well as different forms of media with wired requests for official grace. Telegrams were sent in from all different provinces, levels (local, city, county, provincial, and national), as well as from different types of associations (from women's associations and student alumni organizations to labor unions, agricultural groups, merchant societies, and even military establishments). In Henan province alone, organizations that backed Shi Jianqiao included Kaifeng's Central Labor Organization, the

County's Agricultural Association, its Merchant Association, Woman's Association, the United Merchant Organization, and the Provincial Organization of Women. Each of these organizations had sent a petition for a reprieve not merely to the central government, but also to the city governments of other provinces as well as to other groups, with the intent of encouraging them to support the young assassin.[40] By pleading for clemency, they made their institutional and political presence known and, not surprisingly, the media was quick to acknowledge the power of these groups. In the Shi case, the Shanghai *Shibao*, for example, explicitly credited the appeals from these groups, along with internal lobbying by elder statesmen of the regime, with prompting the government to act.[41]

To be sure, it is possible that not all of these appeals were put forth spontaneously. As I discuss in the next section, militarists such as Han Fuju and Feng Yuxiang mobilized groups to petition the government for pardons in these two cases. While this suggests that many of these telegrams were solicited from above, it does not refute the possibility that as public documents these telegrams still conferred institutional legitimacy on the public groups issuing them. In point of fact, mobilization from above speaks to the growing normative clout of civic associations. The central government, in seeking to justify its decision to sanction violence, sought to mobilize associational authority, and militarists wanting to use the pardons to negotiate political arrangements with the regime would do so as well.

RUMORS, WARLORDS, AND COMPROMISE

Perhaps one of the clearest ways to see how these two pardons enabled the state to negotiate with alternative political sources is by considering the role of two rather notorious politicians in the affairs. Han Fuju, the maverick governor of Shandong, and Feng Yuxiang, a stubbornly independent member of the regime, used the assassination cases to advance their individual interests vis-à-vis the regime. The exact role Han played in engineering the Zheng Jicheng affair and Feng's role in both assassination cases were shrouded in rumor. Both men most likely welcomed the confusion as they sought to obscure the political machinations behind the cases by seeking an official pardon that would sanction the acts not as political murder but as instances of ethical retribution. Both, moreover, mobilized political sentiment to achieve this end. In turn, the pardons became occasions for the regime to respond to these maverick politicians. By granting a reprieve, the regime was in part mollifying these politicians. But on another level, the pardons also allowed the government to reassert its authority and make the claim that it could represent public sentiment and deliver national justice better than any individual political actor.

Jiang Jieshi faced an unruly situation in North China. While wanting to wrest control of North China from semi-independent militarist-politicians, Jiang had insufficient military might to do so. Moreover, Japanese occupation appeared imminent. Rumors were already abounding that regional militarists, while nominally pledging loyalty to Nanjing, were in fact acting in collusion with the Japanese. In this situation the central government no doubt found the mere rumor of autonomous political violence by regional militarists damaging to its reputation. Yet such rumors abounded in these two cases. Speculation regarding the possibility that these acts of revenge were actually political killings proved quite pervasive and heightened preexisting social anxieties about semi-independent militarists and politicians operating just beyond central control.

Both affairs were embroiled in intrigue and speculation. In the Zheng Jicheng case, widespread belief that Governor Han Fuju was behind the assassination fueled much of the buzz. Han had always been notoriously at odds with the central government. Jiang Jieshi had bribed Han with the governorship of Shandong after the Northern Expedition in exchange for his defection from Feng Yuxiang, and Han's allegiance to Nanjing was nominal at best. His tendency to operate with little regard for Nanjing only made his relationship with Jiang all the more tense. The relationship and Han's intentions thus easily became the subject of rumor and speculation.

Talk quickly spread that the filial vengeance was simply a front for Han's political killing of the Dog Meat General. Governor Han had reportedly found Zhang's sudden return to the North China scene in 1931 highly unsettling and was disturbed by reports of a possible coup. Rumor had it that Han, once a close subordinate to militarist Feng Yuxiang, had turned to Feng for advice. At that point, Feng was in temporary "retirement" on Tai Mountain after an aborted attempt to establish the People's Anti-Japanese Allied Army (Guominjun) and return to power. The renewed contact between Feng and Han prompted the Japanese to circulate stories that the two were conspiring to oust Jiang Jieshi (Coble 1991, 64). Rumors that the two were scheming to assassinate Zhang Zongchang quickly followed. It was said that Feng was the one with the insight to recommend Zheng Jicheng, a former cavalry division commander who served in his Guominjun, as a willing assassin, and to devise the idea of presenting the murder as an act of filial revenge to win popular sympathy. Zheng Jicheng's uncle, Zheng Jinsheng, who had been killed by Zhang Zongchang, had ties with Feng Yuxiang from their 1911 revolutionary activities of the New Shandong Native-Place Association (Chai et al. 1957, 334). Many believed that Feng too might have had a personal interest in seeing Zhang Zongchang dead.

Many newspaper accounts participated in this kind of conjecturing. For example, *The North China Herald*, the leading English-language newspaper published in Shanghai, immediately raised questions about the killing of General Zhang. One correspondent wondered why Zhang had even set foot in Shandong when he was fully aware of the innumerable enemies he had there. The writer relayed curious reports about Zhang's visit. He noted that Zhang had begun to act strangely and expressed great discomfort once he knew that governor Han Fuju was not going to appear at the banquet being held in his honor. Three extremely nervous singing girls had reportedly further alarmed the General, who finally announced in the middle of the banquet that he needed to return to Beiping immediately. What struck the reporter as most odd was the manner in which Zhang's assassins, Zheng Jicheng and an aide, were apprehended at the train station. According to the reporter's informant, the police had been ordered to leave their arms behind, and the assassins, though they had made their intention of killing Zhang clear, had been allowed to remain on the platform. He writes, "All this time [during the shooting], not the slightest efforts were made to stop the murderers, who continued quite calmly and unhindered, firing at [Zhang] at close range, until they had emptied their pistols. Then, and then only, were they arrested."[42] As a Western paper, the *North China Herald* tended to report the "goings-on" of the Chinese political world in a way that voyeuristically dwelled on the intrigue. The above account of the Zheng case was one such report, and both reflected and added to the overall buzz surrounding the affair.[43]

According to a recent biography of Han Fuju, these rumors were indeed true, and Han and Feng had gone to great lengths to have the Dog Meat General killed (Lü Weijun 1997, 96–104). That these rumors were true speaks to a real degree of autonomy on the part of regional militarists during this time, something scholars have long noted. Yet, what is interesting here is that Han Fuju, concerned with public sentiment, wanted the regime's help in presenting the killing as an ethically legitimate act of filial revenge. He was thus drawn into negotiations with Jiang Jieshi. For our purposes, then, whether the rumors were verifiable is somewhat beside the point. Rather, it is important to appreciate how the atmosphere of speculation framed the negotiations between Han Fuju and the central regime. It was in the context of rumor and doubt that Han Fuju found the opportunity to push for his agenda with Nanjing.

From the start, Han and his provincial government launched an aggressive campaign to mobilize Shandong public sentiment in support of their cause and to win a quick pardon. Zhang Weicun, the head of Shandong Province's Party Apparatus, spearheaded the efforts and ensured that the pardon was one of the central issues on the table at the 167th meeting of the Shandong Party Committee, held on September 5, 1932.[44] Published in Shandong's main paper, the conclusion drawn at this meeting was that Zheng's revenge was a great act of heroism that had effectively purged the nation of Zhang Zongchang. Members of the meeting also concluded that while the law should be upheld, there was also a need to acknowledge moral sentiment and the principles of reason. Civic groups dispatched a flurry of telegrams to Nanjing, and several provincial notables with national standing voiced their support.[45] Just as the government would eventually use telegrams from civic groups to justify its decision to sanction Zheng's killing of Zhang Zongchang, the activity of associations on the provincial level helped Han Fuju prompt the government to act.

In the face of such aggressive lobbying and widespread speculation, Jiang Jieshi found that he had to address the request for a pardon, yet he did not want to appear to be simply yielding to Han Fuju's pressure. Thus, when Han publicly requested that the government forego the trial and grant an immediate pardon, the center insisted that the case had to follow judicial procedure. Jiang sent a reply telegram to the Shandong governor dated September 9, 1932, in which he stated, "The offender who assassinated Zhang [Zongchang] will have to wait his day in court. Only once the courts mete out a punishment and only if it is [felt to be] too heavy, will we then resort to the procedure of a pardon. Generally, both state law and public opinion can have their say at the same time."[46] Printed in the *Shenbao*, this reply established that the authority of the judiciary would have to be respected, and that only the central government, and not an individual militarist, could use the pardon mechanism to accommodate public sentiment after due process of law. Although national law and public opinion were potentially at odds with each other, both, asserted Jiang, were equally important, and only the executive branch of the government could give both their due attention. Though he did not invoke party doctrine as Ju Zheng would do three years later,

Jiang nonetheless agreed with the logic of the appointed head of the judiciary that only the central regime had the power to reconcile the letter of the law and popular sentiment.

Han Fuju apparently got the message. On September 10, only a day after the Shandong Party had made its request, the governor suddenly reversed Shandong's position and agreed respectfully with the central government that a trial was still necessary. Covering the ongoing give and take between Shandong and the government, the Shanghai *Shenbao* quoted the Shandong governor as stating, "The provincial government is without opinion on the Zhang case. We will abide by the view of the [central government] and the wishes of society."[47] This step back, however, was temporary. After failing to secure an immediate pardon, Han made sure that telegrams in support of Zheng continued to be dispatched, and after the initial court trial, which resulted in a sentence of seven years, Shandong's Official Party Organization requested an official pardon yet again. By late November of 1932, Han's perseverance paid off. Citing public sentiment (*yuqing*), key members of the central government also appealed to Jiang for a pardon, and they met with success.[48] In March 1933, a pardon was finally granted.

What the above exchange between Han and Jiang demonstrates is that there was room in the pardon process for both sides to achieve what they wanted. For the governor of Shandong, a pardon for Zheng Jicheng was eventually secured, and thus a calculated act of political assassination was legitimated by the nation's highest political authority as a righteous act of revenge. For the central regime, a full trial upheld the legitimacy of the courts and at the same time, the pardon served to convey official munificence and establish the Nationalist regime as the final arbiter in the case. Moreover, the official pardon provided a means for the regime to gain some control over upstart politicians like Han. For while Han was allowed to pursue his own goals, kill off a threatening foe, and ultimately negotiate an official reprieve on behalf of his hired gun, he was still forced to acknowledge the final authority of the central government in the process.

Three years later, gossip and hearsay related to the case of Shi Jianqiao helped fuel existing doubts about Nationalist unity and legitimacy once again. A general atmosphere of doubt surrounded the 1935 assassination case. Speculation was rife that Sun Chuanfang's assassination was part of a larger drama of intrigue and politics involving the participants of Shanghai-area politics in the 1920s.[49] There was gossip that Shi Jianqiao was, in fact, an agent of the Military Statistics Bureau and had acted under orders.[50] Suspicion of official engineering of the assassination was perhaps most vividly articulated in a cynical commentary that appeared in the *Qinghua zhoukan*, a weekly publication that regularly included social commentary and political observation. Writing just after the announcement of official sanction, the author of the piece ponders about whether the Shi Jianqiao affair had been engineered from the start. The writer notes that it was little wonder that the perpetrator maintained such a brave front during her trial, given that upon her release from jail, Shi had been met by an official car, received telegrams of support from Nanjing, and continued to win media coverage for her return to Beiping. At one point, the writer states, "It's foolish to hope that the cat will release the rat. However, if in the cat's mouth is its own kitten, then for sure it'll let its prey go." This statement was a play on the saying *mao shu tongmin*, which literally translates as "the cat and mouse sleep together" and figuratively refers to corrupt officials colluding with criminals. As such, it makes clear that the commentator felt Shi Jianqiao's release was due to her connections: if Shi Jianqiao were a mouse, she would never have received a pardon; but as a kitten—that is, as officialdom's own brood—special treatment was a given (Gu 1936).

In contrast to the Zheng Jicheng case, there is little evidence that such rumors of special treatment were true. Yet the general atmosphere of speculation was nonetheless historically significant, specifically because it raised doubt about the degree to which Feng Yuxiang, who was at the time the vice chair of the Nationalist Military Affairs Committee, was following Jiang's agenda. Put slightly differently, if the Zheng Jicheng case invited speculation about Jiang's control over Han Fuju and North China, Shi Jianqiao's case spawned conjecture about the regime's ability to control not regional leaders, but affairs closer to the center. What exactly then was Feng Yuxiang's involvement? Whereas in the Zheng affair, Feng had been behind the scenes as the consultant to Han Fuju from the beginning, in the Shi case it appears that he played a more limited if more visible role in securing the female assassin's freedom. Feng's posthumously published diary, for example, gives no indication that he had engineered the Shi Jianqiao case from the start, and only sheds light on his involvement *after* the killing, when he engaged in considerable backroom brokering to procure a pardon for Shi (Feng 1992, vols. 3–5).

Specifically, Feng Yuxiang's diary entries are fascinating in showing how, even as certain procedural steps were in place to process a pardon, Feng's personal advocacy was crucial in the affair. According to his diary, on November 14, 1935, the day after the assassination, Shi Jianqiao's brother Shi Zefan and cousin Shi Zhongda contacted him. While the terse entry does not reveal more than that they paid him a visit, given the date of their visit, we can reasonably surmise that they came to discuss the possibility of an amnesty for their sister. Indeed, the November 30 entry notes that Feng was already working on pursuing an amnesty (*dashe*) for Shi Jianqiao, meeting with Jiao Yitang, who was the head of the Supreme Court at the time, and Ju Zheng, the head of the Judicial Yuan. On December 21, 1935, Feng met with Jiang Jieshi, at which point he raised the amnesty issue, and on January 27, 1936, he met with Jiang once again, to remind him of the tremendous popular support (*renxin*) for Shi. However, as in the Zheng Jicheng affair, there was no real possibility for an amnesty, and Shi's case was to be tried in the court system. Feng thus had to wait until September 1936, after the legal case ended, to start lobbying for a pardon. On September 21, he was back in touch with Jiao Yitang and Ju Zheng, as well as with Tan Zhen, the vice director of the Judicial Yuan. Once he procured their support for a pardon, he went to the Nationalist Government Council. In a September 27 entry, he records how he had composed a letter supporting the pardon, had eight elder statesmen sign it, and then had it delivered to Lin Sen, the chairman of the government.[51] Feng's determination resulted in a vote for a pardon that took place at 11 A.M., on October 12, 1936, at the Nationalist Government Council meeting. The proposal for a pardon was put on the table early in the meeting, and Feng's letter of support was read, at which point Chairmen Lin said that if there was no opposition, then the pardon would be granted. Fifty-three members voted to approve the proposal. After the announcement of the pardon, Shi Jianqiao acknowledged in an interview that her pardon was in large part the result of this backroom brokering.[52]

Feng's decision to serve as a patron for Shi Jianqiao was inextricably related to his personal agenda of commemorating his 1911 revolutionary status and, by extension, to his complex relationship with Jiang Jieshi. Feng's relationship with Jiang was notoriously tense throughout the Republican period. As one of the strongest and most enduring opponents of the Nationalist regime, Feng joined the central government only under tenuous conditions. In the fall of 1935, Jiang personally persuaded Feng to come out of seclusion from Taishan to return to Nanjing. He invited Feng along with Yan Xishan of Shanxi, another former Nationalist opponent, to participate in the Fifth National Party Congressional meeting, which convened, coincidentally, only a few days before Sun's assassination. Great fanfare marked Feng's return.[53] Media accounts dwelled on how Feng took off the simple peasant clothing of his retirement to don more appropriate wear for his new position as a party statesman.[54] Yet, despite this sartorial gesture, Feng's obligation to Jiang remained ambivalent (Sheridan 1966, 273–80). With his allegiance to Jiang never wholly reliable, Feng did not hesitate to use his new position as a member of the Nationalist regime to advance his individual interests and to portray himself as being more patriotic than Jiang. His insistence on pursuing his own anti-Japanese activities, for example, proved particularly nettlesome for Jiang, who, at the time, was following a highly unpopular policy of appeasing the Japanese.

Feng's role in securing the release of Shi Jianqiao was related to this larger attempt on his part to demonstrate what he believed was his more superior form of patriotism. Publicly, Feng announced that his interest in the Shi Jianqiao pardon stemmed primarily from his loyalty to Shi Congyun, Shi Jianqiao's uncle and Feng's old friend and 1911 revolutionary colleague. Feng and Shi Congyun had both been part of a group of Beiyang army officers that had participated in the tragically fated Luanzhou Uprising, which began on December 29, 1910, lasted only for a few days, and turned out to be an utter disaster. Participants were betrayed, captured, and then executed. Since he had been arrested for unlawful printing of revolutionary broadsides on the day of the uprising, Feng missed the uprising and escaped the tragedy that befell the others.[55]

Feng thus presented his pursuit of a pardon for Shi Jianqiao as related to his agenda to commemorate the Luanzhou Uprising. According to his diary, by early 1936 Feng was simultaneously pursuing both the pardon and the commemoration.[56] Several February entries described the progress he was making with the local governments toward procuring a memorial plaque and a grave for the uprising. By March 3, Shi Congyun, Shi Jianqiao's uncle, was granted official revolutionary martyr status. It was around the same time that Feng recorded his attempt to procure official grace for Shi Jianqiao, with his February 24 entry mentioning that he spoke with Jiang about a possible amnesty. By the fall of 1936, the Luanzhou commemoration had been organized, and Shi Jianqiao's pardon announced.[57] On October 16, Feng writes that since coming to Nanjing, he had accomplished several items that contributed to the mass revolution (*dazhong geming*), including both the Luanzhou memorial and Shi Jianqiao's pardon. For Feng then, a pardon for the heroic niece of Shi Congyun proved timely in bringing more publicity to his commemoration efforts. This twin agenda was not without political meaning. During a period when Jiang's patriotism was under public fire, Feng's commemoration of his role in the 1911 revolution and his active pursuit of Shi Jianqiao's pardon would easily have acquired pointed significance and helped arouse further speculation about the true nature of his loyalty to the central government.[58]

Finally, Feng Yuxiang's involvement in the two cases reveals the importance of human obligation and sentiment (*renqing*) in motivating political relations in early twentieth-century China in general. R. Keith Schoppa (1995) discusses the importance of place and social networks in the making of revolution in China in the early twentieth century. He notes the amazing degree to which political networks and connections of the early Republic were based on personal friendships, school ties, native-place ties, and common revolutionary experience. All such ties were crucial in constituting the complex web of relations that connected Feng Yuxiang with the two assassination cases. Feng's participation in the 1911 revolutionary activities of the New Shandong Native-Place Association, a group that was ostensibly a society for military studies but secretly engaged in revolutionary activity, specifically sealed his commitment to the fate of Zheng Jicheng and Shi Jianqiao. Other participants in the Association included Shi Congyun, Shi Jianqiao's uncle; Zheng Jinsheng, Zheng Jicheng's uncle; and Zhang Zhijiang, one of the key elder statesmen in the Nationalist regime who helped Feng secure a pardon for Shi Jianqiao (Chai 1957, 334). These connections of *renqing* were the basis of Feng's attempts to forward his own political agenda. Using these ties to Zheng Jicheng and Shi Jianqiao, he helped Han Fuju rid Shandong of Zhang Zongchang and also established his own revolutionary standing separate from Jiang Jieshi, even while he had joined the Nationalist regime.

CONCLUSION: THE CASE OF XU DAOLIN

We have seen that the decision to sanction these two instances of ethical violence ultimately proved to be a double-edged sword for the regime. On one level, the nationalist regime was able to flex its executive muscle in these pardons and assert itself as the New Life regime whose legitimacy rested not only on legal foundations but also on ethical authority and martial heroism. The regime used the endorsements to interpret these avengers as New Life heroes, who embodied the national essence and whose acts of violent retribution could bring about national order. These pardons were also occasions for the regime to exhibit the superior authority of party doctrine, and portray itself as the primary voice of public sentiment and as best able to ensure both the pursuit of justice and the smooth working of the state.

Yet, even while providing the regime with opportunities to consolidate its power, on another level, the state sanction of these violent acts generated what were perhaps unintended consequences for the regime. The pardoning process showed that the assassinations provided opportunities for groups both within and beyond the regime to assert their own agendas, often at the expense of the central government. Civic groups used the pardons as a chance to assert their own institutional influence. Individual politicians grabbed the opportunity to create space for their own pursuits, even as they mouthed deference to Nanjing. Insofar as these pardons recognized the authority of appeals by public groups, they clearly served to empower public sentiment as a power potentially distinct from state authority.

It is also worthwhile to briefly consider the 1945 case of Xu Daolin, a dutiful son who decided not to seek violent revenge but pursued satisfaction for his father's murder through legal means. I have used the preceding pardon cases to provide a close-up view of how the Nationalist regime used the process of pardoning ethical violence as a means to negotiate its relations with civic associations, the judiciary, regional militarists, and even Feng Yuxiang, one of its own elder statesmen. While this later case did not involve an assassination or a state pardon, by comparing it with the Zheng and Shi cases, we can take a step back and illuminate the intermingling of power politics, violence, the ethical authority of filial piety, and the role of appealing to the public in pursuit of justice in the Republican era.

In December 1945, Xu Daolin, a high-ranking Nationalist official and renowned legal scholar who had been educated in Germany and had taught in the United States for some years, attracted a great deal of media attention when he brought a legal suit against Feng Yuxiang.[59] In 1925 Feng had had Xu Daolin's father, Xu Shuzheng, assassinated. Known as "Little Xu," Xu Shuzheng had been the most powerful deputy of Duan Qirui from 1912 to 1920 and was the cofounder of the Anfu military clique.[60] On December 30, 1925, Xu was murdered when his train was passing through Langfang, a city between Beijing and Tianjin, which was then occupied by Feng's Guominjun. Immediately after the killing, a public telegram was issued stating that a Lu Chengwu had shot Xu to avenge the death of his father, Lu Jianzhang.[61] Before long, however, there was rampant speculation that Lu Chengwu had not pulled the trigger, and had, in fact, been nowhere near Langfang when Xu Shuzheng was shot.[62]

Many, including son Xu Daolin, held Feng responsible and accused him of hiding behind Lu Chengwu. Though Feng denied any involvement, it was widely believed that he had personal reasons for revenge. Lu Jianzheng had been his patron and relative, and Feng was highly disturbed by his death in 1918. It was also alleged that Feng had concrete political motives in 1925 to want Xu dead, though no substantial evidence for this has been revealed.[63] Again, as in the cases of Shi and Zheng, rumors shrouded Feng's involvement in the Xu case.

Though he held Feng directly responsible for the death of his father, Xu Daolin waited years to take action. In a commemorative volume for his father published in the early 1960s in Taiwan, Xu Daolin claimed that Feng was simply too powerful at the time of his father's murder and he had thus aborted his decision to act immediately.[64] By the 1940s, Xu had become a famous legal scholar and had climbed the official ranks of the Nationalist government to become the secretary-general of the Executive Yuan. In 1945 when Japan was pulling out of China, Xu resigned from his official position to file the lawsuit against Feng as a common citizen. In the end, his legal efforts failed. The Nationalist Courts dismissed the case. Those in Xu's circles alleged that this dismissal occurred because the Nationalist government, which was then engaged in civil war, found Feng Yuxiang indispensable, and that a travesty of justice had been delivered.[65]

Featuring one of the Republican era's leading scholars of law, the failed legal case of Xu Daolin garnered tremendous attention. It was widely known that Xu was haunted by his failure to avenge his father's death either by his own hand or in the courts. He perpetuated this image himself. On the final page of *Xu Shuzheng xiansheng wenji nianpu hekan* (The collected writings and chronological biography of Xu Shuzheng), a collection he compiled in memory of his father, Xu wrote, "I harbored the injustice for twenty years, and was not able to use a knife to avenge my father's death. Nor was I able to use the law to put away a criminal. In the end, I cannot but feel remorse for the rest of my life. I can only pray and hope that history will punish [him]" (1962, 331). The commemorative volume *Xu Daolin xiansheng jinian ji* (A collection of commemorative writings for Xu Daolin) was published for Xu Daolin at the time of his death and, by including essays dwelling on the failed revenge, similarly functioned to keep alive the memory of the affair and his regrets.

Taken together, the cases of Xu Daolin, Shi Jianqiao, and Zheng Jicheng span from the 1920s into the 1940s and collectively shed some light on the conceptualization of justice and violence in the Republican period. Specifically, the three served to raise doubt about whether the legal system was indeed the best way to pursue justice or whether ethical revenge was a more viable alternative. They also provide us with a means to examine the extent to which public sympathy for ethical revenge was an effective antidote to power politics and corruption in the legal arena. At first glance, the results of these cases all seem to suggest that the ultimate deciding factor was Feng's personal political influence. In the Shi and Zheng cases, Feng was the patron of the agent of justice, and his influence was crucial in winning official exemption for the two assassins. In the Zheng case, he helped engineer the revenge from the start. In contrast, in the Xu case the notorious militarist was the target of the legal retribution, and it was widely believed that his position in the Nationalist government was a crucial factor in obstructing legal action.

Yet, attributing the outcome of these legal affairs merely to politics and the power of Feng is not enough. We must also consider the ethical authority of filial piety and public sentiment. Both were consistent forces that were being appealed to by a variety of people and that functioned in complex ways to mediate the ongoing negotiation of power in all three cases. Take, for example, Feng Yuxiang's systematic management of highly popular acts of filial revenge. Even at the height of his autonomous military power during the decentralized era of the 1920s, Feng felt compelled to wrap political murders in the cloak of righteous retribution. In arranging the 1925 murder of Xu Daolin's father, Xu Shuzheng, Feng took pains to find among his subordinates someone whose filial devotion kept alive a grudge against Xu. In the 1932 Zheng case, Feng again manipulated the ethical authority of filial revenge to win public sympathy and disguise the political killing of Zhang Zhongchang. And in the 1935–36 Shi case, Feng once again favored the politics of filial revenge and appealed to public sympathy to bolster his political position vis-à-vis Jiang as he negotiated his entry into the Nationalist government.

The Xu Daolin case is particularly interesting for our purposes because it reveals more starkly than the other two cases how Feng's *modus operandi* of manipulating filial revenge was turned against him, and by extension, against the central government to which he was closely, if not always harmoniously, tied.[66] As mentioned in the discussion of the Shi and Zheng cases, Feng Yuxiang was not alone in recognizing the power of public sympathy with regard to filial revenge. The central state and public groups competed with Feng and Han Fuju, his fellow militarist-cum-politician, in appropriating the authority of righteous revenge and the public sentiment it aroused to pursue their respective agendas. In the mid-1940s, Xu Daolin similarly won tremendous public support by drawing a page from Feng's own playbook. Xu presented his action in the courts as an act of sincere filial duty, and his reputation for filial piety only grew when it was clear that his legal case was doomed. His decision to pursue this impossible task of seeking legal recourse as a common citizen further appealed to the impassioned public. By dramatically stepping down from a position of considerable power and influence to file the legal suit, Xu portrayed his intention to pursue justice as honorable and pure. This gesture stood in sharp contrast with the politically compromised proceedings taking place in the courtroom. Public sympathy for Xu Daolin's filial determination in the face of the unmistakable odds against him in the courts could then function as a searing ethical critique against a legal system, which was perceived by many to have succumbed to politics.

These three cases of filial action also provided the opportunity for contemporary observers to grapple with the legacy of chaos and violence of the 1920s. News about ethical acts of retribution splashed across the pages of urban dailies precisely because they effectively served to right in metaphorical terms the collective wrongs committed by warlords in the 1920s. Furthermore, such cases exposed the degree to which the Nationalist government had failed to disavow the politics of violence inherited from the earlier decade in which it arose. The three affairs underscored the potential contradiction embedded in Nationalist rule between the Nationalists' desire to contain the violent remains of the warlord era and erect an authoritative court system and its other goal of extending party and executive control into the judiciary, and into society more generally, often through sanctioning or tacitly approving violence.

Moreover, it was significant that all three cases featured Feng Yuxiang so prominently. Arguably more than any other political figure of the day, Feng had come to embody the contradiction between the tactics of violence inherited from the 1920s and the desire to seek political legitimacy through erecting civilian institutions in the 1930s. Widely known to be the patron of violent vigilante filial revenge since the warlord period, Feng continued to support filial acts of revenge into the 1930s and, in doing so, perpetuated the tactics of the earlier era. His patronage in the Shi case, for example, was powerfully reminiscent of the political maneuverings and machinations that he had openly engaged in during the warlord period. Such patronage, and the rumors and skepticism it fueled, cast a shadow on the political legitimacy of the regime. As discussed above, Feng's maneuverings behind the scenes in the Shi case put the regime itself in an unflattering light. The regime was criticized for engaging in acts of political violence and shady maneuverings reminiscent of the earlier era, even as it sought to distance itself from its past and establish itself as the legitimate new government of China. In the 1940s case, the irony of Xu Daolin turning the tables on Feng, and winning public sympathy in doing so, only made the ambiguity of the regime all the more apparent.

Finally by examining the Xu case along with the Zheng and Shi cases, we can see more clearly how historical legacy and memory came to be sites for pursuing justice. As mentioned above, in compiling his father's writings, Xu Daolin kept alive the injustice done to his father and thereby let history judge his case. Similarly, in a commemorative volume published at the time of Xu Daolin's death in the 1970s, his sister, daughter, and friends sought, thirty years after the failure of his legal case, to shape his legacy and portray him as a person whose ethical superiority stood in sharp contrast to the corruption of Feng Yuxiang and the Nationalist courts.[67] Writing in memory of her father, Xu's daughter, Xu Xiaohu, for example, pointedly eulogizes his profound sense of filial duty:

> It was your heart-rending love for your father, which made me worship [you] all the more. . . . You rose to high office, becoming Secretary-General of the Executive Yuan, with an office and townhouse in Chungking. And suddenly we saw electric lights and running water again. . . . But, just as suddenly, you resigned from that lofty post in order to bring suit against Feng Yu-hsiang, the warlord and "Christian General," for the assassination of your Father. But you wished to sue as a plain citizen, without the apparatus of power behind you. I was in Nankai Middle School then, and eleven. I was amazed to see that the whole country seemed to tremble in awe at your filial and honorable action. "Oh, your father is an extraordinary man. You will not understand how great your father is till you are older," people said to me. They sighed too. They knew, as you knew, that litigating against the mighty Feng was at that precarious time a totally hopeless cause. (*Xu Daolin xiansheng jinian ji* 1975, 96).

Even if the quotation is culled from a hagiography, it remains illuminating. Xu's daughter continued to portray his nonviolent filial action as honorable. His decision to step down from a high-ranking position was celebrated as an expression of the purity of his intentions. This was a powerful gesture at the time of the legal case, but also worth retelling for the shaping of historical judgment.[68]

In Xu Daolin's case, then, historical legacy continued to foster popular sympathy for his filial behavior and pursuit of justice. In the Shi Jianqiao affair as well, historical legacy was to prove significant after the trial and pardon. As we see in the next chapter, immediately after her pardon, Shi Jianqiao sought to put her legacy to political use during the War of Resistance and took advantage of her reputation of *qing* to mobilize wartime patriotism. During the Cultural Revolution, Shi Jianqiao fared poorly when her reputation as filial avenger made her politically vulnerable. Yet, in the 1980s her legacy was restored posthumously. During a publishing boom that rehabilitated targeted victims of the Mao era as part of a larger move to criticize the extremism of the prior era, Shi Jianqiao's son, like Xu Daolin's friends and family, used biographical writings in an effort to secure his mother's place in historical memory (e.g., Shi and Shen 1985; Shi 1982).

SIX

Beyond the 1930s

From Wartime Patriotism to Counter-Revolutionary Sentiment

In this tragic situation where we are bombed by the Japanese, we have righteous anger (*yifen*); we want to seek revenge for our comrades, we want to bomb those who have bombed us; let us raise money for warplanes!

—Shi Zefan, *promotional material for Hechuan's Campaign to Raise Funds for Warplanes against the Japanese, 1941*

In this final chapter I examine Shi Jianqiao's post-pardon career to inquire into the fate of sentiment beyond the 1930s and to address briefly the question of historical memory. In reviewing Shi Jianqiao's participation in War of Resistance relief efforts, I first offer a few thoughts regarding how Shi Jianqiao's feminized moral sentiment inspired the collective emotion of modern patriotism (*aiguo*) during the Japanese invasion of China in the late 1930s and 1940s. Shi Jianqiao was the perfect candidate to lead a local resistance movement and embody the sentiment of Chinese patriotism. After Japan's relentless bombing campaign of the hinterland from 1938–1941, Chinese patriotism came to draw heavily on the concept of righteous revenge, and Shi Jianqiao, widely known as a courageous and passionate woman willing to sacrifice herself in the name of righteous retribution, was a perfect symbol of patriotism. The second part of the chapter moves away from Shi Jianqiao's experiences during the War of Resistance to consider her fate after the 1949 Revolution. By reviewing two of her autobiographical accounts written in the 1960s, I explore how the politics of the post-1949 era made her embodiment of *qing* highly problematic.

FEMALE SENTIMENT AND PATRIOTISM IN THE WAR OF RESISTANCE

An examination of Shi Jianqiao's relief efforts during the War of Resistance reveals how the relationship between female sentiment and collective emotion so central in the 1930s case of revenge continued to prove significant beyond the Nanjing decade. As a public figure and leader in relief efforts, Shi became a model of resistance who could inspire patriotism among ordinary men and women. In particular, Shi's attributes of self-sacrifice, passion, and courage established during the assassination made her extraordinarily well qualified to symbolize patriotism and selfless love to the wartime Chinese nation. While Shi Jianqiao continued to embody collective sentiment, many differences existed regarding the conditions under which this sentiment was mobilized and the political meaning it acquired. No longer an era when media sensation and melodrama served to universalize individual *qing*, the 1940s saw instead the rise of collective sentiment in a resistance movement that deployed theater, media, and spectacle to gain support for the war against Japan. Furthermore, given the imperatives of war and the existence of an outside enemy, collective patriotism in the 1940s lost the critical edge with regard to the central regime that had been part of the public sympathy in the Shi Jianqiao case.

Shi Jianqiao's participation in fund-raising efforts in the War of Resistance reveals not simply that women contributed to war efforts in China, but also how women's work itself became a sign of a modern nation engaging in patriotic war efforts. As was the case in the United States during World War II, the arenas in which women could participate expanded considerably. In China, women were increasingly encouraged to help with resistance efforts and participate in war work. In such a context, Shi's affective heroism was perfect for mobilizing and symbolizing widespread patriotic sentiment. Her success in leading the organization of a nationally recognized civic movement to raise funds for airplanes showed the ability of this renowned avenger to successfully embody the national desire for revenge against the Japanese.

On October 21, 1936, Shi Jianqiao was released from prison. In the days leading up to her actual release, several newspapers ran misleading announcements of her imminent discharge. Tianjin's *Yishibao* announced on October 20, 1936, that Shi Jianqiao was to be released that day. She was actually released on the next day at 2 P.M., when she was whisked away in a caravan of three cars. According to the Shanghai *Shenbao* a few days later, the earlier reports were purposely leaked to create a smokescreen to protect the well-known prisoner. Feng Yuxiang had pushed for the leak, and both Song Zheyuan, then-garrison commander of Beiping and Tianjin, and Cheng Xixian, the head of the Tianjin Public Security Bureau, had approved the decision. During the Nanjing decade, when the threat of kidnapping was very real, such precautions were common procedure.

The first thing Shi Jianqiao did was to visit her mother in Tianjin. After performing her filial duties, she took a train to Beiping and then proceeded to Nanjing. There she personally thanked Feng Yuxiang, along with Zhang Ji, Jiao Yitang, Yu Youren, Li Liejun, and Zhang Zhijiang, key elder statesman of the Nationalists who had helped procure her pardon (Chen and Ling 1986, 223–24). She expressed her proper debts of gratitude to all those crucial in determining her fate.

In the years following her release, Shi Jianqiao resumed a markedly less publicized lifestyle, yet she did not remove herself from the public arena altogether. During the War of Resistance, Shi drew public attention with her contribution to wartime efforts. Soon after her release from prison, Shi Jianqiao had, along with her family and mother, followed the Nationalists into the hinterland to flee the Japanese and joined in a variety of relief efforts. In 1937 in Changsha, Zhang Zhizhong, the governor of Hunan, appointed her to be the Director of Hunan Province's People's Organizations for logistical support. In the spring of 1938, she was the representative of Hunan at the Hankou Air Force and Army Provisions Conference. From 1941 to 1942, after moving to Sichuan, Shi and her brother Zefan organized a highly successful campaign to raise money to purchase much-needed airplanes for the war effort in Hechuan, a small city outside of Chongqing. Her decision to lead Hechuan's war efforts once again landed her squarely in the national limelight.

The War of Resistance began in July 1937 with the Japanese invasion of China's eastern seaboard. China was subsequently divided into Japanese-occupied territory, Nationalist-ruled areas, and Communist-held regions. While the first phase of the war was the most brutal, lasting for sixteen months until October 1938 with the fall of Wuhan and Guangzhou, the second phase proved more important for the mobilization of Chinese patriotism. During this second phase, the Japanese controlled the major coastal cities and the main railway lines. Japan's superior air power and armed forces forced Jiang Jieshi to adopt a "scorched earth strategy," whereby Jiang traded space for time. Retreating first to Hankou, and then Chongqing, Jiang counted on Japan to overextend itself in China's vast interior. The result was a torturous period of stalemate. While Jiang was unable to expel the Japanese, the Japanese were unable to extend successfully into China's hinterland. Japan could only consolidate its hold on East and North China via collaborative regimes, including Wang Jingwei's so-called New National Government in Nanjing. It also waged an unrelenting air war against the interior cities. Chongqing and other urban centers remained safe from a land attack, but the bombing campaign took a tremendous toll on lives and property as the Japanese used their superior airpower to flatten Chongqing and its surrounding areas.[1]

While Japan's air campaign successfully pounded the interior and placed relentless pressure on the Nationalists, the offensive led to an unprecedented wave of patriotism that was further buoyed by the entrance of the United States into the Pacific Theater in December 1941 after Japan's attack on Pearl Harbor. National unity and patriotism were reinvigorated, and resistance efforts spread quickly. The Second United Front between the Nationalists and Communists, a formal agreement to collaborate against the Japanese, was attempted, if only for a brief period. During this period a large wave of Chinese intellectuals, artists, and playwrights, who had followed the Nationalist government in retreat and had been engaged in staging popular dramas and performances to raise flagging spirits since the start of the war, intensified their efforts with a charged sense of patriotism (Hung 1994, 6). Ordinary citizens' groups also organized and participated in a variety of resistance efforts.

In this period of renewed patriotism, the symbol of the modern Chinese woman as patriot was potent, and mobilizing women for resistance activities became an important aspect of the war against Japan. Seeking to generate patriotism and lift morale among the population at large, the Nationalists placed female mobilization high on its wartime agenda. Song Meiling, Jiang Jieshi's wife, personally led the government's efforts to organize Chinese women, and she came to be known as the moral and active mother of the nation. On May 20, 1938, Song convened the Guilin conference to transform the New Life movement into a platform for female war efforts. At this meeting, it was explicitly stated that Chinese women were to play a supportive but vital role in the war against Japan. Their duties included rear-line operations like caring for war orphans, providing medical care, and staffing relief agencies. Women were also to participate in national reconstruction and the rebuilding of China. They were to secure provisions and supplies for the Chinese armed forces, help ensure female productivity in factories, as well as train and teach the nation's rural citizens about their duties in rural organization.[2]

While there were practical reasons behind the mobilization of women's war work, much of the state's interest in organizing female relief efforts stemmed from its desire to centralize and maintain control over social relief organizations, as well as to ensure that collective sentiment coincided with its own wartime agenda. The 1938 Guilin meeting organized by Song Meiling enabled the regime to unify what had until then been fragmented women's work under its control and, as one account put it, to "harmonize the many-fronted work of the women of China."[3] The Chinese Women's Advisory Committee of the New Life movement was to serve as the central committee, with which all women's organizations were to be affiliated. Led by Madame Jiang, the standing committee was composed of the wives of some of the most powerful leaders in the government, including Madame Feng Yuxiang and Song Ailing, one of Song Meiling's sisters and the wife of the powerful Shanghai financier and then-Minister of Finance Kong Xiangxi.

With war and migration resulting in a considerable expansion of the roles that women could assume, the Women's Advisory Committee actively sought to resurrect the ideology of "Good Wife, Wise Mother" to restrict the newfound public activities of women. Much of wartime work for middle-class women presumed that women's social roles were those of mothers and housekeepers, and female duties on the "home front" were framed in terms of an extension of the domestic realm. Women's work teams continued the moral and hygienic battles women were asked to wage during the Republican-era New Life movement, but with added urgency during the wartime period. Women associated with these organizations fanned out across the Chinese hinterland to teach their sisters how to rear children, combat dirt, and fight against superstition in more scientifically progressive ways. Their mission was infused with the military rhetoric of strategy, rational planning, and efficiency appropriate to a wartime operation.

Song Meiling and the Nationalist women's groups used the press to define this proper female behavior. Most national newspapers were under fairly strict wartime control, and most of the media beyond the Nationalist-controlled press complied quite willingly and appeared to be in full support of the regime's policy on women's relief efforts. During this period of war, local newspapers and journals, flourishing because of the newfound reading public that had migrated to the interior, drummed a highly patriotic beat that matched that of the ruling regime (Hung 1994, 181–85).

During a period of wartime scarcity, journals and newspapers of all stripes used precious paper to encourage ordinary women to be active in war efforts.[4] Entire journals like Hankou's *Zhanshi funü* (Wartime women) and Chongqing's *Funü xin yun* (Women's new movement) and *Zhanshi funü yuekan* (Wartime women monthly) were dedicated to exhorting correct, patriotic, female activity. Articles with titles like "A Discussion of the Work of Organizing Entertainment and Support," "The Road that Wartime Women Should Take," and "How Should Wartime Women Be?" encouraged women to express their patriotism in very specific ways.[5]

With female public activity defined vis-à-vis relief efforts, Shi Jianqiao threw herself into resistance work immediately upon her arrival in Sichuan in late 1940, helping especially to build China's airpower. Her decision to help with China's air force was not arbitrary. Japan's relentless bombing of the hinterland made air strength appear crucial to China's national survival, and providing for the air force was among the most prestigious resistance activities for both men and women. A proliferation of journals and articles dedicated to aviation and the air force spoke to the importance of airpower. Published in Chongqing, *Hangkong zazhi* (Aviation magazine), for example, frequently featured articles such as "From Nazi Germany's Superpower Position to the Establishment and Use of China's Air Force," and "China's Air Force's International and National Characteristics"(Zhou 1941a, 1941b). Zhou Zhirou, the author of these two pieces, explicitly linked a strong air force with China's national and international standing. The abundant articles on the aircraft technology and the appearance of planes on the covers of these journals also speak to the urgency associated with air strength.

Women's magazines specifically promoted the prestige of aviation-related war work for women. Journals such as *Funü gongming* (Women's voices) ran articles that featured heroic women in the air forces of other countries. Listing model female pilots and even entire female air force troupes in England, the Soviet Union, America, France, Italy, Germany, Turkey, and Austria, one article argued that the equality of sexes in this most important sector of the military was something that China should strive for as a modern nation (Shan 1941). The piece proceeded to reprimand China for letting its commitment to developing a female presence in the air force slip after Mme. Jiang had retreated from an active role in this area and concluded by calling for renewed and immediate attention to the matter.[6] The July 1940 cover of the *Funü shenghuo* (Women's lifestyles), which featured a photo of the Soviet pilot "Paulina," smiling in full aviation gear in front of her plane, also emphasized the

Figure 10. Hechuan anti-Japanese resistance activities. Top photo: Shi Jianqiao and Yuan Xueya, the magistrate of Hechuan, presiding over the celebration activities. Bottom photo: crowd watching donated planes flying above. From *China at War* 7, no. 1 (July 1941).

status accorded to heroic female pilots. For those who were not willing to become pilots, other kinds of wartime female work related to aviation were promoted. Articles with titles such as "Urge the Nation's Women to Participate in the Movement to Raise Money for Planes," and "Raise the Discussion and Make Contributions, Women Call for Planes," exhorted Chinese women to raise crucial funds for building China's wartime air force (Yun 1941).

It was in this context that Shi Jianqiao, along with her brother Zefan, established the Hechuan Civic Campaign to Donate Warplanes (Hechuan xianji yundong). Hechuan was a small city in the eastern part of Sichuan that had been bombed four times by Japan between 1940 and 1941. Shi and her brother arrived in Hechuan only a day after it was bombed in July 1940, and part of their motivation to raise money for planes stemmed from witnessing the devastation that resulted. In the preface to *Xianji zhuankan* (Special publication of the campaign to raise funds for warplanes), the promotional literature of the campaign, Shi Zefan described how the second bombing on July 22 was particularly devastating (Shi 1941, 3). One hundred and eight Japanese planes had dropped five hundred bombs, injured two thousand people, and killed seven hundred. Four thousand homes and ninety ships were destroyed.[7] According to the English-language journal *China at War*, Japanese demolition bombs and incendiaries wiped out more than three-fourths of the city.[8]

Faced with this devastation, Shi Jianqiao and her brother were driven to act. In November 1940, on the National Day to Defend the Skies, they gathered together the leaders of various groups and social circles of Hechuan and broached the idea of raising money for warplanes. On December 7, 1940, prominent civic leaders, including the head of Hechuan County, the chairman of the County's Merchant Association, the director of the local branch of the Bank of China, the secretary of the local party organization, and others joined together to establish the Committee to Raise Donations for Hechuan Warplanes. By April 1941 the campaign had raised funds for three airplanes, and by the end of May the Hechuan Movement had gained national recognition. On May 30, 1941, Jiang Jieshi dispatched Air Major-General Chen Qingyun to represent the government and preside over official ceremonies to mark Hechuan's donation of three planes to the national air force.[9] Allotting one hundred and fifty thousand *yuan* to fly the Hechuan jets from Chengdu to Hechuan's airspace and engage in aerial performance, Jiang Jieshi allowed Chen to receive the donated planes with great fanfare.[10]

Although they were few, these planes were nonetheless highly symbolic. Yuan Xueya, the magistrate of Hechuan and coorganizer with Shi Jianqiao of the campaign, linked the modest donation to the larger purpose of patriotic defense, "Without air strength there is no national defense. We can only respond to bombing with bombing. Then we can protect ourselves" (Yuan 1941). In a short commentary on the event, Jiang Jieshi himself wrote that Hechuan's action was "the most powerful kind of response to the enemy—not only are we not afraid of the bombing, but on the contrary, the more they bomb, the more our anger and passions grow" (Jiang 1941). He then proceeded to write of his hopes that the passion so evident in the Hechuan affair would spread to all the counties of Sichuan and, indeed, to all corners of free China.

Much of the success of the Hechuan campaign rested with Shi Jianqiao. To begin with, the famous daughter brought to the movement her organizational and fund-raising skills. Under her guidance, the Hechuan group used several methods to raise donations. First, well-to-do landowners were approached and asked to make special contributions. This approach resulted in one Hechuan farmer turning over a piece of land worth twenty-four thousand dollars and others donating either money or rice.[11] The second method was the "one-dollar" movement, which encouraged each Hechuan resident to donate at least a dollar to the cause. The final method was the organization of dramatic performances whose proceeds would be used for the warplanes. Since Hechuan was a small provincial town, it did not have a sophisticated theater culture. Shi Jianqiao thus used her connections in Chongqing to round up a crew of Chongqing actors, including well-known Peking Opera actors such as Li Fenglou and Tao Shanting, to volunteer their time, travel to Hechuan, and perform for local audiences. Performances were held three nights in a row from February 6 to February 8. According to one campaign report of the event, seats were sold out, and the performances raised more than fifty thousand *yuan*. The report further noted that "the audience's mood was remarkably enthusiastic, feeling that the performance was worthy as art, not to mention that it also served to save the nation" (Yi 1941, 19).

If Shi Jianqiao's organization skills were invaluable to the campaign, so too was her illustrious past. While she had founded the organization with her brother Zefan, Shi Jianqiao served as the public figurehead, and her brother primarily worked behind the scenes. In its announcement of the Sichuan Province–wide Campaign to Raise Funds for One Hundred Warplanes in July 1941, the Nationalists cited the Hechuan movement as source of inspiration and singled out the well-known Shi Jianqiao, along with Yuan Xueya, the Hechuan magistrate, as crucial players in the Hechuan success.[12] Shi Jianqiao also publicly represented the movement in print. The *Zhongyang ribao* coverage of the ceremonial donation of the Hechuan warplanes included a piece by Shi Jianqiao on the campaign along with an article by Chen Qingyun, the Nationalist official in charge of receiving the planes, a longer poem memorializing the movement by Feng Yuxiang, as well as the above-mentioned lines commemorating the affair written by Jiang Jieshi.[13] Finally, Shi Jianqiao's actual ties to the regime no doubt facilitated the success of the movement and ensured official recognition of the affair. The inclusion of the commemorative poem by Feng Yuxiang, Shi Jianqiao's long-time patron, suggests that the national attention paid to the Hechuan donation was at least partially due to Shi's connections to Feng.

Shi Jianqiao's past reputation made her a powerful spokeswoman for the Hechuan campaign in particular and for Chinese patriotism in general. Her heroic commitment to moral causes for which she was willing to act and seek retribution symbolized how Chinese patriotism against the Japanese was being defined and articulated. The Japanese campaign of bombing Chongqing and hinterland cities, intended to weaken Chinese citizens' support for their government, had the opposite effect. The ruthless and indiscriminate nature of the bombing stiffened the resolve of the Chinese and raised cries for revenge. Not surprisingly, the concept of retribution centrally framed the rhetoric of resistance and patriotism in much of the literature related to the Hechuan movement. In his preface to the campaign's promotional material, Shi Zefan writes, "In this tragic situation where we are bombed by the Japanese, we have righteous fury (*yifen*); we want to seek revenge for our comrades; we want to bomb those who have bombed us; let us raise money for warplanes! The Hechuan campaign has raised enough for only three planes and we know that is minimal on a national scale. But, these planes have symbolic value. . . . Comrades of this country, rise together!"[14]

This passage struck an intensely emotional note and was clearly intended to mobilize the Chinese people. What is notable is the language of revenge and righteous anger (*yifen*). Just as righteous anger had been used to justify Shi Jianqiao's act of revenge in 1935 in the courts of law, here righteous indignation is evoked to mobilize patriotism and the desire to seek revenge against the Japanese. At another point, Shi Zefan writes, "We feel toward our enemy that it should be a 'tooth for a tooth,' and a 'punch should return a punch.' Give the Japanese bombers a bomb in return! . . . This is true patriotism [*aiguo zhi xin*]."[15] With patriotism during the War of Resistance being framed in terms of righteous revenge, Shi Jianqiao was a perfect leader of anti-Japanese activities.

In "Respond! Hechuan's Warplanes," a commemorative poem about the Hechuan resistance efforts, Feng Yuxiang similarly adopted this tone of urgency and the rhetoric of revenge. The entire poem was printed in the *Zhongyang ribao* on the day of the ceremonial donation of the warplanes, and part of it reads as follows:

> "Japan's Bandits, . . .
> Raid the skies daily, . . .
> Our revenge is deeper than the sea,
> Our shame is greater than the skies . . .
> Ms. Shi Jianqiao and Zefan,
> Raised funds for planes in Hechuan. . . .
> One county, three planes,
> One province, a hundred planes. . . .
> Our strong air force will rise,
> Proceed to Tokyo and bomb,
> Our shame will be avenged,
> Our Nation and homes will be saved!
> Each one of us is born Chinese!
> Sacrifice and fight to survive,
> Do not let others take our glory,
> Quick, rise and respond![16]

It was no accident that Feng Yuxiang chose the medium of poetry to stir public passions. Poetry, in general, was being used widely as a means to awaken the Chinese masses and instill in them a patriotic consciousness. In his study of recitation poetry, a subgenre of wartime poetry, John Crespi argues that much of the era's poetry was characterized by certain "talkiness," which ensured that the poetry was closely associated with the register of the spoken, and that it was this "apostrophic mode of direct address that in effect 'hail[ed]' an imagined, national audience" (Crespi 2001, 131). In this poem, Feng adopts such "talkiness," speaking directly to his audience, encouraging them to action by telling them to "proceed to Tokyo and bomb" and thus avenge the shame of China. The employment of the language of deep shame and national revenge was further meant to appeal to public sentiment and urge patriotic resistance. His explicit mention of Shi Jianqiao in this context no doubt made the appeal for revenge even more powerful. For readers of Feng's poem, many of whom had migrated from Shanghai and other coastal cities and remembered the affair of Sun Chuanfang well, the connection between Shi Jianqiao as a heroic avenger who had killed a warlord on behalf of her father and country in the mid-1930s and Shi Jianqiao as an effective patriot against the Japanese in the early 1940s would have been easy to make.

Several participants and observers echoed Feng Yuxiang's appreciation of Shi Jianqiao's moral heroism for her expression of wartime patriotism. In the English-language journal, *China at War*, the correspondent covering the movement wrote, "A young woman fired the imagination of Hochwan's [*sic*] energetic magistrate and its population in the 'give planes' movement. Miss Shih Chien-chiao [Shi Jianqiao] crashed into the front pages of the Chinese press a few years prior to the outbreak of the war by assassinating Sun Chuan-fang . . . to avenge her father's death. The case aroused so much popular sympathy that . . . she was granted a special amnesty."[17] By mentioning in one breath her ability to inspire the people of Hechuan during the war and her ability make a splash in the mass media and garner public sympathy in the 1930s, this passage also testifies that Shi's reputation as a sympathy-arousing avenger had not been forgotten. Yuan Xueya, the head of Hechuan County and official representative of the Hechuan campaign, was perhaps most explicit about the point. In a *Dagongbao* article, he stated that as one who had once avenged her father, won the intervention of the state, and embodied the spirit of relentlessly serving the country, Shi Jianqiao was a uniquely inspirational leader for Hechuan's efforts.[18]

If Shi's reputation for having once been a moral avenger was seen as crucial in rousing ordinary Chinese to stand up and resist, so too was her reputation for being passionate. By the 1940s, Shi's *qing* referred not simply to her filial sentiment but more generally to her overall ability to feel deeply. One writer describes Shi as a perfect source of inspiration precisely because she was someone who "when she hates, she really hates; but when she loves she truly loves" (Zheng 1988, 109). Her ability to experience such passions with great sincerity was taken as the basis of authentic love for the country. True patriots were to be like Shi Jianqiao in their ability to hate the Japanese with fervor and love China with a passion.

Just like the public sympathy that Shi Jianqiao had won in the Republican era, the patriotism that she inspired during the War of Resistance was gendered feminine. It was no accident that, as a female patriot, Shi Jianqiao was so effective in stirring patriotism and was ranked among other real-life and fictional women also known to mobilize patriotic sentiment. Xie Bingying, for example, was a particularly famous female patriot. She had participated in the Northern Expedition and in organizing the Hunan Women's War Zone service corps at the start of the war against Japan, and her autobiographical accounts of her harrowing experiences as a female soldier during the Northern Expedition proved popular during the War of Resistance. Chang-tai Hung describes Xie's writings as "no mere flag-waving propaganda pieces about war, . . . [instead they] were often filled with tears and agony (Hung 1994, 75)." Clearly, such writing was able to regale readers, kindle their emotions, and bind them together as a patriotic public. Hung elaborates that heroines of wartime drama differed from their May Fourth sisters in significant ways. Whereas May Fourth women had championed individual subjectivity and romantic love, wartime heroines by the late 1930s and 1940s embodied commitment to the collective goals of the nation and love of the country (76). Xie Bingying's autobiography, *Nübing zhi zhuan* (A woman soldier's own story), literally narrates this shift by recounting her personal transformation from schoolgirl infatuation with the idea of romantic love that was in vogue during her teen years during the May Fourth era to an awakening to the need for commitment to revolution in the late twenties and, finally, to love for the nation as a patriot during the war against the Japanese.[19]

In addition to actual women, fictional heroines also served to mobilize patriotism. In his examination of spoken drama during the eight-year war against Japan, Hung (1994) documents how dramatists played a part in engendering the symbolic power of female patriotism. Bringing spoken drama off the urban stage into the streets of the hinterland to galvanize mass support for the war, these wartime dramatists found that heroic female tropes long familiar to the Chinese population were particularly powerful symbols of resistance. Just as Shi Jianqiao had realized in the 1930s when courting public sentiment for her cause of revenge, playwrights of the 1940s realized that female warriors and patriotic courtesans could excel at mobilizing popular support for resistance efforts. Featuring the traditional female hero, Hua Mulan, Ouyang Yuqian's *Mulan congjun* (Mulan joins the army), for example, was one of the most popular dramas during the war. As Hung argues, the antibarbarian sentiment of the play, along with themes of filial piety, were easily transferred to anti-Japanese sentiment and loyalty to the Chinese.[20]

Patriotism was gendered feminine not merely because women like Shi Jianqiao so effectively embodied the sentiment. Patriots whom she inspired were imagined to be primarily women. One memoir, for example, recounts how Shi's leadership in the Hechuan movement motivated female students in Hechuan's Number Two Girls' Middle School in particular. Upon her visit to the school, Shi encouraged the young girls to study diligently, love their country, and engage in acts of patriotic resistance (Zheng 1988, 109). In turn, these schoolgirls found Shi to be "brave and a hero among women." Just as the public sympathy that Shi elicited in the Republican era was best embodied by school girls who lined up by the steps of the courtroom, the patriotism she inspired during the War of Resistance was best represented by school girls ready for war.

While public sympathy of the 1930s and the collective patriotism of the 1940s were both gendered feminine, they also diverged in important ways. As mentioned earlier, writers in the 1930s criticized the widespread sympathy for assassin Shi among female students in particular. Some even issued dire warnings that such feminine sympathy was a sign of China's failed modern education. In contrast, writers in the 1940s celebrated the public support for patriot Shi. Feminine collective sentiment was no longer something to be skeptical of but had instead become the basis of national strength in a time of war. Another notable divergence between the two forms of collective emotion was their relationship to the central regime. Public sympathy for Shi in the 1930s was based on her being perceived as a vigilante provider of justice, a female knight-errant (*xia*), whose presence could pose an implicit critique of Nationalist rule. Patriotism in the 1940s was arguably also an expression of *xia* chivalry, but not in the sense of functioning as an alternative authority that challenged that of the central regime. Rather, wartime patriotism was a noble force that rallied support for the Nationalist-led nation against the Japanese aggressors. In short, if Shi's female sentiment had been the basis of a potentially *critical* form of public sympathy during the 1930s, by the 1940s it had become the basis of patriotism and love for one's country that promoted the wartime regime's agenda.

SHI JIANQIAO'S FATE IN COMMUNIST CHINA: REVISIONISM AND POLITICAL SURVIVAL

In the Communist era, Shi Jianqiao's fate changed drastically. The prestige and national limelight that Shi Jianqiao enjoyed in the early 1940s disappeared quickly in the post-1949 period. Whereas Shi Jianqiao's reputation of moral heroism was absolute during the war against Japan, the moral significance of Shi Jianqiao's actions and all that they represented proved to be more ambiguous in the post-1949 period. Facing a starkly different political atmosphere, in which the ability to demonstrate one's "redness" or revolutionary credentials was crucial, Shi Jianqiao's embodiment of filial heroism—so useful in the 1930s consumer culture and in the resistance movements of the 1940s—had become a real liability. For the sake of political survival, she found that she had to reinvent her personal history in radical ways. No longer portraying herself as acting out of filial devotion to her father, Shi Jianqiao retold her story to show that she was driven by revolutionary passions to act against feudal and imperialist forces. Evidence suggests that, despite her efforts to recast the past in the politically correct terms of her new present, Shi nonetheless suffered during the Cultural Revolution.

The two initial decades of Chinese Communist Party (CCP) rule constituted a period when China witnessed the heightened politicization of all corners of society. Although Mao Zedong had been sidelined in Shanghai after the failure of the Great Leap Forward in the late 1950s, the early 1960s saw Lin Biao and the People's Liberation Army busily promoting the Cult of Mao on the streets to help Mao regain political power at the center. The mass dissemination of the chairman's Little Red Book and other forms of propaganda helped deify Mao, and his ideas of Permanent Revolution promoted revolutionary progress through the voluntarism of the oppressed classes. The popularity of Mao's idea that certain classes were more revolutionary than others led to an increase in the amount of social and political pressure on intellectuals and those whose class backgrounds were suspect. By 1966, this political struggle and the politicization of society in general culminated in the Great Proletarian Cultural Revolution, a period of tremendous political and social upheaval in modern Chinese history.

Shi Jianqiao had entered the Communist era bearing several crosses. First, she embodied filial piety, which was increasingly identified as feudal and even counterrevolutionary. Second, she had been approved by the Nationalist regime through a high-profile pardon. Third, she had been patronized by Feng Yuxiang, an ex-warlord and member of the Nationalist regime. During the 1950s, however, Shi led a quiet life. After running the Congyun elementary school for underprivileged children in Suzhou from 1946 to 1952, Shi returned to Beijing to nurse her ailing health, and by 1957 she had been elected as a member of the Second Political Congress of Beijing City. It was not until the 1960s that her past became a problem. During this highly politicized decade, Shi was in danger of being identified as having once been part of a "reactionary class" and thus becoming a target in an era of class struggle. To rectify the situation and establish her revolutionary credentials, Shi sought to the best of her ability to present a revised version of her past. Shi produced two autobiographical accounts—one written in 1963, and the other in 1966—in which she continued to demonstrate skill in presenting her actions in politically and morally correct narratives. This decision to clarify her past in appropriate terms for the 1960s was not merely expedient, but most likely necessary for her own and her family's well-being. Yet, while she demonstrated ingenuity in her self-presentation in both accounts, the success she had achieved in the earlier era proved elusive in the politically charged milieu of the 1960s.

Shi Jianqiao was fully aware that among the most appreciated political virtues of the early 1960s was the ability to ferret out class oppression and stand up to feudal forces. Thus, while she was eager to tap into traditions of Confucian heroism in the earlier, nativist period of New Life nationalism, by the revolutionary decade of the 1960s, she carefully avoided any reference to the classic tradition of Confucian martyrdom. Moving away from her motive of filial piety, Shi nonetheless continued to draw from the more popular tradition of knight-errantry. *Xia* heroism, which traditionally emphasized the concepts of action and retribution, was certainly more aligned with modern concepts of revolutionary martyrdom and revolt. For many, the image and ethos of the traditional virtuous assassin, or *xiake*, symbolized revolutionary virtue, and Communist rhetoric frequently invoked the *xia*-hero. Mao himself often cited the traditional novel, the *Shuihuzhuan* (frequently translated into English as *Water Margins*, or *Outlaws of the Marsh*) to demonstrate the existence of the idea of peasant revolution in Chinese history.[21]

Shi Jianqiao was thus acting strategically when she decided to write "Tiebao bu" (A scrapbook) in 1963, in which she emphasized the *xia* qualities of her earlier reputation and presented her behavior in the 1930s as being truly revolutionary in nature. In the piece, she recounts the story of her 1935–36 provincial-level court trial and describes in detail a confrontation with one of the trial judges of the Hebei Superior Court. The account recalls her response to a judge when she discovered that he had suppressed two defense witnesses, Wang Hua'nan and Qu Hongtao, who were to appear in court:

> Wang Hua'nan and Qu Hongtao are important witnesses to this case precisely because they were conscientious and told the truth at the start of the trial. You [judges] bully us weaker ones with your powerful connections by expelling them from the case. You are evil-hearted! The two witnesses are expelled only because of the power and money of the Sun [Chuanfang] family. But, you cannot cover the sky with one hand; nor can you cover up history. Indeed, you cannot deny that I, Shi Jianqiao, killed Sun Chuanfang

> to avenge my father's murder. You all want to overturn [the decision to recognize] my confession and deny me a more lenient sentence. Having sought revenge for my father, I am not afraid to die; do you think I am afraid to sit in jail? You will never be able to change history and in the end, the victory will be mine!"[22]

It is highly unlikely that Shi Jianqiao actually spoke these words. The language, including phrases like "bully us weaker ones," sounds more like the class-struggle discourse of the 1960s than the language that would have been used in the 1930s. The last sentence, "you will never be able to change history," is particularly ironic as that was precisely what the political climate of the 1960s was forcing Shi Jianqiao to do.

To demonstrate further how the rhetorical strategies adopted in this passage were crafted with the politicized atmosphere of the Cultural Revolution in mind, take for example how Shi Jianqiao portrays herself here as a victim of the old feudal forces of the courts and newspapers of the Republican era. The Maoist discourse of the era identified those who were most oppressed and victimized as the strongest and most capable revolutionary agents. No doubt aware of the new political rhetoric, Shi portrayed herself as having once been a victim who stood up against feudal forces, and thus, in the current day, as someone with political credentials. To this end, she portrayed Republican China as feudal and riddled with corruption, and charged the political authorities of the day with being reactionary. Such an image nicely coincided with the prevailing image promoted by the communist regime. The Nanjing decade judge, for example, was identified as unequivocally evil and willing to bully the weak. The powerful Sun family was corrupt in its willingness to use power and money to impede justice. Newspapers were identified as conspirators against the people. In explaining why her outburst against the trial judge was never reported in the press, Shi states, "I now realize that these old newspapers served the reactionary classes; in old society, it was the wronged and those who experienced injustice who could never be victorious." Her explanation thus simultaneously sought to preempt doubt about the veracity of her claim as well as implicate the newspapers. The press, which Shi had so actively courted throughout the Nanjing decade, was, by her account in 1963, conspiring with other reactionary groups in society against the wronged and innocent.

In much of this revisionist account, we can detect her concern to disarm charges that she had been backed by Nationalist figures. As mentioned above, in the political milieu of the1950s and 1960s, Shi Jianqiao's state pardon was a heavy cross to bear. After a brief period of national and economic consolidation in the early 1950s, in which capitalist organizations were mobilized for purposes of national recovery, the CCP started as early as 1951 to initiate aggressive campaigns that targeted politically problematic urban sectors. In addition to thought reform against intellectuals, there was the 1952 *Sanfan* (Three-antis) campaign against bureaucratic corruption and inefficiency, and the *Wufan* (Five-antis) attack on the "bourgeoisie," namely, Chinese industrialists and businessmen, many of whom had close connections with the Nationalists but had decided nonetheless to stay in China. In these campaigns, old Nationalist officials who had retained urban administrative positions and Nationalist-affiliated businessmen suffered the most. By the 1960s, political persecution in general and persecution of those with any previous connection to the Nationalist regime had only heightened. It was in this milieu that Shi Jianqiao attempted to explicitly disavow any connection between herself and the Republican-era regime. For example, the 1963 "Scrapbook" ends with the statement, "In old society, the number who suffered injustices was unthinkable! If I did have the backing of the 'fake government' before the trial, how could it have come to this point? If I think of it today, it is still painful! (Shi 1986, 197)." For Shi Jianqiao, this final claim was meant to dispel rumors that the Nationalists had rigged the Republican-era trial in her favor and that she had once been complicit with "feudal" powers herself.

To suggest that her connections to the Nationalists were never as strong as they might have appeared, Shi Jianqiao not only sought to revise the public interpretation of her trial, but also retold her experiences during the War of Resistance.[23] In an autobiographical chronicle written during the height of the Cultural Revolution in November 1966, Shi launched into great detail about how she had politely declined a request by Song Meiling, the wife of Jiang Jieshi, who was the head of the National Women's Provisions Group during the early 1940s. She told how Song Meiling had been so impressed by her accomplishments in the Hechuan movement that Song had called upon Feng Yuxiang to invite her, Shi, to lead the national Chongqing Movement to Raise Funds for a Hundred Fighter Planes. Shi then said that, despite the honor and prestige of the offer, her final decision was to turn down Song's request. In her son's version of the events, this decision elicited begrudging respect from even Feng Yuxiang, who reportedly uttered, "Jianqiao truly has a backbone" (Shi 1982). This emphasis on Shi Jianqiao's tactful decline of Song Meiling's offer, found both in her own version as well as her son's hagiography, was not without purpose. It was a deliberate attempt to disassociate herself from the right-leaning Nationalist regime.

Shi Jianqiao's revision of her wartime activities also sought to demonstrate how she had actively forged connections with prominent communist leaders even before the 1949 Revolution. During the early 1940s, many key communist figures had not yet joined Mao in Yan'an. Even though the Second United Front between the Nationalists and the CCP had fallen apart as early as 1941, relations between the two did not worsen to the point of civil war until after Japan's surrender in 1945. Many communist leaders and party members thus remained based in Chongqing and the surrounding areas. With her reputation and connections, Shi Jianqiao was able to meet several of them during that period. For example, according to the above-mentioned 1966 autobiographical account, Tao Xingzhi, a fellow Anhui native who was a famous educator, publicist, and activist in anti-Japanese war efforts, introduced Shi to several key leaders of the Chinese left. These included CCP elder Dong Biwu, Zhou Enlai, and Zhou's wife, Deng Yingchao, a famous female revolutionary in her own right and one of about thirty women to have participated in the Long March.[24] The account also describes how Shi met other well-known CCP sympathizers during the 1940s. Those mentioned include Shi Liang, a famous left-leaning female lawyer who, while never becoming a party member, was one of the most important noncommunist members in the communist era, as well as Song Qingling, the only Song sister who was sympathetic to the efforts of the communists. It even mentions how in 1956 Shi Jianqiao had written a letter directly to Mao Zedong himself, reflecting upon current social issues, and that on June 3 of that year, Mao in reply sent someone to provide her with money and told her to take care of her health as she was convalescing in Beijing from an illness.

Merely showing how she had actively forged relations with key leftist figures in the 1940s and 1950s, however, was apparently not enough. In the 1966 memoir, Shi Jianqiao felt compelled to justify further why she did not accompany Zhou Enlai and other CCP revolutionaries to the Yan'an base area. The account went out of its way to explain that upon hearing Zhou Enlai's rallying call to protect the children of workers of the Communist Party, Shi Jianqiao decided to stay behind within Nationalist-controlled territory to establish the Congyun Elementary School of Suzhou. On the surface, the Congyun Elementary School was a legitimate educational facility that targeted children of workers and poor residents of the city as well as orphans (Chen 1991). With help from Feng Yuxiang and educator Tao Xingzhi, Shi Jianqiao raised money for the institution.

One essayist recalled meeting her at fund-raising banquets for the school organized by the Anhui native-place association and noted how truly dedicated she was to raising donations to provide tuition for underprivileged students (Zheng 1992). Another writer noted how, despite one drunken guest who asked her about the rumors that she had political backing in her 1935 revenge, her unequivocal disavowal and truly sincere expression of sorrow for losing her father left such a deep impression that she raised even more money than she otherwise might have (Juan 1967).

Despite these memorable efforts at building a school for underprivileged children, there is evidence that behind the scenes, the school served as a center for covert revolutionary activities. As some post-1949 supporters of Shi Jianqiao argued in retrospect, the school was an organization from which Shi Jianqiao was able to help with the revolution from within Nationalist-held territory. Revolutionary training of progressive youths, the publication of the underground CCP journal entitled the *Guangmingbao*, and the housing of the Suzhou underground communist organization's transmitter-receiver during the 1949 Revolution purportedly all took place at the Congyun facility.[25]

Furthermore, Shi Jianqiao boasted about how she was able to turn her close connections to the Nationalists toward revolutionary ends. In the 1966 memoir, she writes that it was precisely because of her relationship with Feng Yuxiang that the Congyun Elementary School avoided being blacklisted by the Nationalists, so that the above-mentioned covert activities could take place. A sympathetic retrospective account agreed that Shi Jianqiao's unique reputation and connections had enabled her to accomplish things other ordinary people could not during this period. Author Chen Jin (1991) writes that Shi knew she could "use her special status and develop its unique potential" in the service of the CCP within Nationalist-controlled areas. Connections to Feng Yuxiang, he notes, allowed her to move freely and without suspicion so that she was able to engage in covert CCP activities. Qualifying her relationship with Feng Yuxiang was perhaps the most difficult rhetorical task that Shi faced in revising her past, and portraying these relations as expedient for the revolution was clever indeed.

Finally, Shi Jianqiao's involvement in aiding the family of heroic defector Liu Shanben was yet another accomplishment that was frequently cited as evidence of her true Communist colors even while she lived in Nationalist-held territory (e.g., Chen 1991). Flying a B-24 Bomber on June 26, 1946, to Yan'an, Liu Shanben, a pilot of the Nationalist Central Air force, was the first Nationalist pilot to defect to the Communist forces (Chen and Ling 1986, 235). Given that this was the summer in which Jiang Jieshi was planning to launch a general offensive to decimate the communists, Liu's defection caused a tremendous sensation.[26] Shi Jianqiao was involved with the defection, and biographers later emphasized this involvement. They noted that she had helped ensure that Liu's wife and family, whom he had left behind in the Shanghai area, were provided for after the defection. For example, in a hagiographic biography of his mother, Shi Yuyao, Shi Jianqiao's son, claimed that Zhou Enlai had personally entrusted Shi Jianqiao with this task precisely because Shi Jianqiao had connections with upper-level air force figures and could borrow a military jeep to arrange for the financial security of the Liu family (Shi 1982, 10–11). Another memoir recounts how Mao Zedong and Zhou Enlai arranged to have underground agents take care of Liu Shanben's family after his defection. Underground agents included a "Liao Chengzhi, Xia Yandeng, and even female hero Shi Jianqiao, who made her name assassinating warlord Sun Chuanfang. . . . Liu Shanben before his death often talked of this really moving and colorful past, and each time could not avoid shedding grateful, hot tears" (Shi 1987, 519).

During the Cultural Revolution, Shi Jianqiao's efforts to revise her past were to little avail. While the paper trail of Shi Jianqiao's political activities and life grows extremely thin during that tumultuous decade, there is evidence that Shi Jianqiao came under severe attack. The mere fact that she had attempted to rewrite the past through these autobiographical accounts in 1963 and 1966 suggests that she was facing an unpleasant political climate. Furthermore, at the Chongqing City archives, which houses the documents on the Hechuan Campaign to Raise Funds for Warplanes, the catalogue card for Shi Jianqiao has "counterrevolutionary" written in the space for one's "political character" (*xingzhi*). Filed in the summer of 1969, this characterization is a sure indication that Shi Jianqiao was struggled against during the Cultural Revolution.

By the 1970s, however, the attempts by Shi Jianqiao and her sympathizers paid off. Shi was fully rehabilitated by the time she died. Her final years were spent in Beijing, where she had become a member of the People's Consultative Conference to Beijing's City Government. On August 27, 1979, Shi Jianqiao died of colon cancer at age 73 (Shi 1987). Her memorial services were organized by the People's Consultative Conference to Beijing's City Government, and the eulogy read during the memorial characterized Shi's activities during the War of Resistance as heroic and pro-Communist in nature. According to the eulogy, Shi Jianqiao was active in promoting the strategy of the united front of the Chinese Communist Party's national efforts in resisting the Japanese. She was reported to have participated in efforts of organizing entertainment and supplies for the reinforcements or supporting troops in Changsha, Hunan, and was particularly lauded for her ability to defy the Nationalists and help the CCP's famous Route Eight Army by securing fair prices for much-needed supplies. This eulogy noted that Zhou Enlai had commended her efforts when Shi was in Chongqing in the early 1940s, that she had helped the Communist Party after the war when she entered the profession of education with the Congyun Elementary School, and that she had aided the family of CCP hero Liu Shanben at her own risk. In short, by the time of her death, her political credentials were once again reestablished and, for all concerned, Shi Jianqiao had been a Communist Party loyalist since the 1940s. She was furthermore depicted as a true patriot even on her deathbed, where she purportedly indicated that her last wish was to see the eventual unification of Taiwan and the mainland (Chen 1991). No mention was made of her involvement in the Nationalist-endorsed Hechuan Campaign to Raise Funds for Warplanes, nor was it mentioned that she had been branded a counter-revolutionary during the 1960s.

CONCLUSION

The case of Shi Jianqiao continued to ignite the public imagination even after her death in 1979. This social fascination transcended national boundaries, with the case appearing in retrospective accounts published in the PRC, Taiwan, and Hong Kong. It also crossed generic boundaries. The story appeared in memoirs, film, hagiographical biographies, regional and popular histories, unofficial and "wild" histories (*yeshi*), illustrated flipbooks, and, more recently, on the Internet.[27] Notably, the retelling of Shi Jianqiao's story often followed closely the narrative that Shi had already spun to the media during the Republican period. Several accounts simply collected the various clippings of newspaper coverage of the 1935–36 case and printed them. This tendency to conform to the original narrative speaks to the enduring hold of narratives of filial sentiment and female heroic retribution. That said, differences in emphasis and slight revisions appear in some of the accounts. Some of these variances stem from generic considerations, but others suggest that each retelling of the story of Shi Jianqiao served to mediate contemporary concerns and local agendas.

Take, for example, the 1985 publication *Nüjie Shi Jianqiao* (Female hero Shi Jianqiao), a hagiography of Shi Jianqiao written by her son Shi

Yuyao and Shen Yuli (Shi and Shen 1985). This publication was part of a larger trend of political rehabilitation. A swing back from the extreme idealism and radicalism of the preceding era began in the central government in 1978 with a series of politically symbolic acts and ideological shifts that undermined Mao Zedong's legacy. The Third Plenum of December 1978 called for a sweeping "reversal of verdicts" and the rehabilitation of several of Mao's old foes, including Peng Dehuai, a popular general who had been dismissed in 1959 and was widely regarded as having been wronged by the extremism of the Mao era. A torrent of implicit criticism of Mao followed in official channels, and activists who were part of the 1978–1981 Democracy Wall movement published explicit critiques in unofficial journals and wall posters. Those who had once been branded as "rightists" and "capitalist-roaders" during the late Mao era were restored to high cultural and political positions in major cities. The Gang of Four trial, initiated on November 20, 1980, was perhaps the most high-profile reversal of verdicts. Widely televised, the trial, in which four members of the powerful radical clique under Mao were held responsible for the excesses of the Cultural Revolution, constituted a searing indictment of Mao Zedong and the radicalism of the preceding era.[28]

Such reversals of verdicts did not simply take place at the political center. Authors and writers also reflected on the violence and personal trauma experienced during the Cultural Revolution. Much of the literary production was introspective and reflective. Publication of "scar literature," for example, was meant to heal, as its name suggests, and to mediate the transition away from the destructive idealism of the Mao era to a new, more pragmatic era of socialism under Deng Xiaoping. Reportage literature was yet another genre that examined the excesses of the past and prompted readers to participate in the creation of a more rational society. It was in this context of readdressing the excesses of the Cultural Revolution and making amends to the victims of the preceding era that *Nüjie Shi Jianqiao* was published. Along with coauthor Shen Yuli, Shi's son, Shi Yuyao, strove to redeem his mother's legacy through a celebratory biography. It did so by revisiting not only the revenge case of 1935–36, but also Shi Jianqiao's underground activities during the 1940s. To demonstrate how Shi Jianqiao had, in fact, aided the Chinese Communist Party, the biography elaborates upon her building of the Shi Congyun Elementary School as a front for underground CCP activity and her crucial role in mediating Liu Shanben's move from the Nationalist air force to the Communist cause.[29]

Many more popular history publications featuring Shi Jianqiao's case

施羽尧 沈渝丽
女杰施剑翘
北方文艺出版社

Figure 11. Cover of *Nüjie Shi Jianqiao* (Female hero Shi Jianqiao), a celebratory biography coauthored by Shi Jianqiao's son, Shi Yuyao, and Shen Yuli (1985).

followed. With the stabilization of the political situation after the 1970s, the loosening of ideological strictures, and the privatization and renewed focus on the economy in the 1980s, the buying power of the urban Chinese increased significantly, and the market for more popular leisure and entertainment-oriented mass publications expanded rapidly. Jeffrey Kinkley discusses this growing market for popular literary commodities in a recent book on crime fiction and notes that 1984 was a pivotal year. In 1980–81 under Deng Xiaoping's "cultural thaw," translated mysteries by Conan Doyle and Agatha Christie were extremely popular, especially while it was still politically inopportune for Chinese to write about Chinese crime. But 1984 was a time of turning away from the campaigns against spiritual pollution that had arisen in 1983 to suppress the 1979 Democracy Wall movement, and during this period Chinese crime fiction exploded onto the scene. Kinkley notes that even though this fiction was often formulaic, had roots in sensation, was poor in literary quality, and left many social issues unexamined, it was nonetheless upsetting to the

Chinese status quo. He writes, "freer buying and selling of books and magazines after 1984 allowed writers in all genres to 'compete' like prosecutors and defenders, with each other and with the state, and yet live to argue another polemic another day" (Kinkley 2000, 15). These genres became a means for popular authors and their readers to adjudicate the contemporary situation.

Shi Jianqiao's crime case, while not fiction, was a popular history of a legal case that had much in common with the crime fiction discussed by Kinkley. The case of Shi Jianqiao was discussed in the popular histories of the Republican era and allowed readers to address, if obliquely, a sense of injustice in the present day. Indeed, in the People's Republic of China of the late 1980s and 1990s, the sexuality, religion, and violence of China's pre-1949 era were perceived as both lurid and fascinating in contrast to the Communist cultural repression and ideological Puritanism from the 1950s to 1970s. This social interest in the pre-1949 period included nostalgia for the countryside and the past found in "roots literature" (*xungen pai*) and fifth-generation films such as *Hong gaoliang (Red Sorghum)*. Accompanying a fascination with the rural past was a renewed appetite for the urban intrigue and political machinations of the Republican era. Titles such as *Minguo juxiong shou'e da jishi* (The great record of rapacious and evil events of the Republican period); *Minguo mishi* (The secret histories of the Republican era); and *Minguo sifa heimu* (The dark secrets of justice in Republican China) popped onto bookstore shelves. Several such titles focused on extraordinary cases or famous assassinations. Examples include *Daoguang jianying: Minguo ansha jilu* (The glory of the sword: The record of assassination in Republican China); *Minguo ansha yao'an* (Important assassination cases of Republican China [Jing 1996]); *Minguo da'an jishi* (The true account of great cases in Republican China [Jing 1997]); *Jindai zhongguo da'an jishi* (An account of key cases in modern China); and *Jinzui meirenyü—Minguo qi'an* (The drunken mermaid—remarkable cases of the Republican era [Zhu 1986]). All such compilations of assassinations featured the Case of Shi Jianqiao. *Minguo shashou chunqiu* (The annals of assassins in Republican China) included Shi Jianqiao's own essay (Shi 1994).

Even while many of these titles suggest a lurid tale of the Republican past, the books are not necessarily negative. Some are concerned with minute details and, through such minutiae, seek to lure the reader into the intrigue and machinations of the bizarre affair, working much as did Shi Jianqiao's own story and the Republican-era media's detailed coverage of the assassination. Others treated the case as an example of pa-

Figure 12. Print of Shi Jianqiao shooting Sun Chuanfang, included in a 1986 compilation of remarkable Republican-era cases (Zhu 1986).

triotism. In the chapter on the case of Shi Jianqiao in *Cike shi* (The history of Chinese assassins), the author positively assesses the patriotism of Shi Jianqiao's revenge. "From an objective perspective, Shi Jianqiao killing Sun Chuanfang was above all a patriotic action" (Ge 1999, 176). To validate this assessment, the author paints Sun as a traitor by reiterating rumors that the ex-warlord had covertly conspired with Japanese agents during the 1930s to initiate an uprising in Shandong and accuses him of having engaged in religious activities organized by the Japanese. Given that the truth of both claims remains doubtful, the chapter's final assessment lacks objectivity and indicates how Shi Jianqiao's case was being appreciated. In a period of resurgent Chinese nationalism since the 1989 Tiananmen Square incident, Shi Jianqiao's act of *qing* was being notably remembered as an expression of patriotism.

While some accounts celebrated the famous case, others treated it as a colorful foil to the contemporary era. In the late 1980s, a film based on the Shi Jianqiao case, titled, *Cisha Sun Chuanfang* (Killing Sun Chuanfang), was made. Directed by Cai Jiwei, the film featured Yue Hong as

Shi Jianqiao and Sun Feihu, an actor known for playing Jiang Jieshi, as Sun Chuanfang. Unfortunately, I have not been able to locate a copy of this film.[30] The female lead, Yue Hong, however, contributed to a 1988 issue of the journal *Dazhong Dianying* (Mass movies) a short, but revealing article on her experience of playing Shi Jianqiao. She begins her account by distancing herself from the real-life Shi Jianqiao. She notes that many people had advised her not to take on the risky role of a woman whose disposition was that of the "women of the inner chambers" (*xiugui*), a characterization which by the 1980s evoked the feudal persona of elite gentry women of pre-1949 China. She explains that she had nonetheless decided to pursue playing someone whose disposition was so far from her own as a way of self-discovery (*ziwo faxian*). She describes the experience of acting out the passion of hatred necessary for revenge killing and notes how difficult and frightening it was to fire even a prop gun at her colleague and mentor who was playing Sun Chuanfang. Yet she notes that with the guidance of Sun Feihu, her senior colleague, she learned how to *act* hatred and learn diligence. As she writes, "I experienced the taste of being a killer" (Yue 1988). Even half a century after her passions first mobilized the public, Shi Jianqiao's *qing* continued to serve as an effective vehicle for actresses (and others) to experience the intense emotions triggered by the act of assassination.

Conclusion

Given that our contemporary world is characterized by a truly global consumer culture and media economy, it is interesting to cast a glance back to an earlier period when mass media were just starting to shape the political participation of a new mass citizenry worldwide. Transitioning societies throughout the world in the late nineteenth and early twentieth centuries witnessed how high-profile criminal trials and media sensations became arenas in which social and moral issues were subject to scrutiny and examination. 1930s China was no exception. Marked by a rising mass media, a state aggressively trying to centralize, and a fledgling judicial system seeking to establish institutional autonomy, this decade in China saw a flurry of sensational cases, many of which featured passionate men and women. Featuring an extraordinarily media-savvy female assassin, the case of Shi Jianqiao was among the most sensational.

This study has taken her case as a particularly effective vantage point from which to ask how the most intimate structures of the modern self, including morality and feelings, were linked to larger ways of structuring collective identity in the Republican period. Specifically, the case powerfully illuminates how the extraordinary actions of a passionately ethical daughter helped engender a collectivized form of *qing*. The media audience, bound by sympathy to the assassin, came to constitute a critical, communicative entity of "public sympathy," an alternative public of citizens as affective consumers. Once hailed into being, this new public came to shape judicial proceedings, mediate Nationalist strategies for establishing political legitimacy, and deepen the social cleavages between an increasingly invested urban public and the more elite arbiters of taste, politics, and morality.

This study compels us to broaden our understanding of participatory politics beyond institutional channels and recasts the frame within which we examine the relationship between consumerism and politics. It reveals how political participation could occur and expand in the arena of media sensation. As a media event, the Shi Jianqiao case became a forum for public debate, spawning lively dialogue on the role of women in public, and on ways to imagine the nation, define the parameters of modern justice, determine the place of violence in society, legitimate political rule, and, finally, gender modernity. At the heart of these discussions was the question of the modern relevance of *qing*—both in terms of the female assassin's individual *qing* and the collective response of public sympathy, or *tongqing*. Different groups and individuals avidly made public their opinions on the affair. Even members of the population who were traditionally politically disenfranchised could weigh in, even if emotively and as consumers, on hot-button social issues raised by the case.

Different groups reacted to the case differently. The media-consuming public and the central regime found Shi Jianqiao worthy of sanction. During a period when national unity predicated on rational rules of law and state-building remained elusive, Shi Jianqiao's filial courage and her embodiment of the *xia* (knight-errantry) ethos represented a heroic form of national justice. Yet, though both groups celebrated her heroism, their readings of the event were informed by very different politics. The urban audience's celebration of Shi Jianqiao as a chivalric heroine functioned as an implicit critique against ineffectual Nationalist rule. Theater and fictional adaptations celebrated Shi's killing of warlord Sun to render her into a populist female knight-errant hero (*xianü*) whose ability to deliver public justice served as a powerful moral antidote to ineffectual Nationalist rule. With the repeated telling of Shi's tale of gallantry in the mass media, collective sympathy for the heroine intensified and exhibited growing political and moral authority. In contrast, for a regime seeking to legitimate its moral and political legitimacy and authoritarian power, pardoning the avenging daughter was a way to appropriate the renegade hero both in order to contain and to claim the public justice and heroic sentiment she embodied.

There were, of course, critics. In contrast to those who appreciated the moral power of Shi Jianqiao's *qing*, most reformist intellectuals and urban professionals found Shi Jianqiao, her filial sentiment, and the public sympathy she inspired reprehensible. With the new central regime in charge of official cultural and ideological institutions and a well-informed urban public consuming commercial media and popular forms of entertainment, the authority of intellectuals in the 1930s had waned considerably. No longer the final arbiters of a range of issues, including female propriety, the rule of law, and national modernity, these intellectuals and critics sought to affirm their own moral and intellectual authority vis-à-vis the aggressive new regime and the growing mass public. Interested in maintaining their monopoly over defining the direction of modern China, they maligned the sentiment in the case—both in the form of Shi Jianqiao's individual passions and in the collective form of public sympathy—as overly feminine. They targeted *qing* as a dangerous expression of obsolete moralism that was obstructing more rational prescriptions for national strength, including those based on Marxist scientism or the modern rule of law.

Finally, this study uses the sensational case of Shi Jianqiao to reveal changing perceptions about the public's sentimental involvement in state and society affairs as well as in judicial matters. Collective sympathy had become an impressive new moral and political authority that could influence judicial proceedings and debates over the proper direction of modern Chinese law. More generally, this new public had come to represent a form of justice that could prove superior to the one being offered by the corrupt or inept state. Thus, through the particulars of the case, defense lawyers, prosecutors, judges, and, finally, the defendant debated larger questions about the role of sentiment and rites in the definition of modern justice . Jurists were wary of granting too much power to public sympathy in shaping the judicial proceedings of the trial of Shi Jianqiao, yet the defense lawyers in the trial sought to use public sympathy to press their case.

Even though emotional engagement on the part of the public could acquire a critical, antistate connotation in sensational cases like Shi Jianqiao's, the critical power of this public was ultimately precarious. The autonomy of public sympathy was never institutionalized or codified through legal or official means. Indeed, if we argue that the power of public sympathy actually rested in the belief that this "public" was *xia* in nature, then it follows that, by definition, this sentiment-based public could not be systematically provided for, or protected, in legal or institutional terms. Its moral power resided precisely in its spontaneity and in being grounded in *qing*. Furthermore, public sympathy, which arose in the context of a consumer society, was always potentially subject to manipulation through the very institutions of media that created it.

Our discussion of the Nationalist regime's attempt to use its power to pardon to harness public sympathy for ethical revenge in order to legitimate its own rule demonstrates the potential vulnerability of the new public's autonomy. The official pardons cited telegrams written to the central government suggesting that acts of filial revenge, no matter how extreme or violent, could prove symbolically powerful to a centralizing New Life regime. As such, these pardons provided the Nationalists with an opportunity to attempt to "party-fy" the judiciary and constrain the very public it claimed to represent. The regime sanctioned these acts of violence in order to locate final justice in the party rather than in codified law, the legal profession, or the public. Yet, at the same time, these pardons unintentionally served to expose the considerably fractured nature of party-state authority. They revealed how these revenge cases were, in fact, influenced by the machinations of maverick politicians like Shandong governor Han Fuju and semiretired militarist Feng Yuxiang. The pardoning process was part of the ongoing negotiation between the central government and these individuals, in which each side competed in appealing to public support. In short, public sympathy, while gaining authority as a political force, was nonetheless subjected to constant threats of manipulation.

The "autonomy" of collective sentiment became even more vulnerable with the rise of a strong state. As discussed in chapter 6, the Nationalist government acquired substantial control over the wartime press, given the imperatives of the war against Japan. Accordingly, the wartime government was able to mobilize the feminized moralism of collective emotion and have it serve as a powerful basis of resistance and patriotism. During the War of Resistance, patriotism assumed the *xia* mantle in the sense that it came to unite the sentiment of the people and the national government vis-à-vis an outside enemy. No longer directed against Nationalist rule, public *xia* justice had become one and the same with national state justice.

I end with a few brief thoughts regarding how a sympathy-based "public," which by definition resists institutionalization, might have had profound implications for Chinese politics and society into the Communist era. The attempts by the mid-1930s Nationalist regime to use ethical violence to ignite and channel public passions in order to expand party-state authority coincided with many of the Leninist tactics that came out of the political culture of the 1920s. Comintern agents from the Soviet Communist Party, including Mikhail Borodin, had profoundly shaped this culture and had been working with both the communists and the Nationalists. The Nationalists first implemented such tactics of mass mobilization and propaganda in Canton in the 1920s (Fitzgerald 1996). Communists also came to adopt such tactics. First in the Jiangxi Soviet and later at Yan'an, the remote town that served as the base for CCP activities from the end of the Long March to the civil war with the Nationalists in 1947, the Communists proved far more effective than the Nationalists in mobilizing individuals and mass support by appealing to patriotism and anti-Japanese sentiment.

After the establishment of the People's Republic of China in 1949, emotionally driven political campaigns politicized the notion of the "sentiment of the masses," and made it into a powerful force for social justice that could trump any existing form of bureaucratic law. The sentiment of the revolutionary masses in post-1949 politics was often more associated with the sentiment of the rural masses or the revolutionary youth than with that of the urban, media-consuming public that was so influential in the Shi Jianqiao affair.[1] Yet, as I have briefly suggested here, there were key commonalities. The revolutionary sentiment of the masses became, like public sympathy in the Republican era, a forceful moral antidote that could challenge the power of landlord elites, the party bureaucracy, and even the rule of law. During Yan'an, the civil war years, and into the 1950s, "spontaneous" struggle sessions against landlords and other "reactionary" elements of society enflamed the strong affective commitment of the "masses." While often touted as spontaneous by leftist organizers, these struggle sessions were, in fact, carefully orchestrated to conform to long-standing and highly familiar moral narratives of good and evil drawn from China's vernacular storytelling and operatic traditions (Apter and Saich 1994). Though imperial Confucian ritual had long been cast aside as irrelevant to modern society, the participation in struggle sessions against a targeted few was highly ritualized. Such participation thereby powerfully incited and also directed the collective passions of those involved. Peasants, at first hesitant and wary of challenging landowners who had long held power in their villages, soon came to adopt the conceptual tools with which to think about their exploitation and, equally important, to feel entitled to the land and justified in taking power.

The political power of mass sentiment, as well as its susceptibility to manipulation, are perhaps most tragically evident in the Great Proletarian Cultural Revolution. By the 1960s Mao Zedong was calling on the revolutionary ardor of China's youth to overthrow judicial and bureaucratic law completely. Concerned that "bourgeois ideology" was contaminating the party-state apparatus itself, Mao unleashed mass sentiment onto both the bureaucracy and society. Once again, Mao perceived mass sentiment in this case to be a morally superior form of justice that could serve as an antidote to the corrupt "capitalist road" being followed by Liu Shaoqi and the Chinese Communist Party. No longer based on consumerism, this new collective form of emotion was based on "productive" or participatory, performative politics. Revolutionary film and opera, mass rallies held at Tiananmen, and the rituals of self-criticism helped whip mass emotion into revolutionary frenzy, and mass politics thus became imbued with a powerful, if destructive, affective quality. The resulting tumult of the decade demonstrates the more devastating implications of allowing the volatile sentiments of the masses to take priority over legal and bureaucratic rule.

Yet, while public sympathy in the Republican-era case of Shi Jianqiao is a clear precedent to the highly destructive political and moral power associated with the passions of the Red Guards during the Cultural Revolution, it is also a precedent to highly charged forms of collective sentiment that have been widely celebrated as positive expressions of protest against an oppressive and corrupt communist regime. We need only think of the outpouring of grief in 1976 after reformist Zhou Enlai's death that served to criticize the excesses of the Maoist era, and the collective mourning of the death of reformist Hu Yaobang that coalesced into the mass student movement in 1989 to find two such examples. The Chinese Communist Party's authoritarian moves to crack down in both instances attest to the formidable threat that spontaneous mass emotion could pose to those in power.

In this study, I have thus sought to move away from the question of whether China has a civil society, inquiring instead into what the terms were in which critical political participation did occur. I have sought to show that, historically, the moral authenticity of emotions has often been a more powerful normative force motivating collective political participation than rational forms of communicative action, the basis of the Habermasian ideal of civil society in the modern West. In twentieth-century China, collective emotionalism has proven to be a potent, though by no means guaranteed, antidote to authoritarian rule. Public passions, especially when expressed spontaneously, have at times successfully levied a forceful critique of the sociopolitical order. Yet, at the same time, they have remained susceptible to manipulation and have been unleashed in ways that have resulted in disaster. Given these ambivalent yet profound implications, this historical examination of the rise of a sentiment-based public in 1930s urban consumer society continues to be relevant for understanding how moral sentiment shapes political participation in China into the twenty-first century.

By arguing that a sentiment-based public arose in modern China, I do not mean to suggest that China is the exception to the Western norm. In fact, another central concern of this study has been to use the perspective of China to deconstruct universal narratives of modernity that continue to be centrally preoccupied with rational publics. It is time to reconsider rationality-based publics, long privileged in social theory and academic scholarship and often identified as a key constitutive element of Western modernity. Just as classical Confucian thinkers did in their musings about sociopolitical harmony, should we too not think more critically about the ways in which the realm of emotion can enable modern participatory politics? Fashioning herself as a modern, female knight-errant, Shi Jianqiao may have exhibited uniquely "Chinese characteristics." However, as stated at the outset of this study, the appearance of media-savvy women and mass-mediated cases of female passion have hardly been limited to Republican-era China. Similarly, the critical potential of public passions, so sensationally displayed in the Shi Jianqiao case, may alert us to processes that reach far beyond modern China.

Notes

INTRODUCTION

1. Shi Jianqiao was born in 1906 and died in 1979. Sun Chuanfang's dates are 1885–1935. For more biographical information on the two, see chapter 1.

2. A treaty port in the 1930s, Tianjin was physically divided into several districts, called concessions, in which foreign communities resided and enjoyed the privilege of extra-territoriality, which exempted them from Chinese jurisdiction. Many well-to-do Chinese also resided in the foreign concessions, though they were still subject to Chinese law.

3. The information included in this summary of events appeared in all major newspapers the day after the affair. See, for example, *Dagongbao* (Tianjin), 14 November 1935, 4; *Yishibao* (Tianjin), 14 November 1935, 5; *Chenbao* (Beiping), 14 November 1935, 6; *Shibao* (Beiping), 14 November 1935, 4; *Xin Tianjinbao* (Tianjin), 14 November 1935, 5; *Shenbao* (Shanghai), 14 November 1935, 4; *Xinwenbao* (Shanghai), 14 November 1935, 5.

4. *Dagongbao* (Tianjin), 14 November 1935, 4.

5. *Yishibao* (Tianjin), 14 November 1935, 5.

6. *Dagongbao* (Tianjin), 14 November 1935, 4.

7. See Liu 1935, 70. The attempt on Wang Jingwei's life took place in late October 1935 at the Nanjing gathering for the sixth plenum of the fourth Central Executive Committee of the Nationalist government, which was to be followed immediately by the Fifth National Party Congress. While assassin Sun Fengming claimed to have targeted Wang because of Wang's pro-Japanese sympathies and policies, rumor had it that Jiang Jieshi, who had wanted to eliminate Wang without angering the Japanese, was the mastermind behind the assassination attempt (Coble 1991, 253–56).

8. Numerous popular histories feature this case; see, for example, Shi 1986; Ma and Hou 1993; Cao 1994; and Shi 1987.

9. The Chinese is "*Canming yishi, tongyi tongqing.*" See the chapter entitled "Yangquan" in Han 1936, 2:8. For this particular rendering in English, see Watson 1964, 37.

10. For these glosses, see the entry for *tongqing* in the *Hanyu dacidian*. The entry traces the appearance of the term in texts starting from Han Feizi's "Yangquan" to Mao Zedong's *Zhongguo renmin zhanqi lai.*

11. While the phrase "public opinion" continued to be used in the 1920s and 1930s, it lacked the political potential and significance that it had in the late Qing discussions. John Fitzgerald writes about the "downgrading" of public opinion in the political discourses of the 1920s (1996, 206–15). He discusses how this development occurred after Sun Yat-sen decided to reorient Nationalist Party policy away from liberal constitutional politics, denigrated as unruly in the first quarter of the twentieth century, to the politics of a disciplined, mass party.

12. For this earlier debate, see, for example, the special 1993 issue of *Modern China* (19, no. 2), which featured contributions by William Rowe and Mary Rankin, who were proponents of a public sphere in China, and Phillip Huang and Frederic Wakeman, who denied the existence of such a sphere (Huang 1993; Rankin 1993; Rowe 1993; Wakeman 1993).

13. Take, for example, Philip Huang's spatially conceived notion of the "third realm" (1993). For an early critique of the "third realm" as analytically imprecise and vague, see Wong 1993.

14. Bryna Goodman (1995) and Michael Tsin (1999), for example, examine how the relations between the ruling regime and different social groups involved fluid processes of interaction, which were sometimes adversarial and at other times cooperative, with social groups working with the state toward the same goal.

15. Kiely is clearly informed by Louis Althusser's argument that "hailing" can serve to constitute, or, as Althusser says, "interpellate," identity. See Althusser 1971, 170–76.

16. Benedict Anderson's work on national communities and nationalism (1991) has also popularized the idea that political communities have been "imagined."

17. For a discussion of the late Qing notion of "public opinion" as abstract, see Judge 1996. For a discussion of the notion of "urban crowd" in reportage literature, see Laughlin 2002, chaps. 2 and 3.

18. For the late Qing, see, for example, Judge 1996; Fogel and Zarrow 1997; and Karl and Zarrow 2002. For the 1920s, see, for example, Strand 1989 on the politicization of urban Beijing; Tsin 1999 on Nationalist labor mobilization in Guangdong; and Xu 2001 on the flourishing of professional associations in Shanghai.

19. Social critic Lin Yutang (1968), a contemporary of the era, may have been among the first to shape the belief that the Republican-era press and media had little to offer beyond crass commercialism and mindless sensationalism.

20. My thanks to Pablo Piccato for bringing this issue to my attention.

21. An earlier generation of Europeanists tended to view mass media negatively, seeing them as an ideological apparatus that renders the masses passive

and squelches any possibility of an autonomous civil society. Take, for example, one of the most seminal studies of European fascism, George Mosse's *Nationalization of the Masses* (1975), which views the rise of rituals and festivals promoted by the mass media as a means for the bourgeois elites to cooperate with a fascist state by taming the masses and consolidating power. In addition to the Frankfurt school, the influence of Italian Marxist thinker Antonio Gramsci, who is concerned with how a governing power works with the ruling classes to use ideology to win "consent" from those it subjugates, is evident in much of this historiography. More recently, however, Europeanists have started to revise our understanding of the role of the media and consumer culture in supporting authoritarian power or political hegemony. See, for example, Schwartz 1999 and Shaya 2004.

22. As discussed by Susan Buck-Morss (1989), Benjamin's incomplete yet tantalizing *Passagen-Werk* [Arcades project] (Benjamin 1999) explores how the modern city itself is a "phantasmagoria," or an illusion that promises a modern lifestyle for all but in fact functions to elide continued class antagonisms and pave the way for fascist regimes.

23. Europeanists have also recently started to question the obsessive focus on spectatorship in the making of modern society. In a recent article, Gregory Shaya, for example, proposes the importance of the *badaud*, or "gawker," who "partook in a community forged in the spectacle of suffering and outrage to make a new urban crowd" (2004, 76). My theoretical impulse in this study is similar to Shaya's, but my historical and conceptual concern is less with the act of gawking, and more with the act of sympathizing, or *tongqing*.

24. One notable exception is Bryna Goodman's current research on a 1922 social controversy concerning the suicide of Xi Shangzhen, a "New Woman" who committed suicide in her employer's office. Goodman (2005) argues for a "sexualization" of the public. She argues that New Women were themselves exotic in the 1920s, and sensational cases featuring them helped feed the erotic imagination of the public audience consuming news on the affair.

25. For a powerful critique of Frankfurt school theories on mass culture from the perspective of gender, see Huyssen 1986.

26. See Habermas 1989. Feminist critiques of Habermas are numerous. For a few representative articles, see Meehan 1995. See also Landes 1988 for a historical study that responds to Habermas's failure to consider gender. In contrast to Habermas, Landes places gender analysis at the heart of her study of literary salons and the public sphere in seventeenth- and eighteenth-century France.

27. Hu Shi was among the first to use the term "New Woman" (*xin nüxing*). He did so during the New Culture movement, an anti-traditionalist cultural and intellectual movement of the late 1910s. The term referred to an ideal female paragon whose enlightened passions were hailed as virtuous because they represented the cosmopolitan ideals of the new nation. I discuss the concept of the New Woman in more detail in chapter 3.

28. For an in-depth discussion of the shifting definition of *qing* in classical texts, see Yu 1997, especially 56–66. For a discussion of the genealogy of *qing* during the late imperial period, see Martin Huang 2001, chap. 2.

29. The full compound, *renqing*, is difficult to translate and literally refers

to the state of human relationships as felt by people. For convenience, I translate the compound as "human sentiment," "human feelings," or "affective relations." When referring to forms of *renqing* sanctioned by orthodox Confucian discourses during the imperial period, I may also render it as "orthodox sentiment" or "virtue." By definition, ritually disciplined sentiment constituted orthodox Confucian virtues.

30. For a discussion of imperial law and female chastity, see Theiss 2004 and Sommer 2000. For further discussion of imperial law's promotion of filial piety in cases of filial revenge, see chapter 4.

31. The New Culture movement started roughly around 1916 and was led by intellectuals located primarily at Beijing University. The May Fourth movement began with an incident on May 4, 1919, and consisted of a series of urban mass protests that were sparked by China's humiliation in the post–World War I Peace Conference. Many of the New Culture intellectuals and students were leaders of the anti-imperialist demonstrations, and the New Culture movement is generally seen as crucial context for the political events.

32. For example, Maria Hsia Chang and Lloyd Eastman engaged in a sharp debate over the question of whether the Nationalist regime was a fascist regime (see the September and December 1979 issues of *China Quarterly*). Further debate among Eastman, Joseph Fewsmith, and others appeared in 1984 issues of *Republican China*. See also Fewsmith 1985, which compares Nationalist authoritarianism to European interwar regimes; and Wakeman 1997, which argues that Jiang Jieshi's rule, while not purely fascist, was most certainly authoritarian. Wakeman continues to explore the authoritarian nature of the Nationalist regime in his recent monographs, focusing on policing in Shanghai (1995) and the above-mentioned biography of Dai Li, the head of the Nationalist government's Special Services (*Juntong*) organization (2003). By framing the approach to the Nanjing decade with this question of the authoritarian nature of the Nationalists, the inquiry has resulted in the tendency to evaluate the Nanjing decade against a European standard, albeit a negative one, of European fascism. Critics of the Nanjing regime have likened the presence of violence in Nationalist rule to European fascism and authoritarianism in assessing the failure of the regime (e.g., see Eastman 1974; Wakeman 1997). Sympathizers, in contrast, seek to recoup the decade from such an assessment (e.g., Chang 1979).

33. For a discussion of the history of viewing filial vengeance as ritual, see Cheng 2004.

34. See especially the later works of Michel Foucault, such as *Discipline and Punish* (1977) and *The History of Sexuality* (1978).

CHAPTER 1. THE ASSASSIN AND HER REVENGE

1. The seven-character, regulated verse (*qiyan lüshi*) is one of the most standard forms of Chinese poetry. It was developed during the seventh century, and consists of eight lines of seven characters each, with strict rules about rhymes, tones, and antitheses.

2. One observer of the case described Shi Jianqiao's poem as being filled with "boundless emotion"; see *Xinwenbao* (Tianjin), 15 November 1935, 13.

3. This material was published in urban dailies throughout China. For the statement of intent, see, for example, *Dagongbao* (Tianjin), 15 November 1935, 4; or *Shibao* (Beiping), 15 November 1935, 1. For the *GGRS*, see *Shibao* (Shanghai), 26 December 1935, 5.

4. Shi Jianqiao provided a copy of the will at the police station. For the will, see *Dagongbao* (Tianjin), 15 November 1935, 4; or *Shibao* (Beiping), 15 November 1935, 1.

5. *Dagongbao* (Tianjin), 15 November 1935, 4.

6. These interrogation sessions at the public security bureau were also reproduced word for word in the press. See *Dagongbao* (Tianjin), 15 November 1935, 4. While she was detained at the public security bureau after the assassination, Shi Jianqiao explicitly asked for a meeting with reporters; see *Shibao* (Shanghai), 21 November 1935, 5. This was not ordinary behavior for prisoners.

7. See *Dagongbao* (Tianjin), 15 December 1935, 4; 26 December 1935, 4; 12 January 1936, 4 for publications of her poetry. For the interviews Shi granted from the jailhouse, see *Dagongbao* (Tianjin), 12 February 1936, 4; and 6 July 1936, 4. These dates were not arbitrary. For example, the day before the verdict of her first trial was announced, Shi made one of her poems available to the public. The two interviews she granted from her jail cell coincided with the announcements of the verdicts in her second and third trials, respectively. In chapter 4, I explore the relationship between the media and the trial in more detail.

8. See, for example, "Mengzhong hui di" [In my dreams, I meet my younger brother] and "Si Gui" [Thinking of returning home], both printed in *Shibao* (Shanghai), 19 December 1935, 3.

9. For a more precise picture, see the 1935 *Shanghai shi nianjian* [Shanghai City yearbook], which shows that the circulation in 1934 for the *Shenbao* was 150,000 (40 percent distributed in Shanghai, 60 percent outside), the same for the *Xinwenbao*, and for the *Shibao*, 94,000 (47 percent in, 53 percent out).

10. For a photo of headlines in Russian, see Shi 1987, 439.

11. Some still covered the gossip and news of high society. Take for example, Shanghai's long-running *Jingbao* (The crystal). The coverage tended to focus on high-society news, including reports of courtesan circles and anecdotal accounts of famous personages. For an English-language review of *xiaobao*, see Hershatter 1997, 16–17, esp. nn. 48 and 50; and Link 1981. Others published investigative reports and catered to a broader segment of society. Lee and Nathan discuss how Shanghai's *Libao*, a popular paper of the 1930s, had different columns and supplements aimed at broader readership (Lee and Nathan 1985, 374). The *Fu'ermosi* was another example. Less concerned with literati society news, this *xiaobao* was characterized by investigative reporting and thus had a broader readership than that of the *Jingbao* (personal communication from Wang Juan).

12. By 1934, there were a total of 212 magazines published in Shanghai: 29 general, 5 women's, 3 youth, 12 children's, 3 publishing, 6 international, 3 law, 1 police, 1 sociological, 7 educational, 1 aeronautical, 10 economics, 5 communications, 17 industrial, 6 natural science, 6 engineering and architecture, 8 telecommunications, 1 chemical industry, 2 agricultural, 21 medical, 18 paint-

ing, 1 drama, 10 movie, 4 photographic, 2 music, 1 history, and 29 literary (Wakeman 1995, 238–39, n. 75). I focus on the periodical press coverage of the affair in chapter 3.

13. On the rise of the fiction press, see Link 1981, chap. 3. Link argues that such fiction may have reached more than 50,000 readers in commercial papers and, with its adaptation into movies, drama, and even traditional "drum singing," the number may have been in the 100,000s, if not more than 1 million (Link 1981, 12). See Des Forges 1998 for a discussion of the modern, serialized novel in Shanghai. For a general discussion of print culture in 1930s China, see Lee 1999.

14. For theater in modern China, see Mackerras 1975. For the growth of theater in Shanghai, and information on reformed opera in particular, see Meng 2000, chap. 5.

15. On radio, see Benson 1995 and 1996. For a notable discussion of the urban milieu of Shanghai cinema, see Lee 1999, 82–119. On the rise of Chinese film, see Zhang 2005.

16. For biographical information on Shi Jianqiao, see *GGRS* and *Shibao* (Shanghai), 17 November 1935, 8. Other biographical sources include Wu 1990 and Chen 1991.

17. For more biographical information on Shi Congbin, see Boorman and Howard 1967–71, 3:160–62; Chen 1991; and Shi 1986: 188. People of social standing often received a courtesy name, or *zi*, as a public name to be used by those outside the family.

18. For more biographical information on Shi Congyun, see his entry in Huang 1970, vol. 4.

19. For information on her immediate family, see *Dagongbao* (Tianjin), 15 November 1935, 4.

20. *Shibao* (Shanghai), 28 November 1935, 5.

21. *Shibao* (Beiping), 14 November 1935, 1.

22. In a retrospective account, Chen Jin (1991) describes Shi as "a virtuous and genteel occupant of the inner quarters," a description that powerfully invokes a sense of female propriety.

23. See, for example, Shen 1935; and *Xinwenbao* (Shanghai), 15 November 1935, 13.

24. *Dagongbao* (Tianjin), 22 November 1935, 4. At the time, she claimed to have bought the gun for sixty yuan along with six bullets from an army deserter in Tongcheng, Anhui. Thirty years later, Shi admitted that she had obtained the gun from one of her brother's fellow students, who had left it in their Tianjin home during a visit in 1934 (Shi 1987, 514–15).

25. For further discussion on Feng Yuxiang's role in securing her pardon, see chapter 5. In chapter 4, I also discuss the powerful legal team that Shi Jianqiao was able to put together for her defense.

26. For early twentieth-century debates over whether Jiang Jieshi was a soldier or a warlord, see Waldron 1991, esp. 1081–82, 1091–93.

27. For further biographical information on Sun Chuanfang, see Boorman and Howard 1967–71, 3:160–62; Jing 1997; and He and Pan 1997, 219. Jin Yunpeng, who had also been part of the Zhili faction and served as minister of war

and premier for Duan Qirui from 1919 to 1921, retired after Zhang Zuolin took over in Beijing (Boorman and Howard 1967–71, 1:382–84).

28. *Beiping wanbao* (Beiping), 25 November 1935, 4. Sun Chuanfang was indeed the target of Shanghai labor in the 1920s: strikers during the Three Workers' Armed Uprisings shouted, "Down with Sun Chuanfang!" My thanks to Elizabeth Perry for pointing this out to me.

29. *North China Herald*, 20 November 1935, 308.

30. See "Sun Yinyuan ruci xiachang" 1935.

31. This is mentioned in "Sun Chuanfang biaoshi buyuan guowen zhengzhi" 1935.

32. *Beiping wanbao* (Beiping), 25 November 1935, 4.

33. See "Sun Chuanfang biaoshi buyuan guowen zhengzhi" 1935. Despite his denunciations, these accusations that Sun was a collaborator persisted even in post-1949 accounts. One writer asserts that Sun was conspiring with Japanese militarists in the Manchurian Incident in 1931 that led to the Japanese establishment of Manchuko (Jing 1996, 219). Another accuses him of helping to instigate an uprising in Shandong (Shi 1982, 10). Others simply referred to him as a Japanese collaborator, traitor, and even the King of North China (e.g., Zhou 1986, 176; Chen 1991, 140).

34. Her portrayal of Sun as a rapacious warlord who deserved to be assassinated hewed closely to tales of popular fiction. For example, in Zhang Henshui's famous 1929 serialized novel, *Fate in Tears and Laughter* [Tixiao yinyuan], the stock characters include the evil warlord General Liu Dezhu, who was killed by Xiugu, a heroic female knight-errant who sought to avenge his brutal treatment of the modest young girl Fengxu.

35. See *Jingbao* (Shanghai), 22 November 1935, 2.

36. While on the stand during the initial trial in Tianjin, Shi Jianqiao claimed that her father had served the official government of China in the mid-1920s, but when pressed to name the president of China during that time, she was unable to answer. See *Dagongbao* (Tianjin), 26 December 1935, 4. Given the internal chaos in China at the time, international recognition of the "official" government of China during the 1920s was, in fact, rather arbitrary. Often, it simply depended on which warlord was in control of Beijing, the traditional capital. This changed frequently during the period as alliances among Beiyang militarists shifted capriciously and power blocs were constantly forming anew.

37. *Dagongbao* (Tianjin), 15 November 1935, 4.

38. Ibid.

39. Ibid.

40. See her will, printed in *Dagongbao* (Tianjin), 15 November 1935, 4, and *Shibao* (Beiping), 15 November 1935, 1.

41. In the twentieth century, righteous revenge and karmic retribution continued to prevail both as cosmological frameworks and as plot devices in modern vernacular fiction (Chen 1995, 113–14). Popular fiction of the Mandarin Duck and Butterfly school, for example, featured stories of Confucian family drama and karmic reprisal that were often situated in the contemporaneous context of warlord intrigue.

42. Her surrender became the subject of considerable legal debate in her trial, an issue I discuss in chapter 4.

43. For discussions that explain Sun's fate in terms of karmic retribution, see, for example, *Xinwenbao* (Shanghai), 15 November 1935, 13; and *Xinwenbao* (Shanghai), 9 December 1935, 13. Several fictional adaptations also featured this Buddhist cosmological framework. See, for example, the radio play, "Xiejian fotang" [A bloodbath in a Buddhist shrine], which I discuss in chapter 2.

44. Han historians such as Sima Qian were writing about the Warring States period's assassin-retainers, or *cike*. Knights-errant (*xiake*) were also significantly featured in literature in the Tang dynasty (618–906 C.E.), when chivalric tales (e.g., *chuanqi*) flourished.

45. In *wuxia xiaoshuo* (martial arts fiction), the *jianghu* is an imaginary geographical space outside the proper arena of the family and frequently set in opposition to the Court (*ting*) or official arena. For further discussion of the literary and cultural history of *xia*, see, for example, Liu 1967. For late Qing chivalric fiction, see David Wang 1997, chap. 3. For the literary history of the *xia* in the late imperial period and the early twentieth century, see Chen 1995.

46. According to James Liu, when combined with *xia*, as in the compound term *xiayi*, *yi*, or "justice," sheds its orthodox connotation of righteousness and contradicts dominant notions of familial duty and loyalty (1967, 4–5). The late Ming novel, the *Shuihuzhuan*, featured a band of rogue outlaw heroes that seminally defined many of the characteristics of the *xia* hero in the cultural imagination of late imperial China. While the *Shuihuzhuan* did not explicitly feature *xiake*, it played a seminal role in imbuing the *xia* hero with a subversive, antistate quality. Featuring a band of martial outlaws in the northern Song that fights corrupt government officials and general injustice, the novel presents an outlaw lifestyle that becomes intimately associated with the *xiake*.

47. *Jian* is frequently used in combination with other ideographs to connote an unrestrained but virtuous heroism. For example, *jianxia* refers to one who supports the weak in the face of the strong with his or her martial expertise and is practically synonymous with *xiake*, the assassin-retainer.

48. See Pu Songling 1986a, 376–77. The line is "I dare not forget the revenge of my father for a single moment." For discussion of Shi's use of this line, see *Xiao chenbao* (Beiping), 6 December 1935, 3.

49. Of course, this is not to say that filial piety is solely a female virtue. In general it was an ethical ideal for both men and women. Yet, within the *xia* tradition, filial piety figures more frequently in *xia* tales about women than in those about men. Louise Edwards goes so far as to say that for male *xiake* righteousness (*yi*) is the defining characteristic, and for female *xiake*, it is filial piety (*xiao*); see Edwards 1994, 97–103.

50. A story of a daughter who acts heroically outside the household to fulfill her filial duty to her father, the Mulan tale was first featured in a folk song whose origins are generally believed to date back to the Six dynasties (220–589 C.E.). For scholarship on Mulan in literature and drama during the imperial period, see Allen 1996 and Edwards 1995. It is also no accident that Mulan cross-dressed to pass as a man and join the army on behalf of her ailing father. The cross-dressing is the most evident visual symbol of her virtuous dislocation. For a semiotic

analysis of the female warrior's clothing and headgear as markers of her gender in both traditional China and the modern period, see Allen 1996.

51. The heroic standards of virtue demanded of female knights-errant were part of a larger sexual economy underlying China's imperial cosmology, explicit in imperial China's chastity cult, an institutionalized endorsement of female paragons by the state. Celebrated for the trials they underwent to uphold their chastity and fulfill their filial duties, virtuous women served as heroic, physical embodiments of virtue that reinforced political loyalty to imperial rule. For pioneering scholarship on the topic, see Carlitz 1991, 1994; Ko 1994; and Mann 1997.

52. Zeitlin (1993) explicitly contrasts the masculine female hero with the shrew and argues that in the tales of Pu Songling's *Liaozhai zhiyi* the shrew is "hyper-feminine" and thus tyrannical. Indeed, premodern literary and historical discourses have repeatedly blamed the *femme fatale*, with her excessive female sexuality (*yin*), for enticing male rulers, leading the country into disaster, and being at the root of general social and political disorder. For more on how the shrew inverts the conventional power relationship between husband and wife in imperial fiction and was similarly seen to have symbolic consequences for the social order at large, see Wu 1995. In contrast, the "hero among women" perpetuates patriarchal values, is atypical in her masculine essence (*yang*), and is thus highly laudable (Zeitlin 1993, 130). In many cases, these women not only become like men, but also excel their male counterparts. In mid-Qing romance (*caizi jiaren*) novels, this was common. The male protagonist, or *caizi*, is the effeminate, often weak-willed, scholar. In contrast, the female protagonist is often a beautiful warrior who proves to be superior in intelligence and strength.

53. See Pu Songling 1986a, 373–75. Shi cited Shang as her model in her press conference at the public security bureau. See *Dagongbao* (Tianjin), 15 November 1935, 4.

54. *Shibao* (Beiping), 11 November 1935, 1. This Case of the Tongue may have helped Shi Jianqiao to gain the publicity skills so evident in this revenge case.

55. See *Dagongbao* (Tianjin), 15 November 1935, 4. For an example of media coverage that claimed her marriage was simply a means to the final goal of revenge, see *Xin Tianjinbao* (Tianjin), 15 November 1935, 5.

56. "Shi Jianqiao qi jiang wei qifu yu?" 1936, 3326.

57. *Dagongbao* (Tianjin), 26 November 1935, 4.

58. *Shibao* (Shanghai), 28 November 1935, 5. Ironically, her image also conformed to the desexualized, communist "new woman" being promoted in leftist literature and film.

59. Newspapers reporting on the press conference mentioned her breaking down and crying. See, for example, *Dagongbao* (Tianjin), 15 November 1935, 4.

60. *Yishibao* (Tianjin), 15 November 1935, 5.

61. See, for example, *Dagongbao* (Tianjin), 26 November 1935, 4; *Dagongbao* (Tianjin), 29 January 1936, 4; and *Shibao* (Beiping), 26 November 1935, 4. For a more detailed analysis of Shi Jianqiao's performance in court, see chapter 4.

62. *Shibao* (Beiping), 26 November 1935, 4. There was also speculation that Shi Jianqiao prepared these documents with the express intent to publicize her

surrender, which would affect her legal case favorably. See, for example, "Xianü fuchou," *Shibao* (Beiping), 11 March 1936, 4.

63. *Dagongbao* (Tianjin), 15 November 1935, 5.

64. These details are revealed in her will. For a copy of her will, see *Dagongbao* (Tianjin), 15 November 1935, 4, or *Shibao* (Beiping), 15 November 1935, 1. Shi Jianqiao also told of her male relatives' failure to take action in her press conference; see *Dagongbao* (Tianjin), 15 November 1935, 4.

65. *Dagongbao* (Tianjin), 15 November 1935, 4.

66. Much of this information was provided at her initial press conference and then rehearsed again at the initial trial. For press coverage, see *Dagongbao* (Tianjin), 15 November 1935, 4. For verbatim coverage of the trial exchange, see *Shibao* (Shanghai), 28 November 1935, 5.

67. *Yishibao* (Tianjin), 14 November 1935, 5.

68. For coverage of the family's response, see He and Pan 1997, 219.

69. *Dagongbao* (Tianjin), 15 November 1935, 4.

70. *Dagongbao* (Tianjin), 18 November 1935, 4.

71. *Xin Tianjinbao* (Tianjin), 29 and 30 November 1935, 6. For more discussion of supporters, including those on the funeral committee, see He and Pan 1997, 220.

72. *Dagongbao* (Tianjin), 18 November 1935, 4; and *Yishibao* (Tianjin), 18 November 1935, 5.

73. In film, fiction, and political commentary of the Republican period, the modern woman was increasingly a sign of moral decay and ethical turpitude. For discourses on prostitutes as emblems of vice, a health issue, and indicators of moral decay, see Hershatter 1997. For conservative views and policing discourses of the New Woman, see Edwards 2000. For a shift in the public discourse on movie actresses from the 1920s to 1930s, see Chang 1999. Zhang Yingjin (1996) argues that the New Woman was a fictional and filmic symbol of the modern city and all the problems and possibilities associated with it.

74. "Shi Jianqiao'an yu shehui guandian" 1935, 3. I discuss the "highbrow" critics of Shi Jianqiao and her popularity in chapter 3. Here, I am only concerned with those explicitly discussing her ability to manipulate the mass media.

75. One commentator said that Shi was remarkable because she was "not only filial, but also a chaste and chivalric woman" (Shen 1935, 4).

76. Xiao 1936. In addition to this juxtaposition of Shi as delicate woman and her masculine heroism, the contrast between Shi's fragility and Sun as rapacious warlord was also common. This contrast was a stock description used in much of the coverage of the affair and was commonly found in martial arts novels of the time. For example, one account called the affair "news that simply startles!" and then proceeded to contrast Shi as a delicate young woman with the violent episode of killing a warlord. See *Xin Tianjinbao* (Tianjin), 13 November 1935. For a few more examples, see *Shibao* (Beiping), 17 November 1935, 1; and *Chenbao* (Beiping), 28 March 1936, 5.

77. Yi Ji 1935. Note how she appeared manly in contrast to her older brother, whose fragile disposition was repeatedly cited as the reason he failed to act.

78. See for example, the 14 November 1935 article "Zhongguo nü cishou zhi qiji" in *Hushang ribao* (Shanghai), as mentioned in Zhou 1986, 171. Lu Sini-

ang was reportedly the granddaughter of Lu Liuliang, an ardent, anti-Manchu scholar whose corpse was exhumed and dismembered by Emperor Yongzheng because his writings had posthumously become the basis of a plot to usurp the throne. It is commonly believed that granddaughter Lu Siniang escaped the enslavement or exile that befell the rest of the Lu clan, and that she assassinated Yongzheng in an act of revenge.

79. *Xinwenbao* (Shanghai), 15 November 1935, 13.

CHAPTER 2. MEDIA SENSATION

1. For a more detailed discussion of this case, see chapter 5.
2. I discuss this case in more detail in chapters 3 and 4.
3. Some cases of female suicide seemed to rival the sensation stirred by the case of Shi Jianqiao, including the famous 1935 suicide of movie star Ruan Lingyu. The 1928 case of Ma Zhenhua, a woman who committed suicide out of love, was similarly spectacular. In a recent discussion of Ma's case, Bryna Goodman (2006) argues that the media attention of the case engendered a public adjudication of the political significance of love.
4. "Shi Jianqiao shifou xiaonü" 1935, 3967.
5. See, for example, *Liangyou* 11, no. 111 (November 1935): 8; and the *Shenbao huakan*, 25 November 1935, 2.
6. *Fu'ermosi* (Shanghai), 6 November 1936, 1.
7. For Brooks, "melodrama represents *both* the urge toward resacralization and the impossibility of conceiving the sacralized other than in personal terms" (1976, 16).
8. For a critique of Pickowicz's use of *melodrama* and the implicit standard of May Fourth literary modernism by which Pickowicz judges these films, see Hansen (2000), which provides a more theoretically compelling term, *vernacular modernism*, to describe the silent films of early twentieth-century Shanghai.
9. In Wu Jianren's *Henhai*, for example, foreign imperialism and an inflexibly outdated set of Confucian ethics both served as that clear threat. That said, as Haiyan Lee argues, the novel's aim was not to reject in an iconoclastic manner all Confucian ethics. Rather, it seeks to resurrect a more updated ethical system with which to confront the challenges facing China (2002, 83).
10. Denby describes French sentimental literature as "a site of a process of sacralization . . . [that] re-enacts the illuminated communication of the collective religious experience" (Denby 1994, 88).
11. See *Shenbao* (Shanghai), 13 December 1935, supp. sec., 3.
12. For more on the *tanci*, especially as a woman's genre, see Hu 2003.
13. Generally produced as installments for magazines and newspapers, the genre of serialized novels grew along with the rise of modern mass media in the early Republican period. David Wang suggests that publication of fiction in newspapers started as early as the 1870s (1997, 2). Link identifies the 1920s as a turning point. Before the 1920s, urban periodicals dedicated to fiction tended to publish the genre. After the 1920s, with the growth of mass media, more widely read daily newspapers published serialized fiction. Link argues that only at this point could the genre qualify as "popular" (Link 1981, 11–12).

14. For more on court-case fiction, see St. Andre 1998 and David Wang 1997. On detective fiction, see Kinkley 2000.

15. *Shibao* (Beiping), 2 December 1935, 4.

16. There is no evidence that the real Shi Jianqiao had such training.

17. A sudden shift from family melodrama or a love story to an episode of martial adventure was actually a common convention of serialized novels of the time (Link 1981, 30).

18. In addition to using her supreme martial skills, the fictional Shi Jianqiao also threatens to bring the undutiful son and daughter-in-law to court and make their unfilial behavior public. See installments in *Shibao* (Beiping), 6 February 1936, 4; and *Shibao* (Beiping), 7 February 1936, 4. While the threat of a lawsuit had long been a means to "shame" or destroy the reputation of one's opponents in China, what was unique to the twentieth century was the rise of the mass media, which forced legal players to deal with the unprecedented phenomenon of publicity; thus, Shi Jianqiao's threat of making their behavior public makes sense.

19. Glosser 2003 discusses how the Nationalist policy functioned to erode familial authority and allowed for increased state penetration into the family.

20. See the installment in *Shibao* (Beiping), 12 January 1936, 4. Interestingly, although the series portrays Shi's decision to marry Shi Jinggong as initially opportunistic, it veers from the real-life account by describing how Shi unexpectedly falls in love with Shi Jinggong. Shi then claims not to want to put her husband in any danger and decides, in the end, to undertake the task of revenge herself. This detail of Shi Jianqiao's unexpected love for Shi Jinggong adds to the melodrama of the serialization and conforms, perhaps, to the expectations of the reader and generic convention. It also provides the protagonist with yet another opportunity to show off her moral heroism.

21. This segment of the series was featured in the first chapter and ran daily from November 16, 1935 until November 25, 1935.

22. I discuss the Case of the Tongue in chapter 1.

23. Throughout Chinese history, tales about exemplary men and women were powerful didactic vehicles that dramatized the ideal, ethical subjectivity of the Confucian moral individual (*junzi*) and thus the virtues of the collective subjectivity of the Confucian empire, including loyalty. The loyal official and the dutiful son were praised as human paragons to be emulated in imperial Confucian pantheons, and Confucianized Buddhist stories often established the dutiful son as the enlightened religious exemplar. Conventionally cloistered in the inner chambers, the female body had perhaps even greater potential as a site of exemplary virtue. In the late Ming, tales of female virtue became especially dramatic, featuring extreme accounts of daughters who cut their flesh to heal ailing parents or mutilated their bodies to express their devotion to their fathers. For an excellent discussion of self-mutilating tales of female self-sacrifice in the late Ming, see, for example, Carlitz 1994. For the dramatization of virtue in Confucianized Buddhist stories, see Glen Dudbridge's discussion of the tale of Miao Shan, a late Ming, inspirational Buddhist tale that featured a daughter who gouged out her eyes and mutilated her body to save her father from both his physical and spiritual ailments (1978).

24. In a study of Republican-era fiction, Mau-Sang Ng (1994) similarly ar-

gues that so-called "traditional" virtues like filial piety assume a new "generative power" through which they introduce new social norms.

25. See Liang 1987, 386–87. For this English translation, see Fei 1999, 109–10. For more on the late Qing context in which Liang and other intellectuals privileged literature as a field for change, see Huters 2005.

26. See Chen 1987, 460. For this English translation, see Fei 1999, 117.

27. Other contemporaneous news sensations that were dramatized in the 1930s include the attempted killing of Wang Jingwei. See the advertisement for the two-day performance of "The Sixth Plenum: Complete Sensation" in *Xinwenbao* (Shanghai), supp. sec., 19 November 1935, 7.

28. Shanghai papers, including the *Shenbao, Shibao, Xinwenbao,* and *Xishijiebao*, ran advertisements for these performances.

29. *Shenbao* ran ads for this production throughout its run. The change of title took place on December 28, 1935.

30. *Xishijiebao* (Shanghai), 29 November 1935, 2.

31. For a discussion of the characteristics of petty urbanites and their residential spaces, see Lu 1999. For a discussion of them as consumers of early Shanghai film, see Zhang 2005, 64–69.

32. For playhouse ticket prices, see *Xishijiebao*, 4 December 1935, 2. For film prices, see Lee 1999, 83, who cites a 1930 report that says film prices ranged from twenty cents to three dollars.

33. See, for example, ads for *All about Sun Chuanfang*, which in the middle of its run, became *All about the Avenging Daughter*.

34. *Xinwenbao* (Shanghai), 23 November 1935, supp. sec., 2.

35. As mentioned above, Shi's trial was a source of inspiration in fiction. The final chapter of the Beiping *Shibao* series, *Xianü fuchou*, for example, chronicles the trial.

36. For more biographical information on Zhao Junyu, see http://history.xikao.com/person.php.

37. For more biographical information on Zhao Ruquan, see http://history.xikao.com/person.php.

38. *Xishijiebao* (Shanghai), 25 November 1935, 2.

39. See Wakeman 1995 for a richly detailed description of the assassinations of suspected communist organizers and for Nationalist collusion with the Green Gang in Shanghai. For a recent account of the Blue Shirts, see Wakeman 1997. See Coble 1991, 8–9, 283–333, on rising public dissatisfaction.

40. The play began its run on December 20, 1935. Only three days prior, Tianjin's district court had imposed a lenient sentence of ten years. News that Shi Jianqiao intended to appeal the decision was already made public, and public sympathy in her favor was also already evident. The dramatic appeal of the performance was no doubt further enhanced by these developments.

41. The Zhen'e play is a drama set in the final days of the Ming dynasty. It was frequently performed as a drama or turned into *tanci* performances during the Republican era.

42. A political system of patronage continued into the Republican era. For further discussion on the matter, see MacKinnon 1995. For discussion of cen-

sorship under the Nationalists, see Wakeman 1995, 235–40; Xiao 1994; Ting 1974; and Hockx 1998.

43. For new press laws in 1935, see, for example, "Revised Press Law," *North China Herald*, 17 July 1935, 86; "Attempt to Regulate Mosquito Papers Through Law," *North China Herald*, 24 July 1935, 151; "Regulation to Control Newspapers at the GMD National Congress," *North China Herald*, 30 November 1935, 86; "New Press Law Is Opposed: Nanking Journalists Issued Memorandum," *North China Herald*, 7 August 1935, 166; "Growing Defiance of Censorship," *North China Herald*, 4 December 1935, 389.

44. For a discussion of how martial-arts practice of boxing helped transmit the message of uprising, see Esherick 1987.

CHAPTER 3. HIGHBROW AMBIVALENCE

1. For the original quotation, see "Lilun," Wang 1988, 346. For this English translation, see Knoblock 1994, 55. For more on *qing* in Xunzi's thought, see Yu 1997, chap. 2.

2. For further discussion of Confucian sentimentality in sanctifying crucial human bonds in Confucian orthodoxy, see Lee 2002, 44–47.

3. There is a considerable amount of scholarship on the cult of *qing* in the late Ming. See, for example, Ko 1994; Epstein 2001; and Martin Huang 2001.

4. For the rise of ritualism and its role in disciplining the proper expression of filial piety and the increasing tension between personal filial piety and political loyalty, see Kutcher 1999. For the increasing bureaucratization of the chastity cult, see Theiss 2004.

5. Dai Zhen's attack on Wang Yangming did not mean that he endorsed a return to Song *lixue*, the target of Wang Yangming's school. Dai also had problems with Zhu Xi and his incorporation of metaphysical elements into the investigation of things. Instead, what Dai Zhen and his fellow *kaozheng* scholars sought was a practice of the investigation of things that was grounded in exacting, concrete scholarship. For more on Dai Zhen and Ruan Yuan's views, see, for example, Elman 2005, 258–62.

6. For this argument, see Martin Huang 2001, especially 271–314. For other studies devoted to the question of *qing* in the *Dream of the Red Chamber*, see Yu 1997, and Li 1993.

7. Lee (2002) uses Raymond Williams' notion of a "structure of feelings" rather than the ideology of a world view, because the phrase, in her view, better "captures social consciousness as lived experience *in process* or *in solution*, before it is 'precipitated' and given fixed forms" (26).

8. See Chow 1960, 303–7, for a discussion of the two intellectuals and their opposition to filial piety. For original texts, see, for example, Wu 1917.

9. I discuss the May Fourth attack on female chastity below.

10. To be sure, the "woman question" was of paramount importance in the late Qing when radicals, including many female anarchists, such as Qiu Jin, obsessively deliberated over the definition of womanhood and citizenship. For examples of recent, if methodologically divergent, work on this subject, see Judge 2002, and Karl 2002.

11. See Hu 1918. Writing under the pen name, Tang Si, Lu Xun also contributed an article on the topic. See Tang 1918.

12. Hu 1918, 14. Hu portrayed sexual freedom and romantic love as natural endowments to be nurtured to their full potential through the progressive education of the individual rather than through classical sanction, traditional moral cultivation, or legal imposition.

13. For a discussion of how May Fourth writers explored modern subjectivity in the increasingly popular genre of romantic literature, see Lee 1973.

14. Unfortunately, this binary has been the cause of significant semantic and historiographic confusion in recent scholarly debates. The problem has stemmed primarily from translating *gong* and *si* into "public" and "private." These English terms are loaded and unfortunately tend to invoke connotations that are historically specific to European history. To avoid these complications, I have opted to use the Chinese terms instead or translate *si* as "selfish."

15. See, for example, "Shi Jianqiao'an yu shehui guandian" 1935, which argues that there was no basis for Shi's grievance and revenge.

16. "Shi nü ci Sun Chuanfang" 1935. See also the similar argument in Shi 1936.

17. See "Shi Jianqiao'an yu shehui guandian" 1935.

18. Han 1936, 39:3–6. For biographical information on Han Yu, see *Xin Tangshu* 1995, 176:5255–69.

19. Li 1935. For another example, see Wang 1935, 3.

20. See Feng 1938, 349. As I show below, whereas Feng's idea of "society" invoked a spatial correspondence with the nation, the Chinese Left's use of the term more successfully conjured up structural shifts in social reality and modes of production.

21. Arif Dirlik (1978, 4) notes that historical materialism was in vogue among Chinese intellectuals partially due to its ability to alleviate "a crisis in China's historical consciousness," which had resulted from the modernist iconoclasm of a decade earlier that had undermined the authority of traditional Confucian interpretations of the past.

22. See Liu 1935, 70. Liu Shi was one of the better-known leftist essayists of the 1930s who commented on this case and regularly contributed to *Dazhong shenghuo*. Other accounts also took note of the extraordinary number of women in the crowds outside the courtroom. For example, see *Shibao* (Shanghai) 28 November 1935, 6, for an article noting that female teachers and their female students made up the majority of the hundred-plus observers by the door.

23. Wang and Zhu 1992, 486. Continuing the tradition of its predecessor, *Shenghuo, Dazhong shenghuo* was outspoken and critical in its views on Nationalist rule. Established in November 1935 by Zou Taofen in response to public concern over the North China crisis, the journal's coverage regarding the December 9, 1935, student movement so enraged Jiang Jieshi that Jiang had the publication closed by February 1936. But, in March 1936, Zou Taofen began publication of another journal, called *Yongsheng*, which essentially retained *Dazhong shenghuo's* critical agenda. See Yeh 1992, 226, for a characterization of *Dazhong shenghuo* as being increasingly concerned with enlightening the audience on the politically correct ways of thinking in terms of working for the col-

lectivity of the nation. The journal had an estimated circulation of almost 200,000 per issue at its peak (Coble 1985, 294, n. 1).

24. For more on Zou's participation in the National Salvation Association, see Coble 1985, 293–310. The group's activities eventually led to the sensational arrest of its seven major leaders—a case that came to be dubbed the Case of the Seven Gentlemen.

25. See Shiga 1984, esp. 287–88. Also see Fan, Zheng, and Zhan 1992. In chapter 4, I discuss the complicated historical role of sentiment in imperial law in more detail.

26. For more on this debate, see Fan, Zheng, and Zhan 1992, 23–26.

27. See Connor 1993 and 1994 on the schooling and professionalization of early twentieth-century lawyers. See Xu 1998 on the professionalization of lawyers through the bar association. According to Keith Schoppa (1995, 34), the hallmark of early Republican, civilian, elite culture (as opposed to military culture) was an emphasis on law and legal processes, and civilian elites were thus increasingly turning to the legal profession.

28. When the regime applied this Emergency Law in a controversial 1932–33 case against certain individuals for their suspected communist activities, a lively debate over the question of judicial autonomy ensued. The legal journal *Falü pinglun*, for example, ran a series of articles that closely covered the case as well as related editorials, including "Zuihou zhengzha zhong zhi sifa duli" 1932. For the general coverage of the case, see issues of *Falü pinglun* starting from June 1932 (9, no. 36) to October 1932 (10, no. 4).

29. See Zhu 1936. Parks Coble (1991) characterizes the *Duli pinglun* as rather moderate in its stance regarding the Nationalist government's appeasement policy, especially in comparison to more critical, left-leaning journals like the *Dazhong shenghuo*. He describes Hu Shi's personal position as being fairly in line with Jiang Jieshi's, believing that China was not yet prepared to confront the Japanese. Yet, in my discussion, I show how *Duli pinglun* writers did challenge, if implicitly, government policy in its decision to pardon Shi Jianqiao and Zheng Jicheng on the basis of *qing*.

30. Lin Chong and Wu Song are two revenge-seeking heroes of the classic sixteenth-century novel *Shuihuzhuan* (Outlaws of the marsh).

31. I discuss this notion of "righteous anger" and its legal implications in the Shi Jianqiao trial in chapter 4.

32. For a similar opinion on the expansive capacity of law to account for *qing*, see Bu 1935. Bu goes so far as to suggest that since a state pardon may not be forthcoming, it is within the power of the law to remedy the state's failure to recognize the exceptional circumstances in the case.

33. This is not to say, however, that the women's press exclusively printed sympathetic commentary. Several of the critics I have discussed published their critique of Shi in women's publications. See, for example, Li 1935.

34. As several scholars have noted, female liberation started off as primarily a male concern, and writers in the women's press continued throughout the Republican period to be overwhelmingly male. They included young male students or aspiring male writers (Nivard 1984, 46–49; Gilmartin 1995). In my review of the press, I have found that when a female writer or editor made a con-

tribution, her gender was often noted explicitly, suggesting that female writers were still an exception; see, for example, Xiao 1936.

35. Unfortunately, since contributors to the women's press were often unknown writers, little biographical information is available about Xiao Yu, making it difficult to identify her political interests with certainty. Yet, in view of Xiao Yu's appreciation of Shi Jianqiao's classic virtues, it stands to reason that her commentary echoed the views of conservative moralists. And, while morally "conservative" in terms of her endorsement of the female assassin's filial piety, Xiao's views were at the same time arguably progressive in their explicit promotion of female equality. Louise Edwards notes that many of these "moral conservatives" confounded reformist thinkers in their promotion of "traditional" virtues on one hand and their "invocation of feminist-like sentiments" on the other (Edwards 2000, 138–39).

36. See also She 1935, which similarly argued that Shi Jianqiao demonstrated how women were equal to men, and should thus be treated as such in the eyes of the law.

37. For a similar example, see Wang 1935.

38. *Sui* indicates age in Chinese. It does not correspond exactly with the English phrase "years old." A person is one *sui* right at birth, and ages a *sui* each year. So, someone who is ten *sui* is roughly eleven years old.

39. For further elaboration of the critical commentary surrounding the Liu Jinggui case, see Lean 2005.

40. Recent studies of women have also focused on Shanghai dancing girls and movie actresses, typical professions for New Women that were either a part of the media industry or of industries related to the mass media and modern urban Shanghai (e.g., Field 1999; Chang 1999).

CHAPTER 4. THE TRIAL

1. For a copy of the plaint, see *Dagongbao* (Tianjin), 22 November 1935, 4. Unfortunately, I found no legal documents on the case in the Nanjing Number Two Historical Archives, which houses records of legal cases that were appealed to the Supreme Court, nor in the Beijing Municipal Archives, which hold records of cases appealed to the Hebei Superior Court, nor in the Tianjin Municipal Archives, which holds records of local Tianjin District Court cases. But since the case attracted so much attention, the press covered a great deal of the actual courtroom exchanges. The official verdicts were also published in major newspapers, such as the *Dagongbao* of Tianjin and the *Shibao* of Shanghai.

2. *Dagongbao* (Tianjin), 22 November 1935, 4. For the specific articles, see *Zhonghua Minguo xingfa* 1935, 68, 98, and 19 (hereafter cited as *ZHMGXF* 1935).

3. *Dagongbao* (Tianjin), 26 November 1935, 4.

4. For coverage on the appeals process and the arguments for the appeals, see, for example, *Dagongbao* (Tianjin), 17 December 1935, 5; 21 December 1935, 5; 25 December 1935, 5.

5. *Dagongbao* (Tianjin), 7 February 1936, 4.

6. For coverage of the appeals process at this level, see *Dagongbao* (Tian-

jin), 18 February 1936, 5; 22 February 1936, 5; 23 February 1936, 5; 26 February 1936, 5; 1 March 1936, 5; and 8 March 1936, 5.

7. For more comprehensive discussions of the relationship between morality and law in imperial China, see Kinkley 2000, 104–11; and Ch'ü 1961, chap. 6. Jean Escarra's (1936) view of the traditional Chinese conception of law encapsulates the classical Confucian formulation of the relationship between ritual propriety and law. According to Escarra, Chinese orthodoxy traditionally recognized ritual propriety as the normal, essential means to achieve social harmony and viewed law as a means to achieve through punishment what could not otherwise be accomplished through moral teaching. Thus, to the extent that law was a necessary tool of social control, its ultimate goal was to uphold the Confucian ethical order. To this end, the imperial code was replete with ritual differentiation and sanctions according to social rank and family position as ritual propriety (*li*) was over time literally incorporated into the legal code, a process that Ch'ü T'ung-tsu has characterized as the "Confucianization" of the code itself (1961, 267–79). For an examination of how classical texts dealt with the concepts of sentiment (*qing*), Heavenly Principles (*tianli*), ritual propriety (*li*), and law (*fa*), see Fan, Zheng, and Zhan 1992.

8. Michael Dalby (1981) traces the tension from texts of antiquity, including the *Rites of Zhou* and the *Gongyang Commentary*, to legal opinion written in the Tang-Song and then to the legal code of the Ming-Qing period. Ch'ü T'ung-tsu (1961) points out that in the Tang and Song periods, while vengeance was manifestly outlawed, special consideration was still given to cases involving righteous revenge. It was only under Yuan law that revenge was permitted, and he who killed another to avenge the death of his father could avoid punishment. During the Ming and Qing, an avenging child was not subjected to punishment if he killed his parent's murderer immediately after the event.

9. For a more detailed consideration of these conditions, see my discussion below of Jonathan Spence's (1978) examination of a seventeenth-century case of revenge killing that demonstrated how the Qing code carefully restricted judicial tolerance for filial revenge.

10. Alison Yeung (2003), for example, examines the late Qing debate over the new criminal code from the perspective of the amendment of the illicit sex section and the abolition of the Statute of Killing a Wife's Paramour. As Yeung shows, the debate was characterized as a fight between *lijiao* (moral teachings) and *fali* (legal reasoning), which the reformist camp promoting *fali* ultimately won.

11. These efforts at reform accelerated after the fall of the imperial state. Post-imperial reformers discarded the initial work on modern law by the imperial commission and drew instead from the Japanese Criminal Code promulgated in 1907, which was itself heavily influenced by German legislation. In March 1912, they put into force a Provisionary New Criminal Code. In 1928, the Criminal Code of the Republic of China was issued to replace the provisionary code, and in January 1935, a new, revised code was promulgated. It was implemented by July of that year, just in time to be used in Shi Jianqiao's trial. For a detailed history of the codification of China's modern criminal code and the revisions over time, see Escarra 1936, esp. chap. 2 and chap. 3, sec. 4; and Meijer 1967. For a thor-

ough discussion of the revisions of the criminal code under the Nationalist regime, see Li and Ning 1987. Yet, in the end, while changes were implemented, the modifications were piecemeal, and elements of late Qing civil and criminal code remained in the Republican code under the Beijing regime (Li Chen, personal communication, 2004).

12. Jeffrey Kinkley (2000, 104) argues that the 1911 Revolution finally dethroned *li*. Also, it was at this time that the compound *falü* came into fashion to refer to modern law. Lydia Liu (1995, 272) notes that *falü* was a late Qing neologism from Japan that the Japanese had originally borrowed from China and that the compound also appears in classical texts such as *Zhuangzi*, as well as in seventeenth-century Jesuit missionary texts as a translation for "law." Kinkley (2000, 104, n. 15) notes that the term was in official use by May 1904, when the Falü Bianzu Guan (Chinese bureau for the compilation of laws) was installed.

13. This question of the relationship between *li* and law has plagued some of the contemporary scholarship on modern law in China. See, for example, Allyn Rickett (1971, 800), who describes the legal reform of the Republican era as essentially "conservative," citing several articles in the legal codes that continue to uphold Confucian principles as evidence that vestiges of *li* persisted. Yet, I would caution that this sort of assessment problematically assumes the Western definition of modern law as the standard yardstick. Indeed, while "vestiges" remained, the legal reform was still radical enough by the standards of the day to deeply upset staunch conservatives (see Xu 1997).

14. For the definitions of *qing* in Qing civil law, see Shiga 1984, 282–88. Much recent scholarship on imperial law considers whether Qing judges truly relied upon *qing* in practice. I find Thomas Buoye's (1995) argument that Qing judges were at once legalistic and attentive to Confucian compassion in their judgments very compelling. Examining homicide cases, Buoye argues that judges' ability to rely on both legal rule and compassion was literally institutionalized within the dual structure of the criminal judicial system. While the judicial review of homicide cases became increasingly routinized and thus required magistrates to follow the law strictly, they were able to express Confucian compassion in their recommendation of the cases to the autumn assizes, the process whereby the emperor reviewed capital crimes.

15. The *Hanyu dacidian* provides "truth" (*shishi*) as one of the glosses for *qing*. The compound *qingli*, facts or circumstances of the case, builds on this meaning of *qing*. From an English-language perspective, this gloss of *qing* as "truth" might appear odd for a term whose primary meaning is human feelings, or sentiment. Yet, from the perspective of Confucian philosophical discourses, the epistemological dichotomy of objective truth and subjective feeling was not absolute. *Qingli*, the objective logic of events or the rationale behind human behavior, turned on an assessment of the sincere motives of actors involved. The sincerity of intention determined the moral truth of events. *Qingli* was also often the basis of judgment with regard to whether the circumstances of the case, including the degree of sincerity behind the motivations of the actors, accorded with higher truths or principles (*heqing heli, qingli bu tong*).

16. "Cisha Zhang Zongchang zhi falü de guancha," *Shandong Minguo ribao*, 15 September 1932, 3.

17. The relationship between the courts and the public shifted with the rise of new media worldwide, beginning in the late eighteenth century. Sara Maza (1993), for example, has discussed how the publication of *memoire judiciaries*, or trial briefs, in late eighteenth-century France heightened public interest in courtroom proceedings to a degree never seen before, thereby transforming the nature of the relationship between the secluded space of courtrooms and the public arena. Trials of the day, she shows, became more melodramatic, took on broad social and political connotations, and often came to serve as illustrations of both moral principle and legal principle.

18. Chinese reformers drew from the experiences of Western countries and Japan, especially from countries that perceived themselves as late-modernizing nation-states. Though it waned in popularity after its imperialist intentions grew apparent after the 1910s, Japan was a popular model for late Qing Chinese jurists and reformers. As its model of legal reform, Republican China looked to Germany.

19. My thanks to Jonathan Ocko for pointing this out to me.

20. Sei Jeong Chin is working on a Harvard University dissertation that examines the press laws of 1935 and their impact on more overtly political cases such as the 1935 New Life Case of Du Zhongyuan. For coverage of these press laws, see *Dagongbao* (Tianjin), 15 and 16 July 1935.

21. *Dagongbao* (Tianjin), 26 November 1935, 4.

22. Ibid.

23. *Dagongbao* (Tianjin), 7 February 1936, 4.

24. *Shibao* (Shanghai), 28 November 1935, 6.

25. Not all papers covered the trial equally. In Shanghai, for example, the major daily, *Shenbao*, provided minimal coverage of the whole affair. Shi Jianqiao herself had suggested that the Sun family remained powerful in Shanghai and exerted influence over the press (see her "Tiebao bu" 1963, reprinted in Chen and Ling 1986, 197–98, and discussed in chapter 6). That said, other Shanghai papers did not hold back. The *Shibao*, which regularly included news on court cases, was particularly prolific in its coverage.

26. *Shibao* (Shanghai), 28 November 1935, 5.

27. *Shibao* (Shanghai), 26 November 1935, 6.

28. *Shibao* (Shanghai), 28 November 1935, 6.

29. *Shibao* (Shanghai), 28 November 1935, 5.

30. Connor 1994 and Xu 1998 discuss how lawyers, a new professional group in the Republican era, were only starting to develop and institutionalize their occupational identity. A bar association existed, and, according to statistics, Shanghai had the greatest number of members—just over one thousand in 1931. In North China, Tianjin's bar association was the largest, with 518 members, and Beiping had 479 (Escarra 1936, 450).

31. The *Minguo renwu dacidian* (The great dictionary of prominent figures of the Republican era) entry also lists a few of his books, including one on civil law and a reference book on judiciary matters. For more bibliographic information, see Gu Peijun 1980.

32. Her younger brother, Shi Zhongjie, contacted the two lawyers. Other family members were consistent supporters throughout the trial. Her sister, Shi

Youlan, came from Jinan, and her husband came from Taiyuan (He and Pan 1997, 221).

33. The Shi residence in Tianjin was located in the British Concession at 166 No. Ten Road. See *Shibao* (Shanghai), 28 November 1935, 6.

34. *Shibao* (Shanghai), 12 December 1935, 8.

35. Ironically, this journalist mistakenly referred to Yu Qichang as Dai Jimen, another famous lawyer of the day. Other retrospective accounts suggest that trials like Shi Jianqiao's showed that justice in the Republican period was a travesty and that the outcome of most such trials turned on personal relationships between lawyers and judges (e.g., Zhang and Meng 1997). Keep in mind, however, that these authors often aim to depict Republican-era trials as shams and, by extension, to portray the era as decadent and corrupt.

36. One newspaper account stated that the power of the Sun family must have been considerable, given their residence in the foreign concessions. *Shibao* (Shanghai), 12 December 1935, 4.

37. See the member list of *Tianjin shigong hui xunkan* (The journal of the Tianjin attorneys' association) 1, no. 2 (20 March 1933): 1. As an editorial member, Zhang would often write answers for the trade publication's Q&A column. See, for example, *Tianjin shigong hui xunkan* 1, no. 7 (10 June 1933): 5.

38. For press coverage of Shi Jianqiao's charges against Zhang Shaozeng, see Chen and Ling 1986, 197.

39. *Shibao* (Shanghai), 3 December 1935, 6–7.

40. For the original, see the chapter entitled "Qiuguan sikou" in the *Zhou li*. Also, see Lau and Chen 1993, 69. For the English translation, see Dalby 1981, 275.

41. Jonathan Ocko qualifies this more cosmological reading of imperial law and points out that despite different juridical ideologies, similar practical considerations were at work in the law's sanctioning of voluntary surrender in both imperial and Republican eras. In effect, confessions saved authorities time and trouble. Mitigation of a judicial sentence is then both a reward for the help provided to the system and a form of recognition of the accused's ostensible contrition (personal communication, 2001).

42. For the charges made by the lawyers on the Shi side, see, for example, *Yishibao* (Tianjin), 11 December 1935, 5. Extensive discussion of the legal issue of *zishou* in both the District Court and Superior Court trials appeared in the Shanghai *Shibao*.

43. See the defense lawyers' appeal to the Hebei Superior Court, reprinted in Chen and Ling 1986, 201–4.

44. Citing the Tang code, the defense team contended that sending a representative to surrender on one's behalf should constitute voluntary surrender. According to Rickett (1971, 798–99), imperial law did, in fact, recognize this form of surrender, but only under circumscribed conditions. That is, the Qing code recognized the offender's intent to surrender if he or she sent another person *who was privileged by law to conceal him or her* (e.g., close relatives or children) to surrender on his of her behalf. Thus, strictly speaking, by asking the monks, who had no privilege under law to conceal her, to report to authorities on her behalf, Shi did not fulfill these conditions.

45. *Shibao* (Shanghai), 12 December 1935, 8.
46. Ibid.
47. I discuss below the judicial significance of the phrase "then and there."
48. *Shibao* (Shanghai), 3 December 1935, 6–7. The *Gongyang Commentary* is one of the three main commentaries on the *Chunqiu*, or the *Spring and Autumn Annals*, a classical text that has been seen as a repository of the authentic teaching of Confucius. The immediate context of that text's treatment of revenge was the killing of the Chu king by Wu Zixu in revenge for the unjust death of his father and elder brother.
49. For the original, see *Chunqiu Gongyang zhuan* 1936, 25:7b. For the English translation, see Dalby 1981, 273. The "way of [the] thrusting sword" refers to a cycle of retaliation, where an unjust revenge will only lead to yet another act of revenge.
50. Michael Dalby identifies the *Gongyang Commentary* as the *locus classicus* of the long-standing political belief that in times of disorder when the state fails to provide appropriate channels of justice, righteous revenge qualifies as a ritually legitimate alternative (1981, 274–75). For another discussion on the *Gongyang* tradition in English, see Cheng 2004.
51. Li Chen, personal communication, 2005. Also, see Cheng 2004, 40.
52. *Shibao* (Shanghai), 12 December 1935, 8. Wang Anshi (1021–86 C.E.) wrote this commentary under the pen name Wang Jiefu. For the original quotation, see the chapter entitled "Fuchou jie" in Wang 1974, 32:22b. The lawyers also referred to the Tang literary giant, Liu Zihou, also known as Liu Zongyuan (773–819 C.E.), who had also commented on the possibility of revenge in instances of state failure. See *Shibao* (Shanghai), 12 December 1935, 8.
53. *Shibao* (Shanghai), 12 December 1935, 8.
54. Shi Jianqiao's second lawyer, Hu Xueqian, followed suit, arguing that Shi's filial motive should be considered morally relevant. He stated that her crime was not an act of evil intention and thus differed qualitatively from acts of rape and stealing. See *Shibao* (Shanghai), 12 December 1935, 8.
55. *Shibao* (Shanghai), 3 December 1935, 7.
56. *Shibao* (Shanghai), 12 December 1935, 8.
57. The vengeance clause is found in section 323, "Striking in Defense of a Parent," in the Qing criminal code. For the original Chinese, see the *Duli cunyi* (Xue 1970, 962). Staunton (1966, 353) provides the following translation: "If a son or grandson, upon the event of a father or mother, a paternal grandfather or grandmother having been murdered, instead of complaining to the magistrate, takes revenge by killing the murderer, . . . such son or grandson shall be . . . entirely justified, if he kills the murderer upon the impulse of the moment, and at the instant that the murder is committed."
58. Marinus Meijer (1991) discusses the evolution of the legal concept of righteous anger. He argues that the expression "those who kill intentionally, overcome by righteous anger" first became legitimate in 1756. Discussing cases in which the husband murders his adulterous wife, Meijer argues that Qing law identified the husband's anger as noble and absolved him of his crime because he was only punishing the adulterer who had committed the highly dangerous crime of disrupting the social order (Meijer 1991, 56). Likewise, in revenge cases,

the crime was noble because the avenger was correcting a preexisting wrong and thus rectifying the social order.

59. *Shibao* (Shanghai), 3 December 1935, 7.

60. This quotation appeared as a headline in the Shanghai *Shibao's* coverage of the proceedings the following day; see *Shibao* (Shanghai), 12 December 1935, 8.

61. *Shibao* (Shanghai), 11 December 1935, 6.

62. *Shibao* (Shanghai), 12 December 1935, 6.

63. *Shibao* (Shanghai), 21 November 1935, 5.

64. *Shibao* (Shanghai), 28 November 1935, 5.

65. Ibid.

66. *Dagongbao* (Tianjin), 22 February 1936, 4. She also protested this decision to overturn the lower court's granting of leniency based on voluntary surrender by releasing excerpts of her diary to the press. One local Tianjin paper even printed the entire diary. In the diary, she implores, "Where is justice (*gongli*)?" See He and Pan 1997, 225–26.

67. *Yishibao* (Tianjin), 11 December 1935, 5.

68. *Shibao* (Shanghai), 28 December 1935, 5. She dwells upon this situation in an autobiographical account of the case that she wrote in 1963 (Chen and Ling 1986, 197–98).

69. See *Shibao* (Shanghai), 17 December 1935, 6; and *Shibao* (Shanghai), 19 December 1935, 6.

70. For the final decision that upheld Liu's life sentence, see *Chenbao* (Beiping), 28 October 1936, 6. For coverage of the Liu case, see any major newspaper, especially northern ones like the Beiping *Shibao* or Tianjin's *Dagongbao* from March 1935, when the assassination occurred, up until October 1936, when the Supreme Court decision was announced. I discuss the Liu case in more detail below in the conclusion of the chapter.

71. *Shibao* (Shanghai), 12 December 1935, 8.

72. *Shibao* (Shanghai), 17 December 1935, 6.

73. *Shibao* (Shanghai), 19 December 1935, 3.

74. She provided the press with two other poems as well. One is entitled, "Mengzhong hui di" (In my dreams, I meet my younger brother) and the other "Si Gui" (Thinking of returning home), both of which express her desire to return home. See *Shibao* (Shanghai), 19 December 1935, 3.

75. The invocation of Heaven as a witness is an old rhetorical strategy that can imply that the secular authorities are somehow failing to rule righteously.

76. *Yishibao* (Tianjin), 6 December 1935, 5.

77. For coverage, see *Shibao* (Shanghai), 21 November 1935, 5. Lawyers representing the Sun family included Sun Guanche and Zhang Yaozeng. Sun was a powerful jurist in Beiping. He had gone abroad in the late Qing to Japan to study law, had served as a judge in the Supreme Court of Beijing (*Daliyuan*), was the head of the Beiping District Court, and was a famous lawyer (He and Pan, 1997, 221).

78. See Sun 1935. While this lawyer has the same surname as Sun Chuanfang, there is no evidence that they are related.

79. *Dagongbao* (Tianjin), 18 November 1935, 4. The press conference in-

furiated the Shi side. The Shi family accused Lu of manipulating public opinion (He and Pan 1997, 223).

80. In addition to the criminal case, the lawyers of the Sun family also pressed civil charges and demanded a reparation payment of one hundred thousand *yuan* to compensate for costs of damage, the funeral, and costs of rearing Sun's children. See *Shibao* (Shanghai), 28 November 1935, 5. Shi Jianqiao responded that she would never pay and that no amount of money, not even a million *yuan*, could make up for the death of her father. See *Shibao* (Shanghai), 11 December 1935, 6.

81. *Shibao* (Shanghai), 8 December 1935, 8. In a courtroom debate, the Hebei Court's prosecutor similarly charged that the defendant had been misguided by the opinions of old books and the outmoded teachings of Confucian propriety (*lijiao*), implying that the moral teachings of the past should not be used as standards of justice in this case. See *Shibao* (Shanghai), 12 December 1935, 6.

82. *Yishibao* (Tianjin), 7 February 1936, 5.

83. Ibid.

84. *Shibao* (Shanghai), 8 December 1935, 8. The prosecutor also sought to overturn the earlier verdict by arguing that Shi Jianqiao had unsuccessfully established her voluntary surrender according to the letter of law. See *Yishibao* (Tianjin), 7 February 1936, 5. Observers questioned the validity of Shi's voluntary surrender in the press as well. See, for example, "Shi Jianqiao'an yu shehui guandian" 1935, which suggests that Shi had confessed only because she knew she could win a more lenient punishment.

85. For Zhang's argument, see *Yishibao* (Tianjin), 7 February 1936, 5. Also, see the citation of Zhang's argument in the Supreme Court Verdict, Case # 486, 1936, hereafter cited as Verdict #486), issued on 25 August 1936, reprinted in Chen and Ling 1986, 215–16. Newspapers the following day published the full verdict. See, for example, *Yishibao* (Tianjin), 26 August 1936, 5. For the original code, see *Lu hai kong jun xingfa* (1993), also printed in the *Zhonghua Minguo xianxing fagui daquan* (1934). Article #34 reads as follows: "Military soldiers who bring injury to the people shall be punished with death."

86. Superior Court Verdict of a Criminal Matter, 1935, Case #1207 (hereafter cited as Verdict #1207), 18 February 1936, reprinted in Chen and Ling 1986, 206–10. The verdict was immediately printed in the newspapers. See, for example, *Dagongbao* (Tianjin), 22 February 1936, 5. The ruling includes the clause "which the accused should be fully aware of" in order to preempt a defensive appeal to article 16, which stipulates, "Ignorance of the law shall not discharge any person from criminal responsibility; *Provided*, that the punishment may be reduced according to the nature and circumstances of the case. If a person is convinced that his act is permitted by the law and there is justifiable reason so to believe, his punishment may be remitted" (*ZHMGXF* 1935, 6).

87. Verdict #1207.

88. Ibid. This quotation is one of the epigraphs that start the chapter.

89. *Shibao* (Shanghai), 12 February 1936, 5.

90. According to the rules of the appeals process at that time, the Supreme Court did not have to hear all appealed cases, and among those it did hear, it separated out those whose decisions it overturned and returned them for retrial in the lower courts. Shi's case was heard, but not overturned.

91. "Shi Jianqiao'an yu shehui guandian" 1935.

92. For the final verdict, see Beijing Municipal Archives (hereafter cited as BMA) document 65/4/201.

93. In the Liu Jinggui trial, this approach was explicitly laid out in the "Document with Intent to Defend" filed by Liu Jinggui's defense lawyer, Liu Huang. See BMA document 65/4/199, 63–69.

94. For specifics of this argument, see ibid, 64.

95. Ibid., 68.

96. The suspicion of new female emotion coincided with critical commentary on the Liu Jinggui case that cited it as an example of the emotionalism of modern youth running amuck. For further elaboration of how Liu Jinggui's case prompted a public discussion of excessive sentimentalism of new women (in this case, the new figure of the female student) and how this discussion was, in fact, indicative of a more general anxiety regarding the rise of the sentimental masses, see Lean 2005.

CHAPTER 5. A STATE PARDON

1. In his study of merchant elites and the Nationalist regime in the Republican period, Joseph Fewsmith (1985, chap. 6) draws a careful and, for our purposes, highly useful distinction between two parts of the Nationalist government, namely the Nationalist Party and the state. *State*, for Fewsmith, refers to the administrative bureaucratic apparatus, the army, and the vast network of personal relationships linked to Jiang, all of which became the source of Jiang's authority after 1928. The Nationalist Party, or Guomindang, refers to the party organization that coexisted with the state apparatus throughout the 1920s. The decline of the autonomy of the party, or *dang*, in the late 1920s, along with the end of the strategy of mobilizing the masses for nationalist revolution, enabled Jiang Jieshi to gain authoritarian control over the entire regime, including the bureaucracy and the party. Fewsmith prefers the term *state-party* rather than *party-state* to emphasize that Jiang's rise to power indicated the decline of autonomous party power. But given the fact that the term *party-state* has persisted in current scholarship as the conventional term to describe the 1930s regime, I use the phrase *party-state regime* while keeping Fewsmith's distinctions in mind.

2. For more on Zhang, see Boorman and Howard 1967–71, 1:122–27.

3. Zhang killed Zheng Jinsheng after he learned that Zheng had participated in the Northern Expedition. See *Shandong Minguo ribao* (Jinan), 5 September 1932, 5; and *Shenbao* (Shanghai), 7 September 1932, 10–11.

4. *Dagongbao* (Tianjin), 4 September 1932, 5. Accounts described Zhang's departure speech in detail. A few emphasized how ironic it was that Zhang, during what turned out to be the final moments of his life, spoke about wanting to die a hero in his homeland rather than remain a traitor in Japan. Seeking to demonstrate his patriotism, he claimed that the Japanese had offered him thirty million *yuan* and twenty thousand guns to start an uprising in Shandong and that he had refused. He also listed several personal aspirations for China. He challenged North China's brave and righteous soldiers to resist Japan over the long term, called on the government to commit to the fight and not just speak

in empty slogans, and appealed for the resolution of internal division. Zhang concluded by calling for the present-day Shandong government to carry on what he had started during his own rule, namely, confronting imperialists in a united manner without causing the Shandong people any harm. For an example of coverage of the speech, see *Shenbao* (Shanghai), 6 September 1932, 11.

5. See, for example, *Dagongbao* (Tianjin), 4 September 1932, 5.

6. See "Assassination of War-lord, Shanghai Lady's Story of Tsinan Murder: Scene on Platform," *North China Herald*, 14 September 1932, 409.

7. See "Assassins' Calm Behavior," *North China Herald*, 14 September 1932, 409.

8. Zhang Zuolin had named Zhang Zongchang, Sun Chuanfang, Wu Peifu, and Yan Xishan as deputy commanders, though Wu and Yan played no significant role thereafter. Zhang Zuolin ruled north China for eighteen months, during which the coalition was weakened immensely, plagued by extraordinary infighting. For further discussion, see McCormack (1977, 209–15).

9. See Xue 1970, 962, for the vengeance clause in the *Duli cunyi*.

10. The Judicial Yuan was the judicial branch of the Republican government. The Nationalist government was comprised of five branches, or bureaus: the Executive, Legislative, Judicial, Control, and Examination.

11. *Guojia zhengfu gongbao* 1079 (14 March 1933).

12. *Guojia zhengfu gongbao* 2177 (14 October 1936).

13. Both codes are published in *Zhonghua Minguo xianxing fagui daquan* 1934. The brevity of codified regulation may have been intended, since the absence of procedural direction allowed substantial leeway on the part of the executive branch in actual practice.

14. Despite the fact that Lin Sen and Ju Zheng signed the texts, it is not clear whether Lin and Ju were primary movers in the decision to grant the pardons or were simply responding to Jiang Jieshi's directive. Lin Sen had become the Chairman of the National Government in 1931 and held the post until his death in 1943. However, from the start, he was merely the titular chief of state and had few practical responsibilities and little power. His name on the pardon belied the fact that his signature was probably no more than a rubber stamp (Boorman and Howard 1967–71, 2:382). At this point, Ju Zheng was the head of the Judicial Yuan, appointed by the central regime, and his position was most likely similar to Lin's. Their signatures merely signaled that these executive pardons were well within the bounds of law and supported by proper authorities. Such legitimacy became important later when the regime had to defend itself against accusations that it was seeking to extend executive reach into the judicial sphere. I discuss such allegations and the regime's defense further below.

15. Whereas participants in the late Qing "national essence" movement expressed ambivalence toward the West and had been associated with the articulation of an anti-Manchu, Han racial identity, Critical Review members promoted *guocui* as a universalistic humanistic essence of Chinese culture that was grounded in the Western humanist tradition, associated most closely with Harvard professor Irving Babbitt (1865–1933). The latter group promoted "New Confucianism" as a means to locate a common humanistic ground where Eastern and Western essences blended. See Lydia Liu 1995, esp. chap. 9.

16. The quotation appears in Wakeman 1997, 395. It was originally printed in Wilbur Burton, "Chiang's Secret Blood Brothers," *Asia*, May 1936, 209. This speech, which foreshadows the moral economy behind the New Life movement, suggests that the moral discourse associated with the movement can serve as context to our understanding of the 1933 decision to pardon Zheng Jicheng, even though Zheng's pardon was issued more than a year before the official start of the New Life campaign.

17. *Xinwenbao* (Shanghai), 14 December 1935, 7. Local Anhui legal organizations, including those from Anhui counties Tongcheng, Shucheng, and Huaining, were also highly vocal, sending telegrams that emphasized the Zheng Jicheng case as legal precedent. See *Dagongbao* (Tianjin), 6 February 1936, 5.

18. *Zhongyang ribao* (Nanjing), 18 March 1936, 3.

19. *Shenbao* (Shanghai), 13 March 1936, 7. Another women's group, the Yangzhou Women's Organization, called on the United National Women's Organization to take Zheng Jicheng's case as precedent and to plead with the appropriate authorities to exempt Shi Jianqiao from this "political crime." See *Shenbao* (Shanghai), 2 December 1935, 9.

20. For a list of telegrams from different civic groups and individuals, see *Shandong Minguo ribao* (Jinan), 14 September 1932, 5. Among those issuing telegrams in the Zheng case were numerous party organizations. According to Ju Zheng, the head of the Judicial Yuan, telegrams requesting a pardon for Zheng were sent by provincial and city party organizations from Shandong, Jiangxi, and Tianjin; by party organizations in each county in Shandong; by various citizen groups from Shandong, by Yang Minghui, the citizen's representative of Licheng county, and others. See, Ju 1935, 18, n. 1.

21. *Shenbao* (Shanghai), 13 September 1932, 10.

22. *Shandong Minguo ribao* (Jinan), 6 September 1932, 5.

23. *Shenbao* (Shanghai), 13 September 1932, 10. Zheng used this sort of language both in his self-defense right after the murder as well as in retrospective memoirs and autobiographical articles. For accounts of his surrender, see the *North China Herald*, 7 September 1932, 369. For his own description of the affair right after the killing, see *Shenbao* (Shanghai), 7 September 1932, 10. For later accounts by Zheng, see Zheng 1936, 1994.

24. *Dagongbao* (Tianjin), 11 March 1936, 6.

25. *Xinwenbao* (Shanghai), 24 December 1935, 7.

26. *Chenbao* (Beiping), 28 March 1936, 6. For more on the *Gongyang* passage, see my discussion in chapter 4.

27. Zarrow 1990. In contrast, the second generation of May Fourth anarchists was more informed by successful examples of social revolution in Russia and elsewhere and thus preferred mass movements rather than individual assassination as a means to revolution.

28. As mentioned earlier, Wakeman (2003, esp. 176–79) discusses some of the public backlash and how the more high-profile "hits" incited both national and international public outrage and opprobrium against the regime.

29. Zhao 1935. Tang Youren was assassinated on December 25, 1935, in Shanghai's French Concession. As discussed earlier, the attempted assassination of Wang Jingwei, the head of the Executive Yuan, took place on November 1, 1935.

30. See "Ansha," *Dushu shenghuo* 3, no. 2 (1935): 74. I discuss the complicated politics behind the revenge further below.

31. "Xing Zheng de cike" 1932.

32. *Jingbao* editorialist Miao Wei found Sun Chuanfang's choice to behead Shi to be gruesome and his impaling of Shi's head on a stick at the Bangbu, Anhui, train station unnecessarily humiliating and a sign of the chaos of the times. See *Jingbao* (Shanghai), 22 November 1935, 2.

33. For more on Nationalist encroachment into the judicial sphere, see Xu 2001, especially chap. 9.

34. For more on the history of the amnesty, or *dashe*, in Song imperial law, see McKnight 1981.

35. An entry for "teshe" in a 1964 dictionary of legal terms elaborates upon this ideal. Examining the relationship between exemption and criminal policy promulgated in 1953, the entry states that because the legal code is limited in accommodating the endless transformations in the affairs of the people, the executive powers of exemption function to redress and remedy inflexible applications of law (Lin 1965, 429).

36. See Ju 1935. The piece was written in anticipation of the National Judicial Conference held in September 1935 in Nanjing. Prior to 1931, Ju had been estranged from Jiang Jieshi for years, and Jiang even had him arrested at one point for forming a rival government and party organization in North China. By 1931, however, Ju had been brought into the Nanjing fold by his election as vice president of the Judicial Yuan. In March 1932, he became the president of the Judicial Yuan when the incumbent resigned, at which point he no doubt had to tone down any dissenting political views. Thus we must understand Ju Zheng's promotion of party doctrine in the context of his status as the Nationalist head of the Judicial Yuan. For more biographical information on Ju Zheng, see Boorman and Howard 1967–71, 1:473.

37. The entry for *Minsheng* in the *Zhongguo baokan cidian* (Dictionary of Chinese newspapers and journals) states explicitly that *Minsheng* propagated Nationalist views and policies (Wang and Zhu 1992).

38. For further discussion of the extension of party rule in Canton during the 1920s, see Fitzgerald 1996, especially chaps. 5 and 6. See also Tsin 1999, which argues that the Nationalist government in Canton, while it aggressively sought to mobilize society, did not do so effectively.

39. For a discussion of Nanjing's cooptation of merchants, see Fewsmith 1985, and of professional organizations, see Xu 2001. Fitzgerald 1996 discusses the Nationalist tendency to expand its reach into societal organizations, starting in the 1920s. Xu points out that the Nationalist regime required all societal organizations to register with its party organs and bureaucracies by the 1930s (2001, 95–106).

40. *Chenbao* (Beiping), 23 November 1935, 5. It is interesting to note that the earlier pardon for Zheng Jicheng specifically lists party organizations along with other civic groups, whereas no mention is made of party groups in the Shi Jianqiao pardon. The mention of party groups in the Zheng pardon does not necessarily indicate that the central regime was more involved in soliciting telegrams of support for Zheng. Rather, it may reflect the fact that in the early

1930s, the regime was interested in co-opting party autonomy just as much as that of other organizations (Fewsmith 1985).

41. *Shibao* (Shanghai), 17 October 1936, 5.

42. *The North China Herald*, 14 September 1932, 409.

43. Rumors of the affair continued to swirl in post-1949 accounts. Wang Weinong (1960) recalled how he had helped ghost-write *Yingxiong de xiaozhuan* (A hero's pamphlet), a small booklet distributed during Zheng Jicheng's trial and admitted that he had explicitly embellished the facts of the assassination in a manner that favored Zheng. He also recounted how he came across a glaring discrepancy in Zheng's legal defense. Specifically, the contradiction lay between the defense lawyer's argument that Zheng was a heroic assassin, on the one hand, and that Zheng could not have been the true killer since the bullet that had killed Zhang Zongchang was from a rifle rather than a pistol, on the other hand. When he pointed out the flaw in logic to Zheng's defense lawyer, the attorney was, he claimed, remarkably unconcerned, and it was this curious lack of concern that caused him to suspect that the entire trial was rigged.

44. *Shandong Minguo ribao* (Jinan), 10 September 1932, 5.

45. For information on telegrams sent by civic groups, see *Shandong Minguo ribao* (Jinan), 9 September 1932, 5. For information on the provincial notables, see *Shandong Minguo ribao* (Jinan), 10 September 1932, 5. For coverage of Zhang Weicun's telegram to Jiang Jieshi, see *Donghai ribao* (Jinan), 7 September 1932, 2. Fu Sinian, the director of the History and Philology Institute of Beiping's Academia Sinica, and Mao Beihan, another famous figure in the education world, also pleaded for clemency. So too did national players. Li Liejun, who was in an advisory position to the National Government in 1932, issued a telegram in support of pardoning Zheng. See *Donghai ribao* (Jinan), 13 September 1932, 3.

46. *Shenbao* (Shanghai), 10 September 1932, 4.

47. Ibid. The Executive Yuan sent an official telegram ordering the Shandong government to send the case to court on September 23, 1932. For information on this telegram, see *Shandong Minguo ribao* (Jinan), 24 September 1932, 5.

48. *Shandong Minguo ribao* (Jinan), 20 November 1932, 5.

49. See, for example, "Ex-Warlord Shot While [He] Knelt in Prayer," *North China Herald*, 20 November 1935, 308.

50. See Wakeman 2003, 477, n. 34. The author cited there notes that he found no evidence that these rumors were true.

51. Feng had urged key elder statesmen of the Guomindang, including Zhang Zhijiang, a veteran of the Luanzhou Uprising during the 1911 Revolution; Yu Youren, another Revolutionary alliance veteran; along with Jiao Yitang, Zhang Ji, and Li Liejun to lobby personally on Shi's behalf.

52. Cited in Shi 1986, 221–25.

53. Feng had been reinstated as a member of the Central Executive Committee of the Guomindang and was made a member of the State Council in 1931, but in October 1932, he withdrew from formal duties and in 1933, appointed himself as commander in chief of the People's Allied Anti-Japanese army. Facing opposition from Nanjing and Tokyo, Feng was forced into semiretirement from the end of 1933 until he returned to the Nanjing fold in late 1935 (Boorman and Howard 1967–71, 2:42).

54. See articles in the *North China Herald*, 13 August 1935 and 21 August 1935, regarding his return and his change of clothing. For a fuller account, see Jian 1982, 359–60.

55. For a detailed account in Chinese of the Luanzhou uprising and its tragic ending, see Zhao and Ma 2003. For a brief account in English, see Sheridan 1966, 44–48. For more on Feng's account of his near-participation in the uprising, see Jian 1982, 57–59.

56. For the diary entries mentioned here, see Feng 1992, vols. 4–5.

57. The actual commemoration did not take place until May 26, 1937. For coverage of the commemoration event, see articles in Beiping's *Chenbao* and other major newspapers for 21–31 May 1937.

58. It is interesting to note that maverick governor Han Fuju publicly joined Feng to participate in the commemoration and that Wang Jingwei, who was Jiang's strongest rival in the regime at that point, had sent a telegram of support. See *Chenbao*, 26 May 1937, 3.

59. Thanks to Wu Pei-yi and Li Chen for bringing Xu Daolin's case to my attention.

60. For more biographical information on Xu Shuzheng (1880–1925) and for information on his death, see his entry in Boorman and Howard 1967–71, 2:143–46.

61. Xu Shuzheng had shot Lu Jianzhang in 1918, when Lu had been allied with Feng in military struggles against Duan Qirui and his group. Rumor had it that Lu and Feng were threatening an invasion of Anhui. For more on the political situation in 1918, see Sheridan 1966, 67–73. As Sheridan notes, Feng was upset about Lu's murder at the time but was mollified by Duan, who issued a presidential mandate restoring Feng's military rank only two days after the announcement of Lu's "execution." In return, Feng signed a presidential mandate that accused Lu of having incited rebellion and having had connections with bandits (Sheridan 1966, 72–73, and 73n).

62. See Sheridan 1966, 186n, in which Sheridan notes rumors that Lu had been in Shanghai at the time of the murder.

63. Sheridan 1966: 186n. Xu offers his version of the complex warlord politics behind the assassination, which included shifting tensions between Duan Qirui, Xu's patron, Zhang Zuolin, and Feng Yuxiang as they all maneuvered for control of Beijing in Xu 1962, 326–27.

64. See Xu 1962, 329. Xu focused on his studies instead in hopes of eventually establishing himself in a position of power from which to seek revenge. He also claimed that during the period from his father's death until the day he finally filed a suit against Feng, he never spoke Feng's name (329). In a commemorative volume published at the time of Xu Daolin's death in the early 1970s, friends and family also wrote that he had waited reluctantly to seek revenge because China was at war with Japan. See *Xu Daolin xiansheng jinian ji* 1975, e.g., 21, 27.

65. Several contributors to *Xu Daolin xiansheng jinian ji* (1975) argued that Xu had failed in courts because of Feng's political standing.

66. Even though Feng's relations with Jiang were actually very tense at the time of the 1940s trial, the public saw Feng as representative of the central gov-

ernment in the case. Xu Daolin himself notes the tensions between Feng and Jiang Jieshi during the trial (Xu 1962, 330). See also Sheridan's discussion of Feng's increasing alienation in the mid-1940s (1966, 276–80).

67. The publication of this volume in 1975 resonated with the political events occurring in and around Taiwan at the time. Internationally, the second half of the 1970s saw the United States shift its allegiance away from the Nationalists in the Republic of China to Beijing. Domestically, the underground democracy movement and opposition parties were gaining momentum and started to put pressure on the Nationalists to lift martial law. While the turning point in Taiwanese politics did not come until the pro-democracy demonstrations held in Gaoxiong in 1979, discontent with Nationalist martial rule was nonetheless palpable throughout the mid-1970s. It was in this context that this publication gained significance. In re-publicizing Xu's legal case against Feng Yuxiang and, more generally, against Nationalist rule in the 1940s, this commemorative volume might easily have been read as a critique of the legitimacy of the Nationalists in any era.

68. Several other contributors to the volume mention this point as well. See, for example, the entry by Ru Mukai (*Xu Daolin xiansheng jinian ji* 1975, 50).

CHAPTER 6. BEYOND THE 1930S

1. For more information on the War of Resistance, see Eastman 1986 or Hsiung and Levine 1992. Japanese raids hit Guilin, Kunming, and Xian, as well as Chongqing, but the wartime capital and its surrounding areas were hit the hardest. Chongqing itself was bombed 268 times between 1939 and 1941.

2. "Women's Work in China" 1940, 72. Helen Schneider clarifies that Song Meiling was involved in three different yet overlapping social service organizations during the late 1930s, but that the Women's Advisory Committee of the New Life movement became the umbrella group under which other groups, including the National Chinese Women's Association for War Relief and the Wartime Association for Refugee Children, were coordinated (Schneider 2004, 6–7).

3. "Women's Work in China" 1940, 68; see also Diamond 1975.

4. For a discussion of how the exigencies of war affected the press, from the quality of printing and length of issues to the content, see "The Press in Wartime China" 1940.

5. See "Weilao zu gongzuo gaishu" 1941; Li 1938; Liu 1938.

6. Around 1937 Song Meiling had been in charge of reorganizing the Chinese air force as the head of the Aviation Commission (Aeronautics Committee), but had given up the duty in 1938 to focus on "more social problems of war" (Schneider 2004, 6).

7. See the table entitled "Riji lici hongzha woxian chengqu qingkuang jilubiao (Record of all previous occasions of the bombing of our county's city region by Japanese planes) printed in Zheng 1988, 141. The table notes that the office that prints Hechuan's official gazetteer compiled the figures.

8. "Hochwan Gives Three Planes" 1941.

9. *Zhongyang ribao* (Chongqing), 31 May 1941, 3.

10. For a copy of Jiang's text, see Tang 1982, 129.

11. "Hochwan Gives Three Planes" 1941.

12. "Zhongguo hangkong jianshi xiehui zonghui gonghan" 1941.

13. See *Zhongyang ribao* (Chongqing), 31 May 1941, 3.

14. See *Xianji zhuankan* 1941, 6.

15. Ibid, 4.

16. *Zhongyang ribao* (Chongqing), 31 May 1941, 3. Also see a draft version in Feng 1941.

17. "Hochwan Gives Three Planes" 1941.

18. *Dagongbao* (Chongqing), 29 May 1941, 4.

19. For the autobiography, see Xie 1994.

20. Poshek Fu discusses the movie version of *Mulan congjun* (Mulan joins the army) and its intense popularity in occupied Shanghai. He too identifies the mix of the modern quality of strength and power, and the traditional virtues of filial piety and sincerity embodied both by the movie star in the film, Chen Yunshang, and the Hua Mulan protagonist, as crucial in making the film so popular and in reviving the "legendary figure of the past as an allegory for the national crisis of the present" (Fu 2003, 15).

21. Scholars of the late 1950s and early 1960s also interpreted the novel as revolutionary in nature (e.g., Li 1959). Lin Chong, a main character of the novel, is often identified as best able to kindle the desire for revolution among readers.

22. While I do not have a copy of the original account, it is reprinted in Shi Peng 1987, 515–17.

23. I have not been able to locate a copy of the original autobiographical account, but, like the "Scrapbook," it has been reprinted in Shi 1987, 515–17. Shi Peng, who is of no apparent relation to Shi Jianqiao, procured the account from Shi Yuyao, Shi Jianqiao's son.

24. Shi 1987, 515–17. For more information on Tao Xingzhi, see his entry in Wang and Zhu 1992. Deng Yingchao was also known for promoting progressive ideas about marriage and free love during the May Fourth period. She was a CCP representative to the Nationalist government in Chongqing during the forties and a member of the CCP Central Committee and the vice-chair of the National Women's Federation of China after 1949. For more information on Deng, see Qian 1950, 36–37.

25. For more information on the school, its revolutionary activities, and the allegation that Zhou Enlai felt Shi Jianqiao would best serve the CCP from within Nationalist-held territory, see Shi 1982 and Chen 1991.

26. For more on Liu Shanben, see Li 1981.

27. I discuss below some of the memoirs, biographies, popular, and "wild" histories that have featured this case. For an illustrated flipbook, see *Cisha Sun Chuanfang*, 1987, which provides the image for the cover of this book. Yomi Braester and Dorothy Ko each found a copy of this flipbook in flea markets in China, and each was extremely thoughtful to buy a copy for me. The Shi Jianqiao case can also be found on the web. A recent Google search generated countless references to Shi Jianqiao's story.

28. For an excellent study of the role of the Gang of Four trial in mediating

the transition from the idealism of Cultural Revolution era to a new, more pragmatic era of socialist reform under Deng Xiaoping, see Cook, 2007.

29. Other accounts simply reproduced writings by Shi Jianqiao herself, allowing her to make a posthumous case for rehabilitation. A 1980 *Wenshi ziliao xuanbian* (Selected materials of literature and history) compilation, for example, included her essay "Wei baosheng fuchou, shouren Sun Chuanfang" (Shi 1980).

30. The Beijing Central Film Archives, for example, does not have a copy.

CONCLUSION

1. Communists also came to adopt such tactics. First in the Jiangxi Soviet and later at Yan'an, the remote town that served as the base for CCP activities from the end of the Long March to the civil war with the Nationalists in 1947, the Communists proved far more effective than the Nationalists in mobilizing individuals and mass support by appealing to patriotism and anti-Japanese sentiment.

2. Mao Zedong elaborated his populist theory that celebrated the spontaneous revolutionary energies of the rural "people" as early as his February 1927 "Hunan Report."

Glossary of Selected Chinese Names and Terms

aiguo 愛國
aiguo zhi xin 愛國之心
aiqing 愛情
bao 報
Baoding 保定
baoying 報應
beifen 悲憤
Beiyang 北洋
Cai Jiwei 蔡繼渭
cainü 才女
caizi 才子
caizi jiaren 才子佳人
Cao Rulin 曹汝霖
Chen Duxiu 陳獨秀
Chen Jiashu 陳家樹
Chen Qingyun 陳慶雲
Cheng Xixian 程希賢
chou 仇
choudi 仇敵
chounü 仇女
chuanqi 傳奇
Chunqiu 春秋
chunxiao xingcheng 純孝性成
ci 刺
cike 刺客
dafei 大匪
Dai Jimen 戴戟門

Dai Li 戴笠
Dai Zhen 戴震
Daliyuan 大理院
dang 黨
danghua 黨化
dangyi 黨義
dashe 大赦
dazhong 大眾
dazhong geming 大眾革命
Deng Yingchao 鄧穎超
Ding Ling 丁玲
Dong Biwu 董必武
Dong Hai 東海
Dong Hui 董慧
Dong Zhongshu 董仲舒
Du Yuesheng 杜月笙
Duan Qirui 段祺瑞
fa 法
fali 法理
falü 法律
falü lun 法律論
fazhi 法制
fei 匪
Fei Zhen'e 費貞娥
fen 分
Feng Youlan 馮友蘭
Feng Yuxiang 馮玉祥
Fengtian 奉天
Fu Ming 富明
Fu Sinian 傅斯年
fuchou zhuyi 復仇主義
fudao 婦道
ganqing 感情
ganqing lun 感情論
Gao Guoren shu 告國人書
gegu 割股
geren 個人
geren renge 個人人格
gong 公
gong'an 公案
Gongyang 公羊
Gongyang zhuan 公羊傳
guan 官
Guangming 光明
guige 閨閣
guocui 國粹
guodu shidai 過度時代

guofa 國法
guojia ziyou 國家自由
guomin ganqing 國民感情
Guomindang 國民黨
Guominjun 國民軍
guoshu 國術
Han Feizi 韓非子
Han Fuju 韓複榘
Han Yu 韓愈
He Yingqin 何應欽
Hechuan 合川
Hechuan xianji yundong 合川獻機運動
houguo qianyin 後果前因
Hu Shi 胡適
Hu Xueqian 胡學騫
Hua Mulan 花木蘭
Huang Jinrong 黃金榮
hutong 胡同
jian 劍
Jiang Jieshi (Chiang Kai-shek) 蔣介石
jianghu 江湖
jianxia 劍俠
jiao 角
Jiao Yitang 焦易堂
Jin Yunpeng 靳雲鵬
Jing Ke 荊軻
Jing Xingzhen 景星辰
jinguo yingxiong 巾幗英雄
Ju Zheng 居正
junfa 軍法
Juntong 軍統
junzi 君子
jushilin 居士林
kaipian 開片
kemin 可憫
Kong Jiazhang 孔嘉彰
Kong Xiangxi 孔祥熙
li 禮
li 理
Li Fenglou 李風樓
Li Liejun 李烈鈞
Liang Qichao 梁桀超
Lianhua 連華
lianmin 憐憫
Liaozhai tuyong 聊齋圖詠
Liaozhai zhiyi 聊齋志異
lijiao 禮教

Lin Biao 林彪
Lin Chong 林沖
Lin Monong 林墨農
Lin Sen 林森
Lin Yutang 林語堂
Liu Huang 劉煌
Liu Jianying 劉建英
Liu Jinggui 劉景桂
Liu Shanben 劉善本
Liu Shuxiu 劉恕修
Liu Zaihua 劉再華
lixing 理性
lixue 理學
lizhi 理智
longtang 弄堂
Lu Chengwu 陸承武
Lu Jianzhang 陸建章
Lu Ming 逯明
Lu Xiangting 盧香亭
Lu Xun 魯迅
Luanzhou qiyi 灤州起義
Lü Siniang 呂四娘
Mao Beihan 毛準函
mao shu tongmin 貌鼠同眠
Mao Yaode 毛耀德
Mao Zedong 毛澤東
mengshu 盟叔
mengxiong mengdi 盟兄盟弟
Mengzi 孟子
Miaoshan 妙善
minshu 憫恕
Mulan 木蘭
pingtan 評彈
Pu Songling 蒲松齡
qi 奇
qianyin houguo 前因後果
qiao 翹
qing 情
qing ke minshu 情可憫恕
qingdi 情敵
qingli 情理
Qingxiu 清修
qingyu 情欲
qipao 旗袍
Qiu Jin 秋瑾
qiyan lushi 七言律詩
Qu Hongtao 曲鴻韜

qunzhong ganqing 群眾感情
renao 熱鬧
renmin zhengyi 人民正義
renqing 人情
renxin 人心
renzhi 人制
Ruan Lingyu 阮玲玉
Ruan Yuan 阮元
sancong side 三從四德
Sanfan 三反
sanjiaolian 三角戀
Shang Sanguan 尚三官
She Zhengwang 攝政王
shehui 社會
shehui tongqing 社會同情
shehui xinwen 社會新聞
Shen Jiaben 沈家本
shi 詩
Shi Congbin 施從濱
Shi Congyun 施從雲
Shi Gulan 施谷蘭
Shi Hanting 施漢亭
Shi Jianqiao 施劍翹
Shi Jinggong 施靖公
Shi Liang 史良
Shi Liangcai 史量才
Shi Youlan 施幼蘭
Shi Yousan 石友三
Shi Yuyao 施羽堯
Shi Zefan 施則凡
Shi Zhongcheng 施忠誠
Shi Zhongda 施仲達
Shi Zhongjie 施中傑
Shi Zhongliang 施中良
Shiji 史記
shiqing 事情
shishi xiaoshuo 事實小說
shishi xinju 時事新劇
shishi xinxi 事實新戲
shizhuangxi 時裝戲
Shuihuzhuan 水滸傳
si 私
sichou 私仇
sifa danghua 司法黨化
Song Ailing 宋愛齡
Song Meiling 宋美齡
Song Qingling 宋慶齡

Song Zheyuan 宋哲元
sui 歲
Sun Chuanfang 孫傳芳
Sun Feihu 孫飛虎
Sun Fengming 孫鳳鳴
Sun Guanche 孫觀圻
Sun Jiamei 孫家梅
Sun Jiazhen 孫家震
Sun Xinyuan 孫馨遠
Sun Yat-sen (Sun Zhongshan) 孫中山
Tan Xinpei 譚鑫培
Tan Zhen 覃振
tanci 彈詞
Tang Jishan 唐季珊
Tang Youren 唐有任
Tao Shanting 陶善庭
Tao Xingzhi 陶行知
taose qingsha'an 桃色情殺案
Teng Shuang 滕爽
teshe 特赦
Tianchan 天蟾
tianli 天理
Tiebao bu 帖報簿
Tiejia jun 鐵甲軍
ting 庭
tingxi 聽戲
tongqing 同情
tongqing xin 同情心
Tu Zhang 涂璋
tuanti 團體
Wang Anshi 王安石
Wang Hao 王灝
Wang Hua'nan 王化南
Wang Jiefu 王介甫
Wang Jingwei 汪精衛
Wang Yitang 王揖唐
wei fu baochou 為父報仇
wei guo chuhai 為國除害
wei shu baochou 為叔報仇
Wen Renhao 文人豪
wenmingxi 文明戲
wenren 文人
Wu Jianren 吳趼人
Wu Peifu 吳佩孚
Wu Song 武松
Wu Yu 吳虞
Wufan 五反

wuwei 無為
wuxia 武俠
wuyi 武藝
xia 俠
xiake 俠客
xianqi liangmu 賢妻良母
xianü 俠女
xiao 孝
xiaobao 小報
xiaoshimin 小市民
xiaqing xiaoshuo 俠情小説
xiayi 俠義
Xie Bingying 謝冰瑩
xin nüxing 新女性
xin renwu 新人物
xing 性
xingqing 性情
xingzhi 性質
xiugui 秀閨
Xu Daolin 徐道鄰
Xu Jiucheng 徐九成
Xu Shuang 徐爽
Xu Shuzheng 徐樹錚
Xu Yuanqing 徐元慶
Xungenpai 尋根派
Xunzi 荀子
xurong xin 虛榮心
Yan Xishan 閻錫山
yang 陽
Yang Naiwu 楊乃武
Yang Xingfo 楊杏佛
Ye Dejing 葉德椏
yeshi 野史
yi 義
yidang zhiguo 一黨治國
yifen 義憤
yin 陰
yixia 義俠
Yongzheng 雍正
Yosano Akiko 謝野晶子
youxia 遊俠
yu 欲陰
Yu Jiang 于江
Yu Qichang 余棨昌
Yu Youren 于左任
yuan 元
yuan 院

Yuan Xueya 袁雪崖
yuanshou 元首
Yue Hong 岳紅
yulun 輿論
Yun Huifang 惲惠芳
yuqing 輿情
Zhang Ji 張繼
Zhang Shaozeng 張紹曾
Zhang Weicun 張葦村
Zhang Yaozeng 張耀曾
Zhang Zhijiang 張之江
Zhang Zhizhong 張治中
Zhang Zongchang 張宗昌
Zhang Zuolin 張作霖
Zhao Junyu 趙君玉
Zhao Ruquan 趙如泉
Zhao Shitao 趙師韜
Zheng Jicheng 鄭繼成
Zheng Jinsheng 鄭金聲
zhengyi 正義
Zhili 直隸
Zhonghua Minguo xingfa 中華民國刑法
Zhou Enlai 周恩來
Zhou li 周禮
Zhou Zuoren 周作人
zi 字
zishou 自首
ziwo faxian 自我發現
Zou Taofen 鄒韜奮
Zuozhuan 左傳

References

ARCHIVES

Beijing Municipal Archives, Beijing.
Chongqing Municipal Archives, Chongqing, Sichuan.
Academia Historica (Guoshiguan), Taipei, Taiwan.

NEWSPAPERS

Beiping wanbao [Beiping evening post] (Beiping)
Beiyang huabao [Beiyang pictorial] (Tianjin)
Chenbao [Morning post] (Beiping)
Dagongbao [L'Impartial] (Tianjin, Chongqing)
Donghai ribao [Donghai daily] (Jinan)
Fu'ermosi [Holmes] (Shanghai)
Jingbao [The crystal] (Shanghai)
Liangyou [Young companion] (Shanghai)
North China Herald (Shanghai)
Shandong Minguo ribao [Shandong republican daily] (Jinan)
Shenbao [Shanghai daily] (Shanghai)
Shenbao huakan [Shun Pao pictorial supplement] (Shanghai)
Shibao [Truth post] (Beiping)
Shibao [Eastern times] (Shanghai)
Shuntian shibao [Shuntian times] (Beiping)
Xiao chenbao [Small morning post] (Beiping)
Xin Tianjinbao [New Tianjin] (Tianjin)
Xin Tianjin huabao [New Tianjin pictorial] (Tianjin)
Xinwenbao [News post] (Shanghai)

Xishijiebao [Theater world gazette] (Shanghai)
Yishibao [Social welfare daily] (Tianjin)
Zhongyang ribao [Central daily] (Nanjing, Chongqing)

PRIMARY SOURCES

"Ansha." 1935. *Dushu shenghuo* 3, no. 2:74.

"Assassins' Calm Behavior." 1932. *North China Herald* 14 September, 409.

Cisha Sun Chuanfang (The assassination of Sun Chuanfang). 1987. Beijing: Nongcun dushu chubanshe.

Bu Ping. 1935. "Shi Jianqiao zuixing jianmian zhi falü guanjian" (My humble opinion on the law related to reducing Shi Jianqiao's criminal sentence). *Zhongyang ribao*, 31 December, 2.

Chen Duxiu. 1915. "Dong-Xi minzu genben sixiang zhi chayi" (Fundamental differences in thought between the peoples of the East and West). *Xin qingnian* 1, no. 4:283–86.

———. 1987 [1904] . "Lun xiqu" (On theater). In *Zhongguo lidai julun xuanzhu*, ed. Chen Duo and Ye Changhai, 460–62. Changsha: Hunan wenyi chubanshe.

Chunqiu Gongyang zhuan (Gongyang Commentary to the Spring and Autumn annals). 1936. Shanghai: Zhonghua shuju.

"Cisha Zhang Zongchang zhi falü de guancha" (The investigation of the law in the killing of Zhang Zongchang). 1932. *Shandong Minguo ribao*, 15 September, 3.

Da Bai. 1935. "Tan xing ci" (Discussing assassination). *Beiyang huabao*, 16 November, 2.

Da Quan. 1936. "Shu Shi Jianqiao teshe ling hou" (Writing about Shi Jianqiao after the pardon). *Falü pinglun* 13, no. 52:1–2.

"Ex-Warlord Shot While Knelt [*sic*] in Prayer." 1935. *North China Herald*, 20 November, 308.

Feng Youlan. 1938. "Yuan zhongxiao" (The origins of filial piety). *Xin dongxiang* 1, no. 11:345–51.

Feng Yuxiang. 1941. "Xiangying Hechuan xianji shi" (A poem: Respond, Hechuan's warplanes). In "Kangzhan shiliao," no. 1685 (31 March). Academia Historica (Guoshiguan), Taipei.

———. 1992. *Feng Yuxiang riji* (The diary of Feng Yuxiang). Vols. 3–5. Nanjing: Jiangsu guji chubanshe.

Gu Dun. 1936. "Cong teshe Shi Jianqiao shuoqi" (A discussion starting with Shi Jianqiao's pardon). *Qinghua zhoukan* 45, no. 2:61.

Guojia zhengfu gongbao (National government bulletin). 1933. No. 1079 (14 March).

Guojia zhengfu gongbao (National government bulletin). 1936. No. 2177 (14 October).

Han Feizi. 1936. *Han Feizi*. Shanghai: Zhonghua shuju.

Han Yu. 1936. "Lun fo gu biao" (Memorial of the bone of Buddha). *Chang Li xiansheng ji*, 39:3–6. Shanghai: Zhonghua shuju.

"Hochwan Gives Three Planes." 1941. *China at War* 7, no. 1 (July): 66.

Hu Baochan. 1936. "Duiyu Shi Jianqiao cisha Sun Chuanfang yi'an de zong tantao" (A discussion regarding the case of Shi Jianqiao assassinating Sun Chuanfang). *Funü yuebao* 2, no. 10:6–7.

Hu Changqing. 1932. "Zheng Jicheng sha Zhang Zongchang zhi falü wenti" (The legal question of Zheng Jicheng's murder of Zhang Zongchang). *Falü pinglun* 9, no. 50:1–3.

Hu Shi. 1918. "Zhencao wenti" (The question of chastity). *Xin qingnian* 5, no. 1:5–14.

Jian. 1936. "Fayuan ni xianzhi pangting" (The court plans to limit courtroom observers). *Fu'ermosi*, 12 July, 3.

Jiang Jieshi. 1941. "Cong Hechuan xianji shuoqi" (A discussion stemming from the Hechuan Movement to Donate Planes). *Zhongyang ribao*, 31 May, 3.

Jiang Yanfu. 1933. "Ansha yu zhengzhi" (Assassination and politics). *Duli pinglun* 7, no. 57:2.

Ju Zheng. 1935. "Sifa danghua wenti" (The question of the party-fication of the judiciary). *Dongfang zazhi* 32, no. 10 (May): 6–19.

Jun Ji. 1935. "Liang mu lian'ai canju de fenxi" (An analysis of two acts of tragedy). *Chenbao*, 23 March, 11.

Li Xueyun. 1938. "Zhanshi funü ying zou de luxian" (The road that women should take during the war). *Zhanshi funü* 3, no. 4:4–5.

Li Ying. 1935. "Ping Shi Jianqiao nüshi wei fu fuchou" (Commentary on Ms. Shi Jianqiao's revenge). *Funü yuebao* 1, no. 11:2–4.

Liang Qichao. 1987. "Lun xiaoshuo yu qunzhi zhi guanxi" (On the relationship between the novel and popular sovereignty). In *Zhongguo lidai julun xuanzhu*, ed. Chen Duo and Ye Changhai, 385–90. Changsha: Hunan wenyi chubanshe.

Lin Gengbai. 1935. "Liu Jinggui an ganyan" (Thoughts on Liu Jinggui's case). *Chenbao*, 20 March, 2.

Lin Monong. 1980. "Wo zenyang cesheng Dagongbao" (How I made my name at the Dagongbao). *Xuewen ji zhuang* 37, no. 2:116–22.

Lingxiaohangezhu. 1935a. "Beijü wujü" (Tragedy and military drama). *Shibao* (Beiping), 17 November, 13.

———. 1935b. "Fei gongren—Shi nüshi" (Palace Lady Fei—Ms. Shi). *Shibao* (Beiping), 25 November, 3.

Liu Qingyang. 1938. "Zhanshi funü yinggai zenme yang?" (How should wartime women be?). *Zhanshi funü* 3, no. 4:6.

Liu Shi. 1935. "Shi Jianqiao nüshi de yuxiao" (Ms. Shi Jianqiao's ignorant filial piety). *Dazhong shenghuo* 1, no. 3:69–70.

Lu hai kong jun xingfa (The criminal code of the army, navy and air force). 1993 [1929]. In *Liufa liyou panjue*, ed. Guo Wei and Zhou Dingmei, vol. 3. Shanghai: Shanghai faxue shuju.

Lü Zhan'en. 1914. *Liaozhai zhiyi tuyong* (Illustrated songbook of Liaozhai's *Records of the Strange*). Shanghai: Wenhua huaju.

Meng Zhuo. 1936. "Cong xiaofan gegu liaoqin shuoqi" (A discussion stemming from a case of a small peddler cutting his flesh to save his mother). *Shenbao*, 14 January, 1.

Ping Xin. 1935. "Sun Chuanfang bei ci ganyan" (Thoughts on the assassination of Sun Chuanfang). *Dazhong shenghuo* 1, no. 2:52.

"The Press in Wartime China." 1943. *China at War* 10, no. 5 (May): 46–51.

Pu Songling [1640–1715]. 1986a. "Shang Sanguan." In *Liaozhai zhiyi huijiao huizhu huiping ben* (The complete collated and annotated [edition of] Liaozhai's *Records of the Strange*), ed. Zhang Youhe, 373–75. Rev. ed., 1978; repr., Shanghai: Guji chubanshe.

———.1986b. "Xianü." *Liaozhai zhiyi huijiao huizhu huiping ben* (The complete collated and annotated [edition of] Liaozhai's *Records of the Strange*), ed. Zhang Youhe, 210–16. Rev. ed., 1978; repr., Shanghai: Guji chubanshe.

———. 1986c. "Yu Jiang." *Liaozhai zhiyi huijiao huizhu huiping ben* (The complete collated and annotated [edition of] Liaozhai's *Records of the Strange*), ed. Zhang Youhe, 376–77. Rev. ed., 1978; repr., Shanghai: Guji chubanshe.

Shan Jiao. 1941. "Ge guo Kongjun zhong de funü" (The women of the national air force). *Funü gongming* 10, nos. 3–4 (June): 24–26.

Shanghai shi nianjian (Shanghai city yearbook). 1935. Shanghai: Zhonghua shuju.

She Ying. 1935. "Shi Jianqiao ying yuan Zheng Jicheng li teshe" (Shi Jianqiao should cite the Zheng Jicheng pardon as precedent). *Funü gongming* 4, no. 12:2–3.

Shen Si. 1935. "Shi Jianqiao chuyi sharen" (Shi Jianqiao harbors the intent to kill). *Fu'ermosi*, 16 November, 4.

Shi Jianqiao. 1980. "Wei baosheng fuchou, shouren Sun Chuanfang" (To avenge my father, I killed Sun Chuanfang). In *Wenshi ziliao xuanbian*, ed. Zhongguo renmin zhengzhi xieshang huiyi Beijing weiyuanhui wenshi ziliao weiyuanhui, no. 6:159–70. Beijing: Beijing chubanshe.

———. 1994. "Shi wo shasi le Sun Chuanfang" (I killed Sun Chuanfang). In Cao 1994, 8:66–76.

"Shi Jianqiao qi jiang wei qifu yu?" (Shi Jianqiao, is she a spurned woman?). 1936. *Ling Lung* no. 260: 3325–326.

"Shi Jianqiao shifou xiaonü" (Is Shi Jianqiao a filial daughter?). 1935. *Ling Lung* no. 213: 3967–968.

"Shi Jianqiao'an yu shehui guandian" (The case of Shi Jianqiao and society's view). 1935. *Guowen zhoubao* 12, no. 46:3.

"Shi nü ci Sun Chuanfang" (Ms. Shi assassinates Sun Chuanfang). 1935. *Funü shenghuo* 1, no. 6:2–3.

Shi Yin. 1936. "Teshe Shi Jianqiao" (Pardon Shi Jianqiao). *Funü gongming* 5, no. 11:1.

Shi Zefan. 1941. "Hechuan xian bei diji hongzha qingxing ji 'Hechuan hao' feiji chouxian faqi jingguo" (The situation of Hechuan county being bombed and the process of raising money for 'Hechuan' planes). In *Xianji zhuankan* 1941, 3.

Sowerby, A. de C. 1932. "Assassination of War-Lord, Shanghai Lady's Story of Tsinan Murder: Scene on Platform." *North China Herald*, 14 September, 409.

"Sun Chuanfang biaoshi bu yuan guowen zhengzhi" (Sun Chuanfang expresses a disinterest in politics). 1935. *Shenbao*, 20 June, 3.

Sun Guanche. 1935. "Falü shang zhi zishou yiyi" (The significance of voluntary surrender in law). *Shibao* (Shanghai), 21 November, 5.

"Sun Yinyuan ruci xiachang" (How Sun Chuanfang came to retire). *Dagongbao*, 14 November, 4.

Tang Si [Lu Xun]. 1918. "Wo dui jielie zhi guan" (My view on chastity). *Xin qingnian* 5, no. 2:92–101.

Tian Xing. 1935. "Yi jian chousha'an yinqi de wenti" (A question raised by a case of revenge). *Dazhong shenghuo* 1, no. 4:92–93.

Tianjin shigong hui xunkan (The journal of the Tianjin attorneys' association). 1933. 1, no. 2 (20 March): 1.

Wan Sheng. 1935. "Shi Jianqiao you zui hu? Liu wu zui hu?" (Is Shi Jianqiao guilty or not?). *Minsheng* 2 (20 November): 5–6.

Wang Anshi [1021–86]. 1974. *Wang Wengong wenji*. Beijing: Zhonghua shuju.

Wang Guifang. 1935. "Wei Shi Jianqiao nüshi qingqiu teshe" (An appeal for a pardon on behalf of Ms. Shi Jianqiao). *Funü yuebao* 1, no. 12 (December): 3–4.

Wang Shubi. 1935. "Fuchou (Revenge)." *Xinwenbao*, 18 November, 14.

Wang Xianqian, ed. 1988. *Xunzi jijie*. Beijing: Zhonghua shuju.

"Wei lao zu gongzuo gaishu" (A discussion of the work of securing provisions). 1941. *Funü xinyun* 3, no. 1:55–57.

"Women's Work in China." 1940. *China at War* 2, no. 6 (June): 68–74.

Wu Qichang. 1935. "Minguo jiecao yundong" (The Republican era's campaign of morality). *Dagongbao*, 22 December, 2.

Wu Yu. 1917. "Jiazu zhidu wei zhuanzhi zhuyi zhi genju lun" (The old family and clan system is the basis of despotism). *Xin qingnian* 2, no. 6 (February): 1–4.

Xianji zhuankan (The special publication of the Campaign to Raise Funds for Warplanes). 1941. In Chongqing Municipal Archives, 13:56 (April 30).

Xiao Yu. 1936. "Lun Shi Jianqiao ci Sun Chuanfang" (On Shi Jianqiao assassinating Sun Chuanfang). *Funü gongming* 5, no. 2:5.

Xie Bingying. 1994. *Nübing zhi zhuan* (A woman soldier's own story). Beijing: Zhongguo Huaqiao chubanshe.

Xin Tang shu (New Tang history). 1995. Compiled by Ouyang Xiu [1007–1072]. Beijing: Zhonghua shuju.

"Xing Zheng de cike" (Assassins named Zheng). 1932. *Shenbao*, 13 September, 10.

Xiuzheng Zhonghua Minguo guomin zhengfu zuzhi fa (Revised rules of organization for the government of the Republic of China). 1934. In *Zhonghua Minguo xianxing fagui daquan* (The complete laws and regulations of the Republic of China). Shanghai: Commercial Press.

Xu Daolin. 1962. *Xu Shuzheng xiansheng wenji nianpu hekan* (The collected writings and chronological biography of Xu Shuzheng). Taipei: Taiwan Commercial Press.

Xu Daolin xiansheng jinian ji (A collection of commemorative writings for Xu Daolin). 1975. Taipei: n.p.

Xu Shigui. 1935. *Zhongguo dashe kao* (Reflections on the Chinese amnesty). Shanghai: Commercial Press.

Xue Yunsheng. 1970. *Duli cunyi* (Analysis of problems in the legal code). Ed. Huang Jingjia. 5 vols. Taipei: Chengwen chubanshe.

Yang Youjun. 1936. "Minzu zhuyi yu minzu shengcun" (Nationalism and national survival). *Zhongshan wenhua jiaoyuguan jikan* 3, no. 2:381–98.

Yi Ji. 1935. "Guanyu Shi Jianqiao zhi zhong" (About Shi Jianqiao, this type). *Fu'ermosi*, 20 November, 1.

Yi Jing. 1941. "Xianji yundong zhong de zhuanju shangyan" (The performance of special dramas in the campaign to donate planes). In *Xianji zhuankan* 1941.

Yi Mu. 1935. "Liu-Lu'an panjue hou" (After the verdict in the Liu-Lu affair). *Yishibao*, 3 May, 10.

Yu Dacai. 1935. "Lun Liu Jinggui sharen'an" (On the homicide case of Liu Jinggui). *Duli pinglun* 146 (April): 14–15.

Yuan Xueya. 1941. "Hechuan hao ji qun" (Hechuan Planes). In "Kangzhan shiliao," no. 1689 (29 May). Academia Historica (Guoshiguan), Taipei.

Yue Hong. 1988. "Wo yu 'Cisha Sun Chuanfang.'" (Myself and "The Murder of Sun Chuanfang"). *Dazhong dianying* 418 (April): 13.

Yun. 1941. "Wei xianji yudong mian quanguo funü" (Urge the nation's women to participate in the movement to raise money for planes). *Funü gongming* 10, nos. 6–7:1.

Zhang Hongji. 1935. "Shi Jianqiao shizai chujian" (Shi Jianqiao eliminates the traitor). *Jinbao* 8 December, 2.

Zhao Nan. 1935. "Cong Tang Youren bei ci shuoqi" (A discussion stemming from Tang Youren's assassination). *Donghai ribao*, 28 December, 2.

Zheng. 1940. "Tiyi juanxian funü hao feiji" (Raise the issue and make contributions, women call for planes). *Zhongguo nü qingnian* 1, no. 4:1.

Zheng Jicheng. 1932. "Zishu ci Zhang jingguo" (My own account of the killing of Zhang). *Shenbao*, 7 September, 10.

———. 1936. "Wo shasi guozai Zhang Zongchang zhi jingguo xiangqing" (The details of my killing the national criminal, Zhang Zongchang). *Yijing* 7 (June): 42–46.

———. 1994. "Shasi Zhang Zongchang xiongshou de zibai" (The self-confession of the murderer of Zhang Zongchang). In Cao 1994, 8:39–46.

"Zhongguo hangkong jianshi xiehui zonghui gonghan" (The Public Document of the Central Association for Building China's Air Force). 1941. In Chongqing Municipal Archives, 13:718 (July).

Zhonghua Minguo xianxing fagui daquan (The complete laws and regulations of the Republic of China). 1934. Shanghai: Commercial Press.

Zhonghua Minguo xingfa (The criminal code of the Republic of China). 1935. Shanghai: Commercial Press.

Zhonghua Minguo xunzheng shiqi yuefa (Provisional constitution of Republic of China's tutelage period). 1931. Nanjing: Zhongguo Guomin zhongyang zhixing weiyuanhui.

Zhou Zhirou. 1941a. "Cong Nacui de chengba yishi shuodao kongjun de jianli he yunyong" (From Nazi Germany's superpower position to the establishment and use of China's air force). *Hangkong zazhi* 10, no. 8: 1–7.

———. 1941b. "Zhongguo kongjun de guojixing he minzuxing" (China's air force's international and national characteristics). *Hangkong zazhi* 10, no. 11:1–5.

Zhou Zuoren, trans. 1918. "Jiecao lun" (A treatise on chastity). *Xin qingnian* 4, no. 5:386–94.

Zhu Fang, ed. 1936. *Zhonghua Minguo xunzheng shiqi yuefa xiangjie* (Detailed

explanation of the provisional constitution of the Republic of China's tutelage period). Shanghai: Fazhengxue shechuban.
Zhu Wenchang. 1936. "Guanyu Shi Jianqiao nüshi de teshe" (Regarding Ms. Shi Jianqiao's pardon). *Duli pinglun* no. 226:16–17.
"Zuihou zhengzha zhong zhi sifa duli" (The independence of the judiciary in the final struggle). 1932. *Falü pinglun* 9, no. 42 (24 July): 1–6.

OTHER REFERENCES CITED

Abu-Lughod, Lila. 2000. *Veiled Sentiments: Honor and Poetry in a Bedouin Society*. Berkeley and Los Angeles: University of California Press.
Alford, William. 1984. "Of Arsenic and Old Laws." *California Law Review* 72, no. 6:1180–256.
Allen, Joseph R. 1996. "Dressing and Undressing the Chinese Woman Warrior." *Positions* 4, no. 2:343–79.
Althusser, Louis. 1971. *Lenin and Philosophy*. New York: Monthly Review.
Anderson, Benedict. 1991. *Imagined Communities: Reflections on the Origin and Spread of Nationalism*. Rev. ed. London: Verso.
Apter, David F., and Tony Saich. 1994. *Revolutionary Discourse in Mao's Republic*. Cambridge, MA: Harvard University Press.
Armstrong, Nancy. 1995. *Desire and Domestic Fiction: A Political History of the Novel*. London: Oxford University Press.
Baker, Keith Michael. 1987. "Politics and Public Opinion." In *Press and Politics in Pre-Revolutionary France*, ed. Jack Censer and Jeremy Popkin, 204–46. Berkeley and Los Angeles: University of California Press.
Benjamin, Walter. 1983. *Charles Baudelaire: A Lyric Poet in the Era of High Capitalism*. London: Verso.
———. 1999. *Passagen-Werk*. Cambridge, MA: Belknap Press of Harvard University Press.
Benson, Carleton. 1995. "The Manipulation of Tanci in Radio Shanghai During the 1930s." *Republican China* 20, no. 2:117–46.
———. 1996. "From Teahouse to Radio: Storytelling and the Commercialization of Culture in 1930s Shanghai." Ph.D. diss., University of California, Berkeley.
Berenson, Edward. 1992. *The Trial of Madame Caillaux*. Berkeley and Los Angeles: University of California Press.
Bernhardt, Kathryn. 1994. "Women and the Law: Divorce in the Republican Period." In *Civil Law in Qing and Republican China*, ed. Kathryn Bernhardt, and Philip Huang, 187–214. Stanford, CA: Stanford University Press.
Boorman, Howard L., and Richard C. Howard, eds. 1967–1971. *Biographical Dictionary of Republican China*. Vols. 1–4. New York: Columbia University Press.
Brooks, Peter. 1976. *The Melodramatic Imagination: Balzac, Henry James, Melodrama, and the Mode of Excess*. New Haven, CT: Yale University Press.
Buck-Morss, Susan. 1989. *The Dialectics of Seeing: Walter Benjamin and the Arcades Project*. Cambridge, MA: MIT Press.
Buoye, Thomas. 1995. "Suddenly Murderous Intent Arose: Bureaucratization

and Benevolence in Eighteenth-Century Qing Homicide Reports." *Late Imperial China* 16, no. 2:62–97.

Butler, Judith. 1990. *Gender Trouble: Feminism and the Subversion of Identity.* New York: Routledge.

Carlitz, Katherine. 1991. "The Social Uses of Female Virtue in Late Ming Editions of *Lienü Zhuan.*" *Late Imperial China* 12, no. 2:101–24.

———. 1994. "Desire, Danger and the Body: Stories of Women's Virtue in Late Ming China." In *Engendering China: Women, Culture, and the State*, ed. Christina Gilmartin et al., 101–24. Cambridge, MA: Harvard University Press.

Cao Hua, ed. 1994. *Minguo shashou chunqiu* (The annals of assassins in Republican China). Beijing: Tuanjie chubanshe.

Caufield, Sueann. 2000. *In Defense of Honor: Sexual Morality, Modernity, and Nation in Early-Twentieth-Century Brazil.* Durham, NC: Duke University Press.

Ch'ü, T'ung-tsu. 1961. *Law and Society in Traditional China.* Paris: Mouton.

Chai Degeng, Rong Mengyuan, Dan Shikui, Zhang Hongxiang, Liu Naihe, Chen Guiying, and Zhang Cixi, eds. 1957. *Zhongguo jindai shi ziliao congkan* (A collection of materials on modern Chinese history). Vol. 6. Shanghai: Shanghai renmin chubanshe.

Chang, Maria Hsia. 1979. "'Fascism' and Modern China." *China Quarterly* 79 (September): 553–67.

Chang, Michael G. 1999. "The Good, the Bad and the Beautiful: Movie Actresses and Public Discourse in Shanghai, 1920s–1930s." In *Cinema and Urban Culture in Shanghai, 1922–1943*, ed. Zhang Yinjing, 128–59. Stanford, CA: Stanford University Press.

Chatterjee, Partha. 1993. *The Nation and Its Fragments: Colonial and Post-Colonial Histories.* Princeton, NJ: Princeton University Press.

Chen Jin. 1991. "Shouren fandong junfa de qi nüzi" (The remarkable woman who single-handedly killed a reactionary warlord). In *Tongzhan qun ying*, ed. Jin Qixuan and Fan Hong, 7:137–49. Beijing: Zhongguo wenshi chubanshe.

Chen Pingyuan. 1995. *Qiangu wenren xiake meng* (The literati's chivalric dreams: Narrative models of Chinese knight-errant literature). Taipei: Maitian chuban youxian gongsi.

Chen Shangfan and Ling Ren. 1986. "Shi Jianqiao baochou" (Shi Jianqiao seeks revenge). In Shi Peng 1986, 151–237.

Cheng, Anne. 2004. "Filial Piety with a Vengeance: The Tension between Rites and Law in the Han." In *Filial Piety in Chinese Thought and History*, ed. Alan K. L. Chan and Sor-hoon Tan, 29–43. New York: Routledge Curzon.

Chow, Tse-tsung. 1960. *The May Fourth Movement: Intellectual Revolution in Modern China.* Cambridge, MA: Harvard University Press.

Coble, Parks. 1985. "Chiang Kai-Shek and the Anti-Japanese Movement in China: Zou Tao-Fen and the National Salvation Association, 1931–1937." *Journal of Asian Studies* 44, no. 2:293–310.

———. 1991. *Facing Japan: Chinese Politics and Japanese Imperialism, 1931–1937.* Cambridge, MA: Harvard University Press.

Conner, Alison. 1993. "Soochow Law School and the Shanghai Bar." *Hong Kong Law Journal* 23, no. 3:395–411.

———. 1994. "Lawyers and the Legal Profession During the Republican Period." In *Civil Law in Qing and Republican China*, ed. Kathryn Bernhardt and Philip Huang, 215–48. Stanford, CA: Stanford University Press.

Cook, Alexander. 2007. "Unsettling Accounts: The Trial of the Gang of Four and the Cultural Logic of Late Socialism in China, 1978–1981." Ph.D. diss., Columbia University.

Crespi, John A. 2001. "A Vocal Minority: New Poetry and Poetry Declamation in China, 1915–1975." Ph.D. diss., University of Chicago.

Dalby, Michael. 1981. "Revenge and the Law in Traditional China." *American Journal of Legal History* 25:267–307.

Denby, David. 1994. "Sentimental Narrative and the Social Order in France, 1760–1820." Cambridge: Cambridge University Press.

Des Forges, Alexander Townsend. 1998. "Street Talk and Alley Stories: Tangled Narratives of Shanghai from *Lives of Shanghai Flowers* (1892) to *Midnight* (1933)." Ph.D. diss., Princeton University.

Diamond, Norma. 1975. "Women under Kuomintang Rule: Variations on the Feminine Mystique." *Modern China* 1, no. 1:3–45.

Dirlik, Arif. 1975. "The Ideological Foundations of the New Life Movement: A Study in Counterrevolution." *Journal of Asian Studies* 34, no. 4:945–80.

———. 1978. *Revolution and History: Origins of Marxist Historiography in China, 1919–1937*. Berkeley and Los Angeles: University of California Press.

Dong, Madeleine Yue. 1995. "Communities and Communication: A Study of the Case of Yang Naiwu." *Late Imperial China* 16, no. 1:79–119.

Duara, Prasenjit. 1988. *Culture, Power, and the State: Rural North China, 1900–1942*. Stanford, CA: Stanford University Press.

———. 1998. "The Regime of Authenticity: Timelessness, Gender and National History in Modern China." *History and Theory* 37, no. 3:287–308.

Dudbridge, Glen. 1978. *The Legend of Miao-Shan*. London: Ithaca Press.

Eastman, Lloyd. 1974. *The Abortive Revolution: China under Nationalist Rule, 1927–1937*. Cambridge, MA: Harvard University Press.

———. 1979. "Fascism and Modern China: A Rejoinder." *China Quarterly* 80 (December): 838–42.

———. 1986. "Nationalist China During the Sino-Japanese War, 1937–1945." In *The Cambridge History of China*. Vol. 13. *Republican China 1912–1949, Part 2*, ed. Denis Twitchett and John K. Fairbank, 547–608. Cambridge: Cambridge University Press.

———. 1991. "Nationalist China During the Nanking Decade, 1927–1937." In *The Nationalist Era in China, 1927–1949*, ed. Eastman et al., 1–52. Cambridge: Cambridge University Press.

Edwards, Louise. 1994. *Men and Women in Qing China: Gender in the Red Chamber Novel*. Leiden: E. J. Brill.

———. 1995. "Women Warriors and Amazons of the Mid-Qing Texts *Jinghua yuan* and *Honglou meng*." *Modern Asian Studies* 29:225–55.

———. 2000. "Policing the Modern Woman in Republican China." *Modern China* 26, no. 3:115–47.

Elman, Benjamin. 2005. *On Their Own Terms: Science in China, 1550–1900*. Cambridge, MA: Harvard University Press.

Elvin, Mark. 1984. "Female Virtue and the State in China." *Past and Present* 104:111–52.

Epstein, Maram. 2001. *Competing Discourses: Orthodoxy, Authenticity, and Engendered Meanings in Late-Imperial Chinese Fiction.* Cambridge, MA: Harvard University Press.

Escarra, Jean. 1936. *Le Droit Chinois: Conception et Évolution, Institutions Législatives et Judiciares, Science et Enseignement.* Pékin: Éditions H. Vetch; Paris: Libraire du Recueil Sirey.

———. 1961 [1936]. *Chinese Law.* Tr. from the French by Gertrude R. Browne. Seattle: University of Washington Press.

Esherick, Joseph. 1987. *The Origins of the Boxer Uprising.* Berkeley and Los Angeles: University of California Press.

Fan Zhongxin, Zheng Ding, and Zhan Xuenong. 1992. *Qing li fa yu Zhonguoren: Zhongguo chuantong falü wenhua tanwei* (Sentiment, principle law, and the Chinese people: A brief exploration of China's traditional culture of law). Beijing: Zhongguo renmin daxue chubanshe.

Fei, Faye Chunfang, ed. and trans. 1999. *Chinese Theories of Theater and Performance from Confucius to the Present.* Ann Arbor: University of Michigan Press.

Fewsmith, Joseph. 1985. *Party, State, and Local Elites in Republican China: Merchant Organizations and Politics in Shanghai, 1890–1930.* Honolulu: University of Hawai'i Press.

Field, Andrew. 1999. "Selling Souls in Sin City: Shanghai Singing and Dancing Hostesses in Print, Film, and Politics, 1920–49." In *Cinema and Urban Culture in Shanghai, 1922–1943*, ed. Zhang Yingjin, 99–127. Stanford, CA: Stanford University Press.

Fitzgerald, John. 1996. *Awakening China: Politics, Culture and Class in the Nationalist Revolution.* Stanford, CA: Stanford University Press.

Fogel, Joshua, and Zarrow, Peter, eds. 1997. *Imagining the People: Chinese Intellectuals and the Concept of Citizenship, 1890–1920.* Armonk, NY: M. E. Sharpe.

Foucault, Michel. 1995 [1977]. *Discipline and Punish: the Birth of the Prison.* New York : Vintage Books.

———. 1990 [1978]. *The History of Sexuality.* New York: Vintage Books.

Fu, Poshek. 2003. *Between Shanghai and Hong Kong: The Politics of Chinese Cinemas.* Stanford, CA: Stanford University Press.

Ge Chunyuan. 1999. *Cike shi* (The history of Chinese assassins). Shanghai: Shanghai wenyi chubanshe.

Gilmartin, Christina Kelley. 1995. *Engendering the Chinese Revolution.* Berkeley and Los Angeles: University of California Press.

Glosser, Susan. 2003. *Chinese Visions of Family and State, 1915–1953.* Berkeley and Los Angeles: University of California Press.

Goodman, Bryna. 1995. *Native Place, City, and Nation: Regional Networks and Identities in Shanghai, 1853–1937.* Berkeley and Los Angeles: University of California Press.

———. 2005. "The New Woman Commits Suicide: The Press, Cultural Memory, and the New Republic." *Journal of Asian Studies* 64, no. 1 (February): 67–102.

———. 2006. "Appealing to the Public: Newspaper Presentation and Adjudication of Emotion." *Twentieth-Century China* 31, no. 2 (April): 32–69.

Goodman, Dena. 1992. "Public Sphere and Private Life: Toward a Synthesis of Current Historiographical Approaches to the Old Regime." *History and Theory* 31 (February): 1–20.

Gorman, Paul R. 1996. *Left Intellectuals and Popular Culture in Twentieth-Century America*. Chapel Hill: University of North Carolina Press.

Gu Peijun. 1980. "Shi Jianqiao ci Sun Chuanfang an bianhu lüshi Yu Jimen xiaozhuan" (A short biography of Yu Jimen, the defense lawyer in the case of Shi Jianqiao assassinating Sun Chuanfang). *Zhuanji wenxue* 37, no. 4:51.

Habermas, Jürgen. 1989. *The Structural Transformation of the Public Sphere: An Inquiry into a Category of Bourgeois Society*. Cambridge, MA: MIT Press.

Hanan, Patrick, ed. 1995. *The Sea of Regret: Two Turn-of-the-Century Chinese Romantic Novels*. Honolulu: University of Hawai'i Press.

Hansen, Miriam. 2000. "Fallen Women, Rising Stars, New Horizons: Shanghai Silent Film as Vernacular Modernism." *Film Quarterly* 54, no. 1:10–22.

Harrison, Henrietta. 1998. "Martyrs and Militarism in Early Republican China." *Twentieth-Century China* 23, no. 2:41–70.

———. 2000. "Newspapers and Nationalism in Rural China 1890–1929." *Past and Present* 166:181–204.

He Yi, and Pan Rong. 1997. *Sun Chuanfang: Wu sheng lianshi* (Sun Chuanfang: The leader of the Five Allied Southeastern Provinces). Lanzhou: Lanzhou daxue chubanshe.

Hershatter, Gail. 1997. *Dangerous Pleasures: Prostitution and Modernity in Twentieth-Century Shanghai*. Berkeley and Los Angeles: University of California Press.

Hockx, Michel. 1998. "In Defence of the Censor: Literary Autonomy and State Authority in Shanghai, 1930–1936." *Journal of Modern Literature in Chinese* 2, no. 1:1–30.

Horkheimer, Max, and Theodor W. Adorno. 1988 [1944]. *Dialectic of Enlightenment*. New York: Continuum.

Hsiung, James C., and Steven I. Levine, eds. 1992. *China's Bitter Victory: The War with Japan, 1937–1945*. Armonk, NY: M. E. Sharpe.

Hu Hsiao-chen. 2003. *Cainü cheye weimian: Jindai zhongguo nüxing xushi wenxue de xingqu* (Burning the midnight oil: The rise of female narrative in early modern China). Taipei: Maita.

Huang, Jilu, ed. 1970. *Geming renwu zhi* (Biographies of revolutionary personages). Taibei: Zhongwenwu gongyin she.

Huang, Martin. 2001. *Desire and Fictional Narrative in Late Imperial China*. Cambridge, MA: Harvard University Press.

Huang, Phillip. 1993. "'Public Sphere'/'Civil Society' in China? The Third Realm between State and Society." *Modern China* 19, no. 2 (April): 216–40.

———. 2001. *Code, Custom, and Legal Practice in China: The Qing and the Republic Compared*. Stanford, CA: Stanford University Press.

Hung, Chang-tai. 1994. *War and Popular Culture: Resistance in Modern China, 1937–1945*. Berkeley and Los Angeles: University of California Press.

Huters, Theodore. 2005. *Bringing the World Home*. Honolulu: University of Hawai'i Press.

Huyssen, Andreas. 1986. *After the Great Divide: Modernism, Mass Culture, Postmodernism*. Bloomington: Indiana University Press.

Jian Youwen. 1982. *Feng Yuxiang zhuan* (Biography of Feng Yuxiang). Taibei: Zhuanji wenxue chubanshe.

Jing Shenghong, ed. 1996. *Minguo ansha yao'an* (Important assassination cases of Republican China). Nanjing: Jiangsu guji chubanshe.

———, ed. 1997. *Minguo da'an jishi* (The true account of great cases in Republican China). Shanghai: Shanghai renmin chubanshe.

Juan Shi. 1967. "Shi Jianqiao de xiao yu yong" (Shi Jianqiao's filial piety and courage). *Changliu* 13, no. 8:8.

Judge, Joan. 1996. *Print and Politics: 'Shibao' and the Culture of Reform in Late Qing China*. Stanford, CA: Stanford University Press.

———. 1997. "Publicists and Populists: Including the Common People in the Late Qing New Citizen Ideal." In Fogel and Zarrow 1997, 165–82.

———. 2002. "Reforming the Feminine: Female Literacy and the Legacy of 1898." In Karl and Zarrow 2002, 158–79.

Kao, Karl S. Y. 1989. "*Bao* and *Baoying:* Narrative Causality and External Motivations in Chinese Fiction." *Chinese Literature, Essays, Articles and Reviews* 11 (December): 115–38.

Karl, Rebecca. 2002. "'Slavery,' Citizenship, and Gender in Late Qing China's Global Context." In Karl and Zarrow 2002, 212–44.

Karl, Rebecca E., and Peter Zarrow, eds. 2002. *Rethinking the 1898 Reform Period: Political and Cultural Change in Late Qing China*. Cambridge, MA: Harvard University.

Kiely, Jan. 2004. "Performances of Resistance and the Imagined Moral Public: Communist Political Prisoners in China, 1928–1937." *Twentieth-Century China* 29, no. 2 (April): 63–88.

Kinkley, Jeffrey. 2000. *Chinese Justice, the Fiction: Law and Literature in Modern China*. Stanford, CA: Stanford University Press.

Knoblock, John. 1994. *Xunzi: A Translation and Study of the Complete Works*. Vol. 3. Stanford, CA: Stanford University Press.

Ko, Dorothy. 1994. *Teachers of the Inner Chambers: Women and Culture in Seventeenth-Century China*. Stanford, CA: Stanford University Press.

Krebs, Edward. 1981. "Assassination in the Republican Revolutionary Movement." *Ch'ing-shih wen-ti* 4, no. 6:45–80.

Kutcher, Norman. 1999. *Mourning in Late Imperial China: Filial Piety and the State*. New York: Cambridge University Press.

Landes, Joan. 1988. *Women and the Public Sphere in the Age of the French Revolution*. Ithaca, NY: Cornell University Press.

Larson, Wendy. 1998. *Women and Writing in Modern China*. Stanford, CA: Stanford University Press.

Lau, D. C. and Chen Fong Ching, eds. 1993. *A Concordance to the Zhouli*. Institute of Chinese Studies Series, no. 4. Hong Kong: Commercial Press.

Laughlin, Charles A. 2002. *Chinese Reportage: the Aesthetics of Historical Experience*. Durham, NC: Duke University Press.

Lean, Eugenia. 2004. "The Making of a Public: Emotions and Media Sensation in 1930s China." *Twentieth-Century China* 29, no. 2 (April): 39–61.

——— [Lin Yuqin]. 2005. "Liu Jinggui Qingsha'an: Sanshi niandai Beiping de dazhong wenhua yu meiti chaozuo" (Love with a vengeance: media sensation in Republican-era Beiping). In *Beijing: Urban Culture and Historical Memory*, ed. Chen Pingyuan and David Wang, 269–84. Beijing: Beijing University Press.

Lee, Haiyan. 2001. "All Feelings That Are Fit to Print: The Community of Sentiment and the Literary Public Sphere in China, 1900–1918." *Modern China* 27, no. 3:291–327.

———. 2002. "In the Name of Love: Virtue, Identity, and the Structure of Feeling in Modern China." Ph.D. diss., Cornell University.

Lee, Leo Ou-fan. 1973. *The Romantic Generation of Modern Chinese Writers*. Cambridge, MA: Harvard University Press.

———. 1999. *Shanghai Modern: The Flowering of a New Urban Culture in China, 1930–1945*. Cambridge, MA: Harvard University Press.

Lee, Leo Ou-fan, and Andrew J. Nathan. 1985. "The Beginnings of Mass Culture: Journalism and Fiction in the Late Ch'ing and Beyond." In *Popular Culture in Late Imperial China*, ed. Andrew J. Nathan, David Johnson, and Evelyn S. Rawski, 360–98. Berkeley and Los Angeles: University of California Press.

Lewis, Mark Edward. 1990. *Sanctioned Violence in Early China*. Albany, NY: State University of New York Press.

Li Guangcan, and Ning Hanlin, eds. 1987. *Zhongguo xingfa tongshi*. Shenyang: Liaoning daxue chubanshe.

Li, Hsi-fan. 1959. "A Great Novel of Peasant Revolt." *Chinese Literature* 12:62–70.

Li, Wai-yee. 1993. *Enchantment and Disenchantment: Love and Illusion in Chinese Literature*. Princeton, NJ: Princeton University Press.

Li Zhuan'gen. 1981. "Liu Shanben jiangjun" (General Liu Shanben). *Renwu* 5:96–103.

Lin Jidong. 1965. *Xingshifa zidian* (Dictionary of criminal law). Taipei: Zhonghua congshu bianshen weiyuanhui.

Lin, Yutang. 1968. *A History of the Press and Public Opinion in China*. New York: Greenwood Press.

Link, Perry. 1981. *Mandarin Ducks and Butterflies: Popular Fiction in Early Twentieth-Century Chinese Cities*. Berkeley and Los Angeles: University of California Press.

Liu, James J. Y. 1967. *The Chinese Knight-Errant*. London: Routledge and Kegal Paul.

Liu, Lydia. 1995. *Translingual Practice*. Stanford, CA: Stanford University Press.

Liu Shoulin et al., eds. 1995. *Minguo zhiguan nianbiao* (Chronicle of official departments in the Republican era). Beijing: Zhonghua shuju.

Lu Hanchao. 1999. *Beyond the Neon Lights: Everyday Shanghai in the Early Twentieth Century*. Berkeley and Los Angeles, University of California Press.

Lü Weijun. 1997. *Han Fuju zhuan* (The biography of Han Fuju). Jinan: Shandong chubanshe.

Ma Xinhua and Hou Zhigang, eds. 1993. *Zhongguo shi cike waizhuan* (Historical accounts of China's ten most notable assassins). Taipei: Daxin chubanshe.

Mackerras, Colin. 1975. *The Chinese Theater in Modern Times: From 1840 to the Present Day*. London: Thames and Hudson.

———. 1990. *Chinese Drama: A Historical Survey*. Beijing, China: New World Press. Distributed by China International Book Trading Corporation.

MacKinnon, Stephen R. 1995. "Press Freedom and the Chinese Revolution in the 1930s." In *Media and Revolution*, ed. Jeremy D. Popkin, 174–88. Lexington, KY: University Press of Kentucky.

Mann, Susan. 1997. *Precious Records: Women in China's Long Eighteenth Century*. Stanford, CA: Stanford University Press.

Maza, Sarah. 1993. *Private Lives and Public Affairs: the Causes Célèbres of Pre-Revolutionary France*. Berkeley and Los Angeles: University of California Press.

McCord, Edward. 1996. "Warlords against Warlordism: The Politics of Anti-Militarism in Early Twentieth-Century China." *Modern Asian Studies* 30, no. 4:795–827.

McCormack, Gavan. 1977. *Chang Tso-Lin in Northeast China, 1911–1928: China, Japan and the Manchurian Idea*. Stanford, CA: Stanford University Press.

McKnight, Brian. 1981. *The Quality of Mercy: Amnesties and Traditional Chinese Justice*. Honolulu: University Press of Hawai'i.

Meehan, Johanna. 1995. *Feminists Read Habermas: Gendering the Subject of Discourse*. New York: Routledge.

Meijer, Marinus J. 1967. *The Introduction of Modern Criminal Law in China*. Hong Kong: Lung Men Bookstore.

———. 1991. *Murder and Adultery in Late Imperial China: A Study of Law and Morality*. Leiden: E. J. Brill.

Meng Yue. 2000. "The Invention of Shanghai: Cultural Passages and Their Transformation, 1860–1920." Ph.D. diss., University of California, Los Angeles.

Mittler, Barbara. 2004. *A Newspaper for China? Power, Identity and Change in Shanghai's News Media (1872–1912)*. Cambridge, MA: Harvard University Press.

Mosse, George. 1975. *The Nationalization of the Masses: Political Symbolism and Mass Movements in Germany from the Napoleonic Wars through the Third Reich*. New York, H. Fertig.

Nedostup, Rebecca, and Hong-ming Liang. 2001. "'Begging the Sages of the Party-State': Citizenship and Government in Transition in Nationalist China, 1927–37." International Review of Social History. Suppl. no. 46: S185–S207.

Ng, Mau-Sang. 1994. "Popular Fiction and the Culture of Everyday Life: A Cultural Analysis of Qiu Shou'ou's *Qiuhaitang*." *Modern China* 20, no. 2:131–56.

Nivard, Jacqueline. 1984. "Women and the Women's Press: The Case of the Ladies' Journal (*Funü zazhi*), 1915–1931." *Republican China* 10, no. 1:37–56.

Pickowicz, Paul. 1991. "The Theme of Spiritual Pollution in Chinese Films of the 1930s." *Modern China* 17, no. 1:38–75.

Qian Tang, ed. 1950. *Geming de nüxing* (Revolutionary women). Taibei: Huangwen chubanshe.

Rankin, Mary. 1993. "Some Observations on a Chinese Public Sphere." *Modern China* 19, no. 2 (April): 158–82.

Rickett, W. Allyn. 1971. "Voluntary Surrender and Confession in Chinese Law: The Problem of Continuity." *Journal of Asian Studies* 30, no. 4:797–814.

Rowe, William. 1993. "The Problem of 'Civil Society' in Late Imperial China." *Modern China* 19, no. 2 (April): 139–57.

Schneider, Helen. 2004. "'The Mother of China': Song Meiling and Patriotic Women in Wartime Service." Paper presented at the meeting of the Association for Asian Studies, San Diego, 7 March.

Schneider, Laurence A. 1971. *Ku Chieh-Kang and China's New History: Nationalism and the Quest for Alternative Traditions*. Berkeley and Los Angeles: University of California Press.

Schoppa, R. Keith. 1995. *Blood Road: The Mystery of Shen Dingyi in Revolutionary China*. Berkeley and Los Angeles: University of California Press.

Schwartz, Vanessa. 1998. *Spectacular Realities: Early Mass Culture in Fin-de-Siècle Paris*. Berkeley and Los Angeles: University of California Press.

Scott, Joan. 1988. *Gender and the Politics of History*. New York: Columbia University Press.

Shaya, Gregory. 2004. "The Flâneur, the Badaud, and the Making of a Mass Public in France, circa 1860–1910." *American Historical Review* 109, no. 1 (February): 41–76.

Sheridan, James. 1966. *The Chinese Warlord: The Career of Feng Yü-Hsiang*. Stanford, CA: Stanford University Press.

Shi Peng, ed. 1986. *Minguo sida qi'an* (Four remarkable Republican-era cases). Hong Kong: Zhongyuan chubanshe.

———, ed. 1987. *Jinshi Zhongguo shida shehui xinwen* (Ten great social news stories of modern China). Changsha: Hunan renmin chubanshe.

Shi Yuyao. 1982. "Cisha Sun Chuanfang de Shi Jianqiao" (The Shi Jianqiao who assassinated Sun Chuanfang). *Wenwu tiandi* 2 (March): 9–11.

Shi Yuyao and Shen Yuli. 1985. *Nüjie Shi Jianqiao* (Female hero Shi Jianqiao). Harbin: Beifang wenyi chubanshe.

Shiga Shuzo. 1984. *Shindai Chûgoku no hô to saiban* (Law and justice in Qing China). Tokyo: Sobunsha.

Sommer, Matthew. 2000. *Sex, Law and Society in Late Imperial China*. Stanford, CA: Stanford University Press.

Spence, Jonathan. 1978. *The Death of Woman Wang*. New York: Penguin Books.

St. Andre, James. 1998. *History, Mystery and Myth: A Comparative Study of Narrative Strategies in the* Baijia Gong'an *and* The Complete Sherlock Homes. Chicago: University of Chicago Press.

Staunton, Sir George. 1966 [1810]. *Ta Tsing Leu Lee; Being the Fundamental Laws . . . of the Penal Code of China*. Taipei: Ch'eng-wen.

Stoler, Laura Ann. 2002. *Carnal Knowledge and Imperial Power*. Berkeley and Los Angeles: University of California Press.

Strand, David. 1989. *Rickshaw Beijing: City, People and Politics in the 1920s*. Berkeley and Los Angeles: University of California Press.

Tang Weimu. 1982. "Hechuan xian yijiusiyi nian xianji yundong shimo" (From start to finish, the 1941 Hechuan movement to donate warplanes). *Hechuan wenshi ziliao xuanji*, 1 (October): 123–34.
Tang, Xiaobing. 2000. *Chinese Modern: The Heroic and the Quotidian*. Durham, NC: Duke University Press.
Theiss, Janet. 2001. "Managing Martyrdom: Female Suicide and Statecraft in Mid-Qing China." *Nan nü* 3, no. 1:47–76.
———. 2004. *Disgraceful Matters: The Politics of Chastity in Eighteenth-Century China*. Berkeley and Los Angeles: University of California Press.
Ting, Lee-hsia Hsu. 1974. *Government Control of the Press in Modern China, 1900–1949*. Cambridge, MA: Harvard University Press.
Tsin, Michael. 1997. "Imagining 'Society' in Early Twentieth-Century China." In Fogel and Zarrow 1997, 212–31.
———. 1999. *Nation, Governance, and Modernity in China*. Stanford, CA: Stanford University Press.
Van de Ven, Hans. 1997. "The Military in the Republic." *China Quarterly* 150 (June): 352–74.
Wakeman, Frederic, Jr. 1993. "The Civil Society and Public Sphere Debate: Western Reflections on Chinese Political Culture." *Modern China* 19, no. 2 (April): 108–38.
———. 1995. *Policing Shanghai*. Berkeley and Los Angeles: University of California Press.
———. 1997. "A Revisionist View of the Nanjing Decade: Confucian Fascism." *China Quarterly* 150 (June): 395–432.
———. 2003. *Spymaster: Dai Li and the Chinese Secret Service*. Berkeley and Los Angeles: University of California Press.
Waldron, Arthur. 1991. "The Warlord: Twentieth-Century Chinese Understandings of Violence, Militarism, and Imperialism." *American Historical Review* 96, no. 4:1073–1100.
Wang, Ban. 1997. *The Sublime Figure of History: Aesthetics and Politics in Twentieth-Century China*. Stanford, CA: Stanford University Press.
Wang, David Der-wei. 1997. *Fin-de-Siècle Splendor: Repressed Modernities of Late Qing Fiction, 1849–1911*. Stanford, CA: Stanford University Press.
Wang Guilin and Zhu Hanguo, eds. 1992. *Zhongguo baokan cidian, 1815–1949* (Dictionary of Chinese newspapers and journals, 1815–1949). Taiyuan: Shuhai chubanshe.
Wang Weinong. 1960. "Han Fuju de te diedui he Zhang Zongchang de beisha" (Han Fuju's special intelligence troupe and Zhang Zongchang being killed). *Quanguo wenshi ziliao xuanji* no. 5: 135–42.
Watson, Burton, trans. 1964. *Basic Writings: Han Fei Tzu*. New York: Columbia University Press.
Wong, R. Bin. 1993. Great Expectations: The 'Public Sphere' and the Search for Modern Times in Chinese History." *Chûgokushi gaku* 3:7–50.
Wu Shouqi, ed. 1990. *Anhui lishi renwu* (Historical personages of Anhui). Anhui: Huangshan shushe.
Wu, Yenna. 1995. *The Chinese Virago: A Literary Theme*. Cambridge, MA: Harvard University Press.

Xiao, Zhiwei. 1994. 'Film Censorship in China, 1927–1937." Ph.D. diss., University of California, San Diego.

Xu, Xiaoqun. 1997. "The Fate of Judicial Independence in Republican China, 1912–37." *China Quarterly* 149 (March): 1–28.

———. 1998. "Between State and Society, between Professionalism and Politics: The Shanghai Bar Association in Republican China, 1912–1937." *Twentieth-Century China* 24, no. 1:1–29.

———. 2001. *Chinese Professionals and the Republican State: The Rise of Professional Associations in Shanghai, 1912–1937*. Cambridge: Cambridge University Press.

Yang, Lien-sheng. 1957. "The Concept of Pao as a Basis for Social Relations in China." In *Chinese Thought and Institutions*, ed. John Fairbank, 291–309. Chicago: University of Chicago Press.

Yeh, Catherine. 2002. *Wan Qing Min chu de yule xiaobao yu xinwenhua changyu de jianli* (Entertainment press and the formation of a new kind of "cultural field," 1896–1920s). Paper presented at the conference entitled Cultural Field and Educational Vista: From the Late Ch'ing Era to the 1940's. National Taiwan University, Taipei, 7–8 November.

Yeh, Wen-hsin. 1992. "Progressive Journalism and Shanghai's Petty Urbanites: Zou Taofen and the Shenghuo Enterprise, 1926–1945." In *Shanghai Sojourners*, ed. Frederic Wakeman Jr. and Yeh Wen-hsin, eds., 186–238. Berkeley: Institute of East Asian Studies, University of California.

Yeung, Sau-chu Alison. 1997. "Female Criminality in Qing China: Adulteress-Murderesses in Legal and Popular Culture, 1644–1912." Ph.D. diss., University of California, Los Angeles.

———. 2003. "Fornication in the Late Qing Legal Reforms." *Modern China* 29, no. 3:297–328.

Yu, Anthony. 1997. *Rereading the Stone: Desire and the Making of Fiction in* Dream of the Red Chamber. Princeton, NJ: Princeton University Press.

Zarrow, Peter. 1990. *Anarchism and Chinese Political Culture*. New York: Columbia University Press.

Zeitlin, Judith. 1993. *Historian of the Strange: Pu Songling and the Chinese Classical Tale*. Stanford, CA: Stanford University Press.

Zhang Qingjun and Meng Guoxiang, eds. 1997. *Minguo sifa heimu* (The inside story of Republican-era law). Jiangsu: Jiangsu guji chubanshe.

Zhang, Yingjin. 1996. *The City in Modern Chinese Literature and Film: Configuration of Space, Time and Gender*. Stanford, CA: Stanford University Press.

Zhang, Zhen. 2005. *An Amorous History of the Silver Screen: Shanghai Cinema, 1896–1937*. Chicago: University of Chicago.

Zhao Runsheng and Ma Liangkuan. 2003. "Xinhai Luanzhou binjian yu Luanzhou qiyi" (The Xinhai Launzhou soldiers' remonstrance and the Luanzhou uprising). Tianjin: Tianjin renmin chubanshe.

Zheng Jiahuai. 1988. "Shi Jianqiao qiren" (Shi Jianqiao, the person). *Hechuan wenshi ziliao xuanji* 5 (November): 104–110.

Zheng Yimei. 1992. "Cong Ma Gongyu shuo dao Shi Jianqiao" (From Ma Gongyu to Shi Jianqiao). In *Hai shang chunqiu*, ed. Hua Daoyi, 73–77. Shanghai: Shanghai shi wenshi yanjiu guanbian.

Zhou Jiaying. 1986. "Ruonü fuchou ji" (The chronicle of a frail woman's revenge). In *Jiuzui meirenyü*, ed. Zhu Qiufeng, 171–97. Zhejiang: Zhejiang wenyi chuban she.

Zhu Qiufeng, ed. 1986. *Jiuzui meirenyü—Minguo qi'an* (The drunken mermaid—Remarkable cases of the Republican era). Zhejiang: Zhejiang wenyi chubanshe.

Index

Italicized page numbers refer to illustrations.

Text: 10/13 Sabon
Display: Sabon
Compositor: Integrated Composition Systems
Indexer: Sharon Sweeney
Printer and binder: IBT Global